ENDANGERED
PARROTS

ENDANGERED
PARROTS

REVISED EDITION

ROSEMARY LOW

BLANDFORD

A BLANDFORD BOOK
First published in the UK 1994
by Blandford
A Cassell Imprint
Cassell plc, Villiers House
41–47 Strand, London WC2N 5JE

Previous edition published 1984 by Blandford Press

Distributed in the United States by
Sterling Publishing Co., Inc.,
387 Park Avenue South, New York, N.Y. 10016–8810

Distributed in Australia by
Capricorn Link (Australia) Pty Ltd
2/13 Carrington Road, Castle Hill, NSW 2154

British Library Cataloguing in Publication Data
Low, Rosemary
 Endangered Parrots.
 1. Parrots 2. Rare animals
 I. Title
 598'.71   QL696.P7

 ISBN 0–7137–2356–4

Typeset by Litho Link Ltd, Welshpool, Powys, Wales
Printed in Great Britain by The Bath Press, Avon

Picture Credits

Colour plates
Ardea Photographics — Graeme Chapman (16), John Mason (4)
Thomas Brosset (3)
Wolfgang de Grahl (9, 17, 19)
R.H. Grantham (1, 5, 8, 10, 13, 14, 20)
Eric Hosking (7)
Neil Hermes, ANPWS (21)
Carl Jones (15)
Dirk V. Lanning (2)
Don Merton (18)
Muller Verlag Walsrode (11)
Ed Over (12)
James Wiley (6)

Black and white photographs
David Alderton (p. 12)
George Anderdon (p. 135)
Ed Bish (p. 41)
Fred Bohner (p. 115)
Peter Brown (p. 120)
C.B. Studios (p. 49)
Phillip F. Coffey (p. 68)
R.H. Grantham (pp. 67, 69, 70, 79, 83, 96, 97, 100, 136, 158)
Carl Jones (p. 105)
Harry Lacey (p. 167)
Dirk V. Lanning (pp. 17, 18, 47)
Don Merton (pp. 125, 126)
Ramon Noegel (p. 62)
A.J. Pittman and J. Cuddy (p. 103)
Peter Pugh (p. 88)
Michael Reynolds World Parrot Trust (pp. 43, 171)
James T. Shiflett (p. 15)
US Fish and Wildlife Service (p. 89)
Worldwide Fund for Nature (pp. 27, 29)

Other photographs by the author

Maps
Anita Lawrence

*This book is dedicated to Don Merton of the New
Zealand Department of Conservation. He has
found unique solutions to the recovery of critically
endangered bird populations — solutions founded
on his understanding of and love for the birds
concerned. The Chatham Island Black Robin
population, faced with extinction in 1979, with
only one fertile female in existence, increased to
130 birds in February 1991 under his management.
His work is an inspiration to all those who are
actively involved in saving bird species from
extinction.*

Previous pages: Destruction of the tropical rainforest,
habitat of many of the world's most beautiful parrots.

Contents

Acknowledgements & Abbreviations

I am indebted to the ornithologists, aviculturists and others listed below who willingly complied with my requests for information.

Australia: Peter Brown, Murray Bruce, Stacey Gelis, Graeme Phipps, Warwick Remington, Dr W. Wakefield.
Bahamas: Rod Attrill.
Brazil: W.R. Kingston, Ivo Henrique Muniz, Dr P. Scherer Neto, David Oren, Paulo Ken Tomimori.
Channel Islands: David Jeggo.
Denmark: Peter Them.
Dominica: Michael Zamore.
Dominican Republic: Annabelle Stockton Dod.
Fiji: Dick Watling.
France: Abbé R. de Naurois, Dr Henri Quinque.
Germany: Thomas Arndt, Roland Wirth.
Indonesia: M. Noerdjito, I. Made Taman.
Mauritius: Carl Jones.
Mexico: Dr J.P. Ehrenberg, Dr M. Gómez-Garza.
Netherlands: Herman Kremer, Fred Smiet.
New Zealand: David Crouchley, Don Merton, Gretschen Rasch (Department of Conservation), M.D. Sibley (Auckland Zoo).
Philippines: Richard Lewis.
St Lucia: Paul Butler.
South Africa: Neville Brickell, Richard Brooke, David Loubser.
Sweden: Ake Öhman.
Switzerland: Anton Fernhout.

UK: Andrew Gardner, Calvin Bradley, Joe Cuddy, David Holyoak, Dr P.G.H. Evans, Dr C. Imboden, Anna Pavord, Tony Pittman, Peter Pugh, Derek Read, Dr R. Wilkinson.
USA: Ed Bish, Tom Ireland, Dirk Lanning, David Mack, and Sheryl Gilbert (TRAFFIC), Ramon Noegel, R.S. Ridgely, James Wiley, Edwin O. Willis.
Venezuela: Mary L. Goodwin.

Special thanks are due to David Alderton, T.R. Bruce and K. McKenzie who read and commented on the manuscript of the first edition of this book and to Peter Brown, Carl Jones, Don Merton and Dick Watling who gave much valuable advice on appropriate chapters.

I am grateful to Victor Gollancz for permission to quote from *Extinction* by Paul and Anne Ehrlich (published 1982), and to Martin Walters of Cambridge University Press for permission to draw on Carl Jones' material published in *Studies of Mascarene Island Birds*. All quoted references in the text have been dated, and the reader can find all the relevant details in the List of References at the end of the book.

Thanks are due to David Alderton, Thomas Arndt, Ed Bish, Chris Blackwell, Phillip F. Coffey, R.H. Grantham, Carl Jones, Neil Hermes, Dirk Lanning, Harry Lacey, Ramon Noegel, Graeme Phipps, Otto Poschung, Dr H. Quinque, Dr W.C. Wakefield, James Wiley and the World Wildlife Fund for their assistance with the illustrations.

Abbreviations

ABRC	Avicultural Breeding and Research Centre	ICBP	International Council for Bird Preservation now known as Birdlife International
AZZPA	American Association of Zoological Parks and Aquariums	ICI	Imperial Chemical Industries
CEDIA	Center for the Development of the Amazon Indian	IUCN	International Union for the Conservation of Nature
CITES	Convention on International Trade in Endangered Species of Wild Fauna and Flora	MARNA	Ministerio del Ambiente y de Recursos Naturales Renovables
CSIRO	Commonwealth Scientific and Industrial Research Organisation	PBFD	Psittacine beak and feather disease
DoE	Department of the Environment	pers. comm.	personal communication
EEP	Europäische Erhaltungszucht Programm (European Breeding Conservation Programme)	RARE	Rare Animal Relief Effort
		RSPB	Royal Society for the Protection of Birds
FAO	Food and Agriculture Organisation	TRAFFIC	Trade Records Analysis of Flora and Fauna in Commerce
FITT	Fundación Interamericana de Investigación Tropical	UN	United Nations
		WWF	Worldwide Fund for Nature

Foreword to First Edition
David Bellamy

'Pretty Polly, Pretty Polly' and 'Dead as a Dodo' are without doubt two of the commonest catch phrases used in the English-speaking world and they could well become synonymous if something is not done and fast.

Please read this book and listen to the parrots' plea for nothing more than a place in which to live. If action is not taken now the vast majority of the world's species of parrot will join the Dodo in extinction. The reason is habitat destruction on a scale which is almost impossible to comprehend. Forest and scrubland are falling before an onslaught of machetes, bulldozers and fire, most to be replaced with nothing but expanding desert, a miserable 10 per cent planted with exotic species of fast-growing tree. The end result is massive erosion of soil, silting of rivers and estuaries, and the annihilation of much of the genetic diversity of the living earth.

The reasons for that destruction are both need and greed. 1,000 million people plus, the members of the so called third world, live on the brink of starvation and disaster. In their fight for survival they are destroying the forest habitats on which they, the parrots and so many other animals and plants depend. They cannot be blamed; if your wife had to walk 20 km (12 miles) a day to fetch firewood or water and your children were grossly undernourished you would do the same — survival is a desperate situation.

Another 1,000 million (and you are one of them), the members of what can only be called the first world, are destroying mainly out of greed. We (yes, I am one of them too) are already using more than two thirds of the world's resources: food, timber, minerals, fossil fuels — you name it, we use it in a reckless, profligate manner. What is more, we continue to demand more and more, and always at the lowest price; and with starving people on at least part of the supply end all the market forces help us, not them, nor the environment.

Please take a careful look at your own lifestyle. The vast majority of the things we take for granted help to destroy natural habitats and degrade environments both at home and across the world. The timber you are sitting on probably came from the tropics at rock-bottom prices paid to the suppliers, the meat in your hamburger was probably raised on land recently cleared of tropical forest or at least semi-natural vegetation, and the paper pulp which wraps up your throw-away lifestyle may well have had a similar origin. The insurance policy of the third world people consists of large families, in the hope of producing one successful child who will look after them in their old age. The insurance policy which makes *your* old age seem so secure may well be invested in companies which make vast profit from the destruction of natural or heritage landscapes and/or exploits the plight of the third world as cheap labour and resources. What is the use of being a member of a Trades Union which only fights for the rights of the home-based highly paid members of the trade with little thought for those in the sweatshops of the third world in which more and more of the work is now being done?

The trouble is that if you are starving you will do anything to survive, and it would seem that if you are rich you will do anything to get richer.

The whole world is in a terrible mess, caught up in a mad scramble to survive or thrive; and in so doing we are destroying the natural and heritage habitats of this earth at the rate of more than 30 ha (75 acres) per minute, and that destruction is going on every minute of every day. The 1980s can only go down in history as the years of catastrophe for the future not only of the parrots but also of humankind which depends on those resources which are now being destroyed.

This book concerns not only the parrots but also the world. It tells the story of their plight, highlighting the sad fact that the only hope of survival for some of the species is to be bred in captivity until the world comes to its senses and realises the true value of these wonderful living things. And please do not let that be an excuse for unscrupulous people whose only real interest is to own the rarest of the rare to increase the illegal trade of these birds across the world. This vital work can only be done by dedicated experts or under the control of the international conservation bodies. Also please do not let it lead to an outburst from the extreme fringe of conservation who say that no animal should be kept in captivity and that zoos have no role in conservation.

The chips are down, this is survival stakes, and I for one do not want my children to grow up in a world in which there are no parrots and no hope for a meaningful future. Pretty Polly, Pretty Polly, please listen to what this book has to say concerning the parrots and then act by supporting the Worldwide Fund for Nature, Flora & Fauna Preservation Society, Friends of the Earth, Greenpeace or one of the many other bodies who are fighting to save the parrots and all the other living things with which we must learn to share this earth.

David J. Bellamy
Bedburn 1984

Introduction

The assault on nature by one of its products, Homo sapiens, *is massive and continually growing, governed largely by short-term gain and characterized by long-term blindness. Until now conservationists, the people who care what happens to wildlife and who understand its vital importance to our lives, have been a relatively powerless minority fighting a largely losing war. But they have succeeded in having laws passed and international agreements established that will help to protect species from extinction. And in some areas they have at least slowed the lethal march of habitat destruction. If there is continued insistence that these laws and agreements be observed; if others are enlisted to support the goal of preserving natural systems with all their components; if the movement broadens to encompass concerns such as the relationship between rich and poor nations, which are vital to preserving the great reservoirs of diversity in the tropics; if we all strive to instill in others, including our children, respect for and understanding of the natural world, there might be a chance of saving some of it — and ourselves.*

PAUL AND ANNE EHRLICH, IN *EXTINCTION* (1982)

In February 1918 a parrakeet known as Incas died in Cincinnati Zoo. Popular myth has it that he was the last of his race, a race which once numbered millions of individuals — the Carolina Parrakeet or Conure (*Conuropsis [= Aratinga] carolinensis*). Unpublished records of the National Audubon Society, however, confirm that this species existed in the wild until at least 1926, and probably later. Has any parrot species become extinct since then? The answer to this question is unknown. Two species may have done so. One is the Paradise Parrakeet or Parrot (*Psephotus pulcherrimus*) of Australia, which has been the subject of endless speculation among ornithologists. Some of the best informed believe that it may have become extinct in the 1950s; others say there have been unconfirmed sightings since then. If, sadly, the extinction of this beautiful bird has already occurred, it was comparatively recently. The other enigma is the Glaucous Macaw (*Anodorhynchus glaucus*). Was it extinct before the start of the twentieth century or, as some believe, does it still survive today?

If we assume that one of these is extinct but that the other still survives, seven parrot extinctions are known to have occurred since 1844 (when the earliest recorded parrot extinction of modern times occurred, *see* Appendix 1), leaving about 350 species extant. A precise number cannot be given because taxonomists do not always interpret in the same way what constitutes a species or a sub-species. On the face of it parrots may seem to have fared comparatively well in the battle against man's encroachment. Yet this is not so. Many species are struggling for survival in habitats which, in some cases, have been reduced to just a few square miles. Others have populations which are perilously reduced, several consisting of less than 100 individuals — and some of these numbering fewer than 50. During 1992 the International Council for Bird Preservation (ICBP) reviewed the status of all parrot

Carolina Parrakeet (*Conuropsis* [Aratinga] carolinensis), now extinct.

species and suggested that a third, i.e. more than 100, were threatened with extinction. This figure shocked most people who were in any way involved with parrots — but I believe it also heralded the start of a new era. Previously very few parrot conservation projects existed. Subsequently, ICBP embarked on a very ambitious and urgently needed Parrot Action Plan which, it was estimated, would cost about US$10 million per annum for the next five years. Simultaneously, the World Parrot Trust and other conservation organisations were also funding and implementing projects to help specific species.

It is important to bear in mind that, with a few exceptions, population estimates are vague. In most cases it is known that populations are declining but there is no clear idea of the existing population. Just how little is known about parrots in the wild is demonstrated by the fact that, between the publication

of the first and second editions of this book (the decade between 1984 and 1994), three new parrot species have been discovered and named! One can see that, if three species could resist 'discovery' until the 1980s, it would be unwise to state dogmatically that the Paradise Parrot and the Glaucous Macaw is extinct.

Some parrots occur in areas so remote that little is known about them. A classic example is Lear's Macaw. The location of the only known population (in Brazil) remained a mystery until 1978, although it had been known in captivity since at least 1880. In some cases lack of information is due to the fact that few or no ornithologists have visited the region where the species is found. For example, Buru, one of the Moluccan islands, is the only place where the Black-lored Parrot (*Tanygnathus gramineus*) is found. Until recently, visiting the island was prohibited because it served as the main internment camp for thousands of Communist prisoners from Java. Only during the 1980s did field work commence in Indonesia, revealing how many of the region's parrots (nearly all endemic) are threatened with extinction.

The majority of people who read this book will be sympathetic towards the plight of endangered species, or they would not bother to delve between its covers. There are many, many others, however, who cannot appreciate why endangered birds should be saved. What are a few species more or less, they might ask?

As Paul and Anne Ehrlich (1982) have stated, there are four prime arguments in favour of saving species from extinction. Firstly, simple compassion demands their preservation; the needs and desires of human beings are not the only basis for ethical decisions. Secondly, endangered species should be saved because of their beauty, uniqueness, symbolic value or intrinsic interest; in short, for reasons of aesthetics. The third argument is an economic one; many species provide direct benefits to man.

The Ehrlichs point out that the fourth argument 'is rarely heard and even less frequently understood, because it involves indirect benefits to humanity. This argument is that other species are living components of vital ecological systems (ecosystems) which provide humanity with indispensable free services — services whose substantial disruption would lead inevitably to the collapse of civilization. By deliberately or unknowningly forcing species to extinction, *Homo sapiens* is attacking *itself*; it is certainly endangering society and possibly even threatening our own species with extermination.'

1

Why Parrots are Endangered

The most predictable change in natural habitats in the near future is fragmentation. In the next generation, we can expect to see the final fragmentation of the earth from a predominantly natural settled state — a mosaic of settled clearings surrounded by relatively undisturbed ecosystems — to a man dominated state in which natural habitats will remain only as increasingly scattered islands in a sea of development. The latter state is one which most of us are familiar with in developed countries but it is likely to become the normal state of the world very soon.

IAN C.T. NISBET, CONCLUDING REMARKS, *SYMPOSIUM ON MANAGEMENT TECHNIQUES FOR PRESERVING ENDANGERED BIRDS* (1977)

During the twentieth century, habitat destruction has caused populations of countless species of birds to decline and has resulted in the extinction of several others. Some birds can exist in a variety of environments, town and country, marsh and coastal areas, whereas others have more specialised requirements. It is the latter which suffer most as the result of habitat destruction, because they are unable to adapt to other environments. This is especially true of forest-dwelling birds; indeed, two out of three of endangered birds are forest species. When their habitat is destroyed, they have nowhere to go, and their numbers dwindle to extinction. Parrots are especially vulnerable to habitat destruction and disturbance, as the majority are forest-dwellers. Although loss of habitat may be the most

obvious reason for endangerment, there may be secondary causes which are almost equally significant.

Most endangered birds and all endangered parrots are K-selected species — the biologist's term for those which maintain stable populations with a carrying capacity which is called K. Conversely, r-selected species have higher reproduction rates to compensate for substantial fluctuation in population size. A good example is the tit family (Paridae). Tits have as many as eight or more young in one nest, but their life-span is short. Following a population reduction, however, such as is caused by a severe winter, their numbers quickly approach former abundancy.

This is not so with K-selected species, such as the large parrots. They lay smaller clutches (usually two to four eggs), and are not mature enough to breed until they are several years old. After a reduction in the population, such as the result of a hurricane or volcano eruption, their populations take many years to reach their former size — if they ever do. Recovery may be slow and erratic, thus increasing their vulnerability to extinction. An unfortunate example of the latter is the Imperial Parrot (*Amazona imperialis*) whose small population took more than a decade to show any significant sign of recovery following Hurricane David in 1979.

Another problem of K-selected species is that they are unable to cope with rapidly changing environments. Temple (1977) has asked: 'Are endangered species locked into old, unadaptive ways by genetically fixed traits or by tradition? It seems that, in many cases, the problems of endangered species may be the result of unadaptive traditions. Problems relating to habitat selection, nest-site selection, food habits and migration patterns are important components of the unadaptive niches of many endangered birds. They are all strongly influenced by tradition.'

Tom J. Cade, whose legendary success in breeding the Peregrine Falcon (*Falco peregrinus*) in captivity since the 1970s has resulted in it being reintroduced to the wild in greater numbers than any other endangered species, except perhaps the NéNé Goose (*Branta sandvicensis*), forecast that the ingenuity of endangered species biologists will be put to the test repeatedly in the last decades of the twentieth century. He believes in 'creative manipulation' of populations as a means of saving species approaching critically low numbers, 'especially if individuals can be induced to adapt to new ways of living and reproducing in an altered environment' (Cade, 1977).

Field studies of endangered and threatened species are invaluable because, as a result, steps may be taken which arrest their decline. For example, a study of the Thick-billed Parrot (*Rhynchopsitta pachyrhyncha*), funded by the Rare Animal Relief Effort in 1979, showed that its decline could be halted quite easily: by the instigation of a snag management programme. (Snags are standing dead trees.)

This species (see Plate 2) has the most northerly range of any neotropical parrot and it was found in the southern states of the USA (Arizona and New Mexico) until the early 1900s. It was extirpated at about the same time as Wild Turkey, elk, pronghorn antelope and bighorn sheep vanished from the region — and for almost certainly the same reason — it was shot out of existence. It was large enough to qualify as a table item and its noisy social habits made it extremely vulnerable to gunfire. Miners, woodsmen and soldiers were among those who shot it (Snyder, Snyder and Johnson, 1989).

Since the early 1900s its range has decreased significantly; until 1986 it was found only as far north in Mexico as northern Chihuahua and Sonora, and south to Jalisco and Michoacan, the nearest point to the USA border being 150 km (94 miles). Then, in 1986, history was made when it was reintroduced to Arizona. (The story of this release is related in Chapter 21).

Not yet critically endangered, it is vulnerable and increasingly threatened throughout its breeding range by loss of habitat. Until the American ornithologists Dirk V. Lanning and James T. Shiflett commenced their study of this species in 1979, little was known about its nesting ecology. They searched its habitat on foot, using climbing spurs and belt or technical climbing gear where necessary, or by using a four-wheel-drive truck and, for three days, from an aeroplane. They confirmed that the Thick-billed Parrot is dependent on

pines, but not only for nest sites. Pine seeds are its principal food, and the nesting season is timed so that the parrots take advantage of their maturity. The pines, however, are being destroyed . . . .

Commercial logging in the mountains of north-western Mexico commenced in the early twentieth century. It has grown to the degree that in 1979 the pulp mill in Chihuahua was consuming 1,800 tonnes of wood per day. Snags are used for pulp and live pines for lumber. Government regulation decrees that large pines are selectively cut, usually when the girth exceeds 40–50 cm (15–20 in) at 1.4 m (4½ ft). Of the nests in pines referred to below, only one was smaller than 50 cm (20 in) in diameter.

In many forested areas of Chihuahua there are no pines, dead or alive, large enough for parrot nests; the birds now breed only in remote areas or in 'islands' of forest on steep slopes and ridges that are inaccessible or on which logging would be uneconomical.

Fifty-five nests were found by Lanning and Shiflett in 1979 at locations between 2,300 m (7,500 ft) and 3,070 m (10,000 ft). Forty-two were located in Arizona pine (*Pinus arizonica*) and Mexican white pine (*P. ayacahuita*), nine in quaking aspen (*Populus tremuloides*) and four in Douglas fir (*Pseudotsuga menziesii*). Thirty-five nests were located in snags and twenty in live trees.

It was evident that cavities formed by decomposition and by woodpecker foraging and/or nesting activity had been enlarged by the parrots. Forty-two nest cavities (76 per cent) were completely enclosed except for the entrance and were well protected from rain and wind. Ten (18 per cent) had large entrances or cracks where rain could enter. Three (5 per cent) were directly exposed to rain, either because there was no top or because the top contained holes.

During the course of a year nest cavities may deteriorate naturally or due to human intervention. In September 1980 12 cavities in north-western Chihuahua which contained nests in 1979 were re-examined. Eight were in good condition and five of these contained matted beds of grass, lichen, aspen bark and pine needles, also the hairs of Abert's squirrels which had been using the cavities. Holes allowing water to enter had appeared above two nest cavities in pines. Human disturbance was responsible for the loss of two nests (one snag removed, probably for pulp, and one knocked over, probably during logging) and the death of two chicks, found in an aspen cavity disturbed by logging. The latter nest represented the only confirmed re-use of a nest cavity in a subsequent year (Lanning and Shiflett, 1983). Apparently, parrots had nested only sparsely in the area and no conclusions could be drawn as to why so many proven nest cavities had not been re-used.

A step which would safeguard the nesting require-

Habitat of Thick-billed Parrot (*Rhynchopsitta pachyrhyncha*) in Durango.

ments of the Thick-billed Parrot (*Rhynchopsitta pachyrhyncha*) was suggested by Lanning and Shiflett in their 1981 report: guidelines developed by the US Forest Service in Arizona and New Mexico could be adopted for the conifer forests of Mexico, in which snag cutting is not regulated by the government. US recommendations are that five or more good quality snags can be retained per hectare and that provisions can be made for continued recruitment of future snags; spike-topped trees and other large live trees of low commercial value can be left for cavity-nesting species.

'Well-designed forest management practices throughout the forest would have a broad positive impact for nesting Thick-billed Parrots', stated Lanning and Shiflett. Reserves could be created to protect small areas of prime forest habitat and a snag management programme could be instigated 'for the ultimate benefit of both wildlife and the timber industry, especially the unique Thick-billed Parrot.'

Two years after the 1981 Lanning and Shiflett report was made I asked Dirk Lanning if their recommendations had been acted upon. He replied 'There is not yet an effective snag management policy in Mexico. With their current economic problems, there appears to be little interest in long-range planning and management of the nation's forest resources for the benefit of both timber and wildlife. No effective reserves have been created in the Sierra Madre Occidental in the nesting

range of the Thick-billed Parrots. There is also no effective protection of the forests of the Sierra Madre Oriental, home of the Maroon-fronted Parrot.' Mexico is sadly lacking in protected areas. In 1988 only about 0.5 per cent of its total land mass was under some form of protection.

In north-eastern Mexico the Maroon-fronted Parrot (*R. terrisi*) is found. It differs from the foregoing only in the maroon rather than scarlet forehead, silver-grey instead of bright yellow under-wing coverts, and slightly larger and heavier build. In the past it was often considered as a sub-species of the Thick-bill. Its range is limited to the conifer forests of the Sierra Madre Oriental, to an area about 300 km (185 miles) long.

During a period of several months during 1978 and 1979 Peter Lawson and Dirk Lanning studied this parrot and made some important discoveries. (Not all were vital for the survival of this species but were of general interest. They discovered, for example, by taping parrot calls and playing them back to young birds, that the young responded only to the taped voices of their parents and not to those of other birds of the same species.)

The most significant difference in the breeding biology of the two species concerns the nesting site. There are few large trees within the range of the Maroon-fronted Parrot; so they use holes in the many limestone cliffs. In contrast, cliffs within the range of the Thick-billed Parrot contain few holes. In 1979, Lawson and Lanning (1981) estimated that there were 100 Maroon-fronted Parrot nests in 28 km (17 miles) of north-facing cliffs within the study area. They discovered that Ravens (*Corvus corax*) entered known parrot

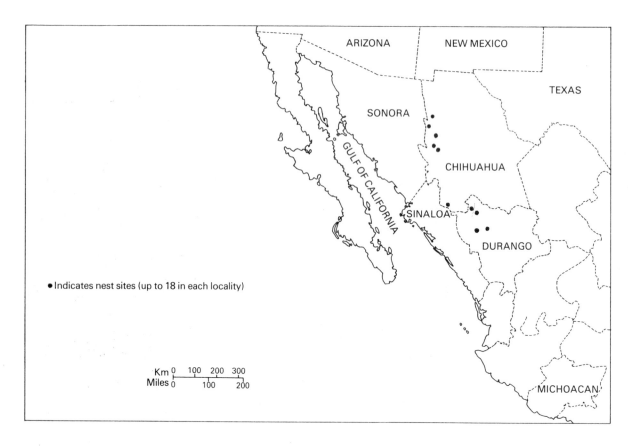

Thick-billed Parrot (*Rhynchopsitta pachyrhyncha*). Study area of Lanning and Shiflett in 1979, in which 55 active nests were found.

nests; as some of these nests failed to produce young, the Ravens were probably taking eggs and/or young.

The Maroon-fronted Parrot is on Appendix I of CITES (Convention on International Trade in Endangered Species of Wild Fauna and Flora). The highest counts of Lawson and Lanning were of 800, 1,400 and 1,600 birds, the latter count being made in January 1978 in the south of the range. This species is unknown in captivity; it is not hunted for food or because it is considered a pest and its nests are inaccessible. It is threatened by one factor alone: habitat destruction. Lawson and Lanning state: 'The mixed-conifer forests of the range are being destroyed by fire, logging, grazing and clearing for orchards and crops. In the past five years fire has claimed about 500 hectares of forest in two of the richest areas of parrot habitat . . ..'

A disastrous series of events follows a mountain fire which may result in the area being laid waste. Loggers salvage the dead trees, grazing of cattle and goats destroys the vegetation and promotes erosion, and the original growth is replaced by a dense chaparral. Attempts at reafforestation may fail because the loss of vegetation which once retained water results in the area becoming more arid. In this way, areas of habitat suitable for parrots may be completely lost.

Few people are more familiar with the Maroon-fronted Parrot than veterinarian Dr Miguel Gómez-Garza. Since he began to study it in 1982, he has noted a significant decrease in its numbers due to the felling of thousands of trees each year in the Sierra Madre Oriental. In his opinion, its population is nowhere near the estimated 2,000 suggested in the Parrot Action Plan. Simultaneous counts at nine sites in September 1991 found only 600 birds. He is familiar with this species at two sites, both of which have mixed forest (an essential source of food for breeding pairs) at the base of the cliffs. In both cases, this forest is being degraded and used as grazing areas for goats and cows. The 'high-rise' area that was studied by Lanning and

Habitat of Maroon-fronted Parrot (*Rhynchopsitta terrisi*) in Coahuila.

Lawson now supports about 25 nests each year. In the second breeding area, Las Cuevas, which he has had under observation since 1983, the number of nests has varied between two and nine. The exception was in 1989, when a road was built there and no birds nested. However, the road was washed away after the rainy season and the next year two pairs returned to nest. Two hundred people live in the 'high-rise' locality and depend on the forest for wood for fuel and house-building. Gómez-Garza commented: 'In this forest it is not unusual to find the remains of *R. terrisi* that were brought down with slingshots by idle herders, or fledglings who, in their first flights, fell to the ground and were eaten by the herders' dogs' (Gómez-Garza, 1991).

In 1992, Dr Miguel Gómez-Garza was appointed director of Proyecto ARA, a long-term project to preserve endangered Mexican birds. The Maroon-fronted Parrot was the first species to receive the attention of the project, which was sponsored by the industrial group Pulsar. Dr Gómez-Garza appointed a council of the Mexican naturalists who knew the species best. Two field studies were approved. One was to be carried out by biologists from the University of Nuevo León, in Cerro del Potosí, in Nuevo León state, and the other by naturalists from the University of Coahuila, in Arteaga, Coahuila state. Both studies will span one year and focus on feeding habits, in order to provide information for future reafforestation programmes. The second aspect of the project was that of conservation education. It was planned to present information about *R. terrisi*, its habitat and the importance of its preservation to all the rural schools in the two regions, in co-operation with naturalists from the University of Coahuila. A proposal was to be made to the governor of the state of Nuevo León that the Cerro de Potosí should be made a biosphere reserve in order to prevent the destruction of more trees. In addition, a way had to be found of protecting the nesting zone of El Condominio.

The mixed-conifer forests of the Sierra Madre Oriental are of particular value to Mexico. They catch and hold moisture, creating a mesic zone in an otherwise arid land. The forests moderate local climate and supply water for drinking, agriculture and industry. Formerly protected by their remoteness and rugged topography, the forests are now being settled, as a result of Mexico's enormous population increases (about 2 per cent per annum) and its total population, in 1990, of 81.25 million inhabitants. Protecting this watershed from deforestation is in the interest of all the

Maroon-fronted Parrots.

people of Mexico; but will the government realise this before the parrot is irretrievably lost?

The Thick-billed, though not common, is fairly well known and has been bred in several collections. For a period, during the early 1970s, trapping for trade did occur. This was short-lived because: a) dealers discovered it was difficult to sell; and b) it was placed on Appendix I of CITES, causing trade to cease. Despite its glowing colours it was not popular because its large beak, destructive habits and shy personality did not endear it to aviculturists. Fortunately, it is still being reared by a few dedicated breeders who realise the importance of maintaining captive stock. To date no one has found this an easy species to rear and numbers are being maintained rather than increased.

Another neotropical parrot endangered solely by loss of habitat is the Yellow-eared Conure (*Ognorhynchus icterotis*). By 1992 it was one of the 19 species categorised as 'critical' (i.e. only those six species given the status of 'critical/extinct' are in a more serious position). This most interesting bird can briefly be described as resembling a Thick-billed Parrot in size and stature, with the areas which are red in the Thick-billed replaced by yellow, which extends over the entire

side of the face. It, too, has a large black bill and is decidedly macaw-like. Furthermore, it possesses the macaw's ability to blush: when excited the flesh-coloured bare skin at the side of the lower mandible becomes red. (*See* Plate 1.)

The Yellow-eared Conure is an example of a declining parrot about which almost nothing is known, except that it is declining. It has never been studied in the field; even a glimpse of this species is a rare event. The American ornithologist Robert Ridgely recorded (1981): 'I considered myself fortunate to see this parrot once (a single pair), this despite spending considerable time in the Moscopan region of Huila, where Lehmann (1957) found them numerous up until the early 1950's.' The fact that Mr Ridgely has observed more neotropical parrots in the field than any other ornithologist provides some insight into the rarity of this particular parrot.

The Yellow-eared Conure has been recorded from several localities in the eastern, central and western Andes of Colombia, and the adjacent Imbabura and Pichincha provinces of northern Ecuador. It may, however, already be extinct in Ecuador. The majority of sites where this species once occurred, such as the Moscopan area of the Cauca division of Colombia, are now largely deforested (King, 1981). The lower temperate zone forests, especially between 2,500 and 3,000 m (8,200 and 9,850 ft) is the habitat of this parrot. So much of this forest has been destroyed, however, that, by 1992, ICBP described this conure as critically endangered. The Parrot Action Plan states: 'The Yellow-eared Conure has declined to a population thought to number less than one hundred, and its specific habitat requirements make it particularly vulnerable.' The largest flock observed in recent years was of 25 birds in the Western Andes in Cauca, in August 1977. Evidence that it still occurred in Imbabura exists in the form of specimens, probably collected in the late 1970s.

In the first edition of this book I wrote that: 'Little information is available regarding the areas in which it does survive. Field work to establish this is urgently required; only then can more positive conservation measures be taken.'

Nothing was done — but the Parrot Action Plan proposed a project which entailed an extensive search for the species, followed by detailed study of its ecology and behaviour. It states that a species recovery programme should be developed and a reserve of the wax palm (*Ceroxylum quindiuense*) should be established, plus an education campaign in the region of Toche, Colombia, to conserve one known remaining population. Large-scale propagation of the wax palm, the species on which this parrot is dependent, and reintroduction of the palms in certain areas, was also recommended. The cost of this programme was estimated at US$370,000. But, one wonders, is it already too late to save this distinctive and interesting macaw-like parrot? What would its population be today, had these measures been implemented a decade ago? Two specimens (and no other references in the literature) were received by a London dealer on different occasions during the 1960s. One of these came to light about ten years later and was purchased by the veterinarian and aviculturist George Smith. I was privileged to look after it for a few months before Mr Smith presented it to Walsrode Bird Park in Germany. A species which is visually unlike any other parrot, its extinction from the temperate forests of Colombia and Ecuador would be a sad loss.

In theory, parrots would benefit from the creation of reserves. In practice, however, reserves are seldom effective in protecting endangered species. Although reserves can be the means of maintaining areas of original habitat, most are either not large enough to be of any significance where large birds such as parrots are concerned, or too large for protection of the birds found within to be feasible. In some countries, such as Colombia, national parks and reserves exist, but there are no laws to protect the fauna within. Colombia and Brazil, whose combined total of parrot species equals a third of the worldwide total, harbour most of the parrot species without protection.

Often, legal protection counts for nothing. Even where birds are protected by law, they may be exploited by the very persons employed to protect them. In the Dominican Republic, salaries paid to game wardens are so small that the wardens were accepting bribes from hunters to take them to places where they could find certain birds (Dod, pers. comm., 1983). On the other hand, in some areas, particularly in the Parque del Este and in the Parque de los Haitises, there was good protection of rare birds, and large flocks of parrots and conures could be seen there, as well as in the two highland parks in the Cordillera Central. In the latter area the habitat was actually being improved by the planting of trees.

In many countries, conservation is either virtually non-existent or the position is not as favourable as it might appear from statistics available. For example, in Panama, which has 21 parrot species, there are nine national parks, watersheds and forest preserves — a combined area in excess of 850,000 hectares (2.1 million acres). This put Panama in seventh position in the world with respect to the total territory under protected status (8.9 per cent) by the early 1980s. Nevertheless, the first of the national parks, Campana, had almost ceased to exist. Due to agricultural encroachment, its original 4,800 ha (11,900 acres) had been reduced to less than 600 ha (1,500 acres).

However, Gale (1983) believed that Panamanian parks and preserves would be better protected in the future. 'That optimism', he wrote in 1987, 'seems to have been justified.'

RENARE, the agency protecting the nearly 810,000 ha (2 million acres) of national parks and reserves, had been understaffed and underbudgeted in its field personnel. However, it was to become an independent institute which would give it greater flexibility and efficiency. Also, in 1985, legislation was ratified creating the Metropolitan Nature Park in Panama City. This is the only forest park in the neotropics located within a metropolitan area. Approximately 200 of its 265 ha (500 of its 650 acres) consist of lowland semi-deciduous forest in which a 26-ha (65-acre) zoo of indigenous species was planned (Gale, 1987). In addition, ANCON, a private conservation organisation was established to protect and manage Panama's national reserves. As in other countries, Panama's national parks have fallen victim to agricultural demands. This bears out a point made by Stonehouse (1981) that: '. . . the concept of static reserves, dedicated simply to being themselves without protection or working policy, has not stood the test of time. People starved of land and protein tend to see reserves as wastelands waiting to be farmed, and protected animals as meat on the hoof; reserves work best when they bring tangible benefits to the local community, as well as to scientists and philanthropists in distant countries.'

In Africa, reserves and national parks are of major importance to the tourist industry, and result in employment and a higher standard of living for the local people. Other countries, however, lack Africa's spectacular show of large game animals; their reserves are not likely to achieve the same kind of popularity and ultimately may be ineffective in protecting the fauna they contain.

Another reason why reserves are not the complete answer to conservation is that the areas around them may be cultivated or developed in some other way so that the reserves become, in essence, islands. It is well known that ecological islands lose species. (Consider, too, natural islands. They invariably support a smaller number of species than comparable continental areas.) Also, colonisation drops because species cannot arrive from the surrounding area. It has been estimated, for example, that when the smaller African reserves are isolated, they will lose about a quarter of their large mammal species in 50 years, two-thirds in 500 years and nine-tenths in 5,000 years. The larger reserves will lose fewer species. Reserves should therefore be as large as possible. The smaller the reserve, the more intensive must be the management in order to maintain stability and to retard loss of diversity.

One of the most important parks yet established in the neotropics is the Manu National Park on the eastern flanks of the Peruvian Andes. Its 15,000 km² (about 6,000 sq. miles) cover areas of forest, mountain and swamp. Virtually undisturbed by man, except for small groups of forest Indians, it contains 400 species of birds, including parrots. The first national park in the Amazon region, it has provided a model on which other reserves in the neotropics can be based. A network of manned guard-posts ensures that virtually no encroachment or poaching occurs.

In this second edition, it is encouraging to include in this chapter a very positive development concerning the Manu Biosphere Reserve which, by 1992, consisted of 18.25 million ha (4.5 million acres). Surrounding it is 25.3 million ha (6.25 million acres) of some of the last very large undisturbed areas of rainforest on earth. These areas will be titled and will serve as a buffer zone. (When land is titled, new settlers are prevented from reaching uninvaded areas.) These activities are part of the goal of CEDIA (Center for the Development of the Amazon Indian) to protect 2.8 million ha (7 million acres) of rainforest, estimated to cost only $292,000 (only 1.7 cents per ha; 4 cents per acre). This work is being supported by Friends of the Peruvian Rainforest (see Appendix 3).

Costa Rica is alone among the Central American countries in having a firmly established conservation movement. The praiseworthy financial commitment of the government of this democratic and stable nation has been supplemented by substantial outside assistance. Many types of habitat are now represented in at least one formally established park or reserve. However, some of the factors which enabled Costa Rica to make these conservation gains in the 1970s, may have negative effects in the 10–20 years after 1982 (Stiles, 1982). These factors include a stable democratic government, a highly literate public and an expanding economy, all leading to a higher standard of living. This, in turn, will lead to pressure on land set aside for parks and reserves because of the need to develop an export-based agro-economy to maintain the standard of living.

An increasingly important role in the survival of some species of parrot will be played by the establishment of reserves, such as the Chiripo Volcano National Park.

In Venezuela the extensive Henri Pittier National Park is situated only a few miles from Caracas, the main centre of human population. Covering 54,600 km² (21,000 sq. miles) of mountain forest, rain and cloud forest, and wastelands, it harbours an immense wealth of flora and fauna and perhaps more species of birds than any similar area in the hemisphere.

Venezuela probably has the most integrated and best established system of national parks and protected areas in South America, and during the past decade its legislation protecting wildlife has been among the best in the world. Rudran and Eisenberg (1982) suggest, however, that the extent and number of protected areas should be increased and that wildlife laws should be more effectively implemented to eradicate devastation caused by illegal activities. Here, too, there was an important development in 1989 when the Parque Naciónal El Guácharo at Caripe, in northern Venezuela, added 166,000 ha (410,000 acres) of pristine tropical forest to the existing 38,750 ha (96,000 acres).

Parrots in Guyana receive no legal protection. As yet that country has no system of national parks or reserves. Niles (1981) noted that about four decades previously the Kaiteur National Park was established by law but nothing had been done to implement or develop it. However, the main threat to the parrots of Guyana is not habitat destruction — there has been little habitat disturbance there — but trade. In 1987 the huge parrot export trade was suspended for a while in order to establish a quota system. Quotas for each species were then set, but these are very high. In October 1987, when trade recommenced, it was permitted to export 35,000 parrots per year. This total included 17,500 Orange-winged Amazons (Amazona amazonica), 2,300 Mealy Amazons (A. farinosa), 2,300 Blue and Yellow Macaws (Ara ararauna) and 480 Hawk-headed Parrots (Deroptyus accipitrinus). The Blue and Yellow Macaw, for example, is a common species, but a slow-breeding one, like all large macaws. As yet, the effect of taking thousands of macaws from the wild over a sustained period is unknown; very little research has been carried out on any of the birds of Guyana.

Suriname (Dutch Guiana), has an excellent system of reserves, notable among which are the Raleighvallen-Voltzberg and Sipaliwino Savanna nature reserves (Pasquier, 1981). A small country and one of the least densely populated in the western hemisphere, the interior is almost uninhabited and covered in undisturbed forest. Suriname is therefore one of the best places to preserve large primeval tracts of forest. None of that country's parrots are endangered. The population of the Dufresne's Amazon (Amazona dufresniana dufresniana) is not high; this fact is worth noting for it does indicate that a species' numbers may be naturally low — not invariably as a result of man's activities.

The creation of reserves may protect large areas from deforestation, but felling is not the sole cause of the loss of immense areas of natural habitat. There is a more compelling reason: flooding. Hydro-electric development can result in the drowning of hundreds of square miles. This has already occurred in Brazil, for example, where further development of that kind is scheduled.

In September 1982, W.R. Kingston informed me of such a scheme in the basin of the Xingú and Tocantins rivers in the south of Pará which would result in the flooding of 2,200 km^2 (850 sq. miles) and the consequent destruction of all wildlife in the area. This includes the endangered Queen of Bavaria's Conure (*Guaruba guarouba*), the threatened Pearly Conure (*Pyrrhura perlata*), also Hyacinthine Macaws (*Anodorhynchus hyacinthinus*), Hawk-headed Parrots (*Deroptyus accipitrinus*), White-bellied Caiques (*Pionites leucogaster*), and two small parrots, the Caica (*Pionopsitta caica*) and the Vulturine (*P.* [= *Gypopsitta*] *vulturina*).

Trade in parrots, like deforestation, commenced several centuries ago, but it is only during the twentieth century that both have been practised on a scale which threatens the survival of a number of parrots. Trade can cause endangerment if the sheer volume is excessive throughout its range, and severe habitat destruction has also occurred, as with the Scarlet Macaw (*Ara macao*), for example; or if a species has a small range and therefore a small total population, although the total number of birds in trade is insignificant compared with other species. The Caninde, or Blue-throated, and the Red-fronted Macaws (both from Bolivia) were, sadly, examples of the latter (*see* pages 50 and 48). Legislation pertaining to trade in endangered species is strictly enforced by many countries. Some countries, however, have a total ban on the export of birds, thus endangerment through export trade cannot occur. Examples are Australia, whose export ban has been in force since 1959, Brazil (1967) and Colombia (early 1970s). Formerly, Colombia had a very large trade in bird and animal export.

Some countries do not wish to prohibit export of parrots because of the revenue this provides. For example, in Guyana exporters pay a 20 per cent tax on all birds exported, and in some Central American countries the tax is a fixed amount per parrot.

During the 1970s the worldwide trade in parrots reached unacceptably high proportions, especially the numbers imported into the USA. This was partly due to the fact that after a ban lasting several years the USA recommenced to import parrots in the late 1960s, after the use of tetracycline was approved to eliminate the public health threat of psittacosis. (For varying periods, however, the ban was reimposed because imported parrots and other birds were found to be carrying Newcastle disease, posing a serious threat to the poultry industry.) Since the late 1970s legislation and the introduction of strict quarantine measures might have reduced the number of parrots and other birds in trade throughout the world, yet this was not the case and the numbers traded remained inordinately high.

Excessive trade is widely cited as a reason for parrots

becoming endangered. This, regrettably, is true in some cases, especially the cockatoos of Indonesia and certain Amazon parrots. The sub-species of the Blue-fronted Amazon from Argentina (*Amazona aestiva xanthopteryx*) is one of the most popular. It used to be a very common bird in the wild but excessive trade has had a devastating effect on its numbers. Bucher et al (1992) describe the factors which led to its decline: 'The impact of habitat destruction from forest cutting and overgrazing is exacerbated by the current method of collecting parrot nestlings. To procure nestlings, the local people usually open a hole in the trunk or even cut the entire tree, which leaves more than 95 per cent of the cavities unusable for future nesting by parrots. Around 100,000 trees have been destroyed or damaged between 1981 and 1989 as a direct result of this practice. Besides destroying the nest cavity, trappers remove the whole brood from every nest they find, resulting in no recruitment of young birds into the population. While a drastic fall in the Blue-fronted population may take some time before becoming apparent due to the parrot's long lifespan, conditions are building for a sudden crash in the remaining population within the next few years.'

The loss of nesting sites is one of the worst aspects of the trade; many parrot species are already under pressure from lack of nesting sites for other reasons, such as extraction of large trees for timber.

Another aspect of trade in rare parrots, which is seldom considered, is that, in some species, trapping and export resulted not from demand but from deforestation. For example, during the 1970s, thousands of parrots of species which were previously very rare or unknown in aviculture were imported from Indonesia and New Guinea. As the forested habitat of certain island parrots was destroyed, they had nowhere to go. They were easy to trap because either they were displaced from their natural habitat or timber extraction opened up previously inaccessible areas to the trappers. Even if they had not been trapped, most of these birds would not have survived because the competition for food and nesting sites would have been too great.

One example is the Amboina King Parrakeet (*Alisterus amboinensis amboinensis*), which suddenly became available during the mid-1970s. It occurs only on Ambon (Amboina) and Seram, in the Moluccas. Ambon is now almost totally deforested. The striking red, green and blue long-tailed parrakeets were refugees in their own home. It was a case of captivity or die — and sadly, in many cases, captivity *and* die. The dealers there apparently had little experience in looking after these birds. Many of those received in Europe were so malnourished that they did not survive, or lived only as a result of intensive care by the few importers who went to great lengths to try to ensure their survival. Today the species survives in aviculture — but not in large numbers.

By the early 1990s, the international trade in wild-caught birds had become a subject for hot debate, attracting the attention of animal rights groups in the USA and Europe. Indeed, in the March 1992 issue of *World Birdwatch*, newsletter of ICBP, Christoph Imboden, Director-General of that organisation, contributed a non-emotive and thought-provoking article on whether this trade should continue. He pointed out that an estimated 1.5 million wild-caught birds are imported into the European Community and more than 0.25 million Amazon parrots enter the USA every year. He stated that, for every bird which reaches a pet shop, several more die during capture or transport — an undeniable fact.

He wrote: 'Although trade is hardly ever responsible on its own for the decline of a bird species, it contributes to the threats facing many, and can become the most critical factor for threatened species that are favoured by aviculturalists.'

What proposals have been put forward to control the problem? The most radical is for a ban on trade, with some exceptions for scientific purposes. Another proposal is for a ban on the importation into the USA and EC countries which 'does not carry the stigma of the rich telling the poor what to do, and leaves them free to continue exporting to countries without such import bans'. (In my opinion, this is no solution, as it might do little to reduce the volume of birds traded. Japan, for example, is believed to import vast numbers of wild-caught birds.) The most sensible proposal seems to be that of a trade or import moratorium, during which time a rational basis for limiting the trade could be developed. However, in the early 1990s, the USA started to phase out the importation of all wild-caught birds.

As Christoph Imboden points out: 'A cornerstone of today's conservation principles is the concept of sustainable development, which recognises the benefit to be derived from natural resources, but also emphasises the crucial importance of keeping any utilisation at a level that does not reduce the resource capital. Relating the well-being of people to their environment provides the best possible incentive for conservation.

'In view of this, should we not allow trade in wild birds, where it can be shown that the consequences of harvesting are not detrimental to the distribution pattern and population levels of these species, or the ecosystems of which they form a part? This is a legitimate line of argument that cannot be easily dismissed, particularly when put forward by developing countries that have been targeted with the sustainability argument by the conservation community. We obviously lose some credibility if, on the one hand, we campaign against the destruction of tropical forests in favour of sustainable use of its many products, while on the other, we seek to ban the trade of all wild-caught birds (including species that are subject to agricultural control programmes funded by international aid).'

Some people are in favour of trade only if it benefits conservation. But, asks Mr Imboden, how does one interpret 'benefit'? Sustainability is more straightforward, less ambiguous and easier to measure. Tested population assessment techniques can be applied.

As the argument raged for or against trade in wild-caught birds, the issue took an unexpected turn. An increasing number of airlines adopted the policy of refusing to carry wild-caught birds. Some airlines did so as a result of pressure from animal rights groups, then others followed suit, probably glad of a reason to carry fewer livestock shipments, many of which were problematical. In some instances, however, this could prove detrimental. Birds will still be traded, by inexperienced or unprincipled carriers who care nothing about transport conditions and delays in shipments. It could well be, also, that more birds will be carried illegally on ships, usually by people who know nothing about their care or welfare, with resulting high mortality.

Whatever one's views might be, for or against the export trade, one fact should be considered. Stopping the trade does not necessarily stop the capture. In some countries taking of parrots for trade, local or export, is a centuries-old tradition. If the export trade ceases, natives will continue to catch larger parrots for food. In South and Central America, for example, macaws (even Hyacinthines) and Amazons are commonly regarded as table items. A total export ban would mean that, without the income from trapped birds, more large parrots would end up in the pot and fewer in dealers' premises. Which, one might ask, is the lesser evil?

An insidious threat to island species, the cause of past extinctions and the reason for dramatic recent declines in some parrot populations is the introduction of mammals. Rats, of course, are the most important of these. A large proportion of oceanic islands or island groups have now been colonised by rats: 75 per cent for islands in the Atlantic, 83 per cent in the Indian Ocean and 81 per cent in the Pacific Ocean (Atkinson, 1985). The grounding of a single ship can have catastrophic results. In 1918 the steamship *Makambo* ran aground off Lord Howe Island, in the south-western Pacific. Five species, more than a third of the island's land-bird fauna, became extinct as a result of this invasion. I can find no reference to the date of extinction of the Lord Howe Island Parrakeet (*Cyanoramphus novaezelandiae subflavescens*) but it may have been one of the victims. In the same region, the parrakeet of Macquarie

Island (*C. n. erythrotis*) became extinct between 1881 and 1890. This was apparently a result of rabbits becoming established there in 1879. The numbers of cats, present since 1820 or before, had been restricted by the scarcity of winter food but the rabbits provided a plentiful food supply year-round; their numbers increased and so did their predation on parrakeets (Moors, Atkinson and Sherley, 1992).

During the 1970s and 1980s, rats have been instrumental in the rapid declines of some of the tiny *Vini* lories of the Pacific region (*see* pages 135 and 137).

In no country have introduced mammals had such a devastating effect on the avifauna than in New Zealand, where 50 per cent of endemic land birds are already extinct. New Zealand's birds evolved without the presence of predatory mammals, thus species which fed and/or nested on the ground had little chance of survival in their company. But it is not only these species which have suffered, some almost to the point of extinction. Some introduced mammals, such as deer, cause no direct harm to bird species, yet their impact on them is extremely serious. These grazing animals help to deplete the food supply. But their impact is negligible compared with that of the brush-tailed possum, introduced from Australia. There are an estimated 80 million of them in New Zealand — and only 3 million people. So serious are their depredations that an increasing number of endemic birds are heading towards extinction on North Island and South Island. Within a very few decades they will probably exist only on a handful of small islands which have been cleared of introduced predators — an enormous task which has cost millions of dollars. Included in this sad category are Red-fronted (Red-crowned) Kakarikis, or Parrakeets (*Cyanoramphus novaezelandiae*) and Kakas (*Nestor meridionalis*).

A biologist with the Department of Conservation in Te Anau, South Island, told me that, although Kakas can be seen, it was suspected that, in that area, they are no longer breeding due to an impoverished food supply. She also told me that a recent study of Yellow-crowned and the Red-crowned Kakarikis suggested that the reason for the decline of the latter was that it feeds at lower elevations in bush or forest; thus it is more susceptible to loss of food plants and to predators than the Yellow-crowned, which is more of a canopy dweller.

In this chapter, the main factors which have contributed to the decline of parrot species and populations are outlined. These factors are varied, difficult to rectify and occur throughout the tropics. As a result, by the early 1990s, the parrots were deemed to be the most threatened group of birds in the world.

Checklist of Species Considered Critically Endangered in 1993

Amazona brasiliensis (Red-tailed Amazon)
A. imperialis (Imperial Parrot)
A. vittata (Puerto Rican Parrot)
Anodorhynchus glaucus (Glaucous Macaw)[1]
A. leari (Lear's Macaw)
Cacatua haematuropygia (Red-vented Cockatoo)
C. sulphurea citrinocristata (Citron-crested Cockatoo)[2]
Charmosyna diadema (New Caledonian Lorikeet)[1]
Cyanopsitta spixii (Spix's Macaw)
Hapalopsittaca fuertesi (Fuertes' Parrot)
H. pyrrhops (Rusty-faced Parrot)
Loriculus catamene (Sangihe Hanging Parrot)
Neophema chrysogaster (Orange-bellied Parrakeet)
Ognorhynchus icterotis (Yellow-eared Conure)
Psephotus pulcherrimus (Paradise Parrakeet)[1]
Psittacula eques (Mauritius or Echo Parrakeet)
Vini ultramarina (Ultramarine Lory)

[1] Or already extinct.
[2] Sub-species of forms not considered critically endangered are not included except for that marked thus.
Source: *Parrots: An Action Plan for their Conservation 1993–1998*, Draft 2, compiled by ICBP.

2

Deforestation: the Crucial Issue

If and when some future Gibbon comes to write The Decline and Fall of Industrial Man, I suspect that one of the fundamental causes of our failure will be held to lie in the foolish belief that the world exists for man's exploitation. The tropical forests represent some of the most important natural features of our planet which still remain, and their rapid destruction by man for short-term ends represents one of the many blatant ways in which we seem determined to demonstrate our unfitness as a species.

D. BRYCE-SMITH, PHD, DSC, CCHEM, FRIC, PROFESSOR OF ORGANIC CHEMISTRY, UNIVERSITY OF READING, IN THE *ECOLOGIST* (JANUARY/FEBRUARY, 1980)

Tropical forests are superb machines, their components beautifully adapted to an almost infinite range of circumstances. The interactions within this ecosystem have been finely tuned over millions of years. The results are spectacular, and represent the most potent source of biological diversity on earth. The complexity of such a system is beyond replication by human ingenuity.

Until this century, the world's tropical forests represented almost insuperable barriers to human movement. Traditional slash-and-burn agriculture made little impression; the forest regenerated quickly. But once we had the technological means, we set out, in our anthropocentric way, to 'tame' this wilderness to serve the immediate needs of our own species' growing population. In Brazil, where north-eastern coastal tropical forests have been reduced to two per cent of their original area, the verb to clear is 'desbravar', literally to tame.

However, what seems so infinitely rich in its wildness becomes no more than impoverished grassland when 'tamed'. The evidence is now irrefutable. Flooding, soil erosion and only transient agricultural productivity have been the results of clearing the forests. The lives of an estimated 500 million people have been disrupted by such unnatural disasters, and the economic costs can be calculated in billions of dollars.

What cannot yet be calculated is the loss of genetic diversity which is also the consequence of deforestation. How can we calculate something based on such a small proportion of the facts? All we can say is that on the available evidence the losses would be astronomic, and for ever.

CHRISTOPH IMBODEN, DIRECTOR, INTERNATIONAL COUNCIL FOR BIRD PRESERVATION, IN THE FOREWORD TO *CONSERVATION OF TROPICAL FOREST BIRDS* (1985).

A number of factors have influenced the decline of parrot populations throughout the world, but they all pale into insignificance compared with the major cause: loss of habitat. Except in Australia, most (but not all) parrot species inhabit tropical rainforest and, to a lesser degree, deciduous forest.

The world's tropical forests lie in a belt centred on the equator, extending 23½° north and south to the Tropics of Cancer and Capricorn. Because of escalating human population as a direct consequence of advances in agriculture, much of it on land cleared from forest, tropical forests worldwide are being cleared at an alarming rate. More than 5 billion people inhabit this planet — but this number is expected to increase to 10–12 billion, according to United Nations (UN) estimates. Inevitably, this will place further pressure on the forests (Holdgate, 1992). According to the Food and Agriculture Organisation (FAO) of the UN, rates of deforestation in the tropics (now detectable using satellites) were severely underestimated in the early 1980s and have accelerated everywhere during the decade which followed. Their figures for 1981 indicated that about 6 million km^2 (2.3 million sq. miles) of forest survived in the neotropics (South and Central America), 2 million km^2 (772,000 sq. miles) in tropical Asia (40 per cent in Indonesia) and 1.7 million km^2 (660,000 sq. miles) in the Afrotropics. Recent estimates of closed tropical forest cover indicate that, in the 1980s, the total area was 11.7 million km^2 (4.5 million sq. miles) — approximately 80 per cent of its original extent. (Note the definition of closed tropical forest and open forest [woodlands], both of which can be separated on aerial photographs and satellite images. Open forests are defined by FAO as forest/grassland formations with a continuous grass layer in which the tree synusia covers more than 10 per cent of the ground; in some woodlands, the trees may cover the ground completely, as in closed forests.)

Holdgate (1992) gives a figure of 180,000 km^2 (69,500 sq. miles) of closed tropical forest destroyed annually, or over 1.5 per cent. It has been estimated (Diamond, in Diamond and Lovejoy, 1985) that about 2,600 of the world's approximately 8,700 species of birds depend on tropical forest. It follows, therefore, that if deforestation continues at its present rate, hundreds of bird species will become extinct.

Tropical rainforest grows where temperatures are high and where consistent rainfall exceeds 2,000 mm (78 in) annually. Approximately 12 per cent of the earth's surface meets this requirement, but much of it has already been cleared. This results in a problem which is increasing over much of the world: desertification due to over-intensive use of land. Hotter, drier climates locally cause what may seem to be an insignificant change in global temperature which could cause massive alterations in the distribution of rainfall.

Ecologically tropical forests are extremely important; they are the richest environment on earth, the source of oxygen for man and other animals to breathe; the cause of climate, the absorber of monsoons. Plants remove dust and other pollutants from the atmosphere; forests therefore could be thought of as giant air filters. As Robin Hanbury-Tenison (1980) wrote, the rainforest is '. . . nature at its most alive, most varied, most energetic. Within it are more species competing to fill more niches and in the process creating, with time, yet more of each. It is an environment not only beautiful and interesting, rich and alive, but also valuable. Unchanged for tens of thousands of years, yet it is developing all the time, with much to teach us about the world we inhabit, what we can make of it and life itself.'

Over 80 per cent of tropical forest biome occurs in only ten countries — Bolivia, Brazil, Colombia, Peru, Venezuela, India, Malaysia, Gabon, Zaïre and Papua New Guinea. According to the ICBP (*Newsletter*, January 1981) the most critically threatened habitats for tropical forest birds in which forest destruction is almost certain to proceed, or has already proceeded to the point where groups of bird species are threatened, are as follows: south-eastern Brazil, the northern-central Andes of Colombia, Madagascar (the Malagasy Republic), the Philippines, Indonesia, Central America, the mainland of south-east Asia, northern Queensland in Australia and East Africa.

The largest area of surviving tropical rainforest is found in South America, covering approximately 470 million ha (1,160 million acres) in the region centred on the adjoining basins of the Amazon and Orinoco rivers. Most of Asia's rainforests lie in the south-east and total about 180 million ha (450 million acres).

Africa has an even smaller area — 175 million ha (430 million acres) — most of which is located in central Africa centred on the Congo basin. Africa is poorer in flora and also has a smaller number of parrot species than any other comparable area in the tropics.

Because of the rapid rate of deforestation, estimates of surviving areas of rainforest must be out of date even before they are published. A bewildering variety of figures can be found regarding the annual rate of loss of tropical rainforest; indeed, formulating accurate estimates of this kind is extremely difficult. Government statistics are not always accurate. As an example, the Philippines claimed that forests covered 57 per cent of its land area but satellite pictures showed the true figure as 38 per cent. By 1991, however, less than 3 per cent of the original forest remained. In 1982 research undertaken by the US National Academy of Sciences and US Government Inter-Agency Task Force on Tropical Forests, indicated that worldwide losses of closed tropical forest totalled between 97,000 and 195,000 km^2 (37,500 and 75,000 sq. miles), or 1–2 per cent per annum.

At the Eighth World Forestry Congress in Jakarta, Indonesia, in 1978, it was stated that tropical moist forests were being destroyed at the rate of about 30 ha (75 acres) per minute. Moreover, the rate of destruction is accelerating. The annual loss was estimated at 15 million ha (37 million acres) — slightly more than the area of England and Wales combined. This is broken down as follows: Africa, 2 million; Asia, 5 million;

Latin America 5–10 million. (The low figure for Africa is explained by the fact that the loss of moist forest is almost total in some areas.)

We are only just beginning to comprehend the meaning of this. India's predicament can serve as an example of what will happen where insufficient rainforest survives: catastrophic flooding. In the summer of 1978 a series of three floods occurred. After the second over 42 million people had been affected and 20 million ha (49 million acres) of land inundated. In the third flood 2 million people were rendered homeless and 600 lives were lost.

As forest cover decreases more water is discharged from catchment areas, resulting in a rise in peak river levels and an increase in the area of seasonally flooded land. During floods the Amazon is rising more than ever before. When I was staying on the Colombian/ Brazilian border in 1976 the river had risen to an unprecedented level and a local Indian village had been abandoned: it was under water.

Deforestation produces less obvious, and totally unforeseen, results. In the state of Paraná on Brazil's east coast, frost struck at the coffee plantations in 1979 with a loss of 6 million of the expected national harvest of 26 million bags. It is not understood whether the spread of frost is caused by local deforestation or by the reduction of the Amazon rainforest. The long-predicted regional climatic and hydrological changes that would be the expected result of Amazonian deforestation had already begun.

One can, perhaps, comprehend that politicians have little interest in saving rainforest for its own sake, yet its destruction is in the worst interests of man. So what argument can ecologists put forward that will halt the dreadful plundering of the world's forests? Harry Knowles, an ecologist who has spent 22 years in the Amazon region, has warned that if deforestation continues at the present rate the Brazilians could create another Sahara. Yet still his words go unheeded.

There is another reason why rainforests are beneficial to man. Already they have yielded numerous useful products: coffee, cocoa, bananas, various spices and rubber, plus chemicals which have been exploited: quinine, curare and strychnine, for example. Pharmacognocists continue to find useful products and undoubtedly many more remain to be discovered where rainforests survive. As has been pointed out (Stonehouse, 1981), 'to destroy this bounty of actual and potential benefits is an act of lunacy that, in the long term, we and our descendants will certainly come to regret'. The tragedy is that the destruction of rainforest is totally unnecessary. The three principal reasons for its annihilation are as follows.

1) Farming — for subsistence and cash crops. This represents very short-term gain: because of the poor quality of tropical soils, cleared areas cannot long sustain human activity. Deforestation for this purpose is therefore a colossal waste.

2) Firewood. It has been estimated that, worldwide, almost half the wood harvested annually is used as firewood, and in underdeveloped countries 80 per cent of wood is burned for fuel. Deforestation for this purpose is a colossal waste because plants can be grown to be burned in power plants or converted to other fuels. Plants (biomass) will be a major future source of energy — when the tropical forests are depleted.

3) Ranching. This is the principal reason for deforestation in the Amazon basin and in Central America. In Brazil 7.8 million ha (19 million acres) of Amazon land were cleared between 1976 and 1978 to make way for 336 ranches running 6 million head of cattle. The beef is destined to be used almost exclusively for hamburgers in fast food chains in the USA. Ironically, although more than a quarter of all Central American forests were destroyed between about 1960 and 1980 to produce beef for the US, *per capita* consumption of beef in Central America has dropped steadily. Deforestation for this purpose is a colossal waste because most ranches located on what was previously tropical lowland forest are proving to be ecologically unstable. The fertility of the land declines so rapidly that raising cattle becomes unprofitable in a decade or so (Ehrlich and Ehrlich, 1982).

Furthermore, what of the cultural effects of deforestation? It has been said that '. . . the destruction of the tropical forests will have profound effects on human culture, for we are inextricably linked to the forest which, in the words of a French forester, "is part of the soul of man although we may not be aware of it"' (Villiard, 1978).

The most immediate effect of deforestation is the destruction of the many forms of life rainforests support. Although they comprise only about a third of the total area of tropical forests, they contain between 2 and 5 million of the earth's 10 million species of plants and animals. Many of these cannot survive outside the forest. For example, of the 460 species of birds known to breed in Peninsular Malaysia, about 60 per cent are incapable of survival outside the forest (Wells, 1971).

Except in Australia, almost all the endangered or threatened parrots are forest-dwelling species. A notable exception is Lear's Macaw from the Brazilian Raso da Catarina, an area of low and often thorny vegetation adapted to the very dry climate (*see* pages 39–40).

Although parrots are found in many types of habitat, they are essentially forest-dwellers. A few can adapt to secondary forest or even other types of habitat, but the majority are doomed to extinction without the forests. Even where substantial areas of forest remain, some of

Large-scale deforestation carried out by hand in Brazil.

the larger species face a serious problem which could lead to their extinction within a very few years: loss of nesting sites.

Some parrots nest in holes in cliffs or rocks but the majority by far need trees, using natural cavities or holes fashioned by woodpeckers or other birds. In selective felling the larger trees may be removed, leaving only those which are too small to contain suitable nesting sites. Practical measures could be taken to prevent this, but they would necessitate the interest and co-operation of either commercial logging companies or conservation organisations, on which it would be optimistic to rely. The loss of nest sites due to the activities of trappers has been mentioned elsewhere (see page 21). Because many parrots nest at considerable heights from the ground, obtaining young is seldom easy. This has led some hunters into the deplorable practice of felling the nest tree to collect the young. Other hunters remove the young by making a hole at the base of the nesting cavity, also rendering the nest unsuitable for future use. The more intelligent hunter leaves the nest intact, and uses a nylon noose to remove the chicks.

I believe that felling or damage to nest trees should be an offence punishable by law. It is true that such a law would be extremely difficult to enforce; but its very existence would at least draw attention to the harmful consequences of such activities.

In Australia the loss of trees containing hollows is widespread, largely because of land clearace for agriculture and an increasing adoption of clear-felling practices. The root-attacking fungus *Phytophthora cinnamomi* and severe outbreaks of defoliating insects also cause significant losses (Forshaw, 1981).

Denis Saunders (CSIRO Division of Wildlife Research) studied the White-tailed Cockatoo (*see* page 28) at two sites in Western Australia. He found that the annual loss rate of nesting hollows were 4.8 per cent and 2.2 per cent which exceeded the rates of formation. At a third site the study had to be abandoned after a number of hollow trees were destroyed during a controlled burning operation in a state forest reserve. Other hollows were destroyed by persons illegally removing cockatoo nestlings. Forshaw commented: 'These findings highlight what I consider to be a major threat to parrots and other hollow-nesting birds.'

Probably no parrot in the world has been subjected to such an intensive field management programme as the Puerto Rican Parrot (*Amazona vittata*). This species survives precariously in an area of about 1,600 ha (4,000 acres) of the Luquillo Forest. When the island was forested, it was found over the entire island; its present range is estimated at 0.2 per cent of its former one. A three-year study of this species during the early 1950s concluded that about 200 parrots survived. In 1968, when the population had plummeted to about 24 birds, it was suspected that one reason for their lack of breeding success might be the scarcity of nesting sites. Over 1,000 trees were examined in the area of the forest inhabited by the parrots: many of the cavities found were too small or too wet to be usable. The conclusion reached was that one suitable nest site was located about every 4 ha (10 acres). The result was that some pairs either failed to breed or their endeavours were doomed to failure. One cavity used was so wet that the incubating female would emerge with slimy breast feathers. There was little chance of her eggs hatching.

Shortage of sites led to lethal battles among pairs. In 1974 two pairs fought for possession of one nest and one member of each pair was killed in the fracas. An attempt to remedy the situation had been made by providing artificial sites in the vicinity; but no interest was shown in them. In later years the parrots were persuaded to use artificial nests because those in charge of the project knew where to provide them through watching the territorial behaviour of the birds.

Another serious problem resulting from habitat disturbance is fragmentation of feeding areas. This can have disastrous consequences for breeding birds. In Puerto Rico in the 1960s Cameron Kepler took up residence in an isolated mountain-top house overlooking the range of the Puerto Rican Parrot. His observations at one nest revealed that the female travelled for as long as 62 minutes to her feeding ground, leaving the nest unattended for a third of all daylight hours and therefore extremely vulnerable to predators. Kepler felt that the parrot went in search of food not found within the forest, thus pinpointing a problem of a species displaced even slightly from its original habitat.

A study made by research biologist Denis Saunders in Australia has shown that breeding populations may be endangered by fragmentation of nearby feeding areas despite a continuing sufficiency in total food resources. His subject was the White-tailed Black Cockatoo, whose poor breeding rate was due to the amount of time the birds were forced to spend foraging away from the nest in the scattered feeding areas. He found that some areas of useful food were not visited by the birds from one year to the next because of their patchy rather than continuous distribution (Forshaw, 1981).

Denis Saunders studied the breeding behaviour of this species at two locations in the wheatbelt of Western Australia, north-east of Perth. At both sites pairs attempted to lay every year but at one production of chicks per pair was half that of the other. In addition, on fledging the chicks weighed less. What factor or factors caused this marked discrepancy? Solely fragmentation of the feeding area. At Coomallo Creek, the successful site, large tracts of uncleared plain country surround the nesting area: the soil, lacking in trace elements, was only recently considered suitable for agriculture. There was an area of 6,750 ha (16,680 acres) in which breeding birds foraged for food. In contrast, at Manmanning, the breeding cockatoos foraged over an area of 48,400 ha (120,000 acres). Little forest remained and the breeding population had decreased from 20 pairs in 1970 to 13 pairs in 1974. During the same period, the Coomallo Creek area was occupied by 75 breeding pairs.

At Manmanning during the period 1970 to 1975, young produced per pair averaged one chick every three years. Fledged young weighed 503 g (83 per cent of the adult weight). At Coomallo Creek the reproductive rate was two young every three years, with fledged chicks weighing 590 g (97 per cent of adult weight). At both localities, all pairs attempted to nest every year. They existed on the same foods — native plants and the seeds of the introduced corkscrew grass.

However, at Coomallo Creek the cockatoos do not have to go far in search of food; they forage within 1–2 km (0.5–1 mile) of the nesting area. At Manmanning shortage of food means that breeding pairs have to spend long periods away from the nest in order to find enough food to survive. Females are forced to leave their nests during incubation and to desert the chicks for long periods during the day, thus exposing them to predators or to other birds seeking nest sites. There are areas containing food not far distant which have not been found by the cockatoos, because of the fragmented distribution of food sources. These unfortunate birds simply do not have time to seek food and to breed efficiently . . . .

The widespread deforestation which has occurred throughout the world's tropical forests in recent years

Clear-felled rainforest in Sumatra.

is, to my mind, the major tragedy of the age in which we live. In Latin America, which has a great wealth of parrot species, the severity of the annual forest loss is influenced by the massive increase in human populations.

In many parts of Central America there has been extensive habitat destruction. The cool, moist highlands which are now densely populated have been transformed for the growing of coffee, tea and quinine, and the Pacific lowlands have been turned over to the production of beef and cotton for export. Conservation has low or nil priority. In Guatemala extensive lowland forests remain only in the remote Peten area; some forest also remains in the south-east. Except for the Tikal National Park, with its fabled Mayan ruins, no important area is protected in any way.

The same situation is found throughout Central America. Only in Costa Rica, the most progressive, democratic and stable nation, is there a firmly established conservation movement. It is fortunate that much has already been achieved, for there is unlikely to be much wild land remaining outside protected areas within a few years. In no other country has forest destruction on the Caribbean side been so extensive. This is due to the fertility of the land which has proved ideal for growing a wide range of crops, including coffee. It has been estimated (Britt, 1981) that of the remaining 1.5 million ha (3.7 million acres) of rainforest, 60,000 ha (150,000 acres) are being illegally destroyed every year.

One factor which has been responsible for a very rapid change in the face of Costa Rica is the Pan-American Highway, completed in the 1960s, which resulted in a great influx of people and the disappearance of forest in the vicinity of the road. Sixteen species of parrots are found in Costa Rica, but how long can they survive outside protected areas at the present rate of forest destruction?

In Panama deforestation has been equally severe. Until the early decades of the twentieth century, the Pacific slope of much of the more humid parts was covered with extensive forest. Today little remains, except along some watercourses and on steep hillsides. Extensive forest remains only in the roadless side of the Azuero Peninsula and in the Darién region, an area of treacherous swamps and trackless jungle which separates Panama from Colombia. Great change is destined for this area, however, for the Darién gap will be opened with the completion of the Inter-American Highway which will allow traffic to pass into Colombia, thus providing an immense highway which will run from Alaska to the tip of South America. The ecological significance of such a highway is daunting indeed.

A similarly depressing story can be told for the tropical forests and other parrot habitats throughout South and Central America. There are additional pressures in some cases, even in sparsely populated areas, such as Ecuador's eastern Amazon lowlands. Covering half of the country's area, its often dangerous fast-running rivers, strewn with hazards such as rocks and rapids, have resulted in much of the area remaining undisturbed and almost unexplored. It might have formed a natural reserve but for one fact — the discovery of oil. Construction of roads and the opening of an airport are already transforming (to the detriment of the fauna) what has been foreseen as one of the richest areas in the whole of South America.

Considering its relatively small size — 270,600 km^2 (104,500 sq. miles), i.e. a little more than twice the size of England or approximately the same extent as the state of Colorado — it is rich in parrot species. Thirty-seven are found there.

The issue of deforestation assumes a magnitude of crucial proportions in the Amazon region, the area of the neotropics where parrots have reached their zenith. The following was pointed out in the *Ecologist* (January/February, 1980): 'In recent years the eyes of the whole world have been focused on the development of the 600 million hectare Amazon rain forests comprising over 54 per cent of the world's tropical moist forests. Three-fifths of the total (360 million hectares) is located in Brazil, but substantial areas are to be found in Colombia, Venezuela, Bolivia, Peru, Guyana and Ecuador. The forests contain on average about 900 tons of living plants per hectare and altogether contain the largest collection of plant and animal species in the world.'

Estimates of deforestation so far vary between a fifth and a third of the total forest area. In Colombia alone it is said that 1 million ha (2.5 million acres) of forest are destroyed annually and, in a report published in 1989, it was suggested that the estimated area of Colombia still under natural forest cover was 38 per cent, most of this being lowland rainforest in Amazonia and Chocó. Ten years ago, little was known of the status of most of Colombia's parrots. It is now known that several are endangered by loss of habitat. These are Branicki's (Yellow-plumed) Conure (*Leptopsittaca branickii*) — also found in Ecuador and southern Peru, the Yellow-eared Conure (*see* pages 18–19), the Flame-winged Conure (*Pyrrhura calliptera*), the Rufous-fronted Parrakeet (*Bolborhynchus ferrugineifrons*), the Spot-winged Parrotlet (*Touit stictoptera*) — also found in eastern Ecuador and northern Peru but most threatened in Colombia and Fuertes' Parrot (*Hapalopsittaca fuertesi*). It has been suggested that the latter may already be extinct (Collar and Juniper, in Beissinger and Snyder, 1992); there has been no confirmed sighting of it since 1911. However, the humid temperate forests on the western slope of the central Andes, where it was reported to occur, have suffered much deforestation. Collar and Juniper state that the Andean valleys (subtropical and temperate zones) of Colombia and Ecuador are one of the three areas in which 70 per cent of the threatened parrots of the neotropics occur.

Massive deforestation has taken place in Ecuador. The effects have been particularly severe in the valley between the Andes, which runs the length of the country. Even where the slopes are too steep for farming, wood is extracted for fuel and for timber. At lower altitudes, tropical forests on the Pacific slope have also suffered serious destruction. One small parrot, unknown to science until 1980 and not formally named until 1988, was known to be threatened by habitat destruction soon after its discovery. It is the El Oro Conure (*Pyrrhura orcesi*), whose known range is humid forest between 600 and 1,000 m (2,000 and 3,300 ft), extending about 100 km (62 miles) in length and 5–10 km (3–6 miles) in width. Another Ecuadorian endemic from the same genus is the White-necked Conure (*P. albipectus*) from the south-east. It is believed to breed in the Cordillera Cutucú.

The Orange-flanked or Grey-cheeked Parrakeet (*Brotogeris pyrrhopterus*) has not declined solely because of habitat loss. For years it was very popular as a pet in the USA and was exported there by the thousand. In 1984 alone 20,000 were exported from Peru, where it is found in the extreme north-west. In view of the limited distribution area of this species, and loss of the deciduous forest in which it occurs, it is most important that it is protected from further trapping. In contrast, the Rusty-faced Parrot (*Hapalopsittaca pyrrhops*) is unknown in aviculture and threatened by the loss of forest to woodcutters and charcoal gatherers, even though it occurs at an altitude of 2,500–3,500 m (8,200–11,500 ft).

In Brazil the situation is even more serious. In the late 1960s the flora and fauna of the Mato Grosso region in western central Brazil were studied by members of an expedition mounted jointly by the Royal Geographical Society and the Royal Society. When the work there was concluded, the forest which had been surveyed was cut down and burned and the land cleared for cattle farming. Despite the pleas of the scientists to preserve their study area, everything was destroyed (Hanbury-Tenison, 1980). Their warnings about the dangerous effects of deforestation were ignored, as they have been throughout Brazil; and their forebodings have been borne out during the past decade as Brazil has continued to waste the vast assets of her forests.

Estimated percentage annual clearance of tropical closed* forest for 1981–85

Neotropics		Asia: insular	
Bolivia	0.2	Indonesia	0.5
Brazil	0.4	Malaysia	1.2
Colombia	1.8	Papua New Guinea	0.1
Costa Rica	4.0	Philippines	1.0
Ecuador	2.4		
Mexico	1.8		
Peru	0.4	Africa	
Venezuela	0.4	Ivory Coast	6.5
		Nigeria	5.0
Asia: continental		Congo	0.1
India	0.3	Madagascar	1.5

*See definition on page 25.

Estimates of tropical deforestation vary due to such factors as definition and the difficulty of interpreting data from remote sensing (satellites). The figures above, prepared by the FAO (1988) are a guide to comparative rates of deforestation in selected countries.

3

South-eastern Brazil: an Ecological Disaster Area

As the situation now stands, the Atlantic forests and their fauna must be considered among the most endangered forest ecosystems on earth. This region presents an international conservation problem of immense proportions that requires action on many different fronts if there is to be any hope of saving what little remains.

RUSSELL A. MITTERMEIER *ET AL*, OF EASTERN BRAZIL, IN
INTERNATIONAL ZOO YEAR BOOK (1982)

Comprising almost half of the total land area of the South American continent, Brazil has 70 species of parrots (nearly 20 more than any other country) within its approximate 8,510,000 km^2 (3,280,000 sq. miles). Larger than continental USA, Brazil includes the great Amazon basin, containing some of the longest and deepest rivers in existence. The broadleaved trees and shrubs of the tropical forests grow to gigantic proportions, with probably a greater diversity of species than any other area on earth, except the rainforests of Borneo. In a British forest, for example, there might be six species of tree to 2.5 km^2 (1 sq. mile); in Brazil as many as 3,000 species have been found in a similar area.

These forests provide optimum conditions for parrots: food is always plentiful, weather conditions are near perfect and there is, in undisturbed areas, a wide choice of nesting sites. It is no accident that parrots have reached their zenith here. This area formed the greatest refuge on earth for members of the parrot family until the recent needless and foolish destruction of the forests.

This has been most severe in a region of special biological interest, the coastal strip in the south. An area of high rainfall, it was formerly clothed in tropical forest from sea level to the tops of all but the highest mountains. The comparatively narrow coastal belt is separated from the immense forests of Amazonia by more arid country inland. The isolation of the area has resulted in the evolution of species and sub-species of birds and animals which are quite distinct from their counterparts elsewhere or which have no such counterparts. The avifauna of this region is therefore quite extraordinarily rich. Unfortunately, nowhere has deforestation been so severe. Huge areas of forest have been eradicated to make way for gigantic centres of human habitation, such as São Paulo with its 6 million inhabitants, and Rio de Janeiro (5 million). These areas have been colonised for more than three centuries, but destruction has been most rapid in the past two or three decades. Probably less than 1 per cent remains in a relatively undisturbed condition (Mittermeier et al, 1982). There *are* reserves — but all are too small and most are already isolated forest islands.

Further south, forest destruction between Bahia and Rio Grande do Sul has resulted in fragmentation of once continuous forest into a mosaic of small tracts. As a result, of the 94 endemics, 21 species and sub-species of birds were known to be endangered by 1977 (King, in Temple, 1977). A 4,000-ha (9,900-acre) area of forest, privately owned by a prominent Brazilian industrialist, is a refuge for 10 endangered species or sub-species of birds — a density unparalleled elsewhere.

Deforestation by 1990 in the Atlantic Region of south-eastern Brazil

State*	Total area in km²	Approx original area of forest in km²	Percentage of forest intact in 1990	Totally protected area in 1990 in km²
Rio Grande do Norte	53 167	2320	14	20
Pernambuco	101 023	18 500	2	60
Sergipe	21 862	9800	1	30
Espírito Santo	45 733	45 500	10	910
Goiás	340 166	38 200	6	–
Rio de Janeiro	43 653	43 500	11	4420
Paraná	199 324	183 000	19	5160
Rio Grande do Sul	280 674	88 900	13	720
Total for all Atlantic states	3 023 316	1 205 780	12	30 950

* States are randomly selected.
Source: Brown and Brown, in Whitmore and Sayer (1992).

It has been estimated that up to 10 million ha (25 million acres) of forest are destroyed annually in Brazil. It therefore comes as no surprise that of the 31 species of continental neotropical parrots considered threatened by Ridgely (1981), 12 are found within south-eastern Brazil. Eleven years later, the second draft of the Parrot Action Plan categorised the species from this area as follows.

Critical or Extinct
Anodorhynchus glaucus (Glaucous Macaw)

Critical
Amazona brasiliensis (Red-tailed Amazon)*

Endangered
Pionus menstruus reichenowi (Reichenow's Blue-headed Pionus)*

Endangered or Vulnerable
Amazona pretrei (Pretre's Amazon)
A. rhodocorytha (Red-browed Amazon)*
A. vinacea (Vinaceous Amazon)

Vulnerable
Ara maracana (Illiger's [Blue-winged] Macaw)
Aratinga auricapilla (Golden-capped Conure)*
Pyrrhura cruentata (Blue-throated Conure)*
P. l. leucotis (White-eared Conure)*
Touit melanonotus (Brown-backed Parrotlet)*
T. surda (Golden-tailed Parrotlet)*
Triclaria malachitacea (Purple-bellied Parrot)

Vulnerable or Safe
Pionopsitta pileata (Red-capped [Pileated] Parrot]

* Brazilian endemic.

It is worth noting that, with the exception of the two *Touit* species (members of this genus are virtually unknown in captivity), all these parrots are from genera which breed very well in captivity. Indeed, three of the species listed are extremely prolific: Illiger's Macaw and the Golden-capped and White-eared Conures. Most of the birds on this list are endemic to Brazil and therefore (as Brazil has not permitted the export of its birds for several decades) all are rare in aviculture, except Illiger's Macaw and the Golden-capped Conure. With the exception of the *Touit*s, whose captive breeding potential is unknown, all the species listed could be saved from extinction by efficient captive breeding programmes.

Some are harder to breed than others. The easiest must surely be the White-eared Conure. When I became curator at the breeding centre of Palmitos Park in 1989, there were ten White-eared Conures of the threatened nominate race: seven males and three females. In that year three pairs were set up for breeding and one pair nested. In the following year, three pairs nested and the year after that the first second-generation young were produced. By the end of 1992 the number had grown to 68 birds; 82 had hatched, 64 had been reared and six had died. Due to space limitations, only four pairs were set up for breeding (due to the refusal of Spanish CITES officials to permit us to export the captive-bred young). Had these young been paired up as soon as they were old enough to breed, by the end of 1992, the total number could easily have been increased to 200. Note that all but three of the young were parent-reared. If hand-rearing had been employed the number could probably have been doubled. So prolific is this species that one clutch contained ten eggs.

During the same period, ie. 1989–92, two pairs of Illiger's Macaws were nesting in the breeding centre at Palmitos Park. One pair reared 13 young and the other pair 15 young. Again, had hand-rearing been employed, the number might have been doubled. Another notable performance by a species on the vulnerable list was that

Golden-capped Conure — endangered by habitat destruction.

of the only pair of Purple-bellied Parrots (a rare species in captivity) at Palmitos Park. They commenced to breed in 1990 when one youngster was reared to independence; in each of the following two years four were reared.

Amazons, alas, are not usually as prolific as *Pyrrhura* conures or small macaws. Nevertheless, captive populations of endangered and threatened species can quickly be built up in competent hands. Many Brazilian parrots are threatened, but the avicultural expertise exists to ensure at least that the species are maintained in captivity and, should suitable habitat survive, *perhaps* even providing the possibility of re-stocking the wild with captive-bred birds.

All the species listed are threatened or endangered solely as a result of loss of habitat. In south-eastern Brazil, the White-eared is now rare and local (other sub-species occur in eastern Brazil and in Venezuela), having suffered a dramatic decline in recent years. It is found in reasonable numbers only in southern Bahia, due to the practice of retaining forest trees for shade in cacao plantations. Its relict distribution is virtually identical to that of the Blue-throated Conure (*Pyrrhura cruentata*), which has fared even worse and occurs in smaller flocks. This, the largest and one of the most handsome of the genus, has no sub-species and occurs only in eastern Brazil. Forshaw (1989) gives its distribution as southern Bahia south to south-eastern Minas Gerais, possibly also coastal north-eastern São Paulo, but there have been no recent records from São Paulo, Rio de Janeiro or southern Espírito Santo. As Ridgely (1981) comments: 'This region has been heavily inhabited for a century or more, and virtually all lowland forest has long since been cut, though the few remaining patches could still harbor small so far undetected populations (this perhaps most likely in coastal northeastern São Paulo).'

Its numbers have suffered a massive decline but it should survive as long as some of its remnant populations exist in protected areas. It is locally common in certain forest localities and persists in smaller numbers in agricultural regions where many forest trees are retained. This is often done to shade cocoa or coffee crops. Indeed, this habit may be the redeeming factor for a large part of the surviving Brazilian rainforest.

At present the stronghold of the Cruentata Conure is the Sooretama Reserve in northern Espírito Santo. In Minas Gerais it may now occur only in the Rio Doce State Park where it was seen in 1977. In southern Bahia it is more widespread and occurs in the zone of most extensive cocoa growing, approximately from the Rio Macuri north to around Una. It also occurs in the Monte Pascoal National Park.

Anyone fortunate enough to be familiar with this conure in captivity would agree that its extinction would be a tragedy. One of the most distinctive of the genus, like most *Pyrrhura*s it adapts readily to captivity and possesses an especially pleasing personality. It is held in few collections; it is fortunate that it is proving prolific.

The third conure endemic to south-eastern Brazil is the Golden-capped Conure (*Aratinga auricapilla aurifrons*) not to be confused with the Golden-crowned Conure (*A. aurea*); the nominate form from north and central Brazil is less threatened. Closely related to the Sun and Jendaya Conures, the Golden-capped has but a recent captive history; indeed, it was unknown prior to the mid-1970s. It is already firmly established in the USA, proving an exceptionally willing breeder in captivity.

At least in the USA the captive future of this conure

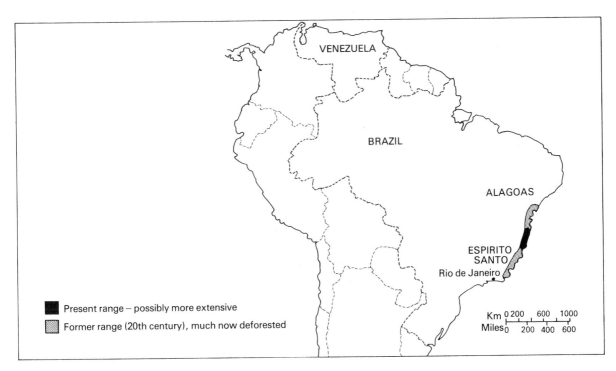

VENEZUELA

BRAZIL

ALAGOAS

ESPIRITO
SANTO
Rio de Janeiro

■ Present range – possibly more extensive

▨ Former range (20th century), much now deforested

Km 0 200   600   1000
Miles 0   200 400 600

Distribution of Red-browed Amazon (*Amazona rhodocorytha*).

looks fairly secure. Alas, the same cannot be said for its wild population. It formerly occurred from Bahia south through coastal Brazil, probably to Santa Catarina, and inland to southern Minas Gerais and Goiás. Its distribution has been greatly fragmented by forest destruction and its numbers have declined substantially in recent decades. This species cannot exist without forest, and thus it seems destined to become even rarer as forest destruction continues.

Ridgely (1981) gives recent records from the following localities: coastal Bahía (the Santo Amaro area south of Salvador, and in and around the Monte Pascoal National Park), eastern Minas Gerais (seen in 1977 in the Rio Doce State Park) and southern Goiás (near Goiânia and Rio Verde). Other small populations doubtless exist but have yet to be located.

Under these circumstances, the present small captive population assumes great significance. It presents an opportunity for aviculturists to prove their ability to establish a species from a limited number of birds.

In contrast to the conures, the *Touit* Parrotlets are small, inconspicuous birds about which very little is

known. They are distributed throughout the tropical part of South America; one species is found in Central America and another, *T. batavica*, includes Trinidad and Tobago in its range. From Trinidad came the only *Touit* Parrotlets I know of which have been kept in captivity outside their native country. They were imported by an English aviculturist, the late Herbert Murray, and lived for some months in his huge, planted aviaries. His experience indicated that they were difficult to keep alive.

Two *Touit*s are found in Brazil and there is no record of either ever having been in captivity. The Golden-tailed Parrotlet (*T. surda*) would appear to be the rarest as it is endemic to the area from Pernambuco south to Rio de Janeiro. This little parrot, which measures only 16 cm (6 in), is attired in different shades of green, with the tail feathers greenish-yellow. There is some golden yellow on the face and olive-brown on the wings.

A small, green, canopy-dwelling parrot, it is extremely difficult to observe in its natural habitat. This may, in part, account for the few records of it; however, the massive deforestation which has occurred in its range makes it seem almost certain that this is a genuinely threatened species. Ridgely (1981) recorded: 'I suspect that, if it has one, the Golden-tailed Parrotlet's stronghold is in southern Bahía, where forest trees have widely been left standing to shade cacao, and where many undisturbed patches of forest also remain (e.g. around Una). I did observe one pair in the Monte Pascal National Park in Sept. 1977; presumably the park harbours a population of unknown size.'

The Brown-backed Parrotlet (*T. melanonota*) bears some resemblance to the Sapphire-rumped Parrotlet (*T. purpurata*) which has a much wider distribution in northern Brazil, the Guianas, Venezuela and Colombia. Both species are notable for their startling black-tipped red tail feathers. The Brown-backed Parrotlet favours humid forests on lower montane slopes, rarely, if ever, descending to the coastal lowlands, where *T. surda* is found. Another victim of forest destruction, its range has been severely fragmented; however, it is believed to be less rare than *T. surda*. Small numbers survive in the Floresta da Tijuca, above Rio; it is also known to occur in the Serra das Oragaos National Park in nearby Guanabara.

There seems little possibility of these *Touit* Parrotlets ever being in captivity: their location and capture would not be easy and even keeping them alive might prove to be very difficult. Strict protection of their surviving habitat seems to be the only hope for their survival which will be precarious at best.

Compared with *Touit*s and other genera of small neotropical parrots, the Amazons (*Amazona* species) are relatively well known. There are about 30 species (taxonomic interpretation of species and sub-species differs) and south-eastern Brazil has more species classified (by ICBP) as endangered or vulnerable than any other part of the neotropics except the Caribbean. The plight of the Brazilian species, marooned by loss of habitat, can be likened to that of the Caribbean island species, all of which are threatened or endangered by forest destruction.

As a group the Amazon parrots are perhaps better known that any other genus of large parrots, because of their popularity as pets. One species, however, is still little-known: the Red-tailed Amazon (*Amazona brasiliensis*). Even its appearance hints at the unusual: the forehead, crown and lores are a unique shade of pinkish-red, and the cheeks, throat and ear coverts are pale brownish-pink, with the tips of the feathers purplish-blue. The tail, the most beautifully marked feature, is banded at the tip with greenish-yellow, preceded by a band of carmine-red and another of purple-blue on the outer three tail feathers near the base.

It now occurs only in the eastern part of the Serra do Mar and its coastal lowlands — in south-eastern São Paulo, Paraná and northern Santa Catarina. The Parrot Action Plan states: 'At least 12 reserves have been created within its range, but trapping, shooting, loss of nest trees to boat builders and land occupation still are major problems.'

A serious and rapid decline led to the Red-tailed Amazon being considered critically endangered by the early 1990s.

Its declining population is estimated at 2,000–3,000 birds. By 1993 it was considered to be critically endangered. (There are two other Amazons in this category: the Imperial and the Puerto Rican.) As it currently has the largest population of any parrot classified as critical, this status reflects its very rapid decline.

Relatively little is known about the Red-tailed Amazon. Pedro Scherer Neto, of the Curitiba Natural History Museum, made it the subject of his MSc thesis in 1989. Its preferred nest tree is 'guanandi' (*Callophyllum brasiliensis*); nest holes are found at a height of 8–10 m (26–33 ft). Nests are located in the forests and also on small islands, from which the Amazons fly daily to the mainland. The result of a census conducted by Scherer Neto suggested that there were about 1,000 Red-tailed Amazons in the state of Paraná in November 1992. At the same time another ornithologist estimated that about 1,000 also existed in the state of São Paulo.

The Red-tailed Amazon was almost unknown outside Brazil until the late 1980s; since then small numbers have regularly been smuggled out. In 1993 Pedro Scherer Neto informed me: 'The illegal trade continues, especially in the state of Saõ Paulo, many of the young going to Europe.'

Another endangered Amazon of this region is *A. rhodocorytha* (there is no agreement on the common name — Red-topped, Red-browed or Red-crowned, all of which could describe other species). Found from Alagoas south to Rio de Janeiro, it may already be extinct in the latter state. As recently as 1935 Pinto described it as common in riverine forest in southern Bahia. In winter it moved into extensive mangroves along the coast. Now rare and locally distributed, it is almost one of the most threatened of the mainland *Amazona*. This has come about as a result of extensive destruction of the coastal lowland forests.

Its declining population, estimated at 2,500 in 1992, survives in some remnant forest areas. The *Parrot Action Plan* suggests that the Porto Seguro Reserve in Bahía must be given total protection and that the authorities in Rio de Janeiro state should take the necessary steps to protect the forest where this species occurs outside existing park boundaries, such as in the Desengano State Park and on Ilha Grande. An education campaign in areas adjacent to breeding sites might reduce the taking of nestlings and the capture and shooting of adult birds.

A field study which commenced in 1991 indicated that the Red-spectacled or Pretre's Amazon (*Amazona pretrei*) is one of the most threatened birds of South America. It has undergone a precipitous population decline during the past 50 years. By the early 1990s it was almost entirely restricted to the forests of Rio Grande do Sul in southern Brazil, although some birds still occurred in Santa Catarina. Its numbers have been reduced by large-scale deforestation during the past 150 years. In recent times removal of young from nests for the local pet trade has further threatened its survival, especially as the nest is often damaged in the process. In 1993 its population was assessed as between 7,500 and 8,500 birds. A number of measures have been proposed for its protection but none have yet been effective. The only roosting site in its range in a protected area suffers disturbance from a shooting club and from families living within the park (at Carazinho).

It has always been a very rare species in aviculture (virtually unknown until the late 1980s) and is represented in few collections. However, there is a chance that it might be established in Europe from a small number of birds there.

4

Blue Macaws: Habitat Specialists and the Lone Survivor

We had travelled several thousand miles through the reported habitat of the Glaucous macaw and realised that there was no chance of it still existing. I believe that the Glaucous macaw has been extinct since the early years of this century, the main cause being the clearance of its main food source, the yatay palm.

TONY PITTMAN, IN *THE GLAUCOUS MACAW. DOES IT STILL EXIST? MAGAZINE OF THE PARROT SOCIETY (1992)*

If the conclusions of Tony Pittman's well-reasoned report are correct, the Glaucous Macaw was the only known species of parrot to become extinct during the twentieth century except, of course, for the Carolina Parrakeet. (Considering the fact that three parrot species became known to science during the 1980s, it is not inconceivable that others existed and became extinct without ever having been formally described.) In recent years, more mystique has surrounded three species of macaws than any other parrots; speculation centred around their continued existence (Glaucous), their unknown origin (Lear's) and, finally, the widely accepted theory that only one bird survived in the wild (Spix's). All three are blue macaws, quite different in appearance to the picture of a large, gaudy, long-tailed parrot which the word 'macaw' conjures to most.

The number of macaw species which survive today is 16, if we accept that the Glaucous is indeed extinct. Another species, the Cuban (*Ara tricolor*) became extinct towards the end of the nineteenth century. With two out of 18 extinct, and another generally believed to

be effectively extinct in the wild, the macaws, it could be argued, have fared worse than any other group of parrots. To understand why, let us examine each case history. Firstly, there is the Cuban Macaw, a medium-sized species, 46 cm (18 in) long, with striking red, orange and blue plumage. Found only in Cuba, its extinction was probably the result of capture for food and clearance of forest for agricultural purposes. It nested in palm trees and fed on their fruits and those of other trees. The last-known specimen to be taken was shot in 1864 but it was suggested that a few survived in the swamps of southern Cuba, at least until the late 1880s.

In contrast, the last-known Glaucous Macaw died in a zoo, but the fact that it *was* the last Glaucous Macaw was unknown at the time. Indeed, the suggestion that it was extinct did not even start to appear in the literature until the 1970s. In *Birds to Watch* (ICBP's world checklist of threatened birds), published in 1988, it was stated to be '. . . almost certainly now extinct'.

During the 1980s rumours persisted that Glaucous Macaws had been located in the wild, but all these rumours were unsubstantiated. In 1991 the controversy raged anew when British aviculturist Harry Sissen was given permission to import two Lear's Macaws from Mulhouse Zoo in France. He made an announcement to the press that one of these birds was probably a Glaucous, his identification being based mainly on its smaller size. Most informed people believed that here was a case of mistaken identity. Nevertheless, it captured the imagination of national and regional press, and TV and radio presenters. It inspired scepticism in the minds of two British macaw enthusiasts, Tony Pittman and Joe Cuddy, who decided to spend their annual leave on a fact-finding mission.

They read all the available literature and an unpublished report by Nigel Collar of ICBP, which summarised reported sightings with map references. When plotted on a map, they formed an almost perfect circle covering Corrientes and Missiones provinces in north-eastern Argentina, Artigas province in north-western Uruguay and Rio Grande do Sul and Santa Catarina provinces in south-western Brazil. Then, on June 30 1992, they left London for Argentina. In the Museum of Natural Sciences in Buenos Aires they photographed and filmed a mounted specimen of the Glaucous Macaw, noting its distinctive plumage colour: 'greenish-blue with a greyish-brown hindneck, throat and upper breast. The head was bluish-grey. We videoed the skin from different angles in the basement room with indirect daylight and perceived an astonishing change in coloration from almost aquamarine to blue. The back plumage close-up, almost seemed to have a brownish edging to the feathers.

In any event, the skin could not possibly be confused with the Lear's . . . .'

Tony Pittman researched nineteenth-century references from the few naturalists who were familiar with the Glaucous Macaw and found that some had been corrupted with interpolations and mistranslations by later writers. The old accounts contained numerous references to the yatay palm (*Butia yatai*) which, he believed, could have been the main food source. He was informed by the Fundación Vida Silvestre Argentina that these palms had nearly all been cleared because they grew on what was good farming land. Indeed, this palm had become so endangered that the government had set up the Parque Naciónal El Palmar near Colón, in Entre Rios province, in 1965, in an attempt to save it. It was Tony Pittman's opinion that the clearing of this palm probably contributed most to the extinction of the macaw.

It is of interest that D'Orbigny, who visited the area between 1827 and 1835, wrote of vast forests of yatay palms stretching along the Rio Paraná creating a bluish expanse. (Could this have been how blue macaws evolved — the colour providing protective camouflage from its most likely natural predator, the Harpy Eagle (*Harpia harpyja*)?) Now these palm forests no longer exist in Entre Rios and Corrientes. D'Orbigny had foreseen that the forests would disappear as soon as the people realised how fertile the soil was. Corrientes province has been progressively settled since the sixteenth century. However, an encyclopedia published in 1866 mentioned that 2,590 km^2 (1,000 sq. miles) of

palm forest still existed. This was perhaps enough to harbour a few pairs which were extirpated when the forest was cleared. If it was a specialist feeder, associating only or mainly with the yatay palm, it may never have been numerous. In 1767 the Jesuit priest, Sanchez Labrador, reported that it was rare in the forests of the Rio Paraguay but apparently abundant on the left bank of the Rio Uruguay.

Tony Pittman and Joe Cuddy travelled thousands of miles in search of the Glaucous. Nowhere in the former range did they find sufficient habitat for such a species. Disturbance in the region has been considerable — forestry, farming, ranching and a giant hydro-electric complex at Salto Grande on the River Uruguay, resulting in the flooding of lowland areas. They spoke to squatters and settlers and encountered genuine astonishment that the Glaucous Macaw could possibly still exist. The region is heavily settled (not remote, like the habitat of Lear's Macaw) and has been subject to military action since the days of the Jesuit settlements in the eighteenth century. Sadly, the Glaucous Macaw is long gone . . . (Pittman, 1992).

The last specimen seen alive was either that in the Jardin d'Acclimation in Paris between 1895 and 1905, or a macaw which might have been *A. leari* in Buenos Aires Zoological Gardens in 1936. The Glaucous Macaw differed from Lear's mainly in the pronounced greyish-green tinge on the head and neck (greenish-blue in Lear's) and in the duller tail coloration (greenish-blue above instead of rich cobalt-blue).

Lear's Macaw was named by Bonaparte in 1856 in honour of the artist, Edward Lear, better known, ironically, for his nonsense rhymes, because painting birds, and especially parrots, was his life's work. In 1831 Lear painted what he believed to be a Hyacinthine Macaw in his *Illustrations of the Family of Psittacidae, or Parrots*. Many years later Bonaparte realised that it was a different species and named it Lear's Macaw accordingly.

For more than a century next to nothing was known about this bird; it was labelled one of the biggest mysteries in South American ornithology. Its origins, rumoured as Brazil, were unknown. A very few birds were offered for sale at such places as Belém and Pará, at the mouth of the Amazon, yet no clue to its precise range was available. This even led to the theory that Lear's Macaw was a hybrid between the Hyacinthine and the Glaucous Macaws. At the time the suggestion was made, it was not known that the Glaucous was almost certainly extinct.

In 1964 the German-born ornithologist from Brazil, Helmut Sick, commenced a systematic search for Lear's Macaw. (*See* Plate 4.) In 1974 he was joined by Dante M. Teixeira, of the Museu Naciónal, Rio de Janeiro. In 1977 they concluded that there was only one spot on the map in which this macaw could have remained undiscovered: an area of north-eastern Bahia known as the Raso da Catarina. They had their doubts, however. 'Could it be,' asked Helmut Sick, 'that this region was so completely overlooked by scientists, and that there could hide, for more than a century, a bird as large as a macaw? It was hardly believable.'

The Raso was reputedly impenetrable. Nevertheless, Sick and Teixeira decided to centre their search on that area. A plateau cut by canyons, there are no settlements and no roads, only dried-up river beds. Most of the area is covered with deep, loose sand and low, frequently thorny vegetation known as *caatinga* which is adapted to the extremely dry climate and intense heat. It remains one of the least known parts of Brazil.

The search commenced on December 18 1978 when they left Rio de Janeiro with Luiz A. Pedreira Gonzaga, also from the Museu Naciónal. On December 29 they obtained the first proof that they were on the right track: the flight feathers of a blue macaw shot some weeks previously by a local hunter. The bird had been eaten. Two days later they finally encountered the object of their search: three 'relatively small dark creatures with a big yellowish area at the base of their mandible, their voice amazingly weak for a macaw' (Sick, 1981).

During the following month, up to 21 of the formerly elusive macaws were observed flying overhead in a single flock. They undertake long flights in search of their favourite foods. These include the small nuts of the licuri palm (*Syagrus coronata*), which the macaws sometimes obtain by walking on the ground. Sick and his companions discovered that they roost in hollows in the upper part of the grotesquely eroded walls of the canyons; they also nest there. They recorded their voices and photographed them as they climbed on the vertical rock face.

The Raso was investigated from the north-east and from the south, in order to delimit the range of this macaw. This achieved, Helmut Sick approached the Brazilian government to enlarge the Raso da Catarina reserve to encompass a larger area of the macaw's range.

For a considerable period before his untimely death in January 1990, Lear's Macaw was studied by a dedicated young Brazilian ornithologist, Alexander Brandt. Funded by WWF, he located eight feeding places of this macaw in an area of 140 km^2 (54 sq. miles). During his observation periods, they spent 50 per cent of their time resting and, during the period that the licuri palm was fruiting, 36 per cent of their time feeding in palms. However, in July, when palm fruit availability was low, they spent 26 per cent of their time foraging on corn crops and only 6 per cent in palm trees in the breeding area where observations were concentrated. They were also seen to feed on the seeds of *Jatropha pohliana*, the flowers of an agave and ripening or dry corn. To what extent, I wonder, have the licuri palms been destroyed by local people in order that they might plant crops such as corn? For about 20 years, the macaws have been feeding on corn, perhaps because their natural food is no longer abundant.

Grazing cattle and goats prevent the recovery of palm stands, thus small areas should be fenced in which the palms could become established. This was the recommendation of Alexander Brandt in 1988. As I write this, it is almost exactly 14 years since the locality and the small size of the only known population was discovered. Alexander Brandt's recommendations should surely have been implemented as a matter of great urgency. I believe that valuable years have been lost. In 1992 Wildlife Conservation International (an arm of New York Zoological Society), which has been funding Dr Charles Munn and Carlos Yamashita to work on the Hyacinthine Macaw, turned their attention to Lear's. It was planned that Charles Munn should make an exploratory expedition to the nesting site of this macaw, to study it over a period of weeks. The expedition would study the licuri palms and design a plan for palm regeneration to commence in 1993. Meanwhile, the cause was taken up by the World Parrot Trust which, in 1992, made one of its largest donations to support this work. It launched a 'Palm for a Parrot' fund, encouraging donations of £10 or US$20 which would be used to found a licuri-palm regeneration scheme. The creation of new feeding areas, identified by the biologists, will eventually occur. At present the macaws must fly further and further over open ground in search of food; during these flights, they would be easy targets for hunters. An education programme is also needed, to achieve the support and sympathy of local communities. Wardens might also be employed. This population must be one of the most vulnerable of all endangered parrots; every possible measure must be taken to preserve it.

An extreme rarity in captivity, Lear's Macaw has been represented in very few collections. In the early 1980s, it could be seen at Birdland, Bourton-on-the-Water in England, and at San Diego Zoo in California and Busch Gardens, Tampa, and Parrot Jungle, Miami, in Florida. The few birds in captivity were exported many years ago; none had attempted to breed, probably because no true pairs existed. Then Parrot Jungle, the famous Miami collection, made a positive move and lent their male to Busch Gardens in Tampa, which is noted for its breeding successes with macaws: 11 species have been reared there. Great was the jubilation there in June 1982 when a chick hatched — almost certainly the first of its species ever to be hatched in captivity. The chick was removed for hand-rearing when a few days old and taken to Parrot Jungle where it was reared by the owners, Mr and Mrs Scherr.

Other chicks were hatched but only one more was reared. This was a great disappointment; I for one had hoped that enough young would be reared to provide partners for the few other Lear's Macaws in captivity. In 1988, the female died. At first the two 1982 young were declared a male and female, and kept for some years in a small cage; their father lived alone, nearby. No attempt was made to pair the old male with one of his offspring (later reported to be two females) before he died in 1992. The situation was incomprehensible to many dedicated aviculturists who saw these birds.

During this period British aviculturist, Harry Sissen, renowned for his successes in breeding rare macaws, was desperately trying to find a way to give the opportunity to breed to the surviving female which had been at Birdland, Bourton-on-the-Water. It was an aged bird; I first saw it and its female companion at Whipsnade Zoo in 1965. The following year they were placed (on loan, I believe), at Birdland. Although Harry Sissen knew that this bird was nearing the end of her breeding life, or perhaps was already too old to breed, in 1988 he raised the very large sum of money which Birdland's owner wanted for her by selling young macaws. He knew that there was a male Lear's Macaw in South Africa and finally located it. The owner, in the spirit of conservation which prevails among those who genuinely care about endangered parrots, agreed to send his male to the UK. The South African authorities issued the necessary papers to allow its export. But the British authorities refused to issue the paperwork to allow it to enter the UK. This situation prevailed for one year. Finally, in desperation, knowing that his chances of ever breeding from the female diminished with every month that passed, he alerted the press and television journalists. They took up the story, nationwide, that two parrots of a critically endangered species were being denied, by bureaucrats, the opportunity to breed. Within days, permission was granted for the male Lear's to enter the UK. Sadly, the female's condition was deteriorating and she died a few months later.

Harry Sissen knew that the number of Lear's Macaws outside Brazil could be counted on the fingers of one hand, but there were two at Mulhouse Zoo in France. The director agreed to send them to him, to bring together the only birds known in Europe. Because so few survive in the wild, a captive-breeding programme is important. Draft 2 of the Parrot Action Plan states: 'Six birds are known to exist in captivity in various places around the world. Efforts to maximise their reproductive and genetic potential should be made, but

Lear's Macaw (*Anodorhynchus leari*) chick, the first hatched in captivity.

the workshop recommended that further wild birds should not be captured.' However, by 1993 it was known that a severe drought was causing a decline in the small remnant population. It was feared there was insufficient food for them; they were flying to areas where they were not normally seen, in search of food, and one or more had been shot. In such circumstances, the population could crash near to extinction, in a matter of weeks.

The third member of the genus *Anodorhynchus* is the best known, the most spectacular and, in addition, the largest of all parrots. In the first edition of this book, I wrote: 'Although it is declining, it is not yet considered to be endangered.' Not long after, the plight of this magnificent bird started to receive a lot of attention. Its range crosses the Brazilian border in eastern Bolivia, where it was not known to ornithologists until 1977. Brazil prohibited the export of birds in the early 1970s but there was a thriving illegal export trade in this macaw, with birds being smuggled out of Bolivia (until 1984, when animal exports were banned), Paraguay and Brazil. In 1986 the Brazilian Government proposed that the Hyacinthine Macaw should be transferred from Appendix II to Appendix I of CITES, which would at least make it impossible for wild-caught birds to enter countries which were signatories to CITES. In order to assess the merits of this proposal, the CITES Secretariat contracted Wildlife Conservation International and TRAFFIC (USA). Their biologists Charlie Munn, Jorgen Thomsen and Carlos Yamashita carried out a field survey from which they concluded that the overall population was probably in the region of only 3,000 birds. The population was actually fragmented into at least three reproductively isolated groups.

The largest was found in the Pantanal of Mato Grosso but there numbers had declined substantially, particularly in the southern part. In north-eastern Brazil the population had been greatly reduced by trappers, so much so that in places the macaws had almost abandoned nesting in trees in favour of less accessible cliff faces. In southern Pará numbers were also substantially depleted. One problem was that indigenous people were killing them for their feathers, used to make head-dresses and other artefacts for sale.

In 1987, this macaw was transferred to Appendix I of CITES. This action often renders even more desirable a parrot which is already known in aviculture and thus, at least initially, may even have the effect of increasing smuggling. The number of Hyacinthine Macaws bred in captivity increased steadily during the 1980s until, by the end of the decade, a substantial number were being hand-reared annually in the USA. Elsewhere there was, fortunately, less emphasis on hand-rearing but fewer were being hatched; nevertheless, captive-bred birds could be found in many countries, albeit at a very high price. While it is certain that some birds are still leaving Brazil illegally, it would now be extremely difficult to smuggle them into most of those countries which are members of CITES. In addition, people in certain areas, such as the Pantanal, are increasingly aware of the value of protecting these spectacular birds.

Da Silva, Munn et al. (1991) explain that: 'Not only should Hyacinth Macaws be able to thrive on properly managed cattle ranches, but they now also may be able to generate substantial incomes for the ranches as tourist attractions. With the explosive world-wide growth in nature-based tourism or "ecotourism" over the past ten years, Hyacinth Macaws themselves already are generating substantial ecotourism income on leading Pantanal ranches. For example, after only four seasons of operating a 22-bed ecotourism hotel at Estancia Caiman, the ranch's annual tourism income now approximately matches that of the decades-old cattle operation . . . . Increasingly, ranchers still fortunate enough to boast healthy populations of Hyacinth Macaws now proudly view their birds as external badges of conservation sophistication, ecological enlightenment, and ecotourism potential. With the new wave of ecological awareness that has swept much of middle- and upper-class Brazil since 1987, and in 1990 the enormous success in Brazil of the nightly, 60-minute TV drama entitled "Pantanal" (which regularly cuts away to actual clips of Pantanal wildlife, including wild Hyacinth Macaws), the future survival of the macaw on the ranches of the Pantanal seems more and more likely.'

Because the Pantanal is flooded for part of the year, its preservation seems assured. In this huge savannah–forest area, extensive cattle ranches have existed for more than a century, yet appear not to have endangered the macaw's two principal food plants, the palms *Acrocomia aculeata* and *Attalea phalerata*. Paradoxically, the cattle may actually assist in the survival of this massive-billed macaw. It is believed that extinct megafauna swallowed the fruits of both species of palm and digested the sweet, sticky mesocarp. The hard nut passed through them undigested, later germinated and grew in the grasslands of the Pantanal. These huge browsing animals maintained the area in its open and semi-open condition, much as horses and cows do today. Macaws habitually feed on the ground, on fallen palm fruits or those which have passed through the cattle.

There is one cause for concern which, it is hoped, the biologists studying this species have already started to correct — the lack of nesting sites. Trees large enough or prone to develop spacious cavities appear to be naturally scarce in the Pantanal, but they are also cut down in order to control vampire bats. Da Silva, Mann *et al.* suggest that ranchers clearing forest or 'tree islands' should leave standing all large *Sterculia*, *Enterolobium*, *Vitex*, *Acrocomia* and *Attalea* as nesting sites. They could go one step further and place protective fencing around small trees of these species, and also erect artificial nest-boxes. The researchers have already taken the latter step and are now waiting to see whether these boxes will be accepted as nest sites. If they are (and I suspect they might be because, in captivity, this species readily accepts any type of nest, unlike some macaws), the future of the Hyacinthine in the Pantanal looks quite promising. This is not so for the population in north-eastern Brazil which, I fear, may decline to extinction unless an aggressive education campaign is mounted.

Soon after its formation in 1989, the World Parrot Trust launched the Hyacinth Fund. Its aim was to raise a large sum, mainly to protect the macaw in the wild. (Those who donate to this fund should note that no administrative or fund-raising expenses whatsoever will be charged to it. All donations go directly to help the macaw.) In order to raise funds, a limited-edition print of a pair of Hyacinthines was produced, also an eye-catching T-shirt featuring this species. Within a year £6,000 had been raised which was used to help fund the field work being carried out by Charles Munn.

Since the publication of the first edition of this book, the attention of conservationists and parrot-lovers worldwide has been focused on a species to which were originally devoted a mere five paragraphs. Since then, the number of words which have been published on its plight could fill a volume. This species is Spix's Macaw (*Cyanopsitta spixii*). An intriguing bird, it is unlike any other macaw in appearance and behaviour and is thus accorded a genus to itself.

Perhaps it was a naturally rare species, even before man interfered with its habitat. The Austrian naturalist Johann Baptist von Spix shot the first specimen known to science — in 1819. Although two or three macaws of this species were known in captivity outside Brazil before the end of the nineteenth century, it was not until 1903 that it was again reported in the wild by an ornithologist. In 1922 came another report. The first and third sightings were from Bahia in north-eastern Brazil and the second from southern Piauí. Incredibly, there was no other published report of sightings until the 1970s. It was made by the great German–Brazilian ornithologist Dr Helmut Sick, who died in 1991. With good reason he was called 'the father of modern Brazilian ornithology'.

He had observed Spix's Macaws near Formosa do Rio Preto in northern Bahia, about 500 km (300 miles) to the west of where von Spix had collected the first known specimen. Then the Swiss ornithologist Paul Roth found a remnant population of five birds at Melancia Creek, near the town of Curaçá, in the same area as von Spix's original discovery. These birds were studied during 1985 and 1986 by Dr Roth of the Universidade Federal do Maranhão. Dr Roth believed that the population there may once have been as high as 60 but that the macaw had suffered from hunting (for sport), the introduction of African bees (which can kill incubating females) and, most of all, from trappers. They were reputed to obtain US$2,000 for each one — far more than for any other Brazilian bird. A Hyacinthine, for example, would earn US$50 for the trapper (Anon., 1986). By 1986 only four Spix's remained at Curaçá. By 1988 all had been taken by trappers. Without wardens, the outcome was inevitable . . . .

Between 1985 and 1988 Paul Roth had made 11 arduous expeditions across the remote and poverty-stricken north-east of Brazil. If another population of Spix's existed, he was determined to find it. But all his expeditions were in vain. Then information about the

Spix's Macaw at São Paulo Zoo.

sighting of a small blue macaw in southern Piauí state was received. This led to ICBP mounting an expedition in 1990. Despite initial encouraging signs and thorough investigations, it turned out to be another fruitless search. The supposed sighting almost certainly related to the common and widespread Red-bellied Macaw (*Ara manilata*). After travelling several thousand kilometres, the research team were reluctant to give up. Then a young man came forward who claimed to have a photograph of a Spix's Macaw which had recently been held by a man in a nearby village. The photograph was produced and showed that the bird was undeniably the subject of their searches. The young man volunteered to take them to a place where he said the species still survived. It was Melancia Creek! And there they found a single Spix's! It was proclaimed to be 'the last wild Spix's' and its photograph, captured by the great Brazilian bird photographer Luiz Claudio Marigo, appeared in newspapers and magazines throughout the world.

Was this the mate of the 'recent captive' and what happened to this captive bird? Why did the ICBP team not start their search at Melancia Creek, the last known habitat? Perhaps their earlier arrival could have prevented the final separation of 'the last wild pair'. Or perhaps they were not a true pair. And perhaps somewhere, unknown to man or to science, there is another pair, or even another population.

There is another question that might be asked. When studying the remnant population at Melancia Creek, Dr Roth noticed the preference of these macaws for woodland dominated by *Tabebuia caraiba*. The gallery woodlands along the watercourses, including Melancia Creek, are dominated by this tree, by far the largest woody species in the area. Why did the ICBP expedition not centre its search on areas with caraiba gallery woodland? Tony Juniper, a member of the expedition, wrote: 'The unique nature of the vegetation and the very obvious preference the bird showed for it left us in no doubt that we should concentrate our future search on areas of similar woodland.

'After enquiring as to the extent of caraiba gallery woodland, we concluded that it was not as widespread as previous reports suggested. Only one other area could be located: Riacho Vargem, about 120 km to the east of Rio Melancia. On arriving at this site, local farmers told us that Spix's Macaw had recently occurred there. However, they said the last individuals had been trapped during the previous year. Although thoroughly sickened by this depressing news, the finding of this new locality did confirm our judgement on the specialised habitat requirements . . .' (Juniper, 1990).

Specialised habitat is the recurring theme in this chapter on the blue macaws. But what factor caused the decline of the caraiba gallery woodland? Tony Juniper explains: 'In only one of the ten 100 m sections of watercourses with mature caraiba trees we studied were young trees found. All other areas had been completely devastated by grazing goats, sheep and cattle. Habitat loss had not previously been considered a threat to Spix's Macaw, but the very limited extent of this apparently preferred woodland may have caused an initial decline in the species, making it vulnerable to trapping.'

It is a tragedy that the ICBP expedition missed finding, by a matter of months, the last two pairs in the last two localities known to have been inhabited by the macaw. Now that it is presumed effectively extinct in the wild, the steps to preserve it, which should have been taken in 1985, are being made. In 1991 IBAMA (the Brazilian Government's environmental agency) sent an ornithologist to study the last bird and the mayor of the nearest town offered whatever assistance the district could provide for a recovery plan. There is said to be 'a strong feeling of support and pride in the macaw locally' — a feeling that was evidently lacking a year earlier when the bird's mate was trapped. ICBP, in conjunction with Kew Gardens in London, was proposing to base a team of four biologists (an ornithologist, an ecologist, a plant taxonomist and an ethnobotanist) in the area for two years. They would study the bird, survey the existing habitat and initiate a management programme to conserve and restore the unusual, threatened forest type in which the species occurs.

These actions would have been laudable if implemented even two years previously. The species might just have been saved. Now the task of saving it will be incalculably more difficult. Unless one or more birds are found in the wild, the recovery plan must involve the release of a captive bird — or more than one. After all, the sex of the lone survivor is not known.

After the expedition, ICBP made the following recommendations on the actions to be taken.

1) If the species becomes extinct, it will be more difficult to reintroduce captive-bred birds at a later date. The locality should therefore be guarded and a scientist should be stationed in the area to keep the bird under observation.
2) A captive bird should be released as a partner for the lone survivor.
3) Sections of the seasonal rivers (i.e. caraiba gallery woodland) must be fenced for five to ten years to enable the young trees to grow out of reach of the grazing animals. (Ultimately, this will be of benefit to the farmers since the mature trees provide renewable food for their animals during the dry season.)
4) To maximise the productivity of the tiny captive population the majority of captive birds must be moved to a new breeding facility to be established within the current range of the species. A second flock of four to six birds should be maintained at one other locality at an already established parrot breeding facility. The captive birds at the local breeding centre should be managed in conjunction with the remaining wild birds, or could be partly managed as a semi-wild population. Proper climatic conditions prevailing at the local site will facilitate breeding success and acclimatisation of birds for release. All captive birds must be brought together in the two breeding localities with no rights of ownership by any individuals.

These suggestions were not univerally commended. Even the World Parrot Trust, in its magazine *Psitta-Scene*, was moved to comment on them (Woolcock, 1990). The opinion was that a single bird was probably safe from the attentions of trappers, but '. . . introduce another bird from a captive collection to create a pair, and the trappers then have a marketable commodity'. As the sex of the lone survivor was unknown, it would have to be caught to determine its gender (by a small operation using a laparoscope, by a blood sample or, if moulting, by taking a blood quill). Two years later, however, there was some hope that a pair might survive the grasping hands of trappers. 'Ararinha Azul' (little blue macaw), as this macaw is locally known, had been adopted as the symbol of the district. The lone survivor had become a focus of interest, not just locally, but worldwide. Perhaps the gamble to release a Spix's for it to mate with would pay off. Perhaps they would nest quite quickly and 'local pride' would protect them and their young. I think the risk should be taken, if the sex of the wild bird can be determined, in the interests of keeping the species extant in its last-known habitat. The risk is high — but desperate measures are called for.

However, few could see any justification for ICBP's suggestion that the majority of captive birds should be moved to a new breeding facility within the current range of the species. I, for one, believe that this would be the quickest way to manage the captive population to extinction. At least three pairs are producing young (in the Philippines, Switzerland and Tenerife). Some of these young are, or soon will be, mature and the breeders can exchange young to make up more pairs. (Unfortunately, DNA blood-testing has shown that some of the breeding pairs are related, but the important factor is that this is known, thus the best possible pairings can be made in the circumstances). Obviously, all were wild-caught birds and, as is usual, it took them several years to settle down or to mature sufficiently to breed. To move them, or most of them, to one location in north-eastern Brazil would be unthinkable. All aviculturists know that the very act of moving successful pairs to another location, let alone another country, is likely to stop them breeding, at least for a couple of years, or perhaps much longer. There are always risks involved in moving birds to a new location; it causes them stress and makes them more vulnerable to disease. Bringing birds from several different locations greatly increases this risk, exposing them to pathogens which they have not previously encountered. Aviculturists with rare birds which are reproducing well do nothing to alter their management or environment without good cause.

These reasons are valid enough for not moving successful pairs but there is another reason. The avicultural expertise to breed such birds does not exist in Brazil. It is sad to tell that more Spix's Macaws have died in the collections of wealthy Brazilian collectors who never even attempted to breed from them, and who could, and did, replace with ease those which died, than the entire total of Spix's Macaws which have ever left Brazil. In addition, there are no avian veterinarians in Brazil; if a local breeding facility ever existed, it would be imperative to have one on the staff, thus adding greatly to the expense of such a facility.

Finally, if there was a breeding facility for Spix's Macaws in the range of the species, it would almost certainly be operated by government employees. It would be quite remarkable if they possessed the experience, the dedication, expertise and avicultural background essential for breeding rare parrots. To most government employees, looking after rare fauna is just a job. A biologist might be studying rare reptiles one year and Spix's Macaws the next; the person cleaning the cages cares little whether it is a hotel bedroom or the home of the rarest parrot in the world — it is a way of earning a living. But to the few private aviculturists outside Brazil who have these birds in their care, Spix's Macaws are of immeasurable importance. These 'owners' possess a burning desire to succeed in breeding them, a desire which is missing in the government employee. In addition, their pride is involved. They know that the eyes of the avicultural world are on them and they will do everything in their power to ensure that they do not fail.

In actual fact, the 'possession' of this macaw is a responsibility so great that few would want it. There were no more than 30 captive birds, seven in Brazil, in 1992. All the known collections outside Brazil had reared young; none in Brazil had done so.

The view that all Spix's Macaws left Brazil illegally and should therefore be returned to Brazil might seem quite reasonable. However, it would not be in the best interests of the birds and this, finally, is what matters more than anything else. I believe that those who currently hold the species should be permitted to keep them, provided that young are not sold for commercial gain but retained within a consortium for breeding purposes. In effect, these birds would have no commercial value because every bird in captivity would be micro-chipped and identifiable, until the day (if ever) when the captive population was large enough for such procedures to be dispensed with.

Private breeding of Spix's Macaw is the only way to ensure it will survive in captivity and, perhaps, ultimately, in its natural habitat, if some of the young produced can be returned to the caraiba gallery forests in remote areas of north-eastern Brazil. Those who prefer the notion of an *in situ* breeding programme organised by the Brazilian Government must acknowledge that 'biologists' are not aviculturists. One cannot do the job of the other. Avicultural knowledge can be acquired but, unless it is combined with observation and instinct and, above all, a love for the birds, it counts for nothing.

5

Macaws: Majestic, Magnificent – and Threatened

. . . unless dramatic moves are made to save them, most of the vast numbers of populations and species now living in tropical moist forests will clearly vanish in the lifetime of many readers of this book.

PAUL AND ANNE EHRLICH, IN *EXTINCTION* (1982)

Large birds are generally more vulnerable to habitat alteration and predation by man than small species. Thus the macaws, the largest and most spectacular of all parrots, have declined greatly as a result of man's interference in their environment. Conspicuous in flight and considered good eating by Indians, they are easy targets for a gun. They require large trees (or holes in cliffs) for nesting and in some areas felling of choice nesting sites has further inhibited population growth.

Much sought after as pets and for aviaries, they have been trapped in unacceptably high numbers. Although they nest readily in captivity and many are being reared each year, numerous large macaws are kept as pets and are denied the opportunity to breed. There can now be no justification for taking the large macaws from the wild; the demand should be met from those already in captivity. A more responsible attitude on the part of traders and aviculturists is essential if the future of some macaw species is to be safeguarded.

All the large macaws have declined over much or all of their range. Some are not yet endangered, simply because their ranges are extensive. This is no reason for complacency, however; as an indication of future trends it is deeply disturbing. Even the most numerous of the large macaws, the Blue and Yellow (*Ara ararauna*) has become rare in some parts of its range. This applies particularly in the Orinoco delta, where it has been very heavily trapped.

It is, of course, species with a small range, such as the Red-fronted Macaw (*Ara rubrogenys*) which are most vulnerable to trapping. In the latter part of 1981 and early 1982 Dirk Lanning carried out a survey on this species and was able to amplify its range slightly to the south. The southern-central part of Bolivia, on the eastern slope of the Andes at elevations from 1,100 to 2,500 m (3,600 to 8,200 ft) is the home of this macaw.

So little was known of it that, when Bolivian animal dealer Rolando Romero opened a hunter's box in 1970 and found this species, he had no idea what it was. At first he believed it might be a cross between a Green-winged and a Military Macaw. It was not until he examined skins at the Natural History Museum, London, that he discovered its true identity.

He started to search for it in the wild and eventually found it, in 1974, in western Santa Cruz department. The area is remote and sparsely settled, being arid and without surface water for most of the year. Unusual terrain for a macaw, there are no forests to speak of but only desert-like shrubby vegetation in the valleys and lower slopes, and taller, though still dry, woodland on some upper slopes and ridges (Ridgely, 1981; Wells, 1981).

During March and April 1977, Robert Ridgely found this macaw, with the assistance of Dr Romero. At the

Habitat of Red-fronted Macaw (*Ara rubrogenys*) in Bolivia.

time of his visit it was feeding on the fruits of various cactus and the seeds of leguminaceous trees in the lower, desert-like zone. It also fed in fields, on ripening corn and on peanuts left after the harvest. The macaws travelled widely within their small range, engaging in long flights to and from their roosting sites. From spring to summer (September to February) they left the valleys, Ridgely was told, to move west, and higher into the mountains. There they nest semi-colonially in cliffs. He estimated that the population consisted of from 1,000 to 3,000 macaws.

Four years later Dirk V. Lanning made a study of this species, for 13 weeks from December 1981. It was funded by ICBP and the New York Zoological Society. Lanning walked 340 km (210 miles) and travelled about 3,000 km (1,860 miles) on trucks in search of this macaw. Its habitat is semi-arid deciduous woodland and scrub on the eastern slope of the Andes down to about 1,100 m (3,600 ft). *Cereus* and *Opuntia* cacti are common in the region. The Red-fronted Macaw's range is bordered by the high grassland of the altiplano to the north-west and south-west, and lies between the Rio Grande and Rio Pilcomayo drainages. To the east and south-east there is humid deciduous forest and woodland.

Before Lanning's survey was carried out, the Red-fronted Macaw was known to range over an area of 100 × 50 km (60 × 30 miles). It has since been observed over a locality extending 150 km (93 miles) west to east and 180 km (112 miles) north to south. The elevations ranged from 1,250 to 2,450 m (4,000 to 8,000 ft). Within the area, however, much of the habitat is unsuitable for this species. The semi-arid woodland which it favours covers about 20,000 km^2 (7,700 sq. miles), from 1,100 to 2,500 m (3,600 to 8,250 ft) elevation, and extends about 220 km (136 miles) west to east and 300 km (186 miles) north to south. It includes south-eastern Cochabamba, western Santa Cruz, northern Chuquisaca and the eastern edge of Potosí (Lanning, 1982).

Lanning concluded that there are from 3,000 to 5,000 Red-fronted Macaws in the wild, and confirmed that persecution and habitat destruction are insignificant threats to their existence. Residents have no way to catch them (very few possess guns or nets), they do not eat them or use their feathers or keep them as pets. Little of the macaws' preferred habitat is suitable for agriculture, but corn and peanut crops are raided by these macaws, making them unpopular with growers. Unlike many parrots, their nesting sites are not vulnerable; the macaws utilise sandstone cliffs which are inaccessible to collectors and not subject to destruction, as are trees.

It was unknown in aviculture until 1973 when very small numbers reached Europe and the USA. In a report produced by the organisation TRAFFIC in 1980, entitled *Macaws: Traded to extinction?*, UK import figures for the years 1970–77 are given. They show 16 *A. rubrogenys* for the year 1973 and none for the other years. Numbers imported into the USA were 16 in 1977, 82 in 1978 and 125 in 1979. Figures are not available for the first six months of 1980; in the second half of that year 81 were imported. In 1981 the total was a record 210. By this time the avicultural demand had been met and the undesirable position reached whereby these macaws were being sold as pets.

During his stay in Bolivia, Lanning sought out trappers and exporters. One exporter estimated that 300 Red-fronted Macaws left Bolivia in 1981. Adult birds as well as young were being trapped, thereby eliminating part of the adult breeding population each year. Local people had observed a marked decline in their numbers. One resident of Saipina told Lanning that five to ten years previously he saw 200 or more macaws in the valley on a good day, but the number had fallen to 30 or 40. There could be no doubt that the population had declined since trapping commenced. Trappers operated (setting mist nests) only in the northern half of the macaw's range; nevertheless, the entire population was at risk because a macaw can easily fly from one end of the range to the other in one or two days.

Lanning suggested that the species should be placed on Appendix I of CITES so that it could not be imported commercially by countries which are signatories to CITES (USA, most of the European countries, and many others worldwide) and would theoretically have the effect of reducing the trade to the point where it was no longer a threat to the species' existence. If, however, there is a demand from even one country which is not a party to CITES, trappers would continue to obtain this macaw. Only a total export ban by the Bolivian authorities (as well as it being added to Appendix I) would safeguard this macaw's future. Lanning suggested that this species should be placed on Appendix I of CITES and this was accomplished in 1983. This alone would not have protected it from trade; Japan, for example, is not a member of CITES and could have continued to import this species. At one time during the 1980s, the Japanese exporter Onishi in Santa Cruz, Bolivia, had more than 100 in his possession. Fortunately, in June 1986 Bolivia introduced a total ban on capture, transport and export of all wild animals. This must have been effective. Boussekey, Saint-Pie and Morvan (1991) reported: '. . . the fortunes of the Red-fronted Macaw appear to have improved. We saw no trapping in the Río Caine, we found no official dealer in Cochabamba and no macaws for sale in the market, and Cordier's trapper had gone back to taxi-driving.

'Although we cannot speak for other parts of the species' range, in the Río Caine the threats to the species are minimal, with no direct persecution, no trapping, and no degradation of habitat, since the human population density of the region is very low (50 Indian families in the part of the valley we investigated).

'The only possible threat to the species in the valley could be the development of a network of local roads to promote tourism at the Torotoro archaeological site 20 km from our study area, albeit in a different valley. At present it is only accessible by lorry in the dry season, or else by light airplane. The consequences of road improvements could clearly be to change the character of life in the valley to the long-term detriment of the macaw.'

In the Rio Caine valley, in northern Potosí department, the Red-fronted Macaw has no great fear of man; it feeds on the ground 100 m (110 yd) from dwellings, follows the plough at less than 30 m (33 yd) and takes flight from an approaching observer at only about 40 m (44 yd). These are clear pointers to the fact that it is not persecuted by man. It is not kept locally as a pet because its ability to mimic is not great.

Boussekey, Saint-Pie and Morvan commented: '. . . the habitat of the Red-fronted Macaw is most unusual for a parrot in a genus largely associated with hot humid lowland forest. The paucity of plants, and the defences most of them possess against being eaten, must have serious dietary repercussions which, combined with a general lack of perches and protective cover, make for a seemingly hostile environment for a relatively large parrot to survive in, and dictate some notable behavioural adaptations.'

They made 26 observations of pairs accompanied by immatures, 24 of which involved a single offspring, one of which involved two and another three. They therefore concluded that the majority of Red-fronted Macaws could only rear one young per year, at best. This would surely be attributable to the extreme dietary impoverishment of the species' natural environment.

It is encouraging to know that what was the main threat to this macaw's existence has probably been eliminated (or occurs on a scale too small to be significant). However, the future threat of increased

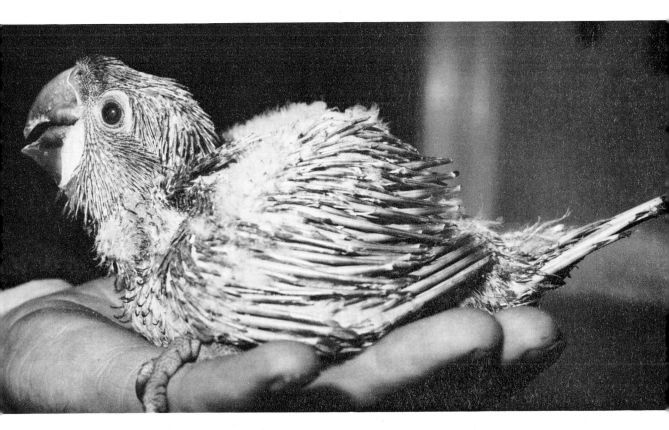

Red-fronted Macaw chick aged 6½ weeks.

access to the area to promote tourism could have serious consequences for this species.

There is still no clear idea of its total population, which has been suggested to be between 1,000 and 5,000 in the wild. In captivity there are several hundred birds, perhaps nearer 1,000. The first captive breeding occurred during 1978 in Wuppertal Zoo in Germany; three young were reared. Ten years later this macaw was still being reared there. Once this species starts to breed it sometimes proves to be very prolific. This is especially the case in the aviaries of Harry and Pat Sissen in Yorkshire, UK. They rear young from three or four pairs every year; between 1984 and 1992 they reared about 130 young. In aviculture, at least, the future of the Red-fronted Macaw is assured.

The 1970s was a decade of important discoveries concerning the range and distribution of several macaw species. One of them was the Blue-throated, or Caninde, Macaw (*Ara glaucogularis*) (Ingels, Parkes

and Farrand, 1981). Very little was known about it at the start of the decade. Its range was believed (Forshaw, 1973) to be as extensive as Bolivia, Paraguay and northern Argentina. On investigation, however, Ridgely (1981) and Ingels, Parkes and Farrand found that the evidence for the extent of its range was non-existent, except in Bolivia. Ingels, Parkes and Farrand were convinced that Azara's description of the macaw he saw in northern Paraguay — the only evidence of its occurrence there — could apply only to the Blue and Yellow Macaw (*A. araruana*). A friend who had Azara's original description of the macaw translated told me that the throat colour indicated that the bird seen was not *A. glaucogularis*.

Thus the only country in which this macaw has been recorded without any doubt in recent years is Bolivia. It has been seen there in extreme south-eastern Beni, south of Trinidad, in the drainage of the upper Rio Mamore. Of particular interest is the fact that it often mingled in flocks of Blue and Yellow Macaws, although it was greatly outnumbered.

Ingels, Parkes and Farrand point out that the known range of the Blue-throated Macaw is restricted to the departments of Beni and Santa Cruz in Bolivia, with a possible additional record at Yacuiba, in the department of Tarija in southernmost Bolivia. According to Lanning (1982), in Santa Cruz it is known only from the north-western corner; this information originates from hunters who work throughout the department. Lanning searched for this macaw in southern Chuquisaca department and in Tarija. He concentrated on the edges of the lowlands and on the lower slopes of the Andes in humid deciduous forest and woodland. It prefers humid lowlands in the tropical savannah, with scattered trees and ribbons of gallery forest along the water courses. He neither heard nor saw any blue and yellow macaws, nor encountered any residents who knew of their existence, although they were familiar with the Military Macaw.

All the recent evidence therefore points to the fact that the range of this macaw is much smaller than was formerly believed, and is probably confined to an area of less than 50,000 km^2 (20,000 sq. miles). In one of its strongholds, the Rio Mamore drainage, it accounts for less than 1 per cent of all the large macaws. Lanning discovered that hunters collect roosting birds with mist nets during May to July, and collect young birds from nests (one or two in each) in January and February. One exporter collecting in the Monteverde region estimated that of the total population of about 1,000 Caninde Macaws, 30 were exported in 1981. Another believed that the total population was only half that, of which he knew that 50 were exported to the USA and 10 to Europe in 1981. If he is correct, 11 per cent of the population was trapped that year.

In the first edition of this book I wrote: 'To safeguard its future, the species must be listed on Appendix I of CITES and, furthermore, the Bolivian authorities must be persuaded to ban its export.' Fortunately, both occurred; like the Red-fronted Macaw, it was placed on Appendix I in 1983 and, in 1986, Bolivia banned the export of all fauna. As with the Red-fronted, a few birds have left Bolivia illegally since then but the numbers involved have probably been very small. Unfortunately, our knowledge of this species in the wild has not advanced; in fact it is almost non-existent. In August 1992 Charles Munn located a small population in Bolivia. This was believed to be the first time that the species had been seen in the wild by an ornithologist. Information had been obtained which was expected to lead to several other populations being located. The Parrot Action Plan suggest that its population is smaller than 1,000 but this is no more than a guess.

The same source estimated its captive population at more than 200. It might be substantially more than this as the species is now being bred very successfully in the USA. However, because nearly all macaws hatched there are hand-reared, and because of the exceptionally appealing nature of this exquisitely beautiful macaw, I believe that many of the Blue-throated Macaws bred there will be kept as pets. At the time of writing its price is still very high, which means that many of the young produced are likely to be bought by breeders. However, this species can still be described as rare in aviculture. The price will almost certainly fall, however, as the indications so far are that the Blue-throated Macaw will be a prolific breeder in captivity. More so than for the Red-fronted Macaw, the demand for captive-bred birds will escalate.

Four other macaws, not mentioned so far, are listed on Appendix I of CITES. The Scarlet (*Ara macao*) was placed on this Appendix in 1985. Its numbers were declining rapidly, also its range. In Mexico and Central America, trapping and loss of habitat has had a devastating effect on its numbers. In Belize there has been a serious population decline; its range is contracting and it is now confined to the south-west. Furthermore, in 1990 it was stated that there had been no documented accounts of young seen in the previous five years. In Honduras, it is common only in the departments of Olancho and Gracias á Dios on the Pacific slope. Its decline is attributed to the use of pesticides in the cotton fields, as well as to deforestation and trapping. In Costa Rica, the 1990 population of this macaw had declined to 50–100 in the Corcovado National Park, about eight in the Palo Verde National Wildlife Refuge and about 200 in the Carara Biological Reserve. Fortunately, the Scarlet Macaw also occurs in the northern part of South America; here it continues to thrive in the more remote forested areas, away from human habitation. The decision to place this macaw on Appendix I was criticised by some traders and aviculturists. However, in my view, it was fully justified because in some areas it was being heavily trapped for export. Undoubtedly, illegal trapping still occurs because certain Indians use the tail feathers, especially those of Scarlet and Military Macaws, in their ceremonial costumes. This occurs not only in Central America but even in the south-western states of the USA, where macaw tail feathers have been used for this purpose for many centuries. One shipment consisting of tail feathers from 150 Military Macaws entered Mexico in 1983 and were sold to Indians living in Arizona.

In *Macaws, A Complete Guide* I recorded: 'In Panama, the capture of macaws for feathers has a long tradition. However, in recent years it has become a serious problem. The feathers are used in the headdresses of costumes worn for local folk dances, whose increasing popularity has led to the formation of dance groups throughout the country. All the dancers seek macaw feathers for their costumes. ICBP-Panama, in collaboration with aviculturists and institutions outside Panama, therefore initiated a project to collect moulted macaw feathers from captive birds. The feathers are hired out for a modest fee.' (Low, 1990). Considering that each head-dress uses 60–80 tail feathers, and that the birds are killed in order to obtain them, it is obvious that illegal capture results in countless macaws losing their lives.

The massive-billed Buffon's Macaw (*Ara ambigua*) was added to Appendix I in 1991. Found in Central America, Panama (but long since extirpated from the Canal Zone), north-western Colombia and Ecuador, its declining population is estimated at about 5,000. Rare in captivity but breeding in a few collections, this species is easily confused with the similarly coloured but smaller Military Macaw. In recent years, in Panama, it, too, has become the victim of feather hunters. To kill these magnificent and threatened birds for their feathers is like killing elephants for their ivory.

This species is especially sensitive to deforestation. It needs large expanses of broad-leaved forest. In Costa Rica its movements are migratory and related to the local ripening period of fruits of *Lysiloma*. No permits for its capture have been issued since 1980. In Honduras it is limited to the wet tropical forests of the Caribbean slope, near the Nicaraguan border. In Nicaragua, the only viable populations are found in the north (near Bosawas) and in the south in the lower watershed of the Indio, Maiz and San Juan rivers. Its habitat has been reduced by agricultural development and felling. In Ecuador, where the sub-species, *A.a. guayaquilensis* is found, it is in danger of extinction. Much of its habitat has been totally destroyed and much illegal trade has occurred.

This race is isolated and restricted to lowland forest in western Ecuador, particularly the hills near Guayaquil — but the area is being invaded by colonists. The decline in its numbers is continuing, being influenced by the selective extraction of timber and the road-building that accompanies such activities.

The future for this species does not look promising. Unlike most other macaws, the captive population is very small. It always has been very rare in aviculture and now it is even more expensive than the Hyacinthine. Breeding successes are occuring but this macaw has yet to prove prolific. To make matters worse, in the USA, hybridising has taken place between this species and the similar, but smaller, Military Macaw.

The Military Macaw (*Ara militaris*) is also declining throughout its range. In Venezuela its status is the most critical of all the four large macaws, according to Desenne and Strahl (1991). They state: 'This species has a patchy and local distribution within Venezuela, and is generally rare within its range. Despite this, it is common in the national pet trade, which gives cause for concern.'

The magnificent Buffon's Macaw has declined because of hunting (for feathers) and habitat loss.

The Green-winged Macaw (*Ara chloroptera*) is declining for the same reasons as the Buffon's. However, it has a much wider range, from eastern Panama and across much of northern South American as far south as Peru, Bolivia, Paraguay and eastern central Brazil. It is already extinct in south-eastern Brazil and Argentina. Although it is widespread it is not numerous, except in some areas of the Amazon region and the Guianas. Fortunately, this macaw is held in large numbers in captivity.

In 1989 the first small species of macaw was added to Appendix I: Illiger's (*Ara maracana*). This is another species which has suffered a drastic decline due to the destruction of the Atlantic forests of eastern Brazil. It may already be extinct in Argentina and is extremely rare in Paraguay. When Paraguay proposed that this species should be added to Appendix I, the researchers described it as one of the least known of neotropical parrots, difficult to investigate due to its rarity. The proposers quoted Nores and Yzurieta (1983) who located only eight or ten specimens in the Paraguayan departments of Canendiyu and Amambay. In 1989 another biologist was able to locate only one pair in the department of Concepción after being in the field for

Illiger's Macaw — the first small species to be added to Appendix I of CITES.

Warren B. King (1977) has forecast that: '. . . there will always be species of special significance, amenable to active management, and worth the effort to some of us. We will need to be increasingly selective in choosing species to manage actively, recognizing management's shortcomings and strengths, and admitting we are not capable of saving everything.' If the sad day ever dawns when it becomes necessary to make such a choice, and if they proved amenable to management, macaw species would surely be among those which are given priority. In their natural habitat they are the most magnificent of avian inhabitants; and it must be recalled that they occur in countries such as Brazil and Colombia which have the richest and most varied avifaunas in the world.

In flight, macaws have an unparalleled majesty. An indelible memory which survives from my first visit to the neotropics is that of macaws flying high over the river Amazon in Colombia, their long-tailed silhouettes outlined against the darkening sky. No one who has seen them flying above the canopy of the Amazon rainforest, in arid mountainous terrain or in the less scenic lowlands, can ever forget the spectacular sight they present: always in pairs, sometimes in small groups, but now almost never in large flocks. Their numbers continue to decline. Should the forests of the neotropics ever be without their raucous cries, mankind will have contributed to the demise of some of the most wonderful and distinctive of nature's treasures. They would continue to exist, for macaws breed well in captivity, but only in their natural habitat can one appreciate the majesty, dignity and splendour of these imposing birds.

eight months. Northern Brazil might be its only stronghold; if it does not survive in good numbers there, it may be extinct within a few years. This is one of the most prolific of all macaws in aviculture and it is puzzling to me why it is not more numerous.

Writing of the future when 'massive forest destruction' will result in 'massive endangerment and extinction',

6

A Conure More Precious than Gold

For wealth of colour and elegance of shape, as well as for general intelligence and docility, the Parrots are scarcely to be surpassed by any of the feathered tribes. From pure white to the deepest shade of black, from scarlet and vermilion to the richest golden yellow, from purple to sky-blue, and from dark grass green to the palest of emerald tints; these and every combination of them are the hues that decorate the plumage of the Psittacidae, among which there is perhaps no more striking looking creature than the subject of the present notice. . . .

W. T. GREENE, OF THE QUEEN OF BAVARIA'S CONURE, IN
PARROTS IN CAPTIVITY (1887)

Its golden plumage, exceptional intelligence and captivating personality sets the Golden, or Queen of Bavaria's Conure (*Guaruba guarouba*) apart from all other conures, and indeed from all other parrots. This imposing bird, 38 cm (15 in) long, has a beak more massive than that of some of the small macaws (*Ara* species). Also known as the Golden Conure, it is said by some to be more precious than gold.

Its scarcity stems from the fact that it originates from an area of northern Brazil, where much of the forest has been cleared for major highways and their ancillary networks. Essentially a forest species, it cannot adapt to other types of habitat and its existence is now endangered by the settlements which have devastated and fragmented its forest home.

The Queen of Bavaria's Conure is found in eastern Pará, also in adjacent and northern Maranhão; its southern limit has not been precisely defined but probably does not extend south of southern Pará (Ridgely, 1981). The known western limit of this species has recently been extended. Consistently given as the river Xingú, Pinto (1978) revised this to the river Tapajós, based on a single specimen collected on the eastern bank. More recently, sight records have indicated that populations exist between the Xingú and Tapajós, also on the western side of the Tapajós, thus extending its range even further to the west (Oren and Willis, 1981). All observations were in hilly upland sites and not along rivers. The records were of groups of 7–12 birds, except the notable record of 27 over Tucuruí, part of which has unfortunately since been flooded by what was then the world's fourth largest hydro-electric project. This resulted in 2,400 km² (925 sq. miles) being flooded. Where once the fauna was rich, there is now only pollution and a forest of dead trees. The Tucuruí dam feeds the Japanese, English and American bauxite industries. Brazil has the third largest bauxite reserves in the world, much of it unfortunately being in the Amazon.

Although Ruschi (1979) states that the geographical distribution of the Queen of Bavaria's Conure was much more extensive in the past and that it formerly occurred throughout north-eastern Brazil, there is no evidence of range contraction. Its presence in north-eastern Brazil was based on the description of a single specimen made by Marcgraf in 1648! Oren and Willis believe that the specimen described 'was a trade bird brought to his base in Recife from Maranhão or Pará, and that the species never occurred in the wild in northeastern Brazil'. Neither is there any evidence of range extension; collectors traditionally kept close to rivers rather than venturing into the uplands; thus birds there presumably went unnoticed until the area was made accessible by the construction of the Trans-Amazon highway.

The preference of this species for *terra firma* rather than *varzea* (flooded forest), which it avoids, is another factor which does not augur well for its survival. Generally speaking, the habitat of parrots which are found along the Amazon and its major tributaries is potentially more secure, as such areas are regularly flooded and therefore remain undeveloped. This species apparently never has been very numerous; it may be unable to adapt to altered habitat; and it is found in an area where human disturbance has had a catastrophic effect on the environment. Its future therefore looks uncertain.

David Oren of the Museu Paraense Emilío Goeldi, in Belém, Brazil, is greatly concerned for its survival. He informed me that it is disappearing in many areas where spontaneous and planned colonisation is taking place. The areas where this conure is most threatened are the zones of rainforest in the Rio Gurupi drainage and the areas extending 150 to 200 km (93 to 124 miles) on either side. This river basin is the last refuge of the species in Maranhão, and there is the chance of a reserve in the area. Already there are several Indian reserves there. The Rio Gurupi is in the middle of waves of colonisation, one from the east in Maranhão and the other from the west in Pará. Oren believes that the massive hydro-electric project at Tucuruí on the Tocantins and associated development will also bring large-scale modification of *G. guarouba* habitat. All areas within 50 km (30 miles) of the Trans-Amazon Highway are subject to habitat change and predation by humans. This conure is regularly shot for food by peasant farmers, especially when it comes to the maize crop in the fields.

'It appears that normal flock size is six to about 30 birds. The identification of flocks of two or three, in my experience, indicates that the species is already doomed in the area, as a healthy reproductive group is larger than this', forecasts Oren. He believes that the Golden Conure is in danger of complete extirpation east of the Rio Tocantins by the year 2,000 without a reserve in the Gurupi.

The westward extension of the known range is therefore of particular significance. Ridgely (1981) had pointed out that no area existed where the Queen of Bavaria's Conure received formal protection; this is no longer true. The Tapajós National Park, the only one in the state of Pará, covers over 1 million ha (2.5 million acres) in the region of the new records. As Edwin Willis pointed out (pers. comm. 1983), however, in other parts of Brazil parks commonly lose part of their area to such uses as hydro-electric projects, and this may well happen in the Tapajós Park, which is well endowed with waterfalls. If minerals are discovered, it could be reduced even further in area.

One must also bear in mind the fact that declaring an area a national park cannot protect its inhabitants from hunters — and this conure is threatened, by local farmers and, apparently, by weekend and holiday intruders. The Brazilian Forestry Institute is training guards for the Park but one wonders how effective they will be in such a large area. Funds are never sufficient to employ enough guards to control sporadic hunting. Nevertheless, the population in the Tapajós National Park may be the best protected throughout the range of this species. Elsewhere it remains threatened by hunting for food and by habitat destruction.

In recent years more than one avicultural writer has made the mistake of equating large numbers of young Queen of Bavaria's Conures in the trade (in Brazil) with the species being numerous.

What has caused the influx? Not any increase in its fortunes; in fact quite the reverse. Two major highways bisect the range of this conure. It is difficult to envisage the devastation that their construction has caused, but consider these figures: Of the area of land officially deforested in the Brazilian Amazon during 1966–75, 1,100,000 ha (2,700,000 acres), 9.6 per cent of the area, was destroyed by the construction of the Belém-Brazilia highway which bisects the species' territory vertically; 675,000 ha (1,700,000 acres), 5.9 per cent, was destroyed to construct the Trans-Amazon Highway which bisects its territory horizontally.

The manpower involved in this devastation may help to emphasise its enormity. In 1971, for example, a Brazilian journal reported that more than 6,000 men were working eight hours daily cutting down trees along the Trans-Amazon Highway. At the same time, another 45,000 men were cutting commercial timber in forests adjacent to the new roads. One estimate was that over 300,000 ha (750,000 acres) of virgin forest were cleared in the Amazon basin in 1970 alone (Davis, 1977).

It should now become clear why the influx of young Queen of Bavaria's Conures has occurred. Every two or three birds on the market represents a nest destroyed and possibly an adult pair whose habitat has gone forever.

Those familiar with the Queen of Bavaria's Conure, who are captivated by its endearing manner and lost in admiration for its golden plumage, can appreciate that the loss of this irreplaceable species would leave a tragic void in the rainforests of Brazil. Few will ever be

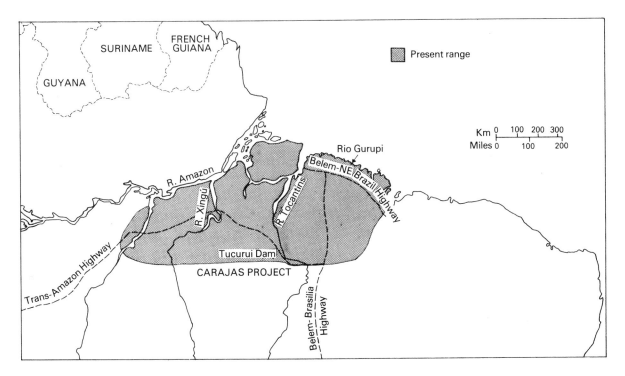

Distribution of Queen of Bavaria's Conure (*Guaruba guarouba*).

fortunate enough to see it there: the knowledge that it survives would be enough.

Because of the type of habitat in which the Queen of Bavaria's Conure occurs, estimating its current population is impossible. There is little doubt that it is declining as a result of disturbance to and fragmentation of habitat but, as yet, there is no reason to believe numbers of this species have been reduced as drastically as that of the island Amazons, for example.

Although the total of specimens in captivity is not high, the species has always been prized, and breeding successes have increased enormously since the late 1970s; thus it can now be considered fairly well established. There is no legal trade in birds from Brazil; yet trade in this conure has been cited as one of the reasons for its endangerment. This was incorrect as trade was formerly minimal; otherwise it would not be one of the most expensive of all parrots. The circumstances have altered, however, and illicit trade is developing to a degree where it could become a serious threat to the species' existence. Much of this trade is domestic but it also involves international smuggling operations (David Oren, pers. comm. 1983). Indians obtain fledglings from nesting trees, but, to their credit, they build ladders to gain access to the cavity, and take only a portion of the young. Often they practise this 'harvest' many years successively at the same nesting tree. The peasant colonists, on the other hand, gain

access to nesting cavities by cutting down the trees which contain them, killing most of the occupants as a result, and destroying existing nesting sites. It is for this reason that aviculturists must buy only birds known to be captive-bred or long established in captivity. The purchase of illegally imported birds directly affects wild populations and will contribute to the extinction of this unique conure.

Captive-bred hand-reared birds command very high prices: they are extraordinarily tame and as playful as kittens. Many retain this tameness throughout their lives and one can handle them without fear of being bitten. As is so often the case of species with fearsome beaks, they are unusually gentle. I once had occasion to trim the overgrown beak of an adult bird of a breeding pair. Docile in the extreme, it lay quietly in a towel and made no attempt to struggle or bite.

It has been my privilege to hand-rear many parrots of varying species, such as Greys, cockatoos and lories, which are among the most intelligent of parrots. But few can compare in this respect to Queen of Bavaria's Conures. As soon as their eyes open one discovers a superior intelligence and awareness, and by the time they are weaned (at four months) a docility and responsiveness perhaps not found in any other parrot. Others who have had the pleasure of rearing this species have remarked on this fact. To me, however, the most remarkable characteristic is the affection which a hand-reared bird returns to its human friends. It will snuggle inside your shirt or otherwise show its appreciation of close proximity, perhaps by climbing up to your face and nibbling it gently.

Greene (1887) described it as 'master of one of the most piercing shrieks that can distress a sensitive ear'. He did not exaggerate; but the endearing personality of the Queen of Bavaria's Conure makes one willing to forgive it this merest detail which, in any other species, would be sufficient to banish it from aviculture!

Perhaps the only writer who has not extolled the virtues of this species was the Marquess of Tavistock, later 12th Duke of Bedford. His four specimens were imported in 1926 and their arrival was described (Anon, 1926) as 'a very notable event in the history of

aviculture', so great was the rarity of this species in captivity. At first he was greatly impressed by them, despite the fact that they were 'possessed of a horrible voice'. He admired their playful disposition and the fact that male and female showed great attachment to each other. He described their 'great games together, hanging upside down from a slender twig by one foot and seeing which can push the other off first by the use of the beak and free foot. They are very gentle in their play and never nip one another or lose their tempers as many other Parrots do' (Tavistock, 1928).

He later discovered, as have other aviculturists to their dismay, that this conure is more prone to feather plucking than any other neotropical parrot. In 1929 he wrote: 'I am compelled to get rid of my Queen of Bavaria's Conures, owing to their tiresome and vicious habits . . .' and offered them to any member of the Avicultural Society 'who would like to have them'. Imagine the response that such a notice would evoke today!

The vicious habit to which he referred was feather plucking by the females: after denuding themselves they would commence to pluck their mates. In despair, Lord Tavistock allowed one pair to fly at liberty. They stayed well but their curiosity led them into the habit of visiting other aviaries and disturbing the inmates.

Captive-hatched Queen of Bavaria's Conure — the result of part of a European breeding programme for this species.

A decade later the first captive breeding occurred, in Sri Lanka (then Ceylon), in the aviaries of Dr W.C. Osman Hill in 1939. The young were accurately described as being paler yellow, with the cheeks streaked with dirty greenish, and the neck, throat and mantle streaked with green (Hill, 1939).

In this species the clutch size is usually three, sometimes four or more. British aviculturist and artist Jim Hayward (1980) recorded the clutch size in his several pairs as usually four, and up to six. The female alone incubates, although the male may spend much of the day inside the nest with the female. The incubation period is about 25 days and young spend nine to ten weeks in the nest.

Young chicks give no hint of the beauty they will possess. Pink and naked after the white down is lost at about ten days, they are characterised by their extraordinary beaks. They have the pronounced raised pads on the sides of the upper mandible found in many neotropical parrots; also, the lower mandible is large and shovel-like, extending beyond the upper mandible (similar to but more pronounced than the bill of chicks of the Grey Parrot [Psittacus erithacus]). When they acquire their feathers, they differ from the adult in having green wing coverts.

Prior to the 1970s no regular breeding successes had occurred in captivity (Low, 1972). This situation has now changed and there are a number of aviculturists who consistently achieve success with this species. However, there are also many non-breeding pairs, perhaps partly because in some collections there are single pairs and this species usually seems to do best within sight or sound of other pairs. Among the most successful breeders were Jim and Pearl Hayward of Carterton, Oxfordshire, UK, who kept a number of pairs in adjacent aviaries. By 1983 they had bred them to the third generation and, in that year alone, reared 24. This was achieved by artificially incubating the eggs and hand-rearing the young (Low, 1983b). In a large proportion of instances, young left with their parents either die very young or are poor specimens, largely due to the unfortunate habit of some pairs of refusing to feed anything but sunflower seed to their chicks, no matter what other foods are available and despite the fact that they have previously consumed a balanced diet. In the USA, virtually all young of this species are hand-reared, then sold as pets. Unless more are retained for breeding purposes, the future of this species in aviculture there, appears far from certain.

This Conure is not the only parrot from northern Brazil which has been adversely affected by loss of habitat. The plight of another conure is far worse. In the first edition of this book I wrote: 'A *Pyrrhura* conure which occurs in the same area as *guarouba* is the Pearly Conure (*P. perlata*). It is not threatened to the same degree, for it is ecologically more tolerant (Ridgely, 1981). It exists in locations which have been partially deforested or where forests are small in extent, thus it is more numerous and widespread than the larger conure.'

Unfortunately, this assessment appears to be totally inaccurate. The race referred to, *P.p. coerulescens*, 'may be extinct or close to extinction in the wild', according to the Parrot Action Plan. It is, or was, restricted to one of the most deforested areas of Brazil: western and central Maranhão. ICBP recommend that: 'A survey should be undertaken of all forest fragments within its historical range, prior to formulating further conservation plans.' It is not known whether any birds of this sub-species exist in captivity.

In northern Brazil there are two Amazons whose populations may be small — but there is little information at this stage. The Marajó Amazon (*Amazona ochrocephala xantholaema*) occurs on the island of Marajó, at the mouth of the Amazon. Its population is estimated at fewer than 5,000 birds. This sub-species was unknown in aviculture until 1984; the number kept outside Brazil is very small; in addition, it is difficult to identify (see Low, 1992a).

One of the least known of Amazons is the Diademed (*Amazona autumnalis diadema*) from north-western Brazil, in the region of the Lower Negro river and the north bank of the upper Amazon. It is known mainly from the Ducke Forest Reserve, north of Manaus. However, there is no actual evidence of a decline. In contrast, the sub-species from western Ecuador, *A.a. lilacina*, is threatened by deforestation and by trapping. Found only in the provinces of Guayas and Manabi, its habitat is gradually being destroyed for agricultural purposes — growing bananas, coffee, citrus, cocoa and yucca; in addition trees are cut for the production of charcoal.

In 1986 Ana and Eduardo Asanza from the Catholic University of Ecuador spent a week studying this Amazon and assessing the threats to its existence. Bird trappers told them that, in many areas where parrots were common three to five years previously, they were scarce and difficult to capture (Low, 1987). A population estimate of 2,000 is suggested in the Parrot Action Plan. The Lilacine Amazon is rare in captivity, having been imported into Europe and the USA for a short period during the late 1970s. It is breeding in a few collections. A concerted effort and the setting up of an international studbook are needed to ensure the captive survival of this beautiful and distinctive sub-species.

7

Island Species: Will they Survive?

The number of endangered birds on islands is disproportionately large because of their limited distribution, small populations, and sensitivity to man's activities and introductions.

WARREN B. KING, IN *ENDANGERED BIRDS* (1977)

The statistics of extinction and endangerment show how very vulnerable are island species. More than 90 per cent of birds which have become extinct in historical times were island species, although less than 20 per cent of all birds are island forms. Islands constitute less than 7 per cent of the earth's surface, yet 53 per cent of endangered birds are found thereon (Mayr, 1965).

An unfortunate example of island parrots in peril is that of the *Amazona* species endemic to the Caribbean. Of the eight extant species, six are endangered, and two of these are considered to be critically endangered (see Chapter 8 and Chapter 10). The St Vincent Parrot (*see* Chapter 9) has a population which is not large, although fairly stable.

Many islands harbour excessively large human populations, resulting in massive or almost total deforestation. Because of this, one Amazon is already extinct, probably since the eighteenth century. It inhabited Martinique and is known only from written descriptions. As the human population expands, as on Dominica, St Vincent and St Lucia, montane forest is encroached upon until parrots survive only in the highest or most remote areas.

Few parrot genera contain a group of species from one area which are so close to extinction as the Amazons of the Lesser Antilles. The over-populated Caribbean islands, among the smallest nation states in the world, lack the financial assets to aid their unique fauna. Politically but not economically independent, they are desperately looking to tourism to improve their economic status, and this escalates the already near-hopeless plight of the endemic parrot.

Of the eight species found in the Caribbean, two are endemic to Dominica. The only other island on which two *Amazona* species occur is Jamaica, home of the Black-billed Amazon (*A. agilis*) and the Yellow-billed Amazon (*A. collaria*). They are now found in the last remnants of the forests which once covered the entire island. In 1988 these forests were believed to extend over less than 540 km^2 (208 sq. miles), only 5 per cent of the total land area. Then on September 12/13 Hurricane Gilbert struck Jamaica. It was recorded as the most powerful storm in the Caribbean this century, with winds in excess of 220 kph (135 mph). The Black-billed Amazon inhabits the heavily forested mountains and valleys up to 900 m (3,000 ft) in the central ridge of the island, especially in the northern areas. Its stronghold is Cockpit Country, the wildest and most inaccessible terrain. A small Amazon, not at all typical of the genus, it is entirely dark green but for the red wing speculum.

The Yellow-billed is more abundant, less shy and probably adapts more readily to disturbed areas. It has two centres of distribution: the northern-central part from Cockpit Country to Mount Diablo, and the John Crow Mountains in the east. In some areas it co-exists with *A. agilis*, but its range is far more extensive.

Steven Gruber, a Jamaican ornithologist with a special interest in the native parrots, estimated the populations in 1977 as 2,500 *A. collaria* and 1,500 *A. agilis* (pers. comm.).

Increasing development, however, is a threat to the existence of both species. Roads are being extended into the Cockpit Country and forestry is encroaching on the central core of the John Crow and the Blue Mountains. Although these areas are designated as national parks, they have never been accurately delineated on the ground or given any special protection (Cruz and Fairbairn, 1980).

Bauxite (aluminium) mining is another factor causing disturbance to parrot habitat. Extensive tracts of the southern Cockpit County have been leased to bauxite companies for exploratory mining. In 1975 I saw for myself the catrastrophic effect this has on the environment, laying waste large areas and resulting in the creation of deadly 'lakes' of waste.

There were already severe pressures on these two

Distribution of (a) Black-billed Amazon (*Amazona agilis*) and (b) Yellow-billed Amazon (*A. collaria*).

---

parrots and Jamaica's 23 other endemic bird species when Hurricane Gilbert struck. Millions of trees were uprooted or damaged. In some places the forest was totally destroyed by landslides. In the John Crow Mountains, which took the full force of the hurricane, 28 per cent of trees were toppled and a further 15 per cent lost their crowns. The government of Jamaica appealed to ICBP to send a team to make an assessment of the endemic forest birds and their habitats. This was carried out between April and August 1989. The result was surprising: these birds appeared to have survived the hurricane well. However, the long-term effect of the hurricane is not yet known. Fruit production by forest trees is expected to be much lower for a number of years and this could result in reduced populations of both parrots and the rare Ring-tailed Pigeon (*Colomba caribaea*). As so many of the largest trees were blown over, it is likely that many parrot nest sites were lost.

Varty (1990) points out that the forests are probably always in some state of recovery; after all, 16 hurricanes have directly hit Jamaica since 1871. The concern now is that forest clearance, timber extraction and hunting could have reduced bird populations to such low numbers that they will be unable to recover from the impact of storms as severe as Gilbert. To make matters worse, many farmers lost their cultivated areas and the resultant demand for new land may have increased the rate of deforestation; so may the misuse

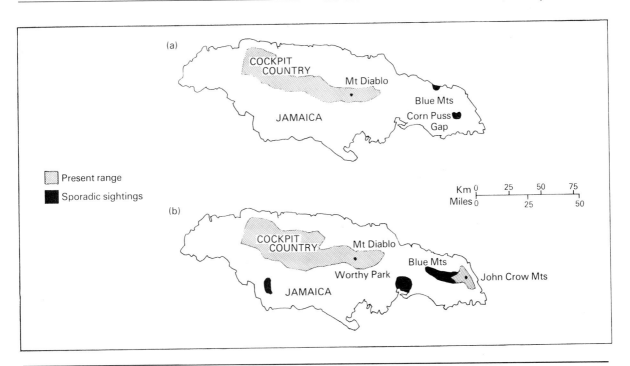

of the many chain saws taken to Jamaica to clean up hurricane damage. However, one outcome of the hurricane may be beneficial to the parrots in the short term: forest trails were blocked, preventing access to shooters and collectors and areas away from paths may remain inaccessible for a long time.

The government of Jamaica has long been aware of the serious effect of reduced habitat on the native fauna; however, it was not until 1989 that firm steps were taken to protect it. In that year an agreement was signed with USAID to establish two pilot national parks, the first of such parks for Jamaica. One of these will encompass a significant portion of the Blue Mountains and the John Crow Mountains. A legal and financial framework for a national park system will be created and a Conservation Data Base will be established at the University of the West Indies. Other areas, including Cockpit Country, so important for the survival of the parrots, may be designated as national parks if the pilot parks are successful.

For a brief period during the late 1970s the Jamaican Amazons were illegally exported in fairly substantial numbers; at no other time have they been commercially available. This regrettable influx provided the hitherto unknown information that the Black-billed Amazon is very difficult to establish. The majority of the *A. agilis* exported (most to the USA, thence a few to Europe) died within a year. Autopsies carried out in the USA indicated that the birds had liver damage and bacterial infections before leaving Jamaica. As a result, only a handful of pairs now exist in collections and, at the time of writing, only one pair had bred. Belonging to Ramon Noegel, they raised one youngster in 1978.

The captive position of the Yellow-billed is only slightly better. Few problems were experienced in establishing this species; but at the time it was available few aviculturists demonstrated much interest in it. A number of pairs exist in collections in Europe and in the USA and a few are regularly producing young in small numbers.

In the USA the Yellow-billed Amazon was first bred in 1972, in advance of the main influx, by Perry Linder of California. The first breeders in the UK were John and Josie Arman in 1982 (Arman, 1983).

To the north of Jamaica lies the 114,500-km^2 (44,200-sq. mile) curve of Cuba, the largest republic in the Caribbean. There are two endemic parrots, the Cuban Amazon (*Amazona leucocephala leucocephala*) and the Cuban Conure (*Aratinga euops*). With its pink and white head markings, the Amazon is an outstandingly beautiful bird. In the past these parrots were persecuted for the damage they caused to banana plantations and other crops. Barbour (1943) noted their decline: 'In the province of Oriente Parrots are still to be found in the forests of the lower mountainsides, but every-where they are growing fewer in number year by year.' The great expansion in cane planting was one factor which caused a major loss of habitat. Hunting these parrots for food and trapping them for pets further reduced their population.

The sub-species *Amazona l. palmarum* is found in western Cuba and what was formerly the Isle of Pines, now called Isla de la Juventud (the Isle of Youth). Collecting parrots for export to the USA was apparently a thriving industry there during the early years of the century. Most parrot hunters were farmers who sold young Amazons to supplement their meagre income. Areas were staked off so that each hunter was allowed a fair share of nests (Noegel, 1978). The island is now nearly totally deforested and the site of boarding schools for over 20,000 students.

In 1978 Dr Abelardo Moreno informed me that, in Cuba, regulations had been made that 'prohibit the capture and exportation of this species, so that its populations will be restored to the numbers existing 50 years ago'. This implied that its numbers had been severely reduced. Cubans who took up residence in Florida at that time stated that parrots were sold in Cuba for food.

The Cuban Amazon population suffered a notable decline during the 1960s (Montaña, 1987). By the early 1990s it still occurred in all provinces but was common only in Ciénaga de Zapata, on the Péninsula de Guanahacabibes, in the Sierra de Najasa (Camagüey) and in some mountainous zones (Sierra Maestra) in Granma and Santiago de Cuba provinces. The largest population was found in the area of San Francisco de la Vega in the Ciénaga de Lanier. In 1988 the population was estimated at 5,000 birds. It had declined in range and numbers throughout Cuba until the late 1970s when the government took measures to control its export (Wiley, 1991). The Cuban Amazon (and all sub-species of *Amazona leucocephala*) has been listed on Appendix I of CITES since 1973, which means countries that were signatories to CITES could not legally import this species. However, Cuba is still not a signatory; thus, prior to the late 1970s, Cuban Amazons could still be imported by countries, such as Japan, which were also not signatories. Whether this occurred I do not know; what is known with certainty is that, during the late 1980s, there was an influx, into Europe, the Canary Islands and the USA, of illegally exported Cuban Amazons, many of them from Russian ships. There were as many as 30 birds in some shipments. Some were confiscated but many others must have passed undetected. Hundreds, even thousands of birds were probably involved. This must mean that they are no longer effectively protected on Cuba. In the Parrot Action Plan the population of the Cuban Amazon is estimated at about 10,000 and its status is described as vulnerable/stable. I fear that this description is over-optimistic.

The status of the red-speckled green parrakeet known as the Cuban Conure (*Aratinga euops*) is now also giving cause for concern. A declining population of fewer than 5,000 is suggested in the Parrot Action Plan. Where an *Aratinga* and an *Amazona* survive in the same area, the conure is generally much more numerous. It is hard to believe that there could be twice as many Amazons unless there was some particular pressure on the conure. If so, what is it? Trapping seems unlikely as it is too small to eat and there is no demand for it as a pet. There are very few in captivity outside Cuba, perhaps not enough to ensure their survival in aviculture. In Germany there are a few pairs.

The Cuban Conure (or Parrakeet) is protected by law — a law which is ineffective on its own. An aggressive education programme is needed if Cuba's two parrot species are to survive. This may be a crucial period in their history — a period when the populations could be stabilised at reasonable numbers *if* an effective education campaign, combined with habitat protection, could be instituted. If this does not occur, both species could decline very rapidly. There would then be a long and costly battle to bring the populations back to the numbers which exist today — if the resources were available.

According to Wiley, the Academia de Ciencias de Cuba has an active captive breeding programme for the Amazon with the objective of returning offspring to the wild. It is difficult to see the logic in this while wild birds are being trapped or deprived of their habitat. Furthermore, the numbers produced for release would be insignificant compared to those which are illegally exported. I believe that the Academia should concentrate its resources on an education programme and leave captive breeding to the aviculturists of Europe and the USA. The demand for it can be met by successful breeders if only Cuba will stop its export.

The Cuban Amazon was rare in aviculture until the 1970s when zoos in eastern Germany started receiving these birds. Now this Amazon is well established in Europe. It is in Florida, however, in the hands of Ramon Noegel, that the most significant successes have been achieved on a scale which has not been equalled with any other endangered parrot. He obtained long-term pet birds from Cuban immigrants in the 1960s. Since 1973 he, and in recent years his partner Greg Moss, have reared more than 200 Cuban Amazons. Fifth-generation offspring have been reared — an unrivalled accomplishment in the annals of captive breeding of endangered Amazons. Great success has also been obtained with the Grand Cayman (*Amazona l. caymanensis*), which is one of the most difficult Amazons to breed.

Approximately 290 km (180 miles) south of Cuba, and the same distance north-west of Jamaica, lie the tiny Cayman Islands. They are better known as a tax haven than for their Amazon parrots; indeed, when I was there in 1975, I discovered that some of the residents of Grand Cayman were unaware that a native parrot existed. It is mainly confined to the mangrove forest in the central and eastern parts of this flat, 37-km (23-mile) long island. It can be seen feeding in gardens and other cultivated areas.

Persecution and development led to a decline in numbers and reduction of range of the Grand Cayman Amazon (*A.l. caymanensis*) since the early years of the century. (*See* Plate 5.) To this day it is shot by Caymanians who regard it as a nuisance when it feeds on their fruit crops; it is also shot for sport.

An American newspaper reported, on October 11 1982, the activities of G. Ray Arnett, the Assistant Secretary of the Interior for Fish and Wildlife. On a four-day business trip to the Cayman Islands, he shot two parrots. He is the man responsible for protecting endangered species in the USA. (According to the same newspaper report, this man has kept the Sea Otter off the endangered species list, allowed the import of kangaroo hides and favours turning over the world's only winter refuge for Whooping Cranes to the state of Texas, which wants to develop part of it for commercial purposes.)

In 1988 I made a brief return visit to Grand Cayman. Parrots were easy to find and it seemed feasible that reports of an increase were true. However, one month later, in September, Hurricane Gilbert hit the Cayman Islands and palm groves and mangrove forests on Grand Cayman were levelled. There was concern for the parrot's survival, but the effect of the hurricane was apparently negligible. The most severe long-term threat to this species is not a natural one but the development of land in association with tourism. However, there have been two positive steps forward concerning the conservation of *A.l. caymanensis*. In 1990 it was removed from the list of game species, a long overdue act but — it can still be shot as a crop pest. Also in 1990, the National Trust for the Cayman Islands and RARE Center for Tropical Bird Conservation commenced a programme of conservation for both the parrots of the Cayman Islands.

When the first edition of this book was published, the population of *caymanensis* was believed to be between 200 and 300 — possibly an underestimate. The 1992 Parrot Action Plan suggested that the population was above 1,000.

The sub-species from Cayman Brac (*A.l. hesterna*) is the smallest race of *A. leucocephala*, with even less pink on the head than *A.l. caymanensis* and, in most specimens, a solid area of vinaceous on the underparts, extending from the breast to the abdomen. It has the smallest distribution of any Amazon parrot, for Cayman Brac is less than 20 km (12 miles) in length and not more than 4 km (2.5 miles) wide. In recent years its population has dwindled to the point where it is seriously endangered. Field work carried out by Ramon Noegel and his assistants indicated that only in the centre of the island are there trees containing cavities large enough for parrot nests.

Before Hurricane Allen hit the island in 1980 there may have been 130 Cayman Brac Parrots; after the hurricane, Noegel estimated that only 50 survived. However, in February 1991 the population was extensively surveyed by the National Trust for the Cayman Islands, resulting in an estimate of 93–134 parrots. Patricia Bradley (1986) had estimated that there were more than 200 in captivity, but some of these were surely from Grand Cayman. Surprisingly, a survey carried out in 1992 resulted in the population being assessed at 300–400 individuals.

There are a number of pressures on this small and vulnerable population; at last, in 1990, the National Trust for the Cayman Islands took an interest in its plight and, with the RARE Center for Bird Conservation, has since implemented a conservation education programme. This is urgently needed; the population is declining and the growth of agriculture on this small island means that, unless action is taken now, there is little hope for its, long-term survival. Recommendations for its conservation include research to determine nest-site requirements and nest availability, and its feeding ecology, including emphasis on the role of fruit crops in the parrot's diet and the removal of feral cats. Wiley (1991) also suggests: 'A carefully managed captive propagation programme seems appropriate in view of the small population size and restricted range.'

Fortunately, Ramon Noegel took a young pair from the island in 1975. In 1981 one chick was reared, the first of its kind to be raised in captivity.

Perhaps due to inbreeding depression, island endemics with tiny remnant populations seldom prove easy to breed in captivity. Reproduction of *A.l. hesterna* has been difficult but continues in this collection. In 1992, four were reared. This may be the only captive group worldwide.

The sub-species from the Bahamas (*A.l. bahamensis*) is distinguished by the fact that the white markings on the head extend behind the eye, as well as around it. In addition, the black margins of the green feathers are more prominent. Most specimens have a greater area and intensity of red on the face and upper breast than the Cuban Amazon. This is, arguably, the most beautiful race of *A. leucocephala*.

Formerly found on several other Bahaman islands, it is most recently extinct on Acklin where it was

Cayman Brac Amazon (*Amazona leucocephala hesterna*), hand-reared by Ramon Noegel in Florida.

reputedly fairly common in the 1940s. Now it is confined to Abaco and Inagua. The two surviving populations are widely spread and represent the northern and southern limits of its former range. Abaco, the northernmost island of the Bahamas, is situated 240 km (150 miles) due east of Fort Lauderdale in Florida; it is 140 km in length and 48 km (30 miles) at its widest point. Inagua, the third largest of the Bahaman islands, is 1,550 km^2 (598 sq. miles) in extent.

Several reasons have been put forward for the decrease of the parrots on Abaco during the 1960s: widespread destruction of pines, the passage of Hurricane Betsy, and shooting. The latter was facilitated by the construction of the first roads in 1959, when pine-cutting recommenced. Previously inaccessible southern areas were opened up to shooters who were primarily interested in the White-crowned Pigeon (*Columba leucocephala*). It is doubtful, however, whether many 'sportsmen' would discriminate between pigeons and parrots, despite the penalties for shooting the latter. In 1968 a heavy fine was imposed for shooting or taking parrots. I visited Abaco in October 1980, soon after the start of the pigeon-shooting season, and was appalled by the number of spent cartridges littering the ground. These were observed not only in the Crossing Rocks region but much further away from the road. The parrots were the wariest I have ever observed. They have undoubtedly learned the wisdom of keeping out of range of humans during the open season for pigeons.

In contrast, they are not at all shy during the breeding season when their unique nesting behaviour can be observed. The Abaco birds alone among neotropical parrots nest underground, as a result of the rarity of large cavities in the native pines. Cavities in the limestone formations which extend underground are the most usual nesting sites. On Inagua the parrots nest in trees.

Increased accessibility on Abaco presents a threat to the parrots there, but on Inagua the situation is quite the reverse; they are protected by the sheer inaccessibility of the greater part of the island. There is no road system and no demand for one. The human population has decreased significantly, from about 5,000 at the beginning of the century, to about 1,200. Farming has declined correspondingly thus reducing the pressure on that population of *A.l. bahamensis*. Several parks have been established by the Bahamas National Trust, including one which encompasses most of the parrot's range. It covers 718 km^2 (277 sq. miles). On Abaco a reserve has been proposed but not implemented.

Although estimates are lacking, it seems that the Inagua population is quite sizeable. The island, largely unspoilt, contains one of the largest flamingo colonies in the Caribbean. The parrot's prospects there are good. On Abaco its survival will depend on the protection of the pines, especially in the 39 km^2 (15 sq. miles) at the south-eastern end of the island, the stronghold for this parrot. There is an equally important factor, essential for their survival, which was not discovered until 1985. In that year Rosemarie Gnam started to study this species in the field — the first biologist to do so. She found that feral cats were the most serious threat to the Bahama Parrot on Abaco. When I met her in 1988 a clearer picture of its breeding biology was emerging. That year only 30 per cent of laying pairs had been successful in fledging young. Fourteen cases of nest predation had been recorded, plus five others where cats may have been responsible. That cats, more than any other factor, determine the success of the breeding season was demonstrated in 1990 when 64 per cent of nests fledged young. During the years 1985–88 an average of 46 per cent of egg-laying pairs fledged young. During 1989–90 fires in the nesting area cleared the forest of its understorey, causing cats to disperse into unburnt areas where more food was available but where few parrots were nesting. Of 34 nests monitored, in underground limestone cavities, eggs were laid in 33. The number of chicks hatched per nest was two; 64 per cent of all nests fledged young and the percentage of nests with chicks which fledged young was 84 per cent — a significant increase on previous years.

In 1990 'Friends of the Abaco Parrot' was launched. This group raises funds for conservation education. Its aim is a well-protected and patrolled parrot reserve, if enough funds can be raised. One of the first projects was the production of a 'Let's get to know the Bahama Parrot' colouring book. The excellent results from involving children in parrot conservation have already been demonstrated on other islands of the Caribbean. Hopefully a whole generation of children will grow up with the awareness that their parrot is unique and important and must be conserved.

How can its conservation be achieved? First, the fight against feral cats must continue. In 1990 a US Fish and Wildlife Service biologist spent a week on Abaco evaluating the cat problem. His recommendations must be acted upon. On an island where unwanted kittens are thrown into the bush, a free programme to spay cats and euthanise unwanted kittens should surely be introduced. Secondly, Rosemarie Gnam's recommendations, resulting from six years of study, must be acted upon by Bahamian government ministries, non-governmental organisations and international conservation groups. Thirdly, if sufficient funds can be raised, some parrots will be translocated to Little Abaco Island (Low, 1992b).

A modest captive breeding programme was envisaged under the auspices of the Bahamas Naturalists' Trust. For this purpose four birds were taken from the wild in 1978 and three in 1979; however, none were ever reared. The export of this parrot is strictly prohibited. Only one legally exported bird is known to exist outside the Bahamas.

The species which, taxonomically, is closest to *A. leucocephala* is the Santo Domingo or Hispaniolan Amazon (*A. ventralis*). It differs mainly in lacking the striking pink facial coloration. It is endemic to Hispaniola (the island which, politically, is separated into the Dominican Republic and Haiti (Hispaniola)). A narrow expanse of ocean separates it from Cuba (to the west) and Puerto Rico (to the east). In common with the parrots of those islands, the major threat to the existence of *A. ventralis* is habitat destruction. This has been most severe on Haiti. In 25 years forest cover has been reduced from 80 per cent of the total area to only 9 per cent. A few parrots are known to survive — but for how much longer?

Woods states: 'The general status of the parrot throughout its range is endangered.' In the Massif de La Selle it is rare and endangered, also in the Massif de La Hotte in the upper mountains, and uncommon but threatened on the Plain of Formon and surrounding mid-elevation areas. In 1975 he had observed large numbers in flocks of up to 80 individuals in the Massif de La Hotte. In the Dominican Republic near the Haitian frontier in the Sierra de Baorucos, at the same elevation as Parc National La Visite, he observed large flocks but in 1985 he found the parrot to be "almost missing" from La Visite. It was common in the mature broadleaved forest of the Plain of Formon where small flocks were easily observed.

Young Hispaniolan Amazon soon after leaving the nest at Palmitos Park, Gran Canaria.

'An active parrot conservation program must be initiated if this species is to be saved from extinction', warned Charles A. Woods in 1987 — but nothing has been done. He stressed the importance of developing and enforcing legislation to prevent exploitation of the species as a household pet and item of commercial value as well as protecting its habitat in the region of the national parks. He suggested: 'Parrots found for sale in market places or by private individuals should be confiscated although it would be too controversial and damaging to the public image of the conservation program to confiscate pet Parrots from households.'

Harvesting of chicks and hunting this species is illegal in the Dominican Republic (under law DR–1975 601) — but the law is not enforced. This republic has been a member of CITES since 1987; Haiti is not a member.

In the Dominican Republic some forest remains, notably in the Samaná Peninsula, on the central part of the north coast, also in the mountains. Parrots have been legally protected since 1975, but shooting and trade continues. Formerly, and by long tradition, considered good eating, large numbers would be shot for food; however, this had less impact on the population than the continuing loss of habitat.

The large-scale collection of chicks for pets is now having a detrimental effect (Ottenwalder, 1978). This occurs in the mountainous regions. Those involved in the trade admit the decrease in numbers; nests have become more difficult to find and prices have increased greatly. One man who had traded in parrots for many years, formerly selling 500–1,000 annually, had had his trade reduced to 300 per year. Although these figures indicate that *A. ventralis* was relatively common by Caribbean Amazon standards, you only have to trace the history of *A. vittata* to realise how rapidly an island species can slide from a seemingly safe level to near-extinction.

This can be triggered by some political happening with far-reaching effects. For example, in late 1991, an economic embargo was declared against the military government of Haiti, one of the poorest nations of the Caribbean. As a result, about 150,000 jobs were lost. The poverty of the peasants was so acute that many sold their few possession in order to buy food. Then there was only one way left to survive: to cut down trees to make charcoal to sell in the market. In some areas no trees survived, so roots were used instead. As the trees go, so do the parrots. But faced with desperate poverty, the people of Haiti are concerned only with the basics of survival — their own survival.

This is not a common Amazon in captivity; but there are sufficient birds to ensure its survival. Since 1971 it has been reared in a number of collections in the USA, also in the UK, Switzerland and the Dominican Republic.

The Hispaniolan Conure (*Aratinga chloroptera*) is also threatened by the destruction of the forests. It was formerly common throughout the island, especially in pine forests and high mountain forests. In the Dominican Republic, it now occurs almost exclusively in remoter areas (especially Sierra de Baoruco, Sierra Neiba, Cordillera Central, Los Haitises and lowlands around Lago Enrilquillo) and sparsely in hills around agricultural areas (Wiley, 1991). In Haiti, its populations are smaller and more restricted in range; numbers may be highest in the Massif de la Selle and Massif de la Hotte.

Like the Amazon, it is uncommon in captivity — in fact, the rarer of the two, held in very few collections. However, it is easy to breed and the low numbers reflect a lack of avicultural interest. The Hispaniolan Amazon is more difficult to breed, but there is more avicultural interest in Amazons. It has never been common in aviculture, but there are probably enough birds to ensure its survival.

Plate 1 (top) Yellow-eared Conure, *Ognorhynchus icterotis* (northern South America).

Plate 2 (left) Thick-billed Parrot, *Rhynchopsitta pachyrhyncha,* at its nest hole (central America).

Plate 3 (above) Red-browed Amazon, *Amazona dufresniana rhodocorytha* (Brazil).

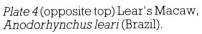

Plate 4 (opposite top) Lear's Macaw, *Anodorhynchus leari* (Brazil).

Plate 5 (far left) Grand Cayman Amazon, *Amazona leucocephala caymanensis* (Grand Cayman).

Plate 6 (centre left) Puerto Rican Parrot, *Amazona vittata*.

Plate 7 (left) Queen of Bavaria's Conure, *Aratinga guarouba* (Brazil).

Plate 8 (above) St Lucia Parrot, *Amazona versicolor*.

Plate 9 (above right) Yellow-shouldered Amazon, *Amazona barbadensis* (Venezuela).

Plate 10 (right) Imperial Parrot, *Amazona imperialis* (Dominica).

Plate 11 (opposite) Red-necked Amazon, *Amazona arausiaca* (Dominica).

Plate 12 (top left) Head of St Vincent Parrot, *Amazona guildingii.*

Plate 13 (above) St Vincent Parrot.

Plate 14 (top right) Black Parrot, *Coracopsis nigra barklyi,* in the wild (Praslin, Seychelles).

Plate 15 (right) Echo Parrakeet, *Psittacula echo,* in the wild (Mauritius).

Plate 16 (opposite top) Ground Parrot, *Pezoporus wallicus* (Australia).

Plate 17 (opposite bottom) Red-breasted Musk Parrot, *Prosopeia tabuensis* (Fiji).

Plate 18 (above) Female Kakapo, *Strigops habroptilus,* feeding her chick (New Zealand).

Plate 19 (left) Orange-bellied Parrakeet, *Neophema chrysogaster* (South Australia, Victoria and Tasmania).

Plate 20 (above) Young Cruentata Conures,
Pyrrhura cruentata (Brazil), captive-bred.

Plate 21 (left) Norfolk Island Parrakeet,
Cyanoramphus novaezelandiae cookii.

The Hispaniolan Conure is threatened by the destruction of its forest habitat.

In contrast, the St Lucia Parrot (*Amazona versicolor*) is unknown in private aviculture. (*See* Plate 8.) It is now confined to an area of 102 km² (40 sq. miles), although once its range extended over the entire island of 609 km² (235 sq. miles). No figures are available, but as with other comparable species the drastic decline has probably occurred since the 1950s. It has been suggested that the population then was as high as 1,000; but there is no evidence to support this. Now, the number of surviving individuals is believed to be between 300 and 350. This is twice the estimate of 'under 150' given in the first edition of this book. It is indeed encouraging to record this — a classic example of a conservation success story. How has this been achieved?

Until the 1970s, hunting was the principal factor in the decline of the St Lucia Parrot. Birds were shot for food and in the hope of 'wing-tipping' to sell as pets. This occurred despite the fact that on St Lucia, also on St Vincent and Dominica, legislation to protect the parrots was introduced at the beginning of the twentieth century, and forest reserves, national parks and conservation areas have been set up. Butler (1990) recorded: 'These actions appear to have failed, and until recent times the populations of their endemic psittacines appear to have continued to decline. Why?

'A fundamental problem in using legislation to alter behaviour is the fact that in small islands, such as those of the Lesser Antilles, the majority of islanders are known to one another. Forest officers and other law enforcement officials are reluctant to take their neighbours to court and, more often than not, a charge is never levied. Indeed, for almost ninety years no wildlife offences were recorded in Saint Lucia during a period when it was estimated that over forty parrots per year were being shot in an attempt to catch them.'

Clearly, more than legislation was needed for an effective conservation strategy. As Paul Butler relates: 'Saint Lucia implemented a comprehensive conservation programme that initiated legislative enactments, reserve establishment, and captive breeding programmes simultaneously and underpinned these by a far reaching and innovative conservation education programme. It incorporates the usual components of a traditional education project plus the innovative use of music, dance, theatre and the interaction between government, non-governmental organisations and local businesses.

'This tri-partite approach, with the external agency serving solely as a catalyst providing core materials and technical assistance, has resulted in a sustainable programme of conservation education which has long outlasted the initial involvement of outside funding. At the same time it has generated a surge of local pride and determined efforts to protect the island's natural patrimony.'

The measures adopted to achieve this result are described on page 170. By 1990, the St Lucia Parrot was the national bird, more than 20 reserves had been established, and St Lucia had become a signatory to CITES. In addition, the number of birds in the breeding programme at Jersey Wildlife Preservation Trust in the Channel Islands had risen from 9 to 22 and two parrots hatched there had been returned to St Lucia. But, above all, the wild population had increased, in the space of a decade, from about 150 birds to more than 250, and since then, has increased even further. The parrot has even expanded its range. Clearly, the story of the St Lucia Parrot has been one of resounding success as a result of involving and educating the people of the island.

Until the 1970s hunting was the principal factor in the decline of the St Lucia Parrot. Birds were shot for food and in the hope of 'wing-tipping' to sell as pets. Any trade of this kind was mainly local; for fewer St Lucia Parrots than any Caribbean species, except those from Dominica, have reached overseas collections.

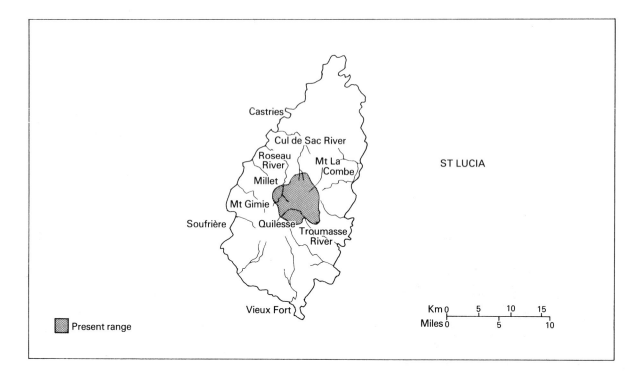

Castries

Cul de Sac River

Roseau
River

Mt La
Combe

Millet

ST LUCIA

Mt Gimie

Soufrière

Quilesse

Troumasse
River

Vieux Fort

Km 0   5   10   15

Miles 0   5   10

Present range

Distribution of St Lucia Parrot (*Amazona versicolor*).

When London Zoo received one in 1874, the country of its origin was unknown but believed to be Cuba. A very few birds (probably not exceeding a dozen), imported singly, reached Europe up to the first half of the twentieth century. From then on it was unknown in captivity outside the island until 1975 when Jersey Preservation Trust in the Channel Islands commenced to work with the Government Forestry Division of St Lucia. A nestling St Lucia Parrot was taken during a field survey that year and six more were obtained in 1976.

The birds at Jersey Wildlife Preservation Trust are, to my knowledge, the only ones outside St Lucia. Certainly the Government has not sanctioned the removal of any others from the island and is unlikely to give permission for any more to be exported. In 1992, the number of captive birds, at Jersey and on St Lucia, totalled 18.

Natural hazards forever pose a threat to island species. After Hurricane Allen struck St Lucia on August 4 1980 it was believed that no serious decline has occurred in the parrot population. This conclusion was reached after comparing sightings, at three study sites, for 1980 and 1982 (Jeggo, Taynton and Bobb, 1982). Parrots had found sufficient food in undamaged and cultivated areas. The forests were severely damaged, however, with an estimated 39 per cent of all trees destroyed and an additional 41 per cent sustaining significant damage (Anon., 1982). Preliminary surveys by members of the island's Forestry Division indicated that large trees were badly affected and that many naturally weakened ones, including those containing cavities, had been destroyed. Such trees had provided the majority of nest sites for the St Lucia Parrot. Now a further step has been suggested to protect the still vulnerable population — the phasing out of certain plantations in favour of reversion to natural forest. If this happens it will be a conservation landmark. At least on one small island sanity will have prevailed — to the ultimate benefit of parrots *and man*.

Unlike the St Lucia Parrot, the Yellow-shouldered (*Amazona barbadensis*) is not exclusively an island Amazon. Unlike the St Lucia, however, its fortunes have suffered a marked decline since the first edition of this book was published. Little was known about its status in Venezuela until 1981, following Robert Ridgely's investigation. Then, he found it to be locally abundant, with no evidence of recent decline, in the areas of Falcón and Anzoategui (Ridgely, 1981). In

July 1988 Thomas Arndt visited the same region and also found it to be locally common. Large numbers were kept as pets; in some areas, one in every four houses kept one. Young could be purchased for the equivalent of only $3. On a plateau nearly 85 km (33 miles) inland, he also found this Amazon to be common. Desenne and Strahl (1991) listed its known breeding areas in Venezuela as the Araya Peninsula, and the vicinities of Puerto Píritu, Paraguaná Peninsula, Dabajuro and Casigua. They stated: '. . . all known populations are under considerable pressure from human activities. The only protected area in which *A. barbadensis* has been sighted in small numbers is a private reserve on the Sierra de San Luis, Paraguaná Peninsula, managed by the Fundación Bioma.'

This Amazon is also found on the islands of Blanquilla and Margarita, which belong to Venezuela, and in the Netherlands Antilles. Nothing had been published about the status of this species on Margarita until Thomas Arndt visited the island in 1988. Margarita is quite a large island, 1,150 km² (444 sq. miles) in extent. It occurred only in the less-developed western part, Macanao, a peninsula reached via a small bridge. Out of the breeding season the Amazons exist in the

Habitat of St Lucia Parrot (*Amazona versicolor*).

dry interior, an area surrounded by mountains and accessible only from the single village there. There are no roads and no agriculture.

More recently, the Yellow-shouldered Amazon has been studied on Margarita by Albornoz, Suárez and Sanz (1992), in one of its main breeding areas, La Quebrada La Chica, on private land. In 1989 no young fledged in this area because all those which survived were illegally removed from their nests. When the study commenced in 1990 the nests were protected; as a result, 35 young left the nest in 1990, 27 in 1991 and 52 in 1992, i.e. 114 in three years. The population was censused at the five roosting sites on the peninsula. It was found that, of a total population of 779 birds, 26 per cent were breeding. In order to carry out this study and conservation programme, wide contact was made with the local people, two young people acted as assistants, and others helped with the census, including university students. However, it will be necessary to deter the theft of young from nests in future years, and

St Lucia Parrot aged 62 days hatched at Jersey Wildlife
Preservation Trust.

to prevent further destruction of its habitat, if this
species is to survive on Margarita. According to
Desenne and Strahl (1991), collecting young for the
local pet trade and perhaps for international commerce, had made a major impact on the population.
Another pressure on the population is sand-mining on
Macanao for construction on the eastern part of the
island. Mining activities are destroying the primary
foraging habitat, as well as roosting areas and nesting
trees.

Another population of the Yellow-shouldered Amazon exists on the small island of La Blanquilla, which
measures only 10 × 5 km (6 × 3 miles). For years I
tried unsuccessfully to obtain information on its status
there. Then in 1992 Franklin Rojas Suárez presented a
short paper on this species at the First Symposium on
the Biology and Conservation of Venezuelan Parrots.

He stated that the total population of *Amazona
barbadensis* on La Blanquilla is less than 80 birds,
distributed over the island. The principal threat to its
existence is the capture of young. A possible threat is
the population of feral cats. He concluded that this was
the population in the greatest danger of extinction;
furthermore, there is some evidence that it should be
treated as an endemic sub-species (Suárez, 1992a).

Until the late 1980s, only the Bonaire population was
studied. It is known to fluctuate between 100 and 400
individuals, this being influenced by climatic conditions, notably rainfall. In 1978, for example, the
population was believed to have been halved by the
severe drought (Low, 1981b). Starving parrots flew into
the main settlement, Kralendijk, looking for food.
Many were shot; others died of starvation. Some were
saved by the importation of mangoes from Venezuela,
at the instigation of a board member of the national
park. The latter covers 2,430 ha (6,000 acres) in an area
known as Washington, formerly a large plantation. It
came into being in 1969 as the result of a bequest to the
Netherlands Antilles Government. When I visited the
island in 1979 I found this Amazon more numerous

outside the park than within it; but in the space of ten days that was largely a matter of chance.

The threat to this species from trade which is now apparent throughout its range, is a recent one, probably dating from the late 1980s. This Amazon was added to Appendix I of CITES in 1981, at a time when there was no avicultural demand for it. Since then, the number of countries legally exporting Amazons has decreased, putting pressure on species which previously were almost unknown outside their native countries. In 1991, Ron Atherton, an Englishman then living in Venezuela, told me that the number of parrots offered for sale in the Caracas area had declined. He sent an item from a local newspaper, the *Daily Journal*, of June 1991. It described how parrots caught locally were smuggled into the Netherlands Antillean islands of Aruba and Curaçao, then shipped out with papers stating that they were native species. According to another newspaper report, of an estimated 1,000 parrots that were illegally imported into Curaçao,

Cadushi cacti and limestone rocks are typical of Bonaire's bizarre yet haunting landscape, inhabited by Yellow-shouldered Amazons (*Amazona barbadensis*).

about 170 a year were being confiscated by customs officials. Sadly, it was the practice to kill confiscated birds until 1991, when MARNR (Ministerio del Ambiente y de Recursos Naturales Renovables) agreed to accept the birds. On at least two occasions the government of Aruba has sent confiscated birds back to Venezuela. After rehabilitation, they were released in the lower coastal area of the Henri Pittier National Park, Estado Aragua (M.L. Goodwin, *in litt*, 1993).

Aruba is an industrialised island, dominated by the oil industry. In the wild, the Yellow-shouldered Amazon apparently became extinct there during the mid-1950s and the species is now represented by a small

Yellow-shouldered Amazons on Bonaire.

number of feral birds. It is not known to have occurred naturally on nearby Curaçao, but a feral breeding colony now occurs there. It originated from birds illegally brought in from Venezuela by fishermen, who released them when approached by Customs officials. When Ramon Noegel visited the island in 1993 he was told that a colony of 17 or more existed in Willemstad, also that this parrot lives in the mountainous areas, from where young are collected and sold to local people.

Some parrots illegally imported from Venezuela leave not via the Netherlands Antilles but from the delta of the Orinoco river. Warao Indians sell to wildlife traders from Guyana and to a lesser extent, Trinidad. A conservative estimate suggests that, during the peak season for trade (February–June), at least 50,000 parrots are exported at a rate of 10,000 per month. According to Desenne and Strahl (1991), 65,000–75,000 parrots are exported annually from the Orinoco delta alone. It appears likely that a major

portion of the legal export quotas for Guyana are filled by birds which were illegally exported from Venezuela. Parrots, obviously including *A. barbadensis*, are being exported in lower numbers from the northern coast and from Margarita, and from here they are sent to other Caribbean islands, North America, Europe and Colombia. From the Colombian ports of Cartagena and Barranquilla they enter Europe and North America.

Since 1988, PROFAUNA, a new governmental organisation within the Ministry of the Environment, has begun to work in conjunction with the National Guard to reduce the illegal trade of wild species. It is composed primarily of professional biologists who are trained in field problems, wildlife management and the conservation of species. Their effort regarding the illegal bird trade first centred on Caracas and adjacent areas and was extended to the Orinoco delta and Margarita. The problem is that fines for illegal trafficking in birds are ridiculously low. In October 1988 the maximum penalty for the possession of any number of wild-caught birds in the Orinoco delta was the equivalent of US$30, with no mandatory jail term. This is equal to the local cost of one pair of Amazons. Unless the fines are increased, reducing the illicit trade will surely be an impossible task.

Although it has been protected by law since 1952 the law is difficult, if not impossible, to enforce. The illegal taking of young from the limestone cliffs in which it nests, including those within the park, is a common occurrence. The export trade is non-existent; the young are taken to satisfy the local demand for pets.

Although many *A. barbadensis* have been captured for export, the species remains rare in aviculture, probably because the majority of birds are sold as pets. Most of the buyers would not be able to identify the species and might believe that it was the Yellow-fronted, or Double Yellow-headed, Amazon (*A. ochrocephala ochrocephala* or *A.o. oratrix*). Consistent success in breeding from more than one pair of this species has been achieved by the partnership of Ramon Noegel and Greg Moss in Florida, and at Palmitos Park, Gran Canaria (in the park's collection and with the author's birds). Due to its aggressive nature, it is not one of the easiest species to breed.

Another parrot from the Netherlands Antilles which is endangered is the endemic sub-species of the Blue-crowned Conure (*Aratinga acuticaudata neoxena*), the only insular form of this species. This large parrakeet, 37 cm (14 in) in length, occurs on the island of Margarita. It was studied there between April and August 1991 (Suárez, 1992b), in the Macanao Peninsula and the Restinga lagoon. Censuses indicated a population of between 180 and 300 individuals. They nest in the black mangroves of the lagoon. Of 21 clutches studied, 14 resulted in chicks. Reasons for failure of the other clutches included predation by rats and flooding. One of the 14 successful nests was probably predated by rats; chicks were stolen from all the other nests to sell as pets. In addition to being endangered by nest robbing, the Blue-crowned Conure is threatened by the holiday complex which has been built in the area of the mangroves. In 1989/90 tourism in earnest came to Margarita, with the possibility of a big increase in tourism as the island becomes better known. Numerous boat trips through the Restinga (seldom in fully occupied boats), are disturbing the environment, as is the sand-mining, already mentioned. Unless an effort is made to conserve this conure, it is surely doomed on Margarita.

8

Dominican Amazons

In the wild grandeur of its towering mountains, some 5000 ft above the level of the sea, in the majesty of its almost impenetrable forests, in the gorgeousness of its vegetation, the abruptness of its torrents, the sublimity of its waterfalls, it stands without rival, not in the West Indies only, but I should think throughout the whole island catalogue of the Atlantic and Pacific combined.

WILLIAM PALGRAVE, WRITING OF DOMINICA (1876)

The place: the forested mountain slopes of Dominica. The date: April 1980, eight months after Hurricane David had ravaged the island. With two companions I was overlooking a deep valley where the Picard river flowed noisily in the ravine below. We gazed expectantly at the lush, dense forest. Here the canopy was intact, protected by the ravine from the hurricane winds which, reportedly, were in excess of 190 mph (305 kph). This was one of the few places where the Imperial Parrot (*Amazona imperialis*) had survived.

Suddenly we jumped to our feet, alerted by the alarm call of a large parrot. Just above the forest canopy a magnificent dark, eagle-like bird soared along the valley on the other side of the river. It was in view for a few seconds, then dropped down into a tree. About an hour later we were rewarded with two more sightings, probably of the same bird travelling back to its nest.

I felt privileged to have glimpsed this magnificent species in the wild, something which would have been impossible without the help of personnel of the Forestry Division. The over-riding emotion of awe at

this sighting, however, was touched with sadness — and apprehension at what the future holds for the Imperial Parrot. Not without reason was it so named. It is the largest, perhaps the most majestic and one of the least typical members of the genus *Amazona*, with plumage which is distinctive and a bearing which is regal. Unquestionably it is the king of the Amazons. The dark green upper parts contrast with the dark underparts in colours which are difficult to describe but give the overall effect of dark purple. Each feather has shadings of brown, pink and blue or purple, reminding one of oil on water. The glossy purple sheen extends over the head, nape and breast. Reddish-brown is the colour of the tail, tipped with vinous or pink. The wing speculum is scarlet and brownish-red. (*See* Plate 10.)

The Imperial is among the most endangered of all neotropical parrots. It is found exclusively in the mountains, which adds to the problems of protecting it, whereas the Red-necked Parrot (*Amazona arausiaca*) favours lower elevations, although there is an overlap in their distribution. The Red-necked is a large, handsome Amazon with plumage which is typical of the genus: basically green. Most of the head is blue, of a violet shade surrounding the eyes, and most specimens have the foreneck or upper breast pink or red. (*See* Plate 11.)

Dominica has a human population of 85,000 — a large number for a mountainous island measuring only 46 × 26 km (29 × 16 miles). There is no industry apart from agriculture (especially banana growing), much unemployment and poverty.

Entirely volcanic in origin, Dominica is composed largely of the rounded cones of extinct volcanoes. It is because of this environment that parrots have survived (albeit precariously) to this day. The inhospitable and, until recently, inaccessible interior was an effective natural protection. The mountains prevented any significant development; and because there is no flat land capable of taking more than a single runway for small aircraft the tourist industry is in its infancy.

The beauty of Dominica's landscape is difficult to impart: it touches one's senses with a deep feeling of wildness and tranquillity. Nevertheless, Dominica's mountains have more than aesthetic appeal; they are her richest natural resources, to be zealously guarded — or so one would have thought.

Until a few years ago they had survived much as they were when Columbus first saw them, five centuries previously. But Dominica's forests were not to escape the axe. During the 1980s deforestation was so severe that it was estimated (Evans, 1989) that in the previous ten years a greater area of forest was destroyed than during the previous thousand years.

Information on former population levels of both species simply does not exist. Probably no estimates were made of *A. imperialis* until the mid-1970s, when Holly Nichols, an American, spent many months on Dominica and St Vincent, in an attempt to learn something of the ecology of the endemic parrots. The total population of the Imperial was assessed at 150–250, with the greatest concentration in the north in the upper Picard river valley along the edge of the Dyer Estate and between Morne Turner and Morne Diablotin. A small number (between 10 and 24) was located in the Morne Anglais area, with a small but undetermined number in the upper Beuse valley. The difficulty of accurately assessing populations in montane rainforest must be borne in mind, however.

From the information available, especially that provided by Green (Anon., 1982), it would appear that until the 1950s the Imperial was found over an area of the northern part of the island which was at least twice as extensive as the current range; the same is probably true of the southern area where Imperial Parrots were found prior to Hurricane David in 1979. Unfortunately, some of these areas have now been cleared for agriculture. The population of *A. arausiaca* in 1950 may well have extended over the entire central part of the island, perhaps over as much as 60 per cent of the total territory. If that was so, it too has had a range retraction of about 75 per cent. In addition, the Imperial was formerly found at lower elevations, according to Green.

Originally the most important factor in the population decline was shooting, especially of the Imperial. It was shot for food and in the hope of 'wing-tipping' so that injured birds could be sold as pets. Sydney Porter, an aviculturist who travelled widely to observe parrots in the wild in the 1920s and 1930s, was almost the only person in that era with the foresight to see the fate of island species. He wrote with concern, especially for the Imperial, after learning from a native hunter: 'Law or no law, we shall always shoot the "Ciceroo" when we can, we pay a licence for a gun and if we go hunting and find no wild pig or agouti and we see a "Ciceroo" we just shoot it because we have no meat.'

Porter was told that, after the hurricane of 1928, a flock of Imperials appeared which numbered between 100 and 200, and was believed by a local man to be the entire population of the species. Porter obtained information from which he could account for more than 38 being killed and captured during the last three months of 1928 and the first two months of 1929 (Porter, 1929). He recorded that only two escaped with their lives, one which he was able to purchase and another which also went to England. If there was no buyer, Imperials were eaten . . . .

It was not until the mid-1970s that hunting pressure lessened on Dominica's parrots — ironically, just before the most serious destruction to its habitat commenced. In 1975 the Forestry and Wildlife Act (Act No. 12) made it illegal to hunt parrots under any circumstances. Peter Evans praised the work of the Dominican Forestry Division, who not only pressed for the passing of new legislation, but regularly patrolled relatively remote areas to enforce the law, at the same time launching an intensive education campaign. After the hurricane of 1979 and 1980, a temporary ban on the hunting of all game animals was enforced. Anyone carrying a gun was automatically identified as acting illegally. Then the law was relaxed so that the hunting of wild pig, agouti and Red-necked Pigeons (*Columba squamosa*) could take place from September to February. The hunting (capture, sale or illegal possession) of parrots carries a penalty of East Caribbean $5,000 and three years' imprisonment. Such deterrents should be adopted (and rigorously enforced, as on Dominica) more widely. Porter had recommended this course of action 50 years previously! The second factor which influenced the population decline was shooting. In the 1970s, one of the nests located by Alphonso Nichols, from St Vincent, and Holly Nichols, was situated in a gommier tree (*Dacryodes excelsa*); the hollow was 90 cm (3 ft) deep, with an entrance 46 cm (18 in) wide and about 21 m (70 ft) above the ground. In the early part of May it contained two unfeathered chicks. When the nest was visited early in July, plucked feathers were found at the base of the nest tree. The parents had been shot. Although the parrots are protected by law, because of the difficulty of surveillance of their habitat that law was rarely enforced.

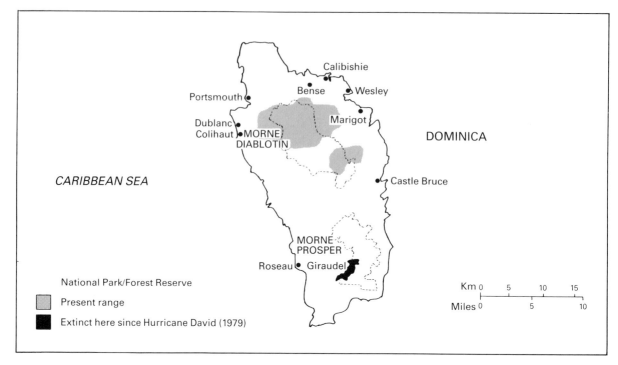

Distribution of Imperial Parrot (*Amazona imperialis*) in 1992. Based on Evans (1993).

A natural catastrophe was the other factor in the decline of the Imperial Parrot: Hurricane David, which struck Dominica in August 1979. It not only reduced the northern population but almost certainly decimated the remnant southern population. The most severe damage occurred in the south-eastern part of the island. In the worst affected area, over 70 per cent of the trees were uprooted or damaged and serious defoliation occurred. Two months after the hurricane Drs Noel and Helen Snyder from the USA made a survey on behalf of the International Council for Bird Preservation (ICBP), and that was their assessment of the damage.

Approximately 40 per cent of the island, including the Morne Diablotin area, the Imperial Parrot's last refuge, suffered only mild to moderate damage. The immediate effect of the hurricane was the destruction of food and nesting sites, and severe pounding of the birds by high winds. One Imperial Parrot was reported in the streets of Grand Bay Village in the south of the island, and another, found by a villager, died before the Forestry Division could reach it (Gregoire, 1981). No Imperial Parrots were sighted within the forests until some time after the hurricane. Then, in desperation to find food, they were seen at low elevations, although the species does not usually occur below about 450 m (1,500 ft). These unfortunate birds almost certainly fell prey to hunters.

Immediately after the hurricane a ban was placed on all hunting; in the face of a long tradition of hunting, it is doubtful whether it had much effect. The Forestry Division did its best to step up the education programme. Officers visited schools to speak on the importance of wildlife and the Wildlife Act and on the urgent need for conservation. Posters bearing the slogan 'Protect the Pride of Dominica' and carrying a picture of the Imperial Parrot were displayed in schools and public places. The same motif was printed on T-shirts (and, two years later, such a T-shirt worn by a young Dominican girl nearly stopped me in my tracks in a Surrey street). The weekly radio programme 'Conservation' alerted Dominicans to the situation and asked everyone to contribute to the conservation effort. Although such education pays dividends in the long term, initially it is unlikely to be very effective. In the 1982 report *Study of Impact of Logging on the Dominica Parrot*, it was suggested that 'an education awareness programme' be expanded in schools and local communities'. Mention was made of a new monthly publication *VWA Diablotin* which covers conservation.

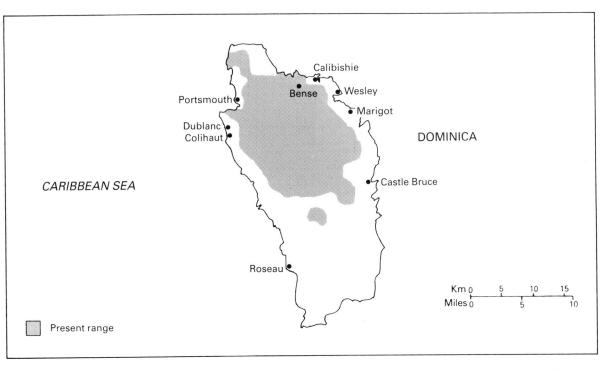

CARIBBEAN SEA

DOMINICA

Present range

Distribution of Red-necked Amazon (*Amazona arausiaca*) in 1992. Based on Evans (1993).

In June 1981 Dr T.D. Nichols and others spent a week on Dominica and, with the help of forestry officers, made an assessment of the populations in two areas. In his report to the ICBP Dr Nichols made the tentative estimate that 40–60 Imperial Parrots survived. It was noted that Devils Valley (upper Picard river) still contained the most important concentration. The post-hurricane population of the Red-necked Parrot was assessed as in 'the low hundreds' by Dr Snyder. The 1981 estimate made by the Forestry Division differed: 75–100 Imperial Parrots and 150–225 Red-necked Parrots.

Estimates varied, but one fact was very clear: Dominica's parrots were facing the worst crisis of their existence. It seemed that, for the Imperial, there was little hope of recovery. Its reproduction rate is, perhaps, slower than that of any other neotropical parrot; it lays only two eggs, perhaps every year, possibly less often.

But worse was to come. Hurricane David was only the beginning of the crisis. Two or three years later commenced a new and urgent threat to its existence: destruction of the area of rainforest which is its last refuge. The area of forest in which both species occur was just outside the Northern Forest Reserve and was then entirely privately owned. Adjoining it are 8,000 ha (22,000 acres) of forest reserve, plus areas owned privately and by companies, some of which had already been converted to banana plantations. Then another area was threatened, the Morne Plaisance Estate. It covered 375 ha (928 acres) of good primary rainforest which was only moderately damaged by Hurricanes David, Frederick and Allen. This estate lies to the south-east of Portsmouth. Generally flat, it ranges from 285 m (935 ft) to 465 m (1,525 ft). By 1982 clearance had been restricted to the felling of trees adjoining the new road that bisects the estate and to some selective felling of gommier trees and bois diable (*Licania ternatensis*). Clear-felling of much of the land was expected to commence between January and March 1983, in preparation for the sale of small lots to farmers. This was to be carried out to stimulate employment and make agricultural land available to small farmers. Geest Industries, the estate owners, in collaboration with the Government, has set aside 80 ha (199 acres) as a watershed protection on the north-west boundary. This does not mean, however, that there will be no felling in the area.

As Anna Pavord pointed out: 'Dominica is a relatively poor country. There are no mineral resources and little industry, and so agriculture is very important.

Given these pressures, conservation will only be feasible if it forms part of an overall strategy of development' (Pavord, 1989). Since 1978 the British conservation biologist Dr Peter Evans has organised a wide-ranging set of studies designed to establish the requirements of Dominica's wildlife (but especially the parrots) and to recommend land-use systems that would allow for forest and wildlife conservation, watershed and soil protection, and sustainable agriculture and ecotourism.

Dr Evans believes that the often contrary demands of agriculture and conservation can be reconciled if certain important rules are established. Most important of these is a system of wide forest corridors between areas of cultivation. In 1989 his work became fully integrated with that of the Forestry Division.

Anna Pavord wrote: 'Dr Evans points out that Dominica is blessed with a Forestry Division that is unusual in its determination to conserve the country's natural resources as well as exploit them. It is recognised as one of the most knowledgeable and best-trained divisions in the Caribbean. It maintains the tortuous trails through the forests, publishes excellent booklets, and wages constant war against illegal encroachment in the reserves.'

In 1988, however, an agreement was signed between the Government of Dominica, ICBP and another conservation organisation, RARE, concerning the purchase of a highly important area of forest adjacent to Forest Reserve, where both parrot species occurred in good numbers. This privately owned land was being encroached upon, at one end by banana and citrus plantations and, at the other, by logging. The purchase of this land was an agreed priority yet when Dr Michael Rand, Programme Director of ICBP, visited the site on July 23 1989, it was being selectively logged. Problems over its purchase had arisen because the land-owners had decided to increase its price; also the Dominica Timber Company has recently moved back into the area and were demanding compensation if they were to stop logging. This company was 49 per cent government owned!

Rapid action followed. The next day the Minister of Agriculture met the representative of the land-owners. The outcome was that 24 ha (59 acres) were donated for parrot conservation and the rest would be purchased for the sum of $83,000. The land was to be owned by the government, ICBP and RARE for three years, after which it became government property, to be held in perpetuity to protect the parrots. It is the responsibility of the Forestry Division and will, it is hoped, be combined with the Forest Reserve to form a future Morne Diablotin National Park. Nature trails have been laid out to enable tourists to visit the forest and an observation tower has been built at a site where views of the parrots are often possible. Eventually, a Nature Centre will be built to facilitate conservation, education, ecotourism, forest management and applied research. In his 1989 report to ICBP Dr Rand wrote: 'When built the Centre will be a unique facility in the Caribbean (possibly the world) providing easy access to rich and pristine tropical rainforest to local people, tourists and ecologists. It could become one of the best-known and studied rainforests in the world.'

The establishment of the national park is vital for the long-term survival of the Imperial and Red-necked Parrots. If the forest of the Morne Diablotin area does not survive, the extinction of the Imperial Parrot will follow. In 1991 ICBP had budgeted $700,000 over a three-year period to establish the park, plus $20,000 per year for research. Funding was being negotiated.

When the first edition of this book was published, in 1984, this chapter was entitled: 'The Dominican Amazons: Zero Point Approaches'. I feared that the Imperial would be extinct in three or four decades, as a result of loss of habitat. Then, the last population estimate before the book went to press, that for 1981, was of 75–100 Imperials and 150–225 Red-necked. It is very encouraging to report that, on almost every front, the situation has improved greatly since then.

In 1989 there was a welcome development regarding the few captive native parrots on the island. An amnesty was instigated for a period of two months. Those keeping parrots were allowed to retain them, provided that they registered them and took good care of them. Each was given a numbered steel leg-band, to assist in identifying any future illegally kept parrots. Five people came forward to register a total of eight Red-necked and one Imperial.

In 1990 Peter Evans was able to report that Red-necked Parrot populations had been showing signs of recovery during the past two years, with an expansion of their range. They were returning to some of the lower-lying areas on the edge of plantations in the north and north-east of the island, and were increasingly being seen south of the road that crosses the island from Pont Cassé to Marigot, in the forested slopes of Morne La Source and Morne Fraser, and in the Maclauchlin area. However, there was little sign of them returning to the slopes of Morne Trois Pitons or further south. In the upper Picard valley, numbers increased between 1987 and 1989, then declined. In neighbouring Dyer, Syndicate and Morne Plaisance Estates, Red-necked Parrots had become more common. In contrast, there was no evidence of an increase in the Imperial population until early 1990. Furthermore, the Imperial had returned to the Syndicate and Morne Plaisance Estates after being virtually absent for ten years (Evans, 1991). The best news I have heard from Dominica since conservation efforts began came when Peter Evans returned from Dominica after the spring of 1990. Maximum flock size, which since 1982 had never exceeded three individuals, had increased to six.

Not until a decade after the hurricanes were the most significant population increases observed. In early 1993 the Imperial's numbers were estimated at 80–120 and the Red-necked was believed to have increased to between 600 and 800. Distribution of the Imperial was still concentrated in rainforest between 550 and 760 m (1,800 and 2,600 ft) on the slopes of Morne Diablotin, with concentrations noted in the upper Picard valley and between Simpa Flats and Diablotin. Red-necked Parrots had expanded their range towards the coast from the slopes of Morne Diablotin and southwards towards Pont Cassé. However, this increase brought with it conflicts between farmers and parrots. Unless crop husbandry changes, the problem will need to be addressed if the shooting of parrots is to be prevented (Evans, 1993).

As noteworthy as the increased populations is the changing climate of conservation feeling in Dominica. This has been achieved by an intensive education programme (*see* page 170). The establishment of the national park will be the final stage of the race against time to save the Pride of Dominica, as the Imperial Parrot has been called. But it will not succeed without the sympathy of the islanders.

Sydney Porter, were he alive today, would have been heartened by the recent turns of events. But he would hope, too, for the survival of most of Dominica's magnificent forests which he immortalised with the words:

'Nowhere do mountains rise so sheer or are the ravines so deep and precipitous. Sometimes the walls of the gorges rise perpendicularly for thousands of feet, covered by the densest tropical creepers and ferns of the most vivid emerald green. From the distance the island looks like a jagged emerald rising up out of the turquoise sea . . . . Giant palms and tree-ferns mix with the other vegetation in the struggle upwards towards the light. Here and there great forest giants lie prone, their great bulk almost hidden by the rank growth of mosses. It is here, in some places impossible for man to penetrate, on the Atlantic slopes of the sinister volcanic peak, Morne Diablotin (Mountain of the Devil) that *A. imperialis* makes its home. Long may it hold its own . . . .'

9

St Vincent's Unique Treasure

. . . in no case should it be necessary to have to choose in favour of either *people* or *parrots. The parrots-versus-people proposition is a false dichotomy. There is room for both on any island, provided only there is the will to work out the way.*

PATRICK FAIRBAIRN, IN *CONSERVATION OF NEW WORLD PARROTS* (1981)

It is fitting that the St Vincent Parrot (*Amazona guildingii*), a bird of singular magnificence, should live on an island of outstanding natural beauty. St Vincent and the Grenadines are in the southern portion of the chain of islands called the Lesser Antilles, which form a barrier between the Caribbean and the Atlantic oceans. All the islands are small and heavily populated and two of them equal or exceed the beauty of St Vincent: Dominica and St Lucia.

These three islands can, between them, boast four endemic Amazon parrots. It has already been related, in Chapter 8, how precarious is the existence of Dominica's two parrots. The St Vincent Parrot population is more numerous, but subject to precisely the same pressures which have brought its congeners so close to disaster.

The St Vincent Parrot is especially intriguing in appearance. The extremes of variation in its plumage are unique, not only within the genus *Amazona* but among parrots in general. It is remarkable for its lack of uniformity and for the fact that most St Vincent Parrots are predominantly tawny-brown. (*See* Plates 12 and 13.) Several colour phases have been described, and one of these is a green morph. This is drab in comparison with the rich colours of birds of the standard morph.

Regardless of body coloration, all St Vincent Parrots have the crown and forehead white, usually with yellow on the crown and, in some birds, also around the eye. On the back of the head the feathers are dull mauve or blue, with dusky edges, and the nape feathers are green or orange-green with even more conspicuous dark margins.

In birds of the standard type, the cheeks are yellow and mauve. Noticeable on close examination of living birds is the almost luminous quality of the few feathers of the ear coverts, which are brilliant light blue at the tip. The body feathers are mainly brown and most are heavily margined with black except those of the abdomen which are broadly edged with green. The rump is brown and the thighs orange and brown.

No written description can do justice to the wing coloration; it can be appreciated only by those who have the good fortune to see this magnificent bird in flight. The spectrum of colours found in the wings includes orange-brown, blue, black and yellow; the speculum is flaming orange. The tail is long for an Amazon and shows three striking bands of colour: orange at the base, a broad band of rich blue and a small amount of green, then a band of yellow.

Plumage descriptions generally make dull reading, but some detail of that of the St Vincent Parrot is necessary if its unusual beauty is to be comprehended.

Habitat of St Vincent Parrot (*Amazona guildingii*).

It has even more to recommend it: a friendly personality with a highly developed sense of curiosity. It seems to be naturally tame and inquisitive. Captive birds lack the aloof quality of the Imperial; if they possessed it, they too could be described as majestic. Instead they have a magnificence which is all their own. The St Vincent Parrot is, indeed, a unique and most beautiful treasure.

There are people who hold the view that no captive bird should be termed 'magnificent'. Although I can understand this viewpoint and even agree that nowhere could this parrot look more splendid than on the forested slopes of St Vincent's mountains, two points should be made with regard to this species in captivity. Firstly, it adapts to captivity extremely well and gives every appearance of enjoying the companionship and attention of its human admirers. Secondly, the great vulnerability of the island to which it is endemic makes it imperative that captive breeding programmes are

established outside that island.

St Vincent measures only 29 × 18 km (18 × 11 miles). Until about the middle of the eighteenth century, when much of the forest still reached to the coast, the parrots nested at low elevations, almost down to sea level. Now they are mainly confined to the ridges and valleys of the mountains in the central part of the island. It has been estimated (Andrle and Andrle, 1975) that their total potential breeding area, in discontinuous localities, encompasses up to 30 km^2 (12 sq. miles), principally at altitudes between 300 and 700 m (980 and 2,300 ft). This figure was based on field work and on map and aerial photographic analysis of sections where large trees occurred. According to one set of observations checked by an altimeter, however, the upper limit was about 400 m (1,300 ft).

According to Butler (1990), 31 per cent of the island is forested and about 25 per cent contains suitable habitat for *A. guildingii*. This is in contrast with the map prepared by Noegel (1993) which shows a smaller area under primary forest and how areas of parrot habitat diminished between 1975 and 1980 (*see* page 80). According to Noegel, forest destruction is estimated at 1 per cent per annum. Noegel points out that: 'Deforestation for charcoal and agriculture has forced the remaining 500± St Vincent Amazons into isolated valleys located in the more inaccessible highlands. These fragment habitats contain six, possibly seven, viable populations of this species. Due to the volcanic ridges and high winds these contained environments act as a deterrent to birds passing from one group to another. This division of the parrots is thought to be encouraging inbreeding because some isolated flocks are small, being represented by as few as thirty birds. Inbreeding on small islands or in confined limited populations is to be expected, but in the case of *Amazona guildingii* it may be producing visible genetic drifts within certain flocks. Observations by researchers suggests variations within the Windward flocks such as a higher pitched call and more visible birds of the green morph as opposed to those reproducing in the Leeward and more dense populations of parrots. Now remembered only in history, a forest once flourished on the island's coastal area. This acted as a natural corridor for integration of the Windward and Leeward flocks of parrots, said to number in the thousands in the last century.'

When I visited St Vincent in 1980, I was fortunate to have as my guide Alphonso Nichols. For about an hour we trekked along an easy track through the mountains, pausing to speak to a woodcutter or to sample wild raspberries. Then we started to climb in earnest; the going was slippery and difficult, with few convenient footholds. After another hour we began to hear parrots and, at last, disturbed one which we glimpsed fleetingly as it flew off, high above us.

We settled down to wait, using leaves as a fan to keep off the mosquitoes which buzzed menacingly around our faces. Parrots on the nearby ridge tantalised us with their calls, and we could only hope that they would cross to our ridge.

As we waited, Nikki spoke about the nesting habits of his native parrot. Over the years he had located many nests, usually situated in gommier trees (*Dacryodes excelsa*). As a result of climbing to inspect them, he knew that the clutch numbers two or three eggs but that only one or two chicks are reared; he knew of no cases of three young being raised. Occasionally he had found a feathered chick, the youngest of two, dead in the nest. This led him to believe that opposums seldom find nests, as these animals would have eaten any dead young. On more than one occasion, a fully feathered youngster had been found below the nest, from where it had fallen before it was old enough to fly.

As we sat still, watching and waiting, I became aware of the coolness of the atmosphere and reflected that many people think of Amazon parrots as birds from the tropics which are used to very high temperatures. Here, thick cloud cover and dense forest canopy effectively eliminated the sun. Nights, too, are cool — and this may explain why *A. guildingii* chicks have thicker down than Amazons found at low altitudes.

After a long wait in vain, we decided to climb to another ridge where a pair were nesting in a tree on a steep incline. The female, who was brooding or feeding young, heard our approach and, screaming loudly, left the nest and glided away down the valley. Later the male, more colourful than the green morph female, flew near to the nest, to be followed by the female.

On the downward climb, more parrots were sighted, including a pair high above. As they emerged from cover and the sunlight shone through their brilliant orange wings, Holly Nichols' description of these birds as having in flight the same kind of beauty as stained glass windows seemed entirely appropriate, their rich colours being unexpectedly illuminated.

Having, at last, seen them in the wild, I wondered how large was the population. Dr I.A.E. Kirby, a Vincentian with a lifelong interest in this species, believed it numbered between 300 and 500 individuals in 1980. The largest flock he ever observed, in about 1956, consisted of 36 birds (Kirby, pers. comm.). In July and August 1982 an estimate was made by an ICBP/University of East Anglia expedition. The conclusion reached was that the population numbered 421±52 (Goriup and Collar, 1983). Flocks numbering up to 24 parrots were recorded. The estimate was made according to localities and can be compared with that of Nichols (1976). See table opposite.

The 1979 volcano eruption and the 1980 hurricane partly account for the decline in numbers in the northern part of the island and probably the Windward population as a whole. Agriculture probably accounts for the loss of the Mesopotamia population. The forest had recently been cleared for the cultivation of bananas. The apparent increase in the Wallilabou-Cumberland area may be due to an influx of parrots from other areas.

Bearing in mind the difficulty of estimating montane forest populations, the figures given above do not necessarily represent a decrease of 20 per cent in six years.

In a report entitled 'The St Vincent's Amazon — Conservation success or dilemma?' (Cuddy, 1993), Joe

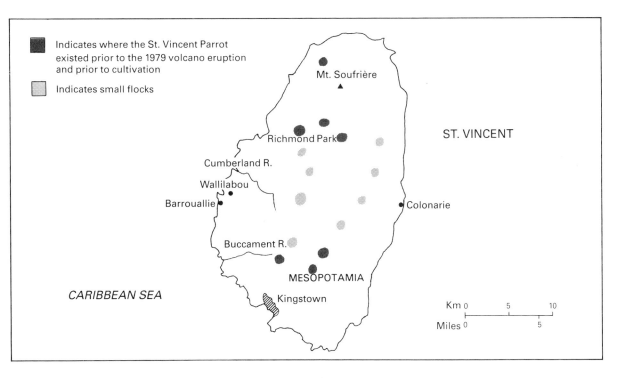

Indicates where the St. Vincent Parrot existed prior to the 1979 volcano eruption and prior to cultivation

Indicates small flocks

Mt. Soufrière

ST. VINCENT

Richmond Park

Cumberland R.

Wallilabou

Barrouallie

Colonarie

Buccament R.

MESOPOTAMIA

CARIBBEAN SEA

Kingstown

Km 0   5   10

Miles 0   5

Distribution of the St Vincent Parrot (courtesy Ramon Noegel and Greg Moss, Life Fellowship).

	1976 estimate Nichols	1982 estimate Univ. of East Anglia
Buccament	80	85±20
Cumberland — Wallilabou	110	186±12
Linley — Richmond Wallibou	130	50
Locust valley to Colonarie valley	150	100±20
Mesopotamia	30	nil
Elsewhere	25	nil
MEDIAN TOTALS	525	421

Cuddy wrote of his visit to St Vincent in December 1992. He visited the reserve in the Buccament valley which was set up in 1987. It consists of 4,350 ha (10,870 acres) of primary forest and secondary vegetation. Recent encroachment had resulted in some forest being cleared for maize and yam crops. (If after only five years some of the reserve had been destroyed for agriculture, what hope can there be for its long-term protection?) Regarding the population trend, Joe

Cuddy reported: 'In 1988 there were believed to be 400–500 birds in the wild. The next census in 1990 indicated that numbers had risen to over 550. The latest census from 1992 would appear to show some 750 birds in the wild.' (However, the population is shown as 400–500 in the Parrot Action Plan.) He also reported the existence of a small population of escaped birds on Barbados. Two were caught by Hallam Edwards, who bought Bill Miller's birds when Mr Miller retired. The following year, the remaining two were accompanied by a young bird which might have been their offspring.

Information concerning the status of this species during the early years of the twentieth century is scarce, so it is difficult to judge whether there had been any significant decline earlier this century. The population had certainly fluctuated, as a result of natural catastrophe. The species was known to be common at the time of the 1898 hurricane. Many parrots were killed and two were picked up dead on the shores of St Lucia.

Before the St Vincent Parrot had a chance to recover its numbers, volcanic eruptions occurred which resulted in it being thought rare and confined to the highest wooded slopes in the centre of the island. Bond (1929) found this species more plentiful than was expected, with a possible total of several hundred birds.

Nearly eighty years later, history repeated itself with a serious volcanic eruption and a hurricane occurring within a short period. The immediate effect of Hurricane Allen, on August 4 1980, appeared not to be serious but the long-term result was: a possible shortage of the principal nest site of the parrot, due to the destruction of large numbers of *Dacryodes excelsa*.

Today the population is fairly stable and numbers between 450 and 500. However, it is still considered critically threatened because of the dangers of hurricanes and loss of forest habitat caused by agricultural encroachment. Much of this is shifting agriculture, occurring on Crown lands and therefore illegal. Goriup and Collar stated that shifting agriculture was most serious in the Windward forests, which are already under great pressure from permanent agriculture. A recent development, a road entering the upper Colonarie catchment from Grieggs valley, is likely to open up the area for banana plantations. Also in the Colonarie valley, and in the upper Buccament, upper Cumberland and Locust valleys, destruction of *Dacryodes excelsa* for charcoal production is common.

Predation — human and otherwise — appears not to be a major problem. Natural predators of eggs and chicks include the Broad-winged Hawk (*Buteo platypterus*), the black rat and possibly the opossum (manicou). Shooting of birds for food had decreased considerably by the 1950s and probably now has ceased entirely. Because parrots are worth much more alive than dead, those injured would have been sold as pets. Most nests are at considerable heights, difficult of access and hard to locate, so it is unlikely that many young are taken from nests. However, Goriup and Collar (1983) believe that at least eight were taken in 1982.

During my stay, I was travelling through the Mesopotamia area, which affords panoramic views over the greenest mountain valleys imaginable, when I heard a parrot call. I asked the taxi driver to stop and soon located two birds. They were housed in a large wine crate on the verandah of a house — without, of course, nesting facilities. Potentially magnificent, their multi-coloured plumage was grimy and tattered and the white feathers of their foreheads grey with dirt. Lack of moisture on their plumage was very evident and one bird had started to pluck the feathers of its upper breast. It would disturb and sadden me to find any parrots kept under such conditions; but it was especially hard to bear the sight of St Vincent Parrots so ill-cared for. They were not exceptions; this was the norm on the island. Fortunately, since then all custodians of this parrots on the island have signed an agreement stating that their birds must be kept according to certain standards; they are inspected regularly. They are forbidden to sell, loan or give away these birds and are instructed that they could be utilised for a captive breeding programme.

The 1982 ICBP/University of East Anglia Expedition located a total of 27 captive parrots, of which 23 were St Vincent Parrots. During the expedition, the first confiscation by the Ministry of Agriculture occurred. This confiscation followed a decision by that department to confiscate all native parrots believed to be under two years old, plus others obviously the subject of illegal trade.

By 1990 all known captive birds had been ringed (banded); there were as many as 81. This included nearly 20 in the government aviaries in the Botanical Gardens, four of which had been hatched there. In 1991 it was reported that the total number reared had increased to nine and, by 1992, there was a total of 28 birds, which included 11 hatched in the aviaries. Nesting attempts were made twice a year, in March and September; clearly most of the attempts were unsuccessful. This was only the fifth location worldwide in which the St Vincent Parrot had been reared; at the time of writing a single bird has been reared in a sixth location, Paradise Park, in Cornwall, UK.

Very few birds have ever left St Vincent legally and most of these were formerly in the collection of Bill Miller who left St Vincent to live on Barbados. Subsequently he bred the St Vincent Parrot on several occasions. Because of the beauty of this parrot, over the years wealthy collectors of birds (I cannot call them aviculturists) have been willing to pay high prices to acquire them, thus encouraging Vincentians to take birds from the wild to be smuggled out of the country. This has occurred; however, I do not believe that large numbers have been involved, unless there was truth in the rumour that on one occasion a group of 20 had left St Vincent.

This is one of the most magnificent and distinctive of all parrots and it would be very difficult to keep this species 'hidden'. The avicultural world is a small one in that the location of rare birds quickly becomes known. The possession of this species would be akin to maintaining an elephant in a suburban backyard! It seems unlikely to me that more than a very small number of St Vincent Parrots are hidden away in private. It seems likely that the number of illegally exported birds is smaller than is often suggested.

Between 1969 and 1989 the official studbook for this species listed 59 birds in 10 collections worldwide; during this period, 14 died. Of the 45 living in 1989, five were reared by Ramon Noegel and Greg Moss in Seffner, Florida, from ten legally exported birds which had been with Bill Miller. Another bird in the studbook

On St Vincent human habitation is extending further into the mountains, approaching the habitat of the St Vincent Parrot.

was bred at Houston Zoo in 1972 — the first-ever captive breeding and the only one to occur there.

In 1979 a consortium was formed of all collections known to keep the St Vincent Parrot. At a meeting in Los Angeles in 1983, at which representatives of all consortium members were present, the total number of birds in the consortium was calculated at 41 in the following collections: Jersey Wildlife Preservation Trust, which never bred this species and later parted with its birds to other consortium members; Paradise Park in Cornwall which, between 1975 and 1992, reared one; Vogelpark Walsrode in Germany which, in 1984 and 1985, reared four at its breeding facility in the Dominican Republic; New York Zoological Society at their premises at St Catherine's Island, North Carolina, which has never bred this species and, indeed, has kept them unpaired much of the time; and Houston Zoo, which bred one during a period of 20 years. At that time there were birds in two private collections; Bill Miller, on Barbados, sent ten of his birds to Ramon Noegel — eight in 1982 and two the following year. Between 1982 and 1992 17 St Vincent Parrots were

hatched and reared at Life Fellowship. In 1992, 16 were alive; one died after injuring itself when a hawk attacked the aviary. Outside the consortium were two males at Loro Parque, Tenerife, and four birds with Robin Pickering in Yorkshire, UK.

The figures alone tell the story: the consortium was not a success. And why? My own view is that there are two main reasons: firstly because most of these birds were in zoos and secondly because of the extraordinary emotions which they seem to arouse. These were summed up by Ramon Noegel (Noegel, Wissman and Moss, 1990) in a way which some might describe as emotive and exaggerated yet, to one who over the years has been aware of developments within the consortium, his description of the St Vincent syndrome seems quite justified: It is: '. . . a malady resulting in functional departure from mental integrity on the part of the few connected with this parrot. Its symptoms are best described as inordinate desire, rapacious eagerness, and lustful longing which culminates in a consuming passion that will stop at nothing to gain control of the few existing specimens outside their native island. Those of us who are immune to its virulence are quite often targeted with invective innuendo by those afflicted . . .. We were not made conscious of the magnitude of fury this disorder can unleash until we became custodians of ten of these Amazons eight years ago. Until then, we happily captive bred West Indian parrots of equal beauty and in some cases, far more endangered, without arousing such vehement anger and opposition.'

Decisions were made by those controlling the consortium apparently without regard to the best interests of the birds themselves. It happened repeatedly. Most of the St Vincent Parrots were not in experienced or sympathetic hands. As Noegel (1993) suggests: 'For the most part those entrusted with various numbers of *guildingii* were able to acquire them not because of their proven expertise with *Amazona*, but because of their being held in high esteem as powerful zoological institutions whose capabilities never seem to be questioned . . .. Life Fellowship is not open to the public, and in its twenty-seven years has not had to resort to soliciting funding. Because of this, it is not subject to the politics and propaganda public-supported institutions must engage in, often to the sacrifice of a captive breeding program.'

How true this is! And there is another, equally or even more valid reason why St Vincent Parrots in private ownership are more likely to breed successfully, and over a sustained period, than those in zoos. In the latter facilities, the hours keepers work are limited, often by unions, and the birds are unattended much of the time. Because of the aggressive nature of this parrot, especially during the breeding season, it needs to be under constant surveillance. 'The key staff members at Life Fellowship live in the middle of the facility. Closed circuit cameras and an unobstructed view of the behaviour of the various species precludes problems that unattended institutions experience' (Noegel, 1993).

In fact at Life Fellowship there are banks of observation monitors. There are very few zoos in the world that could afford these but breeding success at Life Fellowship is so great that the income from the sale of young of other species can be used to ensure that every possible device to safeguard the welfare of the parrots is in operation. (Including a pit bull terrier!)

Sound management decisions play a major part in breeding the St Vincent Parrot. It easily becomes overweight and its diet has to be carefully controlled, with an emphasis on fresh fruit and vegetables. Forming compatible pairs is not easy and involves hours of observation and experimentation. Furthermore, the timing of the introduction of the nest-box is crucial for success. If provided too early, infertile eggs will result, because it is unlikely that both birds are in breeding condition. As Ramon Noegel and Greg Moss discovered and overcame these problems, the productivity of their pairs increased. Success was not easy or accidental but the result of commitment and dedication which is equalled in few collections.

Ramon Noegel commented: 'Since the other programs for this parrot appear frozen in the politics and legal tangle involving this species, we must take sane and practical measures to ensure the future of what Life Fellowship has accomplished in eleven breeding seasons with this species.' To this end, in 1992, Life Fellowship was in the process of setting up a legal trust for the surviving 16 offspring and all future offspring. It was proposed that unrelated pairs would be placed on loan only to qualified breeders of Amazons. These birds and any resulting young would remain under the control of Life Fellowship. In another paper (Noegel, Moss and Dam, 1993) the authors state: 'With 100 St Vincent Parrots known to exist in captivity on the island, there can be no valid reason for returning captive reared birds to their ancestral habitat. If the existing wild population is not increasing, it is obvious that birds outside the island should be maintained in competent breeding programmes for future posterity.'

Without doubt, the St Vincent Parrots thrived where they were cherished and died where they were not. The birds at St Catherine's Island became infected with avian tuberculosis; deaths occurred and birds brought in from other consortium members were exposed to the risk. Furthermore, it is difficult to detect carriers of the disease. A large percentage of consortium birds, excluding those at Life Fellowship, which no longer participates in the consortium, are thus no longer suitable as founders of a captive breeding programme. By 1991, only ten others existed in the USA and five or six in the consortium; in 1992, only 14 birds remained in the consortium outside St Vincent.

It is sad to tell that some of these wonderful birds were moved about like pawns in a game of politics. Fortunately, some of the moves failed when the 'politicians' were revealed as nothing more than ego-boosters. Ignoring the politicians as best they could (except to respond to their more libellous claims) Ramon Noegel and Greg Moss worked undeterred to solve the probems which have made this one of the most difficult parrots to breed, to the point that they now have the only self-sustaining captive population outside St Vincent. They had done it before with other rare Amazons, with giant tortoises and with endangered iguanas. They published their results and freely shared their expertise. Their success was so great that they created a new problem: finding caring homes for these precious endangered animals, homes where their own successes would be carried into second or third generations of captive breeding. Such homes are hard to find, for the truth is that there are few who can give a total commitment to the long-term production of endangered species.

10

The Puerto Rican Parrot: Back from the Brink

Saving endangered species − particularly endangered birds − has become the current cause célèbre in the field of wildlife conservation. Motivated by both the general heightening of environmental awareness during the 1960s and the frustrating realization that most classical wildlife management techniques were less than effective in stabilizing or increasing the numbers of many rare and endangered species, wildlife biologists had to seek new solutions to the problems of saving threatened animals. These solutions, of necessity, had to go far beyond the old standby prescriptions for helping wildlife: legal protection, habitat preservation and education. Instead it became necessary for biologists to devise highly manipulative procedures that intervened directly into the threatened species' life cycle at the precise stage where it had proven vulnerable to adverse environmental pressures. The actual application of such manipulative techniques has been a fairly recent development − most work having occurred during the past 10 years. Owing to the rapid development and proliferation of these management techniques, there has been a certain amount of skepticism and reluctance to accept such procedures as scientifically sound and justifiable. Nonetheless, the initial results of many pioneering efforts at managing endangered species have been encouraging.

STANLEY A. TEMPLE, IN THE PREFACE TO *ENDANGERED BIRDS* (1977)

Everyone interested in the plight of endangered birds knows of the Puerto Rican Parrot (*Amazona vittata*), not as a success story, for it is too early for such an optimistic assessment, but for the enormous sums of money spent in the attempt to save it, almost certainly more than for any other species. (*See* Plate 6.)

Much has been learned in the process; although it is regrettable that the then rarest parrot in the neotropics should have been used as the guinea pig. I believe that, as the years unfold the continuing story of bird conservation, the Puerto Rican Parrot will be cited as an example of many classic mistakes and problems. One could say that the timing was unfortunate, that its spectacular decline was slightly in advance of the conservation movement and that, all things considered, it is nothing short of a miracle that it is still with us at all. On the other hand, there is the belief that, with judicious management of captive birds, the population should by now be very much higher than it is.

The subject of the controversy which has raged around it for nearly 30 years is one of the least distinctive of the Amazon Parrots. At 29 cm (11 in) long one of the smaller species, it is mid-green with most of the feathers edged with dusky-black. The lores and a narrow band on the forehead are dull red and the abdomen is sometimes tinged with this colour. It is certainly not remarkable for its coloration, but it is notable for the fact that it is found only on the island of

Puerto Rico where its current range represents 0.2 per cent of its former range.

Puerto Rico is US territory. Were it not so its parrot would have been the first of the Amazons to become extinct in the twentieth century; the USA possesses the financial resources to pour, reputedly, millions of dollars into the task of saving it, something which no other Caribbean island could afford.

Puerto Rico is at the eastern limit of the group of islands known as the Greater Antilles. The Luquillo forest in which the parrot survives was pronounced a public reserve in 1903, four years after Puerto Rico passed to the US government. It was declared a national forest in 1918 and, since then, its size has been doubled by acquisitions. Nevertheless, it has been extensively cut; of the 11,300 ha (28,000 acres), 2,000 ha (5,000 acres) are believed to be virgin, and the parrot is confined to about 1,600 ha (4,000 acres).

To the east of Puerto Rico is the tiny island of Culebra, whose parrots were given sub-specific status as *A. v. gracileps*, due to their slightly smaller size. This form was apparently common as recently as 1899, extinct by 1912 and not formally named until 1915! Yes, it was extinct 13 years after being described as common! The possibility exists that it may also have occurred on the small islands of Vieques and Mona.

The Puerto Rican Parrot is an unfortunate example of a species whose numbers were reduced rapidly by human intervention. By 1835, and possibly much earlier, a third of the island's forest had been destroyed. Nevertheless, even then great flocks of parrots were reported, and 30 years later they were still described as common. During this era the human population was growing so rapidly, doubling to 1 million between 1850 and 1900, that by then three quarters of the island had been cleared for agricultural use. By 1912 less than 1 per cent of virgin forest remained. Parrots were unable to survive in the small patches of remnant forest, and when Alexander Wetmore made his study of Puerto Rican birdlife in 1911–12 parrots remained only in the rugged limestone hills in the north-west. By 1940 the Luquillo forest was their last refuge. As the lowlands were deforested, the parrots had been pushed into the forested mountains.

Little concern was shown over their plight until the early 1950s when Dr Frank Wadsworth of the US Forest Service urged that there should be an investigation into their numbers. In 1953 a three-year study was commenced by biologist José Rodriguez-Vidal of Puerto Rico's Department of Agriculture. In 1954 he estimated that only approximately 200 parrots survived.

He located the nests of 16 pairs. Their very poor breeding results pinpointed some of the predator problems that they faced. Of the 33 eggs contained in those nests (a low average per clutch), eight were infertile, six were eaten by black rats (*Rattus rattus*), and two by Pearly-eyed Thrashers (*Margarops fuscatus*). The latter, a thrush-sized bird with a long beak, probably began to increase on Puerto Rico in the 1930s and did not appear in the parrot's range until the early 1950s. The parrots had thus had little experience in dealing with these aggressive birds. It was soon discovered that thrashers would not only predate parrot eggs and young but were also competitors for the few nest sites available.

Of the 33 eggs found by Rodriguez-Vidal, 17 hatched and 14 young left the nest. One had been killed in the nest by a rat, another died when the nest tree fell and the third when water filled the nest cavity during a severe storm. In the same year a feral cat not only raided a nest and destroyed the eggs but also killed an incubating female (Rodriguez-Vidal, 1959).

In 1963 Roy Woodbury counted between 130 and 200 parrots on the east side of the forest (Wiley, 1981). This was the last sizeable flock reported and was followed by the biggest decline in the species' history. In December 1966 70 parrots were observed in one flock; thenceforth all population estimates have resulted from consistent observation or, as in November 1968, a comprehensive, simultaneous forest-wide count; it revealed 24 birds.

In the past a number of factors had contributed to the decline, such as shooting to protect the crops and for food, also nest-robbing. These proved to be of little significance in the light of the scale of the habitat destruction which was to follow. In the 1960s, however, the population decline was influenced by several new and unique factors. These were: a) exposure to radiation of a small area of forest near the north edge of the parrots' range; b) military exercises in connection with the Vietnam war; c) testing of herbicides; and d) road construction. In addition, shooting increased during this period as the people became more affluent.

In 1968 a major reason for poor breeding results was pinpointed: lack of suitable nesting sites. The examination of over 1,000 trees in the nesting area revealed that the majority of the cavities in existence were too small or too wet to be of use to the parrots. Ten years later Noel Snyder examined trees in an area of 27.5 ha (68 acres) and found only seven natural cavities of sufficient quality, based on the criteria of depth, internal diameter, height from the ground, and dryness. These factors were based on known, successful parrot nests.

The tree normally used for nesting by Puerto Rican Parrots is palo colorado (*Cyrilla racemiflora*). Although it has little commercial vaue, this species had been affected by a number of events or traditions. These were: a) cutting down of the nest tree by those who robbed chicks from the nest; b) selective removal

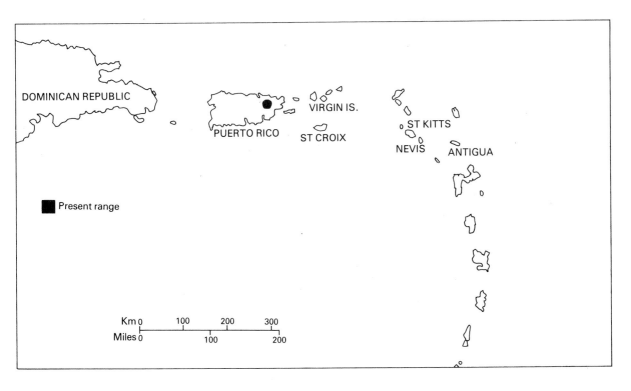

DOMINICAN REPUBLIC

PUERTO RICO

VIRGIN IS.

ST CROIX

ST KITTS

NEVIS   ANTIGUA

■ Present range

Km 0   100   200   300
Miles 0   100   200

Distribution of Puerto Rican Parrot (*Amazona vittata*).

of palo colorado from at least 400 ha (990 acres) of prime forest between 1945 and 1950, for charcoal burning; c) destruction of nest trees during the hurricanes of 1928 and 1932; d) girdling by the Forest Service of palo colorado and other trees in one of the valleys used by parrots commencing in 1935; e) destruction of trees containing suitable cavities by people robbing hives of the honeybee. (Parrots and bees have been known to nest in the same cavity, but not simultaneously [Wiley, 1981].)

A serious problem which resulted from the shortage of nesting sites was fighting. In 1974 two pairs battled for possession of one site and one member of each pair was killed in the ensuing fracas.

A puzzling aspect relating to nest sites was discovered (Snyder, in Temple, 1977). In 1973 two pairs chose territories which lacked good cavities, although the latter were available a few hundred metres away. Both pairs remained in their territories throughout the breeding season. In one case a good site not far from the territory boundary was actually a former successful parrot nest, so it could not be argued that the site was inadequate. It was therefore shown that the failure of some pairs to find good sites depended on more than their overall scarcity, as some remained unused.

By 1974 a major advance by those in charge of the Puerto Rican Parrot programme had ensured that all active wild pairs of parrots were using nests created or rehabilitated especially for them. In addition to providing artificial sites, natural ones had their life-span prolonged by patching with aluminium flushing and fibreglass. In contrast, in 1973 probably only three out of five potential breeding pairs laid. Since 1975 all pairs have laid every year.

In palo colorado trees the upper branches rot and fall, providing access into the trunk and a suitable nesting cavity. In six nests found by Cameron Kepler in 1955 the entrance hole varied between 10 and 23 cm (4 and 9 in) in diameter, and the depth of the cavity between 43 and 63 cm (17 and 25 in). The height of the nest above ground ranged between 7 and 17 m (23 and 56 ft). The altitude was about 650 m (2,130 ft) above sea level.

The only other forest tree large enough to form suitable cavities is the laurel sabino (*Magnolia splendens*), in which at least one *A. vittata* nest has been found. This tree has been subjected to considerable cutting as its wood is suitable for furniture production; this has resulted in the largest and the oldest trees being cut down.

Pearly-eyed Thrasher — a major nest predator of the Puerto Rican Parrot (*Amazona vittata*).

The preference for palo colorado as a nest tree is shared by the Pearly-eyed Thrasher, and head-on encounters between parrots and thrashers over nest sites had been observed. In addition, as already mentioned, eggs and chicks (up to about three weeks old when they weigh about 200 g [7 oz]) are vulnerable to predation by thrashers. Those responsible for the management of the few parrots left in the wild had to find a method of deterring these aggressive birds. At first they actually guarded known nests and shot thrashers which attempted to enter them! A more practical method was eventually found, in the form of a deep thrasher-proof nest-box for the parrots. Studies had shown that parrots selected deeper nests than thrashers. In 1974 thrasher nest-boxes were situated 4 m (13 ft) and 2 m (7 ft) away from the entrances of two parrot nests; in both cases the thrashers used the boxes and kept away from the parrot nests. They also deterred other thrashers which were looking for nest sites. Having established that thrashers dislike deep nests, some parrot cavities were deepened to 1.5 m (5 ft) and provided with an internal bafle so that the bottom of the nest was not visible. As a result of the various measures, there has been no known thrasher predation since 1977. The use of artificial nest sites was a major factor in the remarkable 71 per cent nesting success for wild parrots during the years 1974 to 1978; the previous success rate was very low.

Thrashers are not the only predators; the Red-tailed Hawk (*Buteo jamaicensis*) is believed to be an important factor in parrot mortality. In 1975 two project biologists, Noel Snyder and John Taapken (in Temple 1977), witnessed a Red-tailed Hawk entering a parrot nest which contained two nestlings. Fortunately, Taapken was able to frighten it out of the nest before it took the young parrots. This hawk is apparently the major unsolved natural problem for the Puerto Rican Parrot.

Wiley (1981) gives the normal clutch size as three, eggs being laid in February or March. The incubation period is about 26 days and young spend about 60 days in the nest. Young birds remain with the adults throughout the summer and autumn, but generally disperse from the increasingly aggressive adults during the winter. They begin to breed at three or four years of age.

Since the US Fish and Wildlife Service commenced its conservation programme for the Puerto Rican Parrot in 1968, a mass of data had been collated relating to this species, totally 2,000 pages. It resulted in the publication of the 384-page monograph *The Parrots of Luquillo: Natural History and Conservation of the Puerto Rican Parrot* by Noel Snyder, James Wiley and Cameron Kepler (published in 1987 by the Western Foundation for Vertebrate Zoology), one of the most voluminous and intensive studies of a bird species ever carried out. Another by-product of this intensive study was the admirable film *The Parrots of Luquillo*, produced by the Motion Picture Division of the US Department of Agriculture. This film will be widely shown throughout the Caribbean and will surely result in increased understanding of the parrots of the region. It is an extremely valuable conservation aid.

The concentrated efforts on behalf of the Puerto Rican Parrot have so far produced only scant cause for optimism. In 1979 the pre-breeding minimum was 19 birds, a number which had increased to 25–26 after the breeding season, but had fallen to 19 again by the beginning of 1980. The post-breeding figure was again 26. The 1981 pre-breeding population was 19–22 and following the breeding season it was given as 29–30. In 1979 the total number of captive birds was 15, including four pairs which reared one chick which was released. In 1980 there were 14, including three pairs which reared two young, both of which were released. In 1981 four pairs reared two young; one was released and one retained.

By the mid-1980s the population decline had ceased. There was a slow increase in numbers until, by August 1989, a count revealed a minimum of 47 birds. The following month the Luquillo forest suffered a direct hit by Hurricane Hugo. This had the disastrous effect of reducing the wild population by half; no more than 23 survived the hurricane. Nevertheless by 1991 there was reason for optimism; six pairs established nest sites, the highest number for 24 years, and the population was estimated at 32 birds. The following year the estimate suggested that the population had increased still further, to about 40 birds. The rapid recovery, after the hurricane, augurs well for the Puerto Rican Parrot. Furthermore, by 1992 the only captive population, in the Luquillo forest aviary, numbered more than 60 birds. Improvements to the conditions under which the birds were kept, made in 1989, were beginning to pay dividends. Previously they had been kept in small cages on the second floor of a building. Some of the young hatched in captivity will form the nucleus of a second population. This is to be established in the north-west of the island, in the Rio Abajo forest. In 1993 ten birds from the Luquillo aviary were moved to the Rio Abajo breeding facility.

There is some concern about the lack of genetic diversity because, for about a decade, only four pairs were breeding. On the subject of genetic diversity, Wiley (1981) pointed out: 'Although the four breeding pairs may be genetically diverse individuals and suffer no inbreeding difficulties, future generations may not be so fortunate because of increased probabilities of siblings matings and the tendency of small populations

---

Puerto Rican Parrot emerging from its nest.

---

towards random gene fixation. Widespread fostering of captive-produced eggs and chicks, either in exchange for wild-produced eggs and young or to supplement clutch and brood sizes in these nests, could significantly increase genetic diversity in the wild populations. It is likely that there is already some genetic material in the captive population that is no longer present in the wild as the wild parents of several of the captive parrots are now dead, and it is uncertain whether these same parent birds are represented in the wild by surviving progeny.'

The international cage bird trade has been unjustly blamed for the decline in many species, but this has not been a factor in the decline of *A. vittata*. Although young were regularly removed from nests by local people, very few parrots ever left the island. In the nineteenth century a few were exported; several specimens were exhibited at London Zoo then and eight were obtained by the famous German animal dealer, Hagenbeck of Hamburg. The Puerto Rican Parrot is unknown in twentieth-century aviculture. The only captive specimens in recent times have been those kept under the aegis of the US Fish and Wildlife Service, commencing with the pair taken in 1973. They were exported to the USA, to the Research Centre at Patuxent, Maryland, which necessitated a blood test to ensure that they were free of Newcastle disease. They were — but one died during the test.

This inauspicious start was to set the seal on a far

from successful captive breeding programme which owed many of its problems to the fact that it was administered by personnel totally lacking in knowledge of aviculture. They gained experience with one of the most critically endangered birds in the world.

At Patuxent the single surviving bird was kept with one or both of the two Puerto Rican Parrots which had spent 18 years in Mayaguez Zoo in Puerto Rico. Only infertile eggs were produced and it was believed that both birds were females. The breeding attempt there was abandoned in favour of using the second floor of a building in the Luquillo forest. By 1978 there were 14 *vittata* there, with the most unfortunate ratio of 3 males to 11 females (Pugh, 1978). Because of the disproportionate number of females (a most unusual situation, as in most parrots the reverse is usually true) artificial insemination was considered. In 1979 semen was taken from one male but the quantity was too small to use, and this practice was not continued. There was total infertility among the females until 1978 when one laid three fertile eggs; the following year she produced one fertile egg. The young produced were fostered into wild nests.

In later years the first clutch laid by captive females was removed, to be incubated by Hispaniolan Amazons (*Amazona ventralis*), to induce the Puerto Rican Amazons to lay a second clutch. The *A. ventralis* chicks had been used for another purpose, on occasions. Eggs had been removed from nests of wild pairs which were subject to thrasher predation, and replaced by dummy eggs. At the time the eggs were due to hatch, these were replaced by *A. ventralis* chicks. This was, however, a puzzling and counter-productive strategy. Had the eggs been removed and not replaced, the female would have laid a second clutch, thus doubling the possible number of young produced. It was for practices such as this that the management of these parrots was severely criticised by aviculturists. The most basic techniques for increasing the species' numbers, which would have been practised by any competent aviculturist, were not carried out.

Snyder and Taapken (in Temple, 1977) reported on another technique whereby chicks hatched at the field station (from wild and captive pairs) were hand-fed for a few days, then placed in the nests of wild pairs. The numbers of chicks involved were one in 1974, six from three nests in 1975, five from two nests in 1976 and eight from two nests in 1978. In the latter case the chicks were distributed among three pairs in the wild. They were not returned to their rightful parents in order to introduce new blood to the otherwise isolated eastern and western populations.

The question of returning chicks to the wild at that stage in the conservation programme is one which can be questioned. Mortality among first-year birds was estimated at 32.5 per cent by Snyder (pers. comm.) in 1981. In 1976 the wild population was not increasing, despite increased reproduction. There were then four wild breeding pairs, one of which was lost to predation. In 1980 the number of breeding pairs remained at four.

As it was known that one in three of the young released would not survive the year, the surest way of increasing the overall population would be to retain the immature birds and to release their young — if the captive breeding programme was proving successful. When the total population of a species hovers about the 30 mark, how can the release of the majority of the young produced be justified, when it is known that the chances of one in three living long enough to reproduce are not high? Surely, priority should have been given to increasing the captive population so that these birds could be managed to increase the species' total number as quickly as possible.

Of the 15 birds taken into captivity during the period 1973–79, seven would probably have perished, for various reasons, if they had not been taken to the field centre. Of those taken as eggs or chicks, one first bred at three years, two at four years and two at five years.

In 1983 the captive flock at the Field Centre numbered 17. Of these, eight females laid that year. Of the six paired females, only two produced fertile eggs, eight of the 16 eggs being fertile. Four of the eight chicks were fostered into wild nests, one of which was later taken back into captivity.

Apart from the obvious reason of saving a distinctive species from extinction, it is vitally important that the Puerto Rican Parrot project should be successful. If it fails, the fact will not go unremarked by critics of manipulative conservation or by government officials of nations which can ill afford to spend large sums on conserving endangered species. They will point to this project, and the millions of dollars it cost, and cite it as a total waste of money.

In fact this is not so because, whatever the outcome, a number of valuable lessons learned in the fight to save *A. vittata* can be applied to other species. It seems likely, however, that as long as funding is available the parrot will survive and, it is to be hoped, increase to the point where once again a viable population will breed and flourish in what survives of Puerto Rico's forests.

11

Africa: Still the Vast Unknown?

While biologists and conservationists wrestle with the massive problems facing the parrots of the Neotropics, we need to turn our attention to the parrots of Africa, and more specifically southern Africa. As far as I could establish, with the assistance of the PSG management, there is currently nobody working on the parrots of this huge continent! Consequently, the biology, ecology and status of the various species are very poorly known, and the volume of international trade in wild caught indigenous birds is certainly unknown.

ANDRÉ BOSHOFF, IN 'WHAT IS HAPPENING TO THE PARROTS OF SOUTHERN AFRICA?', *BIRD FOKUS* (1991).

Africa, the vast 'dark continent' has many problems — political, social, economic and ecological. Little wonder, as one conservation scientist admitted, that 'conservation has taken a bit of a back seat'. If we hear nothing about the threatened parrots of Africa, it is not because they do not exist, but because, as André Boshoff commented: '. . . nobody is working on the parrots of this huge continent'.

Africa is poorer in flora and also has a much smaller number of parrot species (22, including the three in Madagscar) than any other comparable area of the tropics. It also has less rainforest than any other tropical continent — about 1.75 million km^2 (675,000 sq. miles), most of which is located in central Africa, centred on the Congo basin. In some other areas of Africa, total deforestation has occurred. In 1978 it was estimated that, if the trend of that time continued, by about the year 2040 no tropical moist forest would survive, except where protected in national parks or where the terrain made access difficult. A serious problem in Africa is grazing by domestic stock, especially in montane forests, where it results in enlarged clearings and prevents forest regeneration.

In the first edition of this book, little more than one page was devoted to Africa and its parrots, because of lack of knowledge. Now, a decade later, not a lot more has been learned about their status. What has emerged is that the most endangered, as a group, are the Lovebirds (*Agapornis* species). Eight species inhabit Africa and one is found in Madagascar. Only one of these, Swindern's (*A. swinderniana*) is unknown in aviculture. Three species, the Peach-faced, Masked and Fischer's Lovebirds, are extremely popular and are bred in extremely large numbers. Peach-faced Lovebirds are produced in countless mutations; colour breeding is a popular hobby, similar to that with Budgerigars.

Reference to the *1991 Breeding Register of the Parrot Society* (of Great Britain) shows that, in that year, members (but not all members) reported breeding, 2,290 normally-coloured Peach-faced Lovebirds, plus 1,947 mutation specimens, 38 Abyssinian Lovebirds, 60 Nyasa Lovebirds, 28 Black-cheeked Lovebirds, 152 normal Fischer's Lovebirds plus 65 mutation specimens, 781 Masked Lovebirds and 755 mutations of Masked Lovebirds. This shows that only Peach-faced and Masked Lovebirds are reared in substantial numbers and that the species which produce mutations (i.e. the most prolific) are the most popular. In the event of, for example, the Peach-faced Lovebird becoming endangered or extinct in the wild, it would probably be impossible to find a pure-bred bird for re-stocking the wild population because they are all 'split' (heterozygous) for at least one other colour.

Little is known about the ecology and status of Lovebirds, but two species give especial cause for concern. It has long been suspected that the population of the Black-cheeked Lovebird (*A. nigrigenis*) never recovered from very heavy trapping for export during the early years of the twentieth century, before which it was unknown in captivity. By the early 1980s this species was confined to an area of only about 6,000 km^2 (2,340 sq. miles), almost exclusively in southern Zambia. It also extended along the Zambezi in northern Zimbabwe, where it is now believed to be extinct. Formerly it possibly occurred in northern Botswana and Namibia's Caprivi Strip, but its existence there now is unconfirmed.

The Parrot Action Plan described the Black-cheeked Lovebird as Africa's most endangered parrot, its decline having been caused by habitat alteration and illegal trapping, and possibly also by hybridisation with introduced populations of Nyasa Lovebirds (*A. lilianae*). A project is planned to ascertain the present distribution and to identify and evaluate the threats limiting the recovery of the Black-cheeked Lovebird.

It is very regrettable that the once very common Fischer's Lovebird (*A. fischeri*) has declined rapidly — in abundance and range — as a result of large-scale trapping for export. This Lovebird nests readily in captivity; demand should have been met by breeders, not by importers. However, the authorities in Tanzania should surely take the blame, as this is the only country in which it is found — not including the introduced population in Kenya. Not until 1992 did Tanzania impose a trade ban on this species. Tanzania is the second largest bird exporting country in Africa; estimates of its annual bird exports vary between about 200,000 and 3 million.

Lovebird breeders must be made aware of the endangered status of Black-cheeked and Fischer's Lovebirds. There is scope here for small breeders who have limited space and finances but who wish to breed with a purpose rather than for pleasure or profit. Such breeders could concentrate on producing strains which are pure-bred (not produced from mutations) and free of hereditary disease. Trapping has played a major part in the decline of both species — not habitat destruction; thus re-stocking their habitat with captive-bred birds might be feasible in the future.

Little is known about the Black-collared (Swindern's) Lovebird (*A. swinderniana*). It is believed to feed on figs and has never been kept alive for more than a few days in captivity. It is believed that the nominate race may now be very rare. In this instance, trade is not to blame but the reason for its decline is unknown. It comes from the Ivory Coast, Liberia and southern Ghana; the sub-species *A.s. zenkeri* is found from Cameroon and Gabon as far as western Central African Republic and Zaïre.

The Lovebirds are the smallest of Africa's parrots. The largest (excluding the Greater Vasa of Madagascar) is one of the best known of all parrots, worldwide, the Grey (*Psittacus erithacus*). At the time of writing, the only African parrot on Appendix I of CITES was the sub-species *P. princeps* from the islands of Príncipe and São Tomé in the Gulf of Guinea. Its inclusion on Appendix I is illogical because it is not known to be endangered and cannot be distinguished from the nominate race. In 1992 a proposal was received by the CITES nomenclature committee to downlist it (transfer it to Appendix II).

There are only three genera of parrots in Africa (a fourth in Madagascar), the third being *Poicephalus*. This contains nine or ten species, depending upon one's taxonomic viewpoint. From the conservation aspect, it is preferable to treat the nominate race of the Cape Parrot (*P. robustus*) as a separate species, in order to emphasise its threatened status and the fact that it is the only endemic parrot of South Africa. Its population is estimated at fewer than 1,000. The West African Cape Parrot (*P. fuscicollis*), from the Gambia and southern Senegal to northern Ghana and Togo, may also be declining. The sub-species *P.f. suahelicus* has the widest distribution, from Mozambique, Zimbabwe, northern Botswana and northern regions of Namibia to Angola, southern Zaïre and central Tanzania.

The South African Cape Parrot is distinguished by its browner (not silvery) head coloration. It inhabits mainly montane forest in subtropical and temperate regions, whereas the other forms prefer woodland and wooded savannah. It reputedly may fly over 100 km (60 miles) in search of food. Boshoff (1991) states: 'They do not exhibit regular feeding patterns; for example, flocks may feed and roost at a locality for days, weeks or even months before vanishing for months and even years. Flocks often return nightly to their traditional roosting and breeding sites in the montane forests. The species is normally gregarious and flocks of up to 20, or even 40 or 50 are usually seen . . . .'

Numbers have apparently decreased greatly in the eastern Cape and Transkei but less so in Natal (where it is specially protected) and perhaps hardly at all in the Transvaal, where it was always scarce. Three factors are responsible for this decrease. The first is destruction and alteration of habitat — the coastal and montane evergreen forests — that has occurred during the past 150–200 years. Secondly, Cape Parrots are sought for the local cage-bird trade, adults and nestlings being taken. Thirdly, the parrots are persecuted because they damage crops.

According to Boshoff, most of the large areas of montane evergreen forest now enjoy a relatively good conservation status, thus the main breeding localities are probably secure. Trapping is now the most serious threat to their existence, according to Dave Loubser, of the Eastern Cape Scientific Services (Loubser, *in litt.*, 1992). Outside South Africa the nominate race of the Cape Parrot is extremely rare in captivity. Boshoff states: 'A large number are held in captivity', i.e. in South Africa. This is extremely unfortunate, because the mortality rate among adults of this highly nervous species must be high. They do not make good pets unless obtained young; many of the birds trapped would not be suitable as pets and few aviculturists are interested in them.

There are different opinions on the seriousness of the persecution of birds which attack crops. Dr Chris Kingsley believed that it could endanger the survival of the species, because pecan-nut orchards were being planted in areas where this parrot occurs. An East London resident had informed him that they were regarded as a pest by growers and destroyed and caught in large numbers. On the other hand, Dave Loubser informed me: 'The problem caused to pecan nut crops, in the eastern Cape Province, has concerned us for many years and I have consequently been doing some investigation as to the extent of the problem. I discovered that pecan nuts are a marginal crop with only a handful of serious pecan farmers. Questionnaires were sent to them to determine the extent of the damage to their crops. The returns that I have received so far indicate that there is no problem at all. I know this to be not entirely true as I have seen parrots in pecan plantations causing damage, but it appears to have been exaggerated. The major pecan nut area in South Africa is in the north-eastern Transvaal where *suahelicus* is found; the farmers in that area have absolutely no problem with parrots raiding their plantations.'

In the eastern Cape the species is unpopular with fruit growers. Boshoff states that commercial pecan growers are 'angered by the high wastage factor' because Cape Parrots discard many fruits. 'Control methods to date include shouting and throwing sticks, and the use of gas guns, catapults, fire-crackers, pellet guns and salt-filled shotgun cartridges to frighten the birds away. However, some farmers have been observed shooting at the birds with high-powered rifles, and anecdotal evidence suggests that this practice is more common than is thought.'

Boshoff states that a public awareness campaign and an investigation of the non-destructive and ecologically acceptable methods of control of the species that do cause crop damage must be carried out.

The *South African Red Data Book* states of *P. robustus*, under the heading of 'Breeding potential in captivity', that it is 'not good'. I was fortunate to breed *P. suahelicus* in my own collection and to have several pairs of *P. fuscicollis* produce young in my care at Palmitos Park, Gran Canaria, and Loro Parque, Tenerife. I do not agree with this assessment. In my experience the Cape Parrot nests readily, produces three eggs per clutch and normally proves to be an excellent parent. All young are parent-reared. However, it is important to house these shy birds where they are free from disturbance or the near presence of noisy or threatening birds. I have never used suspended cages for this species as I believe they need the security of an aviary with at least one solid wall.

Perhaps one has to know this big-beaked bird to understand its fascination and to appreciate its beauty; for many, it does not have instant appeal. For me, the silvery-headed males are among the most beautiful of parrots. And the chicks, with their snow-white down and contrasting emerging green and orange feathers are, to my eyes, second to none for beauty, except perhaps newly hatched *Calyptorhynchus* cockatoos (with their mass of dense daffodil-yellow down). Capes have the additional advantage of being the quietest parrots which one could own.

The taxonomic status of the South African Cape Parrot (separate species or sub-species) may soon be confirmed by mitochondrial DNA studies being carried out at the time of writing. Whatever the outcome, a captive breeding programme should surely be implemented for this bird. Unlike *P. fuscicollis*, which is represented in aviculture, although in small numbers, there are extremely few outside South Africa — if any. Some people who keep Cape Parrots cannot distinguish the sub-species and few have any knowledge of the threats which face these birds. In competent hands, Cape Parrots are not difficult to breed; a carefully managed captive breeding programme would at least ensure their survival in aviculture. In addition, there should be some kind of collaboration among breeders of *P. fuscicollis*, or an EEP (European breeding programme) or a studbook. Shortage of females and the high price which they command has resulted in inadequate results with this species to date.

In the hands of competent private aviculturists, all the African parrots, if endangered, could be saved from extinction by captive-breeding, with the exception of the previously mentioned Swindern's Lovebird and the Red-faced Lovebird (*Agapornis pullaria*). The latter breeds in termite nests. Although a few captive pairs have used nest-boxes, most of the few successes have occurred in simulated termite nests (usually using cork panels). However, not enough young have been reared for this species to be established in aviculture. One of the problems has been the high death rate within a few weeks or months of capture. Wild-caught birds should not be expected to thrive on hard seed but should be given soft foods, soaked seeds and seeding weeds.

The less easily bred Lovebirds, such as the Madagascar (*Agapornis cana*) and the Abyssinian (*A. taranta*) could be bred in larger numbers if more breeders would specialise in them, instead of keeping perhaps one or two pairs. The more common Lovebirds, like Budgerigars, are bred not by aviculturists but by fanciers who are primarily interested in colour mutations; many also like to exhibit their birds at shows. (I define an aviculturist as a breeder of species which have not yet been captive-bred for many generations, and fanciers as breeders of domesticated species such as Budgerigars, Canaries, Zebra Finches, Cockatiels and Peach-faced Lovebirds, in which mutations and exhibiting

play an important part.) However, in the UK, the Lovebird Society, which was founded in 1989, has a Rare Species Scheme. It exists to promote the breeding of the five rarer species, Nyasa, Black-cheeked, Abyssinian, Madagascar and Red-faced (listed in descending order of known population in the UK). Captive-bred young are placed with interested persons by a co-ordinator, rather than being advertised on the open market. Owners of these species are encouraged to register them with the co-ordinator who, at the time of writing, was Calvin Bradley. He told me that in 1992 one member had bred 60 Black-cheeked Lovebirds and was offering them for re-stocking their natural habitat, if this was feasible. This is an example of the part which private aviculture has to play in parrot conservation. However, there are many problems associated with reintroduction (or 're-stocking') and these are discussed in Chapter 21.

12

The Black Parrots of Praslin

This is one of the few inhabited places left in the world where nature has been allowed to run wild; where you can wander among the tall trees and overhanging greenery, breathing-in the musty, hot-house fragrance and experiencing momentarily what it must have been like at the beginning of the world. Nowhere is this feeling more easily evoked than in the mysterious, primeval atmosphere of the Vallée de Mai *at the centre of the island. Here in a 50-acre nature reserve are forests of coco-de-mer, a unique species of palm. Its vivid green leaves are shaped like a knife-pleated skirt and it produces a strange double nut resembling a female pelvis (the nuts are now collector's items costing anything from R 600). There are more than 4,000 trees, some of them 100 ft high and hundreds of years old. There are many other interesting species in the valley, and it is also the only habitat of the Praslin black parrot.*

SEYCHELLES (BRITISH AIRWAYS BOOKLET, 1983)

The sun was setting over the Indian Ocean, streaking the clouds with orange and yellow. The scene was one of utmost tranquillity and unsurpassed beauty, the mood-changing mountains rising steeply from the coast. They brooded darkly without the sun, or lit up to reveal a hundred shades of green. The forest comprised many species of palm, tree ferns, giant bromeliads, creepers with small bright green leaves winding their way skywards and, towering above them all, the long straight trunks of the coco-de-mer palms.

A melodious whistling — a sound I had grown to love — alerted me to the presence of Black Parrots (*Coracopsis nigra barklyi*). There they were: two pairs swooping and diving into the sunset, silhouetted against the darkening sky. Something about their flight suggested the *joie de vivre* that is typical of this little parrot. (*See* Plate 14.)

Its habitat is one of absorbing beauty and interest. After visiting the Vallée de Mai, General Gordon pronounced his belief that this was the Garden of Eden. The Vallée existed virtually in a virgin state until the 1930s; and no one who spends a few hours inside it (the only coco-der-mer palm forest in the world) can fail to be touched by its primeval qualities. Perhaps this is accentuated by the silence, broken only by the occasional trickle of a stream, the frequent clashing of giant palm fronds in the breeze and the noisy calls of the excitable endemic Bulbul (*Hypsipetes crassirostris*). Sometimes, too, the joyful whistling of the parrots will be heard.

Something about their appearance suggests that they are among the most primitive members of their family, of which there is one other species. One of the unique features of the *Coracopsis* is their plumage, which is greyish brown or grey throughout. In coloration these are the dullest parrots in the world.

Little is known about the *Coracopsis* parrots in general, and the Praslin race in particular. Is it endangered? How many survive? Is it declining? These were among the questions which I hoped might be answered by visiting Praslin in April 1982, for the literature referring to Black Parrots is sparse.

The population of the Black Parrot (*Coracopsis nigra barklyi*) is centred on the Vallée de Mai. Its beauty and primeval qualities resulted in General Gordon declaring the Vallée the original Garden of Eden.

The Bristol University Seychelles expedition of 1965 drew world-wide attention to the birds of these islands. It resulted in an article by Malcolm Penny in *Animals*, in which he suggested that the population numbered 30 to 50 parrots. He based this figure on an August night spent in the Vallée; at dawn five people counted the number of birds seen leaving and returning to the Vallée. A similar exercise, conducted once and involving six members of the Aberdeen University Expedition to Praslin in 1976, resulted in an estimate of 90 parrots, plus or minus 20 (Evans, 1979). Coastal areas were not included in this study, however, and parrots do occur there, in the south-eastern part of the island. A similar estimate to that of the Bristol expedition had been made in 1970 by members of the Young Scientists' Society from Seychelles College.

An estimate in the region of 100 seems a reasonable one, although much lower figures have been suggested; but there is no accurate way to count the population.

Although the Black Parrot is conspicuous in flight over valleys and when it makes its presence known by its whistling call, at other times, when perched, it can be hard to locate. When moving around in foliage, its small size and grey coloration renders it liable to confusion with the endemic bulbul (a common bird in the Vallée de Mai) to the inexperienced observer.

Occasionally parrots perch boldly in the bare limbs of a dead tree or the exposed topmost branch of a living one, to observe their surroundings, silhouetted against the sky. Much more often though, they are lost among the foliage of a tree, their sombre plumage making them difficult to locate. Having located feeding Black Parrots, however, they can often be approached within a few feet, especially when feasting on bilimbi trees (*Colea seychellarum*).

It is fascinating to watch them feed. They nip off a fruit, which grows from the trunk in small clusters, and sit nearby holding the green fruit in the foot. Working rapidly, they take large bites from the fruit to remove the seeds, drop it after perhaps half or two-thirds have been eaten, select another fruit and repeat the process. The ground beneath a fruiting bilimbi is littered with partially-eaten fruits. Out of curiosity I sampled one: juicy but amazingly acid. A common endemic tree, the bilimbi is found all over the island.

The Black Parrot is often difficult to observe when feeding in dense, dark vegetation.

Another endemic tree on which the parrots feed is latanier latte (*Verschaffeltia splendida*), a species of palm. There are many specimens of it inside the Vallée de Mai National Park, where the closely knit forest canopy makes parrot-watching difficult. One day I saw two parrots not far from the westernmost point of the nature trail, from which visitors can explore the Vallée. They were soon lost from view in the dense vegetation, and although I could neither see nor hear them I knew that they were very close. Eventually they were right above us. Their arboreal trail could be followed by means of the small fruits of the latanier palm, which were raining down around us and hitting the ground, or the dead fronds covering it, with a crack. When at last they took to the wing, we discovered with some surprise that they had been only a few feet away from us. They had fed in total silence and had not revealed their whereabouts.

For those prepared to make the climb, there is a vantage point in the National Park which provides an excellent view over a large area. Anyone who spends a little time there, even in the heat of midday, will before long be rewarded by their whistling calls, and will probably see them winging their way across the Vallée, little more than specks in the distance.

This, however, was too remote to be satisfying, and I always yearned for the close approach which is possible when they are busy feeding. Then, they were perfectly aware of our presence but showed no alarm as long as we kept fairly still.

Late one afternoon we explored new land in the presence of Victorin Laboudallon, who is employed by the Ministry of Agriculture. He has achieved local fame as a singer and told me of the folk song he had written about the Black Parrot, explaining why it has no bright colours.

Victorin took us up a steep unmade track of rutted red soil which is used by the forestry department for timber extraction. Before long we came across a large tree laden with round orange-yellow fruits which Victorin identified as santol (*Sandoricum indicum*). Here the huge fruit bats and the parrots were busy feeding during the hour before sunset. As the setting sun coloured the clouds with yellow and orange, the parrots flew out of the tree in pairs, their small wings seeming to beat furiously against the darkening sky. Yet at other times their flight seemed of a different species, as they swooped and dived with effortless ease.

Like many parrots they are immensely curious; but unlike almost all other parrots their voice is a melodious whistle. We were able to turn both these

The plumage of the Black Parrot is in fact not black at all, but a dark shade of brown.

factors to our advantage. The Black Parrot has several different call notes, all of which are far-carrying whistles. My companion became adept at imitating the usual contact call — to the degree that curious parrots would fly in from a considerable distance to investigate. Situated as we often were high up on a forestry road overlooking the valley, we could observe flight movements over a considerable distance. Thus there was no doubt that parrots were responding to his whistles, for on several occasions they located us precisely, either landing in a nearby tree or observing us as they flew overhead.

I will always recall the first pair we ever saw, perched in the exposed branches of a dead tree. They preened and whistled for some minutes, one perched a few feet above the other. When we had gazed our fill, my companion clapped his hands in order (as we thought) to film them in flight. They peered down, curious, and did nothing but give a melodious whistle. They even answered when he mimicked their call . . . .

Such incaution is not found in parrots which suffer human persecution (Low, 1982a). The attitude towards conservation in the Seychelles is encouraging. Within the previous decade the people have become increasingly aware that their avifauna contains species found nowhere else in the world. They also realise that it attracts tourists.

During the past two decades the outlook for the parrot has become appreciably brighter. Up until the late 1950s dead parrots could be seen by the roadside, the victims of children with catapults. This never occurs now. Although there is no evidence that shooting of parrots occurred, the confiscation of firearms in June 1970, for political reasons, must also be in the parrot's favour. All endemic birds are protected by law, with fines or imprisonment not exceeding one year, under the Wild Animals and Birds Protection Act.

It appears that human predation is a thing of the past — so do parrots have to contend with any other predators? It is known that rats have taken young in the nest, but at that time only four nests had been found; one of these was predated by rats. Rats could be the most significant factor in retarding the population growth, if indeed it is retarded. They are attracted to nests on hearing chicks being fed. Metal guards will therefore be placed around the base of all known nest trees. The extent of rat predation needs further study. In view of the difficulty of locating nests, this would not be easy to carry out.

Was it true, I asked Lindsay Chong Seng of the Seychelles Department of Agriculture, that the introduced Barn Owl takes parrots? He thought not — that these nocturnal owls prey on light-coloured birds. That seems logical — yet on Praslin there are no light-coloured birds, except the extremely rare White-eye

(Zosterops). The Fairy Tern has been wiped out by the owl. It seems unlikely, however, that Barn Owls present a serious threat to the parrots, although this possibility should not be dismissed.

Having covered the subject of predation, I considered other factors which could limit the population: food supply and nesting sites. The former is plentiful, the latter an unknown quantity. Both Evans (1979) and Penny (1965) believed that the absence of suitable nesting sites, i.e. standing dead trees, might be the factor limiting the population growth. Penny suggested the provision of nest-boxes and Evans, a little more realistically, believed that leaving dead *Albizia* and *Acacia* trees standing was the best policy.

Could it be that the parrots are competing for nest sites with other species? It was only after an intensive study was made of the Puerto Rican Parrot (*Amazona vittata*) that it was discovered it was losing the quest for nest sites in competition with a recent colonist, the Pearly-eyed Thrasher (*Margarops fuscatus*). Could the same type of problem be occurring here, with the introduced Common Mynah (*Acridotheres tristis*) playing the role of villain? I would have thought not, as there are few mynahs in the Vallée itself; they prefer areas of human habitation. In addition, parrots can and do utilise deep nesting sites; mynahs cannot.

Nevertheless, Andrew Gardner, a zoology student at Aberdeen University, who spent a year on Praslin studying geckos, informed me of the following incident. 'I watched a group of three parrots investigating a hollow *Pandanus hornei* stump on November 18 1980. One bird went inside, then hopped out and performed a head-bowing display and appeared to be fed by one other, ruffling its head feathers in the process. A few days later, however, it became obvious that mynahs had taken over the hole.'

It seems unlikely that lack of nesting sites is inhibiting population growth but, as a precaution, Victorin Laboudallon of the local Department of Agriculture had placed a number of 1.5 m (5 ft) tree stumps in the ground to rot for potential nesting sites, in 1983.

Remarkably little is known of the nesting habits of the Black Parrot. It has been suggested that nests might be found during most months of the year, yet it seems that eggs are most commonly laid towards the year end.

The first two nests described were found by a forestry worker in November 1963 (Legrand, 1964). One, in the trunk of a dead *Pandanus hornei*, was destroyed when the tree fell. It contained three young. The second nest, in a dead *Albizia falcata*, was examined closely. It contained two white eggs which has been deposited on a layer of rotten wood dust at the bottom of a hollow cavity about 1.2 m (4 ft) deep. One of the nests was found in the Vallée de Mai, the other outside it.

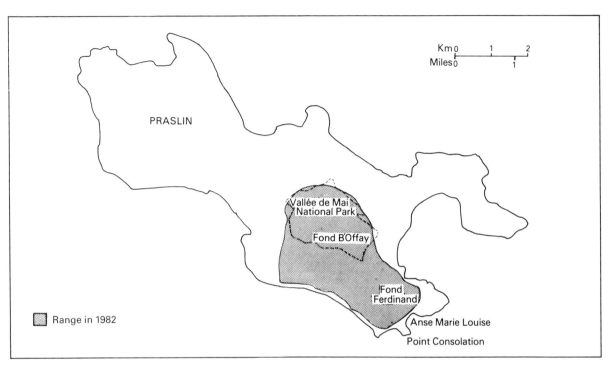

PRASLIN

Km 0   1   2
Miles 0   1

Vallée de Mai
National Park

Fond B'Offay

Fond
Ferdinand

Anse Marie Louise

Point Consolation

Range in 1982

Distribution of Black Parrot (*Coracopsis nigra barklyi*).

In November 1982 a nest was discovered in a coco-de-mer stump about 4.2 m (14 ft) high. It was situated by the side of the path of the nature trail which runs through the Vallée de Mai. The nesting cavity was about 3.6 m (12 ft) from the top and had a diameter of about 26 cm (10 in). The nest litter consisted of debris from the palm to a depth of 6 cm (2.5 in). When the nest was discovered, by Victorin Laboudallon on November 17, it contained one egg. The next day there were two eggs. He recorded that both had hatched by December 6. Both chicks fledged during January.

Victorin showed me the nest tree on my return visit to Praslin in October 1983. He climbed to the top to establish whether it was in use; cobwebs over the entrance indicated that it was not.*

Black Parrots are not dependent on the Vallée for food or for nest sites and range quite widely over the eastern part of the island in search of fruiting trees. They are not conspicuous birds; and it seems that some local people are unaware of their presence outside the Vallée. One October afternoon I had been exploring

the coast road near Point Consolation and observed two parrots in a garden a few feet from the road. Two men came by. I asked them if there were parrots in the area, and the parrots began to call as I did so! One replied 'Vallée de Mai' and the other indicated that they were found all along the coast road.

Observations made by observant local people over a period of several years can be a valuable indicator of the state of the local parrot population. The Figaro family, of Fond B'Offay, near the National Park, observed that the number of parrots visiting their garden to feed on the guava trees had increased during the four years they had resided there. They frequent the garden daily, often as many as ten to twenty.

Mr Figaro, who is employed by the Department of Agriculture, told me that double that number could be seen at Marie Louise, near the southern tip of the island, more than a mile outside the Park.

There are, however, extensive areas which they do not visit. Perhaps they never have made use of the lowland forest, which contains few trees to their liking. Andrew Gardner told me that he spent much time in the remnant patches of natural forest behind Cote d'Or, in the northern-central part of the island, and at

*A decade later, he estimated the population as at least 61 birds and stated that there are also regular sightings on the small island of Curieuse (*Birdwatch*, 1/93, issue no 5). To overcome the problem of lack of suitable nest sites, artificial nest-boxes have been introduced and have proved successful. Three of the eight boxes were in use when reported. In addition, three natural nests were also occupied.

Mr Figaro holds the only Black Parrot in captivity.

Anse Kerlan on the west coast. During a period of more than a year, he never saw parrots there. The vegetation and character of the Point Consolation area is similar to that of the Vallée de Mai, which doubtless accounts for their presence there.

During my first visit to Praslin the Figaros' house was a site of particular interest since there could be seen the only captive Black Parrot on the island. A young bird, it had been picked up several months previously with a broken wing. Extraordinarily gentle, it was removed from its cage and sat contentedly on my hand while I scratched its head. On being taken from shade to sunlight it adopted the sun-bathing posture, with one wing outstretched, which I have seen in captive Vasa Parrots (and, on one occasion, observed in a wild parrot). It welcomed the sun in a manner more reminiscent of a pigeon than a parrot.

In this instance a bird in the hand was worth many in the bush, for it enabled me to examine it closely.

Everything about the Black Parrot is brown; even the feet, nails and the iris of the eye. If ever a bird was erroneously named it was this *Coracopsis*. The only part of its plumage which is not brown is the underside of the wing which is whitish. This was often noticeable in birds in flight, especially in strong sunlight.

We measured this little parrot; its total length was a mere 24 cm (9½ in). The head and bill are small in proportion to the body. Praslin's Parrot, the smallest member of the genus, is a sub-species of *Coracopsis nigra*, the Lesser Vasa Parrot, from Madagascar and the Comoro Islands.

Very little is known about *C. nigra* and the size of its population. Less plentiful than the Greater Vasa Parrot (*C. vasa*), the only other member of the genus, it is a woodland bird, favouring denser forest than the Vasa. Madagascar has suffered very severe deforestation; however, it is a large island, 592,000 km^2 (228,600 sq. miles) in extent. Slightly smaller than Texas or two and a half times larger than Great Britain, it is the fourth largest island in the world, 1,600 km (1,000 miles) in length with an average width of 400 km (250 miles). Yet according to one source (Anon., 1974), only 39,000 km^2 (15,000 sq. miles) of forest had survived. This area is immense in comparison with suitable habitat in other parts of its range, yet there is no guarantee that *C. nigra* will survive on Madagascar. During the decades of the 1970s and 1980s, Madagascar's population soared from 5 million to 22 million. In that period 80 per cent of its rainforest was destroyed. It seems surprising that in the Parrot Action Plan the Lesser Vasa's status is described as stable, with an estimated population in the region of 30,000.

The Comoro race (*C.n. sibilans*) is highly vulnerable, being found on two small islands, Grand Comoro and Anjouan. Possibly it is persecuted locally as Benson (1960) was told that the parrot was a pest in cocoa plantations, attacking young pods in which the seeds had not formed, and sucking the sweet milk of the forming fruits. In 1956 it was less common than the Greater Vasa Parrot. The latter was usually seen singly, or in small flocks of up to six. *C. nigra* was associated with evergreen forest and, as in Madagascar, kept much more to the interior than *C. vasa*. It was never noticed flying above the forest, as was the Vasa. Benson thought that despite its marked association with evergreen forest it might be able to survive where forest had been destroyed, provided that some large trees were left standing.

Ngazidja, the largest island of the group and that with the largest area of evergreen forest, was the subject of population studies on endemic bird species in 1985 and 1989. Their abundance during these two years was compared (in September of 1985 and November–December 1989). It was concluded that the Lesser Vasa

In an attempt to heighten awareness of the bird's situation, the Black Parrot is featured on one of the coins of the Seychelles.

has increased, probably due to the abandonment of exploitation of the forest. It was found in gardens as well as in the Karthala forest (Stevens, Herremans and Louette, 1992).

Grand Comoro (950 km²; 365 sq. miles) and Anjouan (378 km²; 145 sq. miles) are large islands by comparison with Praslin, which measures only 11 × 3 km (7 × 2 miles). The parrot's range on Praslin is small, probably about a third of the island; the human population is large. Yet the parrot has survived, with a population of about 100 in 1992, which was believed to be stable. Two fortuitous events helped to conserve it: the creation of the Vallée de Mai National Park to protect the world's only forest of coco-de-mer palm (*Lodoicea maldivica*) and the banning of firearms for political reasons. Since then, education of the people of Praslin has resulted in pride in the parrot's existence and a desire to protect it. Nevertheless, the small size of the population and the limited area of its range means that it is one of the most vulnerable parrots in existence. There are none in captivity. Perhaps its population never was large. Perhaps as long as the National Park survives so will the parrot. Let us hope so. For me, the Garden of Eden would lose its charm without this cheerful, inquisitive and diminutive denizen.

Members of the genus *Coracopsis* were extremely rare in aviculture until the 1980s when deforestation in Madagascar resulted in commercial export. Behaviourally Vasas differ from other parrots in a number of respects. For some years no breeding successes occurred; then in the early 1990s success became more frequent but was still far from common. Although single pairs have reared young in some collections it seems that success is most likely in a colony aviary where males outnumber females. The young grow at an enormous rate, more rapidly than any other comparable parrot. The female appears to need more than one male to provide her brood with sufficient food. In the event that captive breeding was ever deemed necessary for Praslin's little parrot, the expertise of a few dedicated breeders of Vasas is there to be applied to the rarest of them all.

13

Mauritius: the Last Echoes

The echo parakeet Psittacula echo *is the rarest and most endangered bird in the Mascarenes. It is likely that this, the last surviving endemic parakeet from a western Indian Ocean island, will soon become extinct.*

CARL JONES, IN *STUDIES OF MASCARENE ISLAND BIRDS* (1987)

What an appalling indictment it is, what a disgrace to mankind, that the road to his so-called civilization should be built on the memories of extinct species and species on the way to extinction.

THE RIGHT HONOURABLE EARL OF JERSEY, SPEAKING BEFORE THE 1972 CONFERENCE ON BREEDING ENDANGERED SPECIES

Some of the earliest parrot extinctions caused by the activities of man occurred on the Indian Ocean island groups of Mascarene and Seychelles. The Mascarene Islands comprise Mauritius, which extends over 1,865 km² (720 sq. miles), Réunion (2,600 km², 1,000 sq. miles) and Rodrigues (111 km², 43 sq. miles). They lost about 30 species of birds, either through direct persecution or as their forests were destroyed. The number is uncertain as reports of some species are of doubtful provenance, and others are known only from their bones. During French supremacy the trees on Mauritius were felled for boat-building. During the 1880s the British brought back about 12,000 ha (30,000 acres) of forest (Wright, 1974) but by then irreversible

damage had occurred. The Dodo, the symbol of extinction, had long since disappeared, having last been seen in the 1660s. Other victims included species of duck, grebe, rail, goose, flamingo and heron, and the Mauritius Parrot (*Lophopsittacus mauritianus*). The latter, a large bird said to have been grey or blue, is known only from bones and from incomplete accounts by travellers.

The skin of another extinct parrot, *Mascarinus mascarinus*, can be seen in the National Museum of Natural History in Paris. The species was found on Réunion, possibly also on Mauritius. About 35 cm (14 in) in length, this parrot is reputed to have been mainly brown with the face black, the head greyish-lilac and the beak red (Forshaw, 1989). However, photographs of a skin in the natural history museum in Vienna show quite clearly that '*Mascarinus*' was a Vasa Parrot (*Coracopsis*): its plumage was typical of that genus, except for black feathering on the face. There is no evidence that the beak was red. Furthermore, the label on the specimen shows that in 1873 Wagler had named the species *Coracopsis mascarina*. It is claimed that the last known living bird died in the gardens of the King of Bavaria in 1834 (Greenway, 1967).

Mauritius, a volcanic island 870 km (540 miles) east of Madagascar has a population of over 1 million people. It measures 60 × 46 km (37 × 29 miles) and over half of it is devoted to the growing of sugar cane, a crop which survives the regular cyclones. Originally the island was an evergreen hardwood forest except for a small area of palm savannah on the coast, the home of the *Lophopsittacus* parrots and the Dodo, and an upland area of stunted scrub and marshland. A few areas of original forest have been preserved as nature reserves, especially in the south-western part of the island. It is here that the rarest parrot in the world is found — the Mauritius or Echo Parrakeet (*Psittacula eques*, formerly *P. echo*). Although its range is 50 km^2 (19 sq. miles), it spends most of its time in an area less than half this size, centred on the Maccabé Forest.

It has survived for nearly a century longer than its congener in the Seychelles, *P. wardi*. Formerly classified as a sub-species of the Alexandrine Parrakeet (*P. eupatria*), the Seychelles bird is now considered to have warranted specific status. The three skins of *P. wardi* in the Natural History Museum, London, collected in 1880 and 1881, show that it was smaller than the Alexandrine Parrakeet. The red on the wing was variable but generally less extensive and less dense. It should perhaps be pointed out that Cooper's plate in Forshaw (1973) is misleading; the small beak of the bird depicted lends it the appearance of a Ringneck, when in fact it was an Alexandrine, with the large beak typical of that species. The male differed from the male Alexandrine in lacking the pink half-collar but differed from the Ringneck in its darker shade of green and in having the red wing patch.

The exact distribution of the Seychelles Parrakeet is unknown, but it certainly occurred on Praslin and on Silhouette. When I was in the Seychelles in 1982, I learned of an optimistic ornithologist who had searched the relatively undisturbed forest on the tiny island of Silhouette (a few miles north-west of Mahé) in the hope of finding that the parrakeet still survived. Such was not beyond the bounds of possibility; but, alas, it was not to be. It would not have been the first Seychelles bird to be reprieved: in 1962 the Zosterops (a small inconspicuous insectivorous species) was rediscovered, after being declared extinct in 1936.

The fate of the Seychelles Parrakeet was sealed by its habit of raiding maize plantations (resulting in it being shot) and in the destruction of its forest habitat during the nineteenth century. When the ornithologist Michael Nicoll visited Seychelles in 1906, he failed to find the parrakeet. Its extinction must have occurred during the closing years of the nineteenth century.

At about the same time yet another western Indian Ocean *Psittacula* was lost to us forever. On the small island of Rodrigues existed Newton's Parrakeet (*P. exsul*). From the only two specimens ever collected, the last in 1875, it appears that it differed from other *Psittacula* parrakeets in its blue plumage, much like a cobalt Ringneck, although an early account suggests that there may also have been a green phase.

A much earlier loss was that of the parrakeet on Réunion, *P. eques*, which disappeared in about 1800.

Eighteenth-century skin (faded) of *Mascarinus mascarinus* in the National Museum of Natural History, Paris.

Apparently it was identical to the Mauritius species.

The loss of these parrakeets was not heeded by the inhabitants of Mauritius; it was to be many years before the conservation movement was established. From the turn of the century for the next 50 years or more, the tropics were ravaged without any thought of the fate of the fauna.

The Mauritius or Echo Parrakeet was formerly classified as a sub-species of the Ringneck Parrakeet (*P. krameri*) but ornithologists who have studied it most closely give it specific status. Furthermore, recent studies suggest that the Echo Parrakeet is more closely related to the Alexandrine than to the Ringneck. Its long isolation has allowed it to evolve distinct morphological, behavioural and ecological characteristics.

From written descriptions it can be difficult to visualise the difference between closely related species and it was not until I compared the skins of *P. eques* and *P. krameri krameri* that I appreciated how distinct these two are. The Mauritius bird is much larger in body size than the common Ringneck, a fact which is not evident from comparison of total measurements. *P. krameri* has a very long tail, whereas that of *P. eques* is shorter and broader, the feathers being about 2.5 cm (1 in) at the base (twice the width of those of *P. krameri*). The body is about 25 per cent larger and heavier.

The plumage, too, differs appreciably. In *P. eques* the shade of green throughout is much darker: mid-green, not light apple green as in *P. krameri*. Males have pronounced blue margins to the feathers of the crown, or crown and nape, extending to a lesser degree to the mantle. In addition, there is a pronounced yellow line beneath the black throat. The bill coloration differs in that females have the beak entirely black; in males the upper mandible is red, as in *P. krameri*. Immature birds have the beak red (not black, as stated by Forshaw, 1973); the beak changes to black at between three and four months. In males the upper mandible becomes red when they are aged one year or more (Jones and Duffy, 1991). This is of interest, as among the *Psittacula* parrakeets such a change in beak coloration is found in the Derbyan Parrakeet (*P. derbiana*) from China and from Assam, in northern India, and not in the Ringneck. Another characteristic which sets the Echo Parrakeet apart from the Ringneck is its voice, which differs in pitch, cadence and stridence; also, it is less vocal. In addition, its habitat is solely forest, and upland scrub, rather than open country. In common with most Mauritian birds, and unlike the Ringneck, the Echo Parrakeet shows little fear of man and can be approached to within 3–5 m (10–16 ft) before it takes flight.

Severe habitat destruction occurred in the eighteenth century on Mauritius (as in the Seychelles), commencing about 1753 and continuing until 1880.

The last record from the eastern part of the island is contained in a report by Newton and Newton (1876); even then the parrakeets were declining, but there is no indication of what kind of numbers survived. Early reports, however, suggest that they were always thinly distributed. Between 1835 and 1846 more than half the surviving forests were felled. By 1880 only about 3.6 per cent of the island was covered by primary forest. In the 1930s Echo Parrakeets were still found over an extensive area of the upland plateau but in the 1940s some areas were cleared for tea plantations.

Cutting of the upland scrub and forest on Plaine Champagne forced displaced birds into the remaining areas of native forest in the south-west. The numbers recorded in the early and mid-1970s therefore represented an elevated population density and led to the belief that Echo Parrakeets were more common than was the case. With some of the best foraging areas

destroyed, they had to search intensively within the surviving habitat to find sufficient food.

By the 1970s the situation on Mauritius for all native fauna has become critical. ICBP, the Worldwide Fund for Nature and the New York Zoological Society therefore funded the appointment of a full-time scientist and, with considerable foresight, developed a captive breeding project for the endangered endemics. The first scientist/aviculturist was an American, Stanley Temple. He believed that between August 1973 and December 1974 the population consisted of between 32 and 58 individuals. He noted: 'The recent downward trend . . . is ominous'.

In 1972 55 km² (20 sq. miles) were planted with tea and other areas of Echo habitat were cleared for plantations of pine and other soft woods. According to Jones and Duffy (1992): 'The most devastating blow for the parrakeet was the clearing of key areas of dwarf forest on Plaine Champagne and surrounding areas between 1973–1981. This last project, largely financed by the World Bank, destroyed 3.6 square km of important foraging habitat. In 1973, at the start of this project there were probably 30 or more parrakeets; by 1981 when this work was completed there were less than ten birds known.

In 1975 W.A. Newlands from Britain took over the work. He believed that the population pre-cyclone Gervaise was 40 plus, and had observed more than 20 individuals during a morning spent on Macabé ridge. In 1976 an American, David McKelvey, had taken over Newland's position and, at the end of the year, believed that there were about 45 birds. In 1977 McKelvey and France Staub, a Mauritian ornithologist, thought the population to be between 35 and 45 birds. In 1978 Fay N. Steele was certain that there were less than 20, probably fewer than 10. Dr Staub, who had been watching the parrakeets for many years, was certain that the population had declined rapidly during the previous four or five years. He was almost certainly correct; and the extent of the decline had not been noted by the project managers.

There was, unfortunately, almost an annual turnover of managers until 1979 when Carl Jones, a Welsh aviculturist, took over. Jones, who is also an ornithologist and a field biologist, has remained on Mauritius and is committed to conserving the endangered wildlife. As a result of his dedication and knowledge, the captive breeding project is now achieving great success with breeding colonies of the rare Mauritius Fruit Bat (*Pteropus niger*) and the endangered Rodrigues Fruit Bat (*P. rodricensis*). The greatest achievement has been in breeding the Pink Pigeon (*Columba mayeri*), a species which is highly endangered in the wild state; due to the success here, there are now more than 150 in captivity worldwide.

The captive breeding of the Mauritius Kestrel (*Falco punctatus*) was at first problematical but is now hugely successful. From 1984 to 1991, 71 captive-hatched chicks were released. When the conservation programme started in 1973 the critical status of the Echo Parrakeet was not appreciated and valuable years were lost concentrating on other species. It was not until Carl Jones censused the population in 1979 that the extremely vulnerable state of the species was fully realised. Jones could account for only six or seven individuals. although it now seems probable that there may have been as many as ten or twelve. At the end of 1979 cyclone Claudette hit the island, bringing winds of nearly 224 kph (140 mph) and 390 mm (15 in) of rain within 24 hours. After the cyclone the parrakeet population was disrupted and few birds could be located, although a group of six birds was later seen.

In 1980 observations of Echo Parrakeets were only half as frequent, per hour of field work, as in 1979. Occasionally, up to June 1981, a group of five or six were observed on the Macabé ridge. During 1982 fewer sightings were made and Carl Jones believed that

Macabé Forest, Mauritius, habitat of the Echo Parrakeet.

the population had declined even further.

As seasonal food shortages played a large part in the decline of the population, feeding stations were set up. This was first attempted in 1979 but the foods — seeds and fruits — were ignored. Then grapes and chillies were hung from trees in known feeding areas but it was difficult to prevent monkeys from taking them. Success came with placing wire feeding baskets in trees in an area frequented by a group of parrakeets. They learned to eat apples, green beans, acorn squash, also one of their favourite natural foods was taken — star fruit (grown commercially and available for six months of the year).

Which factors were responsible for the catastrophic decline that occurred during the 1970s? Loss of habitat has already been mentioned. In addition, natural disasters, including Cyclone Gervaise in 1975 and cyclone Claudette in 1979, resulted in population reductions. Mortality was probably direct, rather than the result of starvation. The cyclone may have destroyed nesting cavities; instead of seeking new nesting sites, some pairs apparently remained close to the original cavity and made no further attempt to nest that year. Temple claimed that the cyclone in 1975 destroyed nine of the 24 known parrakeet nesting cavities (Temple, 1978) or eight out of 14 (Temple,

1976). Cyclone damage, however, is known to contribute to cavity formation. Because the older trees containing cavities are lost in cyclones, it is important that native forest trees are able to regenerate and produce new trees that can mature and form cavities.

A serious problem, directly attributable to man's influence, is the presence of the Ringneck Parrakeet, introduced into Mauritius about 1886. Today the population is widespread and high, with a roost of several hundred birds within the Black River gorges. They are wary of humans and do not usually approach habitations.

Jones (1980) suspects that the two parrakeets are ecologically incompatible. They utilise different areas of the Black River gorges and this lends support to the idea that there is some form of competitive exclusion. The Echo frequents ridges and forested slopes, the heads of valleys and the native scrubforest of the plateau, whereas the Ringneck is found in disturbed areas and plantations at the mouths of the gorges and along river and stream valleys. Jones' observations indicate that the two species are not 'overtly aggressive'. He writes: 'It is tempting to speculate that there has been competitive exclusion between the two species of parakeets. *P. echo* has possibly undergone niche contraction, or perhaps more likely 'niche restriction', as a result of competition from its more ecologically generalised congener.

'It is probable that the ring-neck parakeet is preventing the echo parakeet from modifying its feeding ecology and adapting to an increasingly altered forest. The echo parakeet's arboreal nature and dependence upon mature forest do, however, preclude it from entirely occupying the niche now occupied by *P. krameri.*'

The most severe form of competition is over nest sites. Temple (1978) cited two cases of territory-holding pairs of native parrakeets relinquishing their nesting cavities to Ringnecks. This was carried out passively, without engaging in physical defensive behaviour. Dr Staub had observed that the two parrakeets often compete for nest holes and Temple, Staub and Antoine (1974) noted that two out of seven *P. echo* nests were taken over by Ringnecks in 1973.

Nest-site competition is a constantly recurring theme in these chapters, and the Mauritius Parrakeet has a number of such competitors. These include bees, White-tailed Tropicbirds (*Phaethon lepturus*), Common Mynahs (*Acridotheres tristis*), black rats and possibly bats. Native parrakeets have been seen to defend a cavity successfully against prospecting Tropicbirds, whose clumsiness in trees places them at a disadvantage. Tropicbirds, perhaps the most spectacularly beautiful of all seabirds, breed throughout the year and have been known to take possession of a

cavity formerly occupied by parrakeets. At least one former nest was occupied by Tropicbirds in 1974.

The aggressive mynahs have also been known to displace parrakeets; one pair had used a cavity for four years before mynahs took possession. As the forest became progressively degraded and the canopy developed gaps, mynahs invaded the forest and became serious nest competitors. Of the other competitors, probably only rats presented a real danger, both as competitors and predators of eggs and young. A failed nest in the 1990–91 season contained rat droppings and the broken remains of two eggs. Some of these competitors used nest-boxes which were erected for, and ignored by, the Echo Parrakeets.

Loss of nesting sites by Echo pairs had serious consequences for the species and aided its rapid decline. In three cases pairs which had lost their nest stayed in its vicinity but failed to nest that year, although there were suitable cavities within 200 m (656 ft) of the original site (Temple, 1978). This is an interesting observation as a similar phenomenon has been observed in the Puerto Rican Parrot (*see* page 87). In 1975 seven of the pairs of Mauritius Parrakeets which had nested in the previous year lost their cavities as a result of the cyclone in February. During the following breeding season, over six months later, at least four pairs did not attempt to breed, despite the proximity of suitable nesting sites.

Imbalance in the sex ratio is another important factor in the population biology of this species; in a tiny remnant population it becomes critical. In the mid-1970s an excess of males was noted, especially around the nests of active pairs, where as many as five male 'helpers' have been seen. This must have been partly due to the fact that habitat destruction displaced many non-breeding birds into a small area. In many species of parrots in aviculture an excess of males is apparent (not only in imported birds but also among those hatched in captivity) and this is most notable in the Ringneck Parrakeet. During 1976/7 McKelvey saw 18 unpaired males and only three pairs.

Of 24 tree cavities inspected during the period from 1973 to 1975, it was found that 13 were used by parrakeets, four had been used in the past and seven had been prospected but not used. Trees usually selected were living *Calophyllum*, *Canarium*, *Mimusops* or *Sideroxylon* with a diameter of at least 75 cm (30 in) at breast height. Preferred cavities were at least 10 m (33 ft) from the ground, did not face north (where they would be affected by prevailing winds), and had an overhang or other feature that prevented rain entering. Entrances to cavities varied between 10 and 15 cm (4 and 6 in), depth was a minimum of 50 cm (20 in) and diameter a minimum of 20 cm (8 in) internally. Holes in horizontal limbs were preferred to those in vertical trunks, although the latter were used. Another preference was for trees that either emerged above the forest canopy, or were on a steep slope, exposing most major limbs.

Observations made since 1973 indicated that breeding activities commenced in September. Most nesting failures occurred during the incubation period. Potential predators of the two- or three-egg clutch, and of chicks, are mynahs and rats. There is no direct evidence of monkeys (macaques) raiding parrakeet nests according to Carl Jones.

As in all parrakeets, incubation is carried out by the female only. Observation at one nest in 1974 revealed a surprising fact: during a two-day period the eggs of one pair were left unattended for 32 per cent of daylight hours, the longest period being of 64 minutes. During a full day's watch at a nest containing young approximately two weeks old, the chicks were fed at intervals that averaged 79 minutes; the food-bringing parent, male or female, remained at the nest for an average of 11 minutes per feed. Nestlings were therefore left unattended for most of the day. They lunged and bit at intruders and were probably capable of deterring most of these after the age of two weeks. It should be noted that the lengthy absences of the parents may have been caused by fragmentation of the feeding areas, as has occurred in the White-tailed Black Cockatoo (*see* page 28).

During the period 1973 to 1975, young Echo Parrakeets left the nest between November 14 and January 4, but usually in December. After fledging they were fed by their parents for two to three months, until as late as March in some cases.

Although there is some overlap between their diet and that of the Pink Pigeon and Mauritius Bulbul (*Hypsipetes olivaceus*), the diet of the endemic fruit bat (*Pteropus niger*) shows much more similarity and must have some impact on the food available to the Echo Parrakeet. The most destructive and important food competitor is the macaque, which frequently rips off all the fruit before it is ripe, rendering it unavailable. There is little known competition for food between the native parrakeet and the Ringneck; the latter rarely feeds in native forest, but usually prefers forestry plantations, orchards and maize fields in the lowlands. Even Ringnecks which nested in the forest fed in areas of exotic vegetation.

It is believed that reduction in the diversity of plant species in the native forests has had a severe impact on the feeding ecology of Echo Parrakeets. Carl Jones (pers. comm. 1983) has pinpointed the loss of native food plants as a major cause of its decline.

Of the other factors involved, habitat destruction (especially the upland scrub lands) was surely the most important. Trapping or killing, for whatever reason,

has been rare in recent times, although Guerin (1940) claimed that they were killed for food, being considered a delicacy by the rich inhabitants of the island. As recently as 1972 two Echo Parrakeets were shot by a hunter who had them mounted; but such incidents have been rare.

What could have been an effective conservation measure, the transloction of birds to the island of Réunion, has not been attempted. This was an ecologically sound idea, as Réunion has more surviving forest and no Ringneck Parrakeets; nevertheless, any introduced birds could have been threatened by hunting which occurs there. It is now too late for translocation. Jones and Duffy (1991) stated: 'In future we intend to take eggs from pairs that have laid early in the season to encourage them to lay replacement clutches. Captive Echo Parrakeets have not done as well in captivity as we had hoped, and until we have their management well worked out we will refrain from taking young when we feel there is little likelihood of the parents recycling.' In 1974 two of the five young which fledged were removed. In 1975 two more were taken. All were short-lived. A five-month-old male died from visceral gout; a one-year-old female died in December 1975 from traumatic injuries as a result of panicking in the aviary and in January 1976 a female died due to a severe infection of *Staphylococcus aureus* and *E. coli*. The fourth, another female, died in July 1975. The only lesions found on post mortem were some haemorrhage and inflammatory foci in the kidneys.

At the 1980 meeting of ICBP's Parrot Working Group the belated recommendation was made that all the remaining Echo Parrakeets should be captured; it was further suggested that they should be sent to a collection specialising in the breeding of parrots. In the event, it proved impossible to catch the survivors.

In the first edition of this book I wrote: 'Anyone can be wise in retrospect but there is little doubt that had captive breeding by experienced aviculturists or relocation been undertaken in the 1960s the story of the Echo Parrakeet would not be destined to end in the 1980s. The moral must not be allowed to escape biologists and conservationists working with other critically endangered parrots: captive breeding must not be a last-ditch decision but one that is implemented with birds of genera which are free-breeding in captivity as a matter of course.'

Fortunately, I was totally wrong on two counts. Experience with captive Echo Parrakeets has shown that, unlike the Ringneck Parrakeets kept at the same site as their foster parents, they are not easy to maintain. They seem to have an ability to utilise a high percentage of the nutrients present in food and, if fed on high-energy items, soon become overweight. Seeds and nuts were thus excluded from their diet, which consists entirely of fruit, vegetables and leaves, including star fruit, bilimbi, badamier, ochra, peas, green beans, apple, orange and pomegranates. In addition to altering the diet, a large aviary is planned, L-shaped, 62 × 4.7 m (200 × 15 ft) and 3.7 m (12 ft) high. Smaller breeding aviaries will be attached to this. It will thus be possible to keep the captive birds together as a flock, enhancing pair formation and social behaviour.

My prediction that the story of the Echo Parrakeet was destined to end in the 1980s was also wrong, although precariously close, with only two females known to survive. By 1992 the population had increased to 15–20 birds, which included four pairs. In the previous four seasons 16 young had been hatched, seven of these in captivity from eggs laid or chicks hatched in the wild. Unfortunately, not all of these survived and, in 1992, there were four birds in the breeding aviaries. By February 1993 the picture looked much brighter. The wild population was in the region of 20–25 birds, including five known pairs, and the captive population stood at seven (Jones, *in litt.*, 1993). The

earliest attempts to keep Echo Parrakeets in captivity had failed.

One aspect of the wild management of the Echo Parrakeet was proving very successful: the weeding of experimental plots of forest because native forest is being degraded by exotic weeds, rendering it unsuitable for most native birds. These plots are favoured parrakeet feeding and roosting sites.

The Echo Parrakeet has the second-smallest known population of any parrot. But its future is no longer without hope. The wild population is slowly increasing, much has been learned about its captive management, which should lead to successful breeding, and, finally, the parakeet's forest habitat is to be protected through the designation of the National Park for Mauritius.

'One of the very positive results from our work on Mauritius is that the Government has increasingly realised that it must look after the habitat so that the birds can be looked after in their proper environment and there will always be somewhere to release captive produced birds back into . . .' (Jones and Duffy, 1991).

14

Australian Parrots in Danger

A nation's animals and plants are among its own finest works of art. Each species is as individual as any creation of the artist or artisan. Particularly where the degree of endemism is so high there should be a commensurately respectful cherishing of the national heritage entrusted to each nation's care. Destruction of any species or its life-support system is vandalism indeed.

PATRICK FAIRBAIRN, IN *CONSERVATION OF NEW WORLD PARROTS* (1981)

Judged by its parrot populations, in some respects Australia is the richest country in the world. Its 52 parrot species are surpassed only by Brazil, which has 70 species. No other country, however, has such a diversity of forms. Neotropical parrots are a homogeneous group, with great resemblances between various genera, whereas Australia can boast a number of dissimilar groups: white cockatoos, black cockatoos, genera of parrakeets which differ widely in appearance and habits, lorikeets and the true short-tailed parrots such as *Eclectus* and *Geoffroyus*.

In Australia parrots have adapted to almost every type of habitat: coastal heathland, eucalyptus forest, tropical rainforest, agricultural land, localities around watercourses and lakes in the otherwise arid interior, saltbush plains and mallee forest. In other continents parrots are seldom easy to observe; indeed I have encountered people in the Caribbean who were unaware that parrots existed on the island where they had spent their entire lives. In Australia, however, even the visitor with no particular interest in wildlife cannot fail to be aware of the presence of parrots. Even

if they never leave the towns they can see the Gang Gang Cockatoos (*Callocephalon fimbriatum*) feeding on hawthorn trees in Canberra or Scaly-breasted Lorikeets (*Trichoglossus chlorolepidotus*) in flowering coral trees (*Erythina indica*) in the streets of Sydney.

During the past two centuries agriculture has significantly changed the face of Australia. As in Brazil there has been severe loss of habitat in the coastal regions where urban development has been concentrated. No habitat type has been totally eradicated but great changes have been brought to many areas, and the tropical rainforest has been seriously depleted. The bird most affected by destruction of the rainforest in north-eastern New South Wales and south-eastern Queensland is Coxen's Fig Parrot (*Cyclopsitta diophthalma coxeni*). It is now extremely rare and confined to less accessible areas.

Its declining population is estimated at fewer than 200 individuals. (In 1993, the population was estimated at fewer than 50 birds.) The largest winter flock seen during the decades of the 1970s and 1980s consisted of only eight birds. A shortage of winter food is suspected and habitat fragmentation may be preventing access to food trees. ICBP has budgeted $250,000 for a recovery plan. They suggest that planting of food trees should be encouraged and further studies of its ecology should be made in the valleys of the Lamington Plateau. Traditional feeding trees and stands of dry rainforest must be preserved. Coxen's Fig Parrot is a sub-species of the Double-eyed which is less rare in two other areas, the Cape York Peninsula and north-eastern Queensland. It also occurs in New Guinea. This diminutive species, only 14 cm (5½ in) long, remains one of the least known of Australia's native parrots.

Considering the habitat destruction which has occurred, it is surprising that, at most, only one parrot species has become extinct in Australia — or has it? The Paradise Parrakeet (*Psephotus pulcherrimus*) remains the supreme mystery of Australian avifauna. The last confirmed sighting occurred in the Burnett river area of southern Queensland in 1927. Its rapid decline over a period of 40–50 years was probably the result of a combination of drought and over-grazing. In the meantime, rumours persist that the Paradise Parrakeet survives, apparently being backed up with photographic evidence. Through conversations with knowledgeable ornithologists in Queensland and New South Wales, my own view is that it probably became extinct in the 1960s. However, in 1991, ICBP planned to budget US$30,000 to search in suitable areas, notably in northern Queensland.*

Australia is such a vast country that populations can survive undetected for many years. In 1912 a Night Parrot (*Geopsittacus occidentalis*) was collected at Nichol Spring in Western Australia. This specimen, which was poorly prepared and rotted away, was the only evidence that the Night Parrot had existed in the twentieth century. Then in June 1979, at a place called Coopers Creek in north-eastern South Australia, four Night Parrots were seen. This was not a chance event but the result of a camel-borne expedition to search for this species, led by Rex Ellis and Shane Parker. Forshaw (1981) commented: 'This rediscovery of a species in a vast area of undisturbed habitat augurs well for the future, though there is little doubt that the birds have disappeared from many parts of their former range.'

In 1990 came further proof that the Night Parrot still survived — a story so improbable it could only be true! In October, Walter Boles, Collection Manager of the bird department of the Australian Museum in Sydney, was returning from a six-week trip into the outback with two other ornithologists. They were travelling south of Mount Isa when Boles stopped his vehicle to ask the driver of the other one if he had had a good look at some interesting birds further back. As he returned to his vehicle, he looked down at his feet. There he found the remains of a Night Parrot which had probably been lying at the roadside for more than three months. For the first time in history, the oppor-

tunity was provided to carry out DNA testing and to study the skeleton of this species. Only 23 skins are known in museums worldwide — all study skins which lack skeletons.

In 1989 the publisher of *Australian Geographic Magazine* had offered a prize of A$50,000 to the first person who could confirm the Night Parrot's existence. The Australian Museum was planning to use the reward money to finance a network of ornithologists throughout Australia who had four-wheel drive vehicles and could quickly reach the area of a reported sighting. If a live bird is found, it will have a radio-transmitter attached to it so that its movements can be monitored (Patrick, 1991–92).

The Night Parrot is terrestrial, nocturnal and probably nomadic. It is known from widely scattered localities in the arid interior. Few men ever set foot in many of these areas, thus the possibility exists that it is not actually endangered, that small populations survive in remote areas and that they will continue to do so as these localities are inhospitable to man. More populations may come to light before the close of the century; meanwhile, the important fact is that it survives.

Apparently there is a close association with Night Parrots and spinifex (*Triodia* species). Parker wrote to Forshaw (1981) that he suspected that these birds move seasonally from samphire-succulent belts and inland salt lakes or flood plains out to areas of seeding *Triodia*, then back again when the seeding has finished. Unless the interior suffered a succession of catastrophic droughts, it would seem safe to conclude that if the *Triodia* (on whose seeds it feeds) survives, so will the parrots.

If it was known to be endangered, could it be maintained in captivity? One can only speculate on this, since next to nothing is known of it as a captive subject. The little available information is derived from a single bird kept at London Zoo in 1867. It moved about in a series of jumps. It readily accepted the usual greenfoods, thus there would appear to be no practical reason why this species should not survive in a carefully constructed aviary.

The same might also be true of the Ground Parrot (*Pezoporus wallicus*). (*See* Plate 16.) This species is endangered solely by loss of its specialised habitat. An inhabitant of coastal and adjacent montane heathlands, estuarine flats and swamps, in some areas it is also found in grasslands and pastures.

The Ground Parrot is a small, slender bird, with a long tail which accounts for nearly half of its total length of 30 cm (12 in). Its green plumage, intricately marked with yellow and black, is not unlike that of the Night Parrot; but the latter has a short tail. Each species is accorded a genus to itself, although some taxonomists claim that the differences between them

---

*Just before this book went to press, a short report appeared in the September 1993 issue of *Wingspan*, the newsletter of the Royal Australasian Ornithologists' Union, of sightings of the Paradise Parrakeet. Reputedly, five birds were seen daily during a period of eight weeks, from late February to mid-April 1990. They visited a homestead garden with Pale-headed Rosellas (*Platycercus adscitus*) and fed on native grasses growing around the house.

are insufficient to warrant this (Serventy and Whittell, 1976). There is no doubt that these very interesting birds are closely allied.

A considerable contraction in range has occurred in the case of the Ground Parrot. It was once plentiful in areas now occupied by the cities of Sydney and Wollongong in New South Wales and Adelaide in South Australia. Urban and agricultural development is sounding its death knell. Tasmania is the last stronghold of the Ground Parrot. There it is found inland, mainly at higher altitudes, as well as in coastal localities. It is now extinct on Flinders Island in Bass Strait. The Ground Parrot was formerly much more widespread along the south-western coastline of Western Australia, also on the east coast, where it has now almost been extirpated from Queensland.

Forshaw (1981) reported: 'Coastal swamps and estuarine flats have been lost through drainage schemes or expanding pastoral development, thus leaving heathlands as the important habitat for this species, particularly on the mainland. Our surveys at Barren Grounds Nature Reserve indicate that mere reservation of a heathland fosters a generally tall, dense vegetation, with a predominance of woody perennials, which is unsuited to the parrots and is extremely vulnerable to wildfire. On the other hand, heathland cannot be subjected to heavy grazing or too frequent burning. A mosaic pattern of controlled burning, whereby sections of the heathland area are burnt at intervals of eight to ten years, would ensure that optimum habitat is always available to the parrots.'

Comparatively little is known of the habits of the Ground Parrot. As a terrestrial species whose plumage provides excellent camouflage, and a shy and elusive one, it is not easy to observe in the wild. The population of the nominate race of the Ground Parrot in south-eastern Australia and Tasmania has been tentatively estimated at 5,000±. That of the sub-species *flaviventris* in the south-west (Western Australia) is believed to be fewer than 450 birds in two isolated populations, in Fitzgerald River National Park and Cape Arid National Park. Fire is blamed for their decline. ICBP recommend that management guidelines for suppression of fire should be developed. Predation by introduced cats and foxes may also be significant threats. Translocation to Two Peoples' Bay Nature Reserve might also be considered (draft Parrot Action Plan, 1992).

At Barren Grounds Nature Reserve, south of Sydney, regular censuses of the Ground Parrot have been made since 1982. In the 2,000-ha (800-acre) reserve, the population is estimated at between 70 and 100 birds (Sempe, 1992). Telemetry (5-g [0.2-oz] transmitters are attached) has been used on 12 birds, including one pair. The nest fledged two young and was recorded on videotape. Much new data emerged, including the fact that the pair fed only during the daytime.

According to Eva Sempe: 'The species will become extinct without sympathetic management of Reserves like Barren Grounds. A management strategy is necessary to preserve the bird and must include recognition and methods of maintaining suitable habitat and population density, assessment of vegetation for food, plant density and adequacy of cover, including a fire management plan . . .. The fate of the Ground Parrot relies on the whim of legislation to provide Reserves and the skill of Wildlife Managers to maintain them.'

The nomadic nature of some of Australia's parrots, which move around in search of seasonal seeding or flowering plants and trees, has led to certain species being declared endangered when in fact this is not so. At one time it was widely believed in avicultural circles that the Scarlet-chested Parrot or Splendid Parrakeet (*Neophema splendida*) was extremely rare, perhaps even approaching extinction in the wild. Then large flocks began to appear in the wild; in 1960 one flock of an estimated 800–1,000 birds was seen in a tract of mallee forest north of Barmera, eastern South Australia.

Prior to the 1950s the Splendid Parrakeet was a rare bird in aviculture. Now it is so numerous and inexpensive that it is considered suitable for those without extensive experience of bird-keeping. Since the mid-1970s over 1,000 have been bred annually in the UK alone; in 1991, 253 UK members of the Parrot Society bred 2,020 normally-coloured Splendids, plus 1,063 mutations. This total would have been exceeded in some European countries such as the Netherlands and Germany. The annual total reared in aviaries throughout the world is therefore very considerable, and it is feasible that there are more in captivity than in the wild.

It should be pointed out that, as Australia prohibited the export of its native fauna in 1959 (except to *bona fide* zoos, and these would not need to import this species), all these birds are descendants of those which have been aviary-bred for many generations. It is unlikely that any catastrophe would overcome the species in the wild; but if it did it would survive in aviculture.

However, since the 1980s, an increasing number of mutations have been bred, with a subsequent decline in the numbers of 'pure' birds and the suitability of captive-bred Splendids for reintroduction, in the unlikely event that this might be necessary.

In 1992, a nomadic species which previously had not received the attention of conservationists, became the subject of concern. The Swift Parrakeet (*Lathamus* discolor), a small species from south-eastern Australia, has a breeding range which is confined to Tasmania and some adjacent islands. Largely nectar- and pollen-feeding (but not a lory), this species feeds extensively on eucalyptus. In early 1993 a research officer was about to be appointed, after the population size had been estimated at only 1,500 pairs. This species is quite uncommon in aviculture in Australia, yet fairly well established in Europe.

Of the species of Australian Parrots officially described as endangered, one is quite well known in aviaries, especially in Europe. This is *Psephotus chrysopterygius chrysopterygius*. The nominate race, known as the Golden-shouldered Parrakeet, is found in the tropical part, the Cape York Peninsula in northern Queensland, whereas the Hooded Parrakeet (*P.c. dissimilis*) inhabits the north-eastern part of the Northern Territory.

According to Forshaw (1981) both have declined markedly since the turn of the century. Contraction of their ranges has been noted, resulting in their disappearance from some areas and therefore fragmentation of the population. Forshaw states: 'This fragmentation of the population, with resultant loss of interchange within the genetic pool, threatens the viability of the species. Local extinction is a real danger because there appears to be no immigration into areas from which birds have disappeared, and this highlights the vulnerability of each breeding population.'

Peter Chapman, an aviculturist who has bred this species to six generations, as well as having observed it in the wild, believed that, by 1989, it was locally distributed in an area measuring only 160 × 60 km (99 × 37 miles). Agricultural activities, especially burning of the ground coverage, had markedly reduced its range (Chapman, 1990).

Forshaw further states that although the decline is generally attributed to trapping for the bird trade, he believes the primary cause to be interference with ground cover, particularly seeding grasses, through grazing and persistent dry-season burning. The latter occurs when there is maximum dependence on the food supply. It was the late Joe Mattinson, a well-known aviculturist, who observed: 'the seeding grasses growing right outside the nesting hole — a sort of millet, and the parents feed this extremely green feed, and in fact I have never observed the nesting Golden-shoulders to eat dry seed' (Mattinson, 1976). Mattinson wrote this after studying the species in the wild for ten seasons.

This parrakeet has extremely specialised nesting requirements and uses only special types of termitaria. Within its habitat there are three types, only two of which are suitable, because the temperature within the third rises so high that eggs and chicks would not survive. A biologist called Mark Weaver examined 848

termitaria of the meridian type; only two had been excavated by the Golden-shouldereds; however, of 80 of the conical type examined, seven had been excavated. The conical type is associated with a soil on which grows the seeding grasses on which they feed. The Musgrave cattle station is well known for its breeding population of Golden-shouldereds — but cattle and horses graze in the immediate vicinity of the nests, trampling and eating the vital food supply. As the known breeding range is so small, an effort should surely be made to protect this vital area from hoofstock. The population there is declining, according to Mark Weaver, and it has been suggested that feral cats might be contributing to the decline. If this is true, the Golden-shouldered population could decline with dramatic speed, as happened to the Kakapo population on Stewart Island (about 50 per cent per annum at one stage). A programme to protect this population, probably the only one in existence, must surely be implemented as a matter of urgency. ICBP have budgeted $200,000 for such a programme. Let us hope there is action before it is too late.

In recent years, aviculturists, especially in Australia, have experienced a greatly increased degree of success in breeding Hooded and Golden-shouldered Parrakeets, by catering for their particular requirements. These birds are inhabitants of tropical regions and appear to take many generations in captivity to adapt to cold, damp climates. (This is in direct contrast to the neotropical parrakeets, for example, which are extremely hardy when acclimatised.) In Europe a special type of aviary, which can be heated, described by Groen (1962), is used for these birds. It is completely enclosed, except for a window in the back and the sloping front constructed of glass panels which fit over wire netting. They can be removed to admit direct sunlight. The sloping front has the advantages of admitting some rain and of preventing birds from roosting on the wire at night.

The unusual nesting habits of these parrakeets give rise to another problem. The terrestrial termite mounds in which they nest in the wild are so hot inside that there is no need for the female to be in constant attendance at the eggs. In the heat of midday eggs and chicks will be left for several hours. Unfortunately, in captivity this behaviour persists. Also, although the female will sit alongside the young, she will not brood them, as under natural conditions this would be unnecessary.

In Australia, the late Joe Mattinson found a way to overcome these problems. He used electrically heated nest-boxes so that eggs and young did not become chilled. He had found that females varied in their brooding habits; some incubated continuously while others left the nest for three hours at a time. Young spent between four and five weeks in the nest, the most critical period being at about ten to eleven days, between the down and pin feather stages. One of the first breeders of this species in Australia, Sir Edward Hallstrom, achieved success by covering the aviaries with plastic and installing radiators. Another measure which increased breeding success was to fit the nest-box with a funnel entrance 10 cm (4 in) long and 5 cm (2 in) square. A similar idea was adopted by Joe Mattinson who used natural spouts from trees as nest entrances. He found that some birds were reluctant to enter boxes without these.

Breeding Hooded Parrakeets has been more successful. A remarkable pair of Hooded Parrakeets was owned by A.H. Gardener of Sydney. By 1950 they had reared over 60 young to maturity during a period of 16 years. The male lived for at least 30 years.

One of the most consistent breeders of this species is the noted Swiss aviculturist, Dr R. Burkard, who produced 12 generations in 21 years. In Europe, hundreds are reared annually, especially in the Netherlands.

It should be emphasised that even in Australia most parrakeets are derived from aviary stocks of long standing. Aviculturists there resent the assumption that most birds in their aviaries are wild ones. Phipps (1983b) points out: 'An example is the Princess of Wales parrot, which, while being listed as an endangered bird, has a very large captive population. There has not been in the memory of any bird dealer a wild caught Princess parrot offered for sale. Nevertheless, some wildlife departments would prefer that we do not hold Princess parrots, and other species which are declared rare in the wild, and seek their removal from the list of permitted species. It may not currently be considered important to the conservation of the Princess parrot to release captive birds, but who is to say that in 100 to 200 years it may not be so desired? To eliminate the aviary population of Princess parrots now, on the absurd basis that this will in some way be a positive thing for the protection of wild living Princess parrots is to eliminate a management option of the future. I am totally opposed to this cruel example of bureaucratic expedience and ignorance.'

Graeme Phipps points out that aviculture is being cited less and less for the demise of wild populations in Australia, as more information becomes available. At a symposium held in Canberra in 1982 on endangered species, however, both the Golden-shouldered and the Hooded Parrakeets were cited as being threatened by illegal capture. This is definitely no longer the case; the Golden-shouldered is well established in aviaries in Australia, with over 200 birds held by members of the Avicultural Society of New South Wales alone. As for the Hooded Parrakeet, it is such a common aviary bird that the 1992–93 suggested price of the Avicultural Society of Australia for aviary-bred pairs was only A$250. Unregistered wild-caught birds would be almost worthless.

Graeme Phipps comments on the illogical situation that exists in Australia: 'Not only is the wild population [of Hooded Parrakeets] under no threat of illegal capture from the aviary bird trade, but anyone wanting to obtain them can buy them at any birdshop in Sydney, no questions asked. Such is the inconsistency in our laws that bird dealers are not restricted as to whom they may sell rare birds, but aviculturists are restricted as to what they may trade.'

The answer to this anomaly is quite simple, he suggests. Most aviculturists would be willing to fit closed rings on young birds, as proof that they were aviary-bred, if ringed birds could then be traded freely throughout the country.

This is unlikely to happen, partly because each state has its own laws regarding species found within its boundaries. John Bowden (1983) suggests that in the past there was less concern for the welfare of species from other states which may have led to increased removal from the home state. Interstate co-operation would therefore lead towards prevention of the interstate disposal of illegally obtained birds. Bowden commented: '. . . in their overzealous efforts to appear to be doing something positive, the conference of state conservation authorities has overstepped its conservation role and has instead greatly decreased the chances of preservation of some species.'

The Golden-shouldered Parrakeet is an example of a species whose survival has been jeopardised in this way. Rare and endangered, it is considered by many to be on its way to extinction in the wild, states Bowden. 'What good will it do,' he asks, 'if the Golden-shouldereds in aviaries in each state are isolated from those in other states. The fewer there are in the aviaries of any one state the less the chances of survival of aviary stock in that state.' Eventually they will die out, especially if the movement of offspring is made difficult. This policy would make it much easier for the various parks and wildlife services to monitor the movements of the species in their state and to detect any attempts to move the birds across state borders.

Few would disagree with Graeme Phipps' opinion. 'It is particularly important to be able to show that traffic in aviary birds had no deleterious effect on wild populations, because if there is such an effect, it should be stopped. However, if, as I suspect, it is shown to have no effect, wildlife authorities will have to look elsewhere for answers as to what is happening to our rare birds. People are already coming to the realization that the bird trade is at best a secondary pressure on wild bird populations.'

15

A Future in Jeopardy: the Orange-bellied Parrakeet

It is possible that the total population of the Orange-bellied Parrot is now at so low a level that management of the key environments may prove insufficient and that the species may continue to decline regardless of any measures taken . . . . It will be necessary to take the decision either to allow it to slide into eventual extinction, or to undertake a captive breeding programme.

BROWN AND WILSON, IN *A SURVEY OF THE ORANGE-BELLIED PARROT* (1980)

In the first edition of *Australian Parrots*, published in 1969, Joseph Forshaw adopted a somewhat optimistic outlook with regard to the status of *Neophema chrysogaster*, the Orange-bellied Parrakeet, or Parrot, in Australia, where no distinction is made between long-tailed and short-tailed species. He suggested that the abundance reported between 1838 and the turn of the century might have been brought about by irruptions in certain areas throughout its range, with birds moving as far afield as the Sydney region. Just over a decade later, in 1981, the second edition of the book was published. Studies carried out in the intervening years showed that the species was seriously threatened, a fact acknowledged by Forshaw in the revised edition.

The term 'seriously threatened' was an understatement: seriously endangered was then nearer the mark. From counts carried out annually, between 1978 and 1982, in winter and during the breeding season, involving up to 150 volunteers from Tasmania, Victoria and South Australia, the population had been assessed. It was considered that the total no longer exceeded 200 individuals. The Orange-bellied Parrakeet was therefore the most endangered parrot in Australia, unless the Paradise Parrakeet was still extant. By 1992 the wild population was estimated at 150 birds. In 1982 the whereabouts of 30 to 35 pairs were known (although only eight nests had been located) and it was estimated that no more than 40 breeding pairs existed.

Until recently it was the least known member of the genus *Neophema*, a group of ground-frequenting parrakeets averaging about 20 cm (8 in) in length. Five of the seven species are among the best-loved of all Australian birds by aviculturists and are extensively reared in captivity. The Rock Parrakeet (*N. petrophila*) and the Orange-bellied, however, are and always have been, virtually unknown in captivity; the exception is the small number of Rock Parrakeets in Australia.

The two latter species exploit the coastal food resources, whereas the Elegant and the Blue-winged, the two most successful *Neophema*s, have a range which extends far inland. It includes open grasslands, mallee and semi-arid salt-bush country.

A little larger than a Budgerigar, and not unlike it in shape, the Orange-bellied Parrakeet (*N. chrysogaster*) is bright grass green above. It is greenish-yellow on the breast, merging into bright yellow on the abdomen and under-tail coverts. There is an orange patch in the centre of the abdomen; in females and juvenile birds the orange and yellow areas are less extensive. The primaries and the shoulders are violet-blue and the male has a broad frontal band of deep blue, bordered by a narrow pale blue line. The female's frontal band is less extensive and lacks the light blue border. (*See Plate 19.*)

Although there is some variation in the shade of green of the upper parts (brightest in the pre-breeding plumage of the adult male), the shade is most distinctive and does not tend towards the olive green of the three similar species. As its name suggests, the orange patch on the abdomen is brighter and more extensive than in the other members of the genus.

The first Orange-bellied Parrakeet was recorded in 1773, at Bruny Island, south-eastern Tasmania, probably on Captain Cook's second voyage. There appears to be no further mention in the literature until Gould (1848) reported it in abundance during a visit to the Actaeon Islands, off south-eastern Tasmania, in 1836. In the summer of that year, in 1886 and 1918, large numbers, even 'several thousand', were seen in coastal South Australia. These irruptions, occurring at long intervals, gave a false impression of the species' population. It was not until the turn of the century that a steady decline was apparent, when significantly fewer birds were observed at well-known wintering areas. In 1917, in *Birds of Australia*, Gregory Mathews pointed out the rarity and apparently endangered status of this parrakeet. He was the first to do so.

The Orange-bellied Parrakeet makes an annual migration between its breeding grounds in Tasmania and the Australian mainland through Bass Strait and King Island. This commences in early March, with coastal movements northwards up the western coast of Tasmania in pairs and small groups. Beyond the north-western coast the birds 'island-hop' across Bass Strait. They have been recorded from most of the major islands in the Hunter group, especially Hunter Island itself. By contrast, the migration route of the similar Blue-winged Parrakeet appears to be a direct one; it flies over Bass Strait and is seldom encountered on King Island. There would be insufficient food resources on the islands to support the many thousands of Blue-wings on migration but there is ample food for the small numbers of Orange-bellieds.

The major wintering location of the Orange-bellied is in Victoria, in Port Phillip Bay. A further important wintering area is in south-eastern South Australia. In a number of localities there groups of up to 20 occur. It is of interest that there the feeding habitat is totally different to that used by the species in Victoria.

There is some overlap in the overall range, but not in the breeding distribution, of the Blue-winged and Orange-bellied Parrakeets; remarkable similarities occur also in their behaviour and habits and, to some extent, food requirements. The Blue-winged, however, has adapted to and benefited from the clearance of

The critically endangered Orange-bellied Parrakeet breeds only in south-western Tasmania.

forest and increase of pasture, whereas the Orange-bellied prefers unaltered coastal habitat. Where the two species are found feeding in the same salt marshes on the mainland, they seldom mingle. On beach frontages their separation is obvious, although they may feed within 50 m (165 ft) of each other.

In 1978 ICI announced its intention to build a huge petro-chemical plant at the Point Wilson wintering area. This resulted in an outcry by naturalists who realised the pressure such an undertaking would place on the parrakeet. Much correspondence on the subject appeared in the national press, but ICI went ahead with its plans. It was not until three or four years later that they announced their decision to defer indefinitely the building of the plant, on the grounds of reduced world demand for petro-chemical products.

Unwittingly, ICI had helped to aid the survival of this bird. Attention having been focused on its plight, an investigation was commenced into its numbers. The results were startling. Brown and Wilson (1982) describe how the initial counts were made: 'In 1978 Richard Loyn began the first attempt at determining the numbers of overwintering birds in Victoria and South Australia. He enlisted the support of many volunteers in undertaking a co-ordinated search on a single pre-determined date, of potentially suitable coastal habitat between the Gippsland Lakes in the east, and as far west as Adelaide.' On this occasion no more than 80 birds were located.

Regular searches have since been made in winter in order to identify other localities used. It was found that, other than three birds in the breeding area in the south-west during June/July 1982, there is no evidence that many parrakeets overwinter on the Tasmanian mainland. Small numbers spend the winter on King Island: one in 1980, four in 1981 and two in 1982. In the past it appears that the majority of the population wintered in South Australia, but from recent records it seems that approximately two-thirds now remain in Victoria and in particular Port Phillip Bay, with only small numbers in Westernport and east to Lake Jack Smith in Gippsland.

The most important overwintering locations within Port Phillip are near Werribee (up to 74 birds during the winters of 1980–82) and Swan Bay/Bellarine Peninsula (up to 30 birds). They arrive at Werribee earlier (late March) than at Swan Bay (June and July) and usually remain in both areas until September or October, occasionally November, before returning to Tasmania.

Until the studies were carried out, very little was known about the situation in South Australia. It brought to light the fact that between 30 and 50 birds were usually scattered along the coast in small groups between the Victorian border and Coorong.

In producing winter totals for this species two figures were given (shown below); the first indicates its minimum number recorded on the day of survey, and the second (where applicable) the maximum, including possible double counts and birds recorded from other locations.

There is ample evidence to suggest that as recently as

State	1978	1979	1980	1981
Victoria	83–91	65–80	82–96	68–74
South Australia	–	7–25	7–27	5
Tasmania	–	–	1	4
	83–91	72–105	90–124	77–110

the 1960s the Orange-bellied Parrakeet was considerably more numerous than it is today. The most recent records of numbers apparently greater than today's are of 35 at Salt Creek in the Coorong for 1962/3, and up to 100 birds on Mud Island in Port Phillip Bay in the early 1960s. However, Orange-bellied Parrakeets seldom inhabit either locality now. It must be borne in mind that below a viable minimum (which is unknown in this case) a population struggles for existence, and when its habitat is interfered with it can plummet to extinction in a very short space of time.

In Victoria this species has specialised habitat requirements: coastal saltmarsh and adjacent grasslands. Saltmarshes worldwide have long been considered areas of useless wasteland and, historically, have been reclaimed for farming, used for industrial and other development or as recreation areas. In contrast, most sightings in South Australia are from beach front or dune vegetation. There have been occasional records of single birds up to 100 km (62 miles) from the coast; however, 95 per cent of all sightings in recent years are within 6 km (3.7 miles) of the coast or saline harbour (Macquarie Harbour and Port Davey/Bathurst Harbour in Tasmania). Very few inland sightings have occurred.

In Tasmania this parrakeet is to be found in coastal sedgelands, heath and eucalypt. It uses only a small proportion of potential habitat: 100 km (62 miles) of coastline in South Australia and 400 km (248 miles) of coastline in Tasmania (Anderson, Dedman and Doughty, 1980). In Victoria plenty of saltmarsh survives but that at Port Phillip is greatly reduced. Saltmarsh and adjacent grassland is critical habitat, as is the buffer of herbland, sand dunes and woodland. In particular, the habitat at Werribee is seemingly irreplaceable for this species, and over 80 per cent of the known population has been seen at the Spit, near there.

In 1989 I was fortunate enough to be at the Spit in April, a few days after the first Orange-bellieds arrived from Tasmania. I had the good luck to be in the company of Andrew Isles (known worldwide for his natural history bookshop which almost certainly stocks a greater number of bird titles than any bookshop ever opened). It seemed so strange to drive a few miles outside a large city (Melbourne), park the car by the roadside, walk for 20 minutes or so across saltbush scrub (causing a flock of Pelicans to take off from the water's edge) to reach the habitat of not just a parrakeet but one of the rarest in the world.

We continuously scanned the bushes ahead with binoculars as we stepped over dead, stranded fish. After nearly an hour, we were both becoming a little despondent. Then suddenly Andrew gave a shout of excitement. He had spotted a couple of Orange-bellieds some distance away feeding in a bush. He

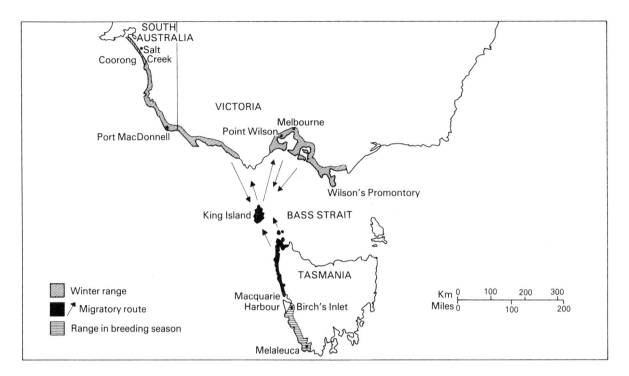

Distribution of Orange-bellied Parrakeet (*Neophema chrysogaster*). Brown and Wilson, 1982.

handed me the binoculars; I could marvel at their vibrant shade of green and observe their watchfulness. They kept an eye on us as they fed and we knew we could not approach too closely. There were five feeding in the salt bushes and at their bases, on the ground. We could watch them only briefly, but that morning provided a memory I will always cherish.

Had ICI's development gone ahead, the groundwater and drainage changes could have altered significantly this critical area. Levels of noise, lighting and airborne chemicals would have been most harmful. It is not realistic to believe that a species whose total population numbers about 150 could have survived industrial development near its principal wintering area.

Brown and Wilson (1982) believe that although much apparently suitable winter habitat exists, subtle factors such as age, height and density of the saltmarsh plant called beaded glasswort (*Salicornia quinqueflora*), the presence of grey glasswort (*Artrocnemum halocnemoides*) and alternative food sources there and in the adjacent sewage filtration paddocks are responsible for the importance of Werribee as overwintering habitat. Despite the area of apparently quality saltmarsh in the Coorong and the frequency of Orange-bellied Parrakeet sightings there during the past 20 years, very few birds have been recorded from saltmarsh. For several decades they have been known to use disturbed areas or failed pasture in at least three locations behind the dunes of the Younghusband Peninsula.

The reason that coastal Victoria is now preferred to South Australia may be connected with land reclamation. Prior to drainage in the early 1960s much of the hinterland on the Coorong, in South Australia, between Meningie and Kingston, was composed of mallee woodland interspersed with swamps and large lakes. This area is now close-cropped pasture and may have affected the food plants available.

A further cause of concern is created by the Blue-winged Parrakeet as a food competitor. The draining of saltmarshes in north-western Tasmania has reduced their quality and quantity. Stock has access to most of these marshes and renders large areas unsuitable for the Orange-bellied. On the other hand, the Blue-winged has increased markedly due to increased adjacent grassland. Although the breeding ranges of the two species do not overlap, their requirements on migration are very similar and may be placing increasing pressure on saltmarsh food resources for the endangered parrakeet in north-western Tasmania.

The saltmarsh on King Island is not used by the Blue-winged, but if it encroached on this small area the future of the Orange-bellied would be further jeopardised.

In 1980 the post-breeding population was believed to consist of approximately 170 birds: 80 breeding adults, 22 non-breeding birds and 68 young. Of nine nests reported by Brown and Wilson, three failed and the other six produced at least 15 young, giving a minimum production rate of 1.7 per nest. The number of breeding pairs was estimated at 40; apply the 1.7 per nest and the result would be 68 young. That the species bred successfully is borne out by the discovery of the 40–50 migrating juvenile birds on King Island in April 1980, of which 34 were seen in one flock.

The breeding range of this species is restricted to south-western Tasmania, south of Macquarie Harbour in the mid-west. It nests mainly along the coastal fringes and usually within 10 km (6 miles) of the coast or the margins of the large natural harbours of Macquarie and Bathurst/Port Davey, never being found far from water. Fortunately, the breeding locality falls within either the World Heritage Area or the South-west Conservation Area. No nest had been located more than 100 m (330 ft) from a forest margin. The nest site invariably overlooks a large open area of buttongrass sedgeland plain (Brown, 1991).

A number of factors may adversely affect breeding results. Although mineral exploration is carried out in the known breeding area, the harsh climate of south-western Tasmania restricts human activity. Illegal burning and wild fires are an annual hazard, usually occurring when the parrakeets are nesting. The coastal plains are burned to provide fresh growth in open country for wallabies which are then shot for bait by fishermen. In January 1976 an extensive fire swept through a large area south of Macquarie Harbour, including the area where four nests were found in 1979/80.

Orange-bellied Parrakeets apparently prefer small copses and tree-lined creeksides for nesting (Brown and Wilson, 1980); however, many copses are of insufficient age to provide adequate nest sites, shortage of which could be an important factor inhibiting population growth. One nest was located on the edge of a large tract of rainforest and another in a thickly wooded mid-river island. Understorey varies from myrtle, blackwood, celery-top pine and ferns of closed forest to open bracken and tea-tree scrub.

Several nest competitors and predators are known. On one occasion an attempt to take over a nest by eight Tree Martins (*Cecropis nigricans*) was observed. The martins flew in turn at the entrance, occasionally entering and behaving aggressively towards the parrakeets. No harm came to the nest, however. Probably the most important nest competitor is the Green Rosella (*Platycercus caledonicus*), a species which is particularly abundant in south-western Tasmania. Brown and Wilson observed these Rosellas inspecting five nests. The Orange-bellieds made no attempt to drive the larger birds away and were plainly afraid of them. At one nest a Black Currawong (*Strepera fuliginosa*), a large crow-like bird with a huge bill, made repeated attempts to enter, presumably to predate the young.

Starlings (*Sturnus vulgaris*), which have been introduced to Tasmania, are abundant and widespread in eastern Tasmania but as yet are uncommon in the west. In 1980, however, a pair of Starlings attempted to oust a pair of Orange-bellied Parrakeets from a nest they occupied, in which they had successfully reared young in the previous year. Direct conflict lasted a whole morning before the Starlings gave up and left the area.

On their return to Tasmania, nest-hole cleaning is an activity immediately engaged in by previously successful pairs. Brown and Wilson (1982) have observed that they leave the roost one to two hours after sunrise for the nest tree. The female occupies the hole for periods of up to one hour, while the male perches nearby. Only the female incubates the clutch of five to six eggs (as in all parrakeets), while the male gathers food for both birds. Incubation starts from the laying of the first egg.

Watches at nesting sites resulted in some interesting data being collected, not least of which was the frequency of visits by the male to feed the incubating female. Of 22 successive visits at five nests, the average time between each was 2.9 hours; the shortest period was 55 minutes. After the chicks hatched in one nest and the female was assisting with the feeding, the average of 20 successive feeds was 1.3 hours apart. The feeding routine changed when the female assisted with food gathering; until then the male was not permitted to enter the nest, but thereafter he did so.

In the nests studied in 1979, the young fledged in late January and early February. It has been observed at Melaleuca that juvenile birds join creches of up to 15 individuals. Adult birds commence migration soon after, leaving their young to shelter in scrub along creeks and to experiment with various food sources. These include new growth of *Eucalyptus nitida* and fallen seed in recently burnt areas. They generally start to migrate in March; the last bird had left the study area by March 11 in 1979, and in 1982 by March 16 — unusually late. The northward migration takes places over two to three months in most years, sometimes over a longer period. It occurs between March and June, the peak being April and May. A few birds may winter in Tasmania and on King Island in the Bass Strait, which lies approximately half-way between Tasmania and the mainland. In 1979 most birds had

Data of five nests studied by Brown and Wilson (1980) in south and mid-west Tasmania

TREE SPECIES	HEIGHT OF TREE	HEIGHT OF NEST ENTRANCE	DIAMETER OF ENTRANCE	NEST DEPTH	FACING	LOCATION
1) *Eucalyptus nitida*	18 m (60 ft)	8.5 m (28 ft)	24 cm (9½ in)	49 cm (19 in)	due W	1 ha (2.5 acres) forest patch
2) *Eucalyptus nitida*	24 m (78 ft)	18 m (60 ft)	10 cm (4 in)	60 cm (24 in)	SW	5 ha (12 acres) forest patch
3) *Eucalyptus nitida*	20 m (66 ft)	11.4 m (37 ft)	22 cm (8½ in)	46 cm (18 in)	due E	7 ha (17 acres) forest patch
4) *Eucalyptus ovata*	20 m (66 ft)	18 m (60 ft)	approx 6 cm (2½ in)	–	S	forest in sedgeland plain
5) *Eucalyptus nitida*	40 m (131 ft)	25 m (82 ft)	8 cm (3 in)	–	N	copse of 25 ha (62 acres)

Of the five nests above, one contained six eggs. Clutch size of the others was unknown.

returned to south-western Tasmania by the beginning of November and nesting had commenced by the middle of the month at Macquarie Harbour and Port Davey.

These two main breeding localities in south-western Tasmania have in common large, open, low-lying sedgeland plains which drain into large harbours. It has been found that the food plants are used by the Orange-bellied Parrakeets according to the period when they were last fired. An area at Birch's Inlet fired seven years prior to 1980 was used as a congregating and feeding area by newly arrived birds in 1980 and 1981. A marked increase in growth (especially *Melaleuca* and *Leptospermum* species) has since occurred and it was predicted in 1981 that this area would be unsuitable as a food source in three to five years. Seldom have these parrakeets been observed in vegetation more than 15 years old. Coastal plains are probably fired less frequently than formerly, when aboriginals regularly worked this coast during the summer months. A plan of fire management of coastal buttongrass is therefore required, particularly in key Orange-bellied Parrakeet areas.

In the wintering locations habitat alteration of a different kind has occurred; this has been most marked in Port Phillip Bay. The construction of industrial complexes has resulted in degradation and destruction of saltmarsh, along the shores between Melbourne and Geelong. Brown and Wilson (1982) commented: 'The fact that this bay is still used by Orange-bellied Parrots at all gives testimony to the tenacious nature of the species.'

They point out that areas unaffected by industrial growth, particularly those used by the parrakeets, must be protected and improved if the winter strongholds are to be maintained intact. The sewage farm at Werribee was fortuitously sited in that it has prevented industrial development in the area, but its presence has had a dramatic effect on the ecology. It has also attracted a wide variety of birds, including predators.

Great alteration has also occurred on Mud Island, in Port Phillip Bay, which was formerly frequented by many Orange-bellied Parrakeets. Up to 100 were recorded there in the 1960s but five is the most seen since 1978. This is due to the increasing colony of Silver Gulls, which numbered less than 1,000 during the 1960s; now 100,000 use the island, causing changes in vegetation.

Conversely, in the Bellarine Peninsula a new feeding area has evolved from an artificially created island, resulting from the dredging out of a channel near Queenscliff. The birds feed on *Salicornia* there. This is an important development for it indicates that similar new feeding areas could be created.

As more was discovered about the habits of this species, the problems besetting it were being identified. Brown and Wilson suggested that management proposals for the most important sites in Tasmania, on King Island, at Werribee and Bellarine Peninsula in Victoria, and in south-eastern South Australia, should be drawn up by state authorities with assistance from the survey team, that a fire management plan should be produced for the key breeding and feeding areas, and that management of food resources should be undertaken, possibly including a food-plant propagation programme.

In 1980 implementation was made of some of the recommendations. All planned forest protection burns of buttongrass sedgelands were suspended in areas where the occurrence of Orange-bellied Parrakeets was suspected, south of Strahan, during the breeding season.

The Forestry Commission undertook to consult the National Parks and Wildlife Service prior to any proposed burns on the migratory route and to take account of any recommendations made by the survey. A more concrete step was that of the purchase by the National Parks and Wildlife Service of two blocks of privately owned land on King Island, totalling 250 ha (620 acres). They form part of the saltmarsh used by the migrating parrakeets. As the rest is Crown land, the area is now reasonably protected from habitat alteration.

Perhaps the most important conservation measure would be to halt the reduction and reclamation of saltmarsh in areas used by this species. Failing that, captive breeding may be of increasing importance. The survey officers of the National Parks and Wildlife Service started to prepare for this eventuality in 1983 when Rock Parrakeets and Blue-winged Parrakeets were installed in the aviaries built at the research centre near Hobart. These birds were wild-caught and were to be used in breeding trials. Aviculturists might be surprised that such a cautious approach is necessary

Birch's Inlet, habitat of the Orange-bellied Parrakeet (*Neophema chrysogaster*).

when other members of the genus are reared in aviaries in such large numbers. Nevertheless, the fact is that the Orange-bellied is little known in aviculture; therefore working with the two species whose ecology most closely parallels that of the Orange-bellied first is highly commendable.

The first record of a captive bird relates to 1907, when one was exhibited at a show in Sydney. It may not have been until the 1940s, however, that as many as 'a few dozen' (Brown and Wilson, 1980) were available commercially. Small-scale trapping continued in the 1950s and into the 1960s. It probably continued into the early 1970s when several pairs reached Europe; these are unlikely to have been aviary-bred. Regrettably, the species was not established in aviculture; in Australia breeding successes were recorded on only three occasions. In Europe, the first was achieved by van Brummelen in the Netherlands in 1971, when three young were reared from five eggs. In the following year another Dutch aviculturist, J. Postema, reared a single youngster. Since then the species seems to have completely died out in aviculture, which suggests that it may be much more difficult to breed than the other *Neophema*s, although, of course, in comparison, very small numbers indeed have been maintained in captivity.

Following a meeting of the Orange-bellied Parrakeet Recovery Team held in November 1985, ten birds were taken from the wild to inaugurate the captive breeding programme. A serious problem surfaced the following

May when yellow feathers started to appear in the plumage of some of these birds. Eventually it was realised that they were suffering from psittacine beak and feather disease (PBFD), a serious condition which resulted in the death of seven of the ten. (In wild-caught birds — many species are affected — this disease is not apparent until the first moult in captivity.) The surviving two females produced a total of four young, paired to the same male. Two of these young later died from PBFD.

In the meantime, six more birds were taken from the wild and the following season eight young were reared in three nests. The next year, 1988/89, seven of the eight females laid and a total of 22 young were reared. Losses were still occurring from PBFD, however, and it was decided to relocate the breeding complex to a climatically better site, because the cold winter conditions caused some stress to the birds. The move took longer than anticipated; thus only three young were reared the following year.

During the 1990/91 season 14 young were reared from six females, two of which were double-brooded. It was the coolest summer since the breeding programme had been operating, and this may have contributed to its success. In October 1991 the first release of captive-bred birds was made. Eleven were released at Melaleuca (*see* page 165). There were then 52 birds in the aviaries and the recommendation was made to release 15 more during 1992/93. It was also suggested that a second captive population should be established.

During the six years (to 1991/92) that the programme had been operating, 81 young had been reared and 16 birds had been taken from the wild, to give a total of 97 birds. The stock then consisted of 52; 36 had died and 11 had been released, thus the original stock of 16 had increased by almost 300 per cent. The percentage of young reared which were visibly affected by PBFD had declined each year. It appeared to be a mild form of the disease, becoming apparent only at the first moult and not developing after this period.

The success of the 1992/93 breeding season augurs well for the future; 37 young were reared to independence. This excellent result was achieved despite the fact that no females laid second clutches. During 1992 a further 14 were released, several of which bred that year. Another encouraging aspect was the rearing of 11 in the wild in four nest-boxes erected by the Department of Parks and Wildlife (Peter Brown, *in litt.*, 1993).

It is too soon to view the future of this species with total optimism. One might expect a significant increase in the wild population by the mid- to late 1990s. If this does not occur, it might be because there is still some aspect of the biology of this species which remains to be unravelled. However, there is no evidence that such exists, just a fervent hope that the tide is turning for the Orange-bellied Parrot and that, within a few years, its population will have doubled.

Continued research is required to define all the problems facing this parrakeet. If all the recommendations for its survival are implemented, if the annual census continues, and its wild 'management' is carefully considered, and when put into practice it is monitored for effectiveness, there is a good chance that it will survive.

16

Kakapo: Unique among Birds

Its intelligence commands respect, and its helplessness sympathy, while its genial nature endears it to all who know it well. It repays kindness with gratitude, and is affectionate as a dog, and as playful as a kitten.

HUTTON AND DRUMMOND, OF THE KAKAPO (1905)

Some very significant progress has been made in spite of the fact that the kakapo must be one of the world's most difficult animals to study. It inhabits some of the most isolated and inhospitable country, seldom calls, and is nocturnal, solitary, secretive, cryptically coloured, and exceedingly rare.

DAVID MCDOWELL, DIRECTOR GENERAL, NEW ZEALAND DEPT OF CONSERVATION, IN *PROCEEDINGS OF A WORKSHOP ON THE CONSERVATION OF KAKAPO* (1992)

The loss of any species is a tragedy because each one is unique and can never be re-created. Yet the loss of some creatures is, or would be, a greater tragedy than that of others which may have closely related forms, differing little in essential characteristics. Judged by this criterion the greatest loss would therefore be of the species which differed most from all others extant. Indisputably, unique among parrots is the New Zealand Kakapo (*Strigops habroptilus*). So greatly does it differ from all others that some taxonomists place it in a special subfamily or even accord it a family of its own. (*See* Plate 18.)

A large bird, over 60 cm (2 ft) in length, it is by far the heaviest parrot in existence; males vary in weight between 1.5 and 3.4 kg (3 lb 5 oz and 7 lb 8 oz) and females weigh considerably less, between 0.9 and 1.6 kg (2 lb and 3 lb 8 oz). The mean weight is 2 kg (4 lb 6 oz) for males, and 1.2 kg (2 lb 10 oz) for females.

Its unusually soft plumage is barred and streaked throughout with brown and yellow, being mainly green above and greenish-yellow below. It is sometimes called the Owl Parrot because of its facial disc of modified bristle-like feathers. While walking, the head is held very low so that the cat-like whiskers brush the ground in horizontal stance.

The head is rounded. Although the neck is long, at rest there is no marked constriction between neck and trunk. The normal stance is near horizontal but Kakapo sometimes assume an upright attitude, the body being supported by the strong, decurved tail. The erect stance is adopted when the bird is alert and defensive or aggressive.

The mainly nocturnal Kakapo usually endeavours to hide in some secluded and well-shaded corner during the day, squatting on the entire length of the very short tarsus. It often roosts in relatively light situations, however, and does occasionally sun itself.

Strange and unique though the Kakapo is in appearance, it has other characteristics which set it apart from any other parrot ever known to exist — and indeed from birds of other families. It is, for example, the only known flightless lek bird (Merton, Morris and

Atkinson, 1984); a lek is a mating system in which males clan together and perform courtship displays from traditional display grounds.

Consider, too, these unique or rare aspects.

1) It is the only lek parrot.
2) It is the only lek bird to have evolved in the absence of predatory mammals.
3) It is the only flightless parrot. It is capable of short, steep downward wing-assisted leaps and parachuting; but its virtually keel-less sternum makes it incapable of flying in the true sense, the maximum 'flight' being 3–4 m (10–13 ft).
4) It is one of the few truly nocturnal parrots. ('Kakapo' means 'parrot of the dark' in Maori language.)
5) It possesses aberrant soft plumage, with facial disc, otherwise found only in owls.
6) It is the only parrot to have an inflatable thoracic air sac, and to make a booming call.
7) Unusually, although probably not uniquely for a parrot, it does not breed annually; the entire population nests synchronously every two to four years, coinciding with plentiful food supplies.
8) Unlike most parrots, which are highly social, its habits are solitary.
9) Its unique bill structure is adapted for grinding food finely; the gizzard, the organ in which food is ground in most parrots, is small and degenerate.

The Kakapo is therefore the most aberrant of all parrots. Its extinction would be a loss of incomparable proportion. In mid-1982 less than 50 Kakapo remained and the species was in steep decline, according to Don Merton, Endangered Species Officer of the New Zealand Wildlife Service. To those interested in the fate of endangered species, his name is synonymous with that of the Kakapo. I am indebted to him for most of the contents of this chapter, which originate from his papers (published and unpublished) on this species.

Before discussing the events of the subsequent decade, let us look at the reasons for the near-extinction of this species. Subfossil remains indicate that the Kakapo was formerly widespread on the main islands of New Zealand where it is now extinct. It last occurred only in Fiordland, South Island. An ecological island, surrounded by sheer escarpments, it escaped most of the alien influences which so radically altered other parts of the mainland. The Milford region was known to harbour eight birds, all males. Until 1977 it was thought that they were the sole survivors of their species, which was therefore doomed to extinction. Then, in January of that year, a population which included females was discovered in the south-east of Stewart Island.

The Kakapo has been in decline for a long time.

Being flightless, lacking any form of defence, and unfortunately considered excellent eating, it stood no chance against a host of mammalian predators, the chief of which was, initially, man.

Even before Europeans set foot in New Zealand, Maoris were hunting Kakapo. Reputedly, in the early 1770s, Maori chiefs took their habitat into consideration when dividing land, for the skins of these parrots were highly valued. On feast days Maoris would wear Kakapo heads hanging from their ears. Cloaks were fashioned from Kakapo feathers; an example in Perth consists of 11,000 feathers attached in twos on alternate lines of wefts. The cloak measured over 1.2 m (4 ft) long and 84 cm (33 in) along the right side. The soft Kakapo feathers were also used to fill mattresses; and one in the Dominion Museum contains 20–30 per cent of this species' feathers.

Kakapo was the principal food of Ngatau natives, before the potato was introduced to New Zealand, according to one early explorer. They were hunted at night by torchlight. The unfortunate parrots were then still numerous in mountainous areas on the mainland.

The predation of the Kakapo population by Maoris was probably insignificant compared to that which occurred when Europeans arrived in New Zealand. In 1845 the first Kakapo was found by a white man; its fate was to be repeated over and over until it was extirpated from most areas — it was eaten. The skin of the first victim was sent to England, where it was described by Gray. Its arrival dispelled the idea that the Kakapo might be a member of the Cuculidae (cuckoo family). It excited much interest among taxonomists.

Meanwhile the slaughter of Kakapo was reaching unprecedented proportions. During the gold rush of the 1860s and 1870s the diggers reputedly lived on Kakapo, and ate the meat until they were tired of it. Wild cats, dogs and rats introduced by Europeans also feasted well on the defenceless parrot. Exploring parties made Kakapo the principal item of their diet and, later, when cruising tourists visited New Zealand from other continents, they shot and ate Kakapo which they found to be 'as good eating as a barnyard fowl'.

In a paper read to the Zoological Society of London in 1852, Dr David Lyall, surgeon on a survey ship which had sailed around New Zealand, had described the flesh as white and 'generally esteemed good eating'. After visiting Kakapo habitat in 1861–2, Sir James Hector had written: 'The Kakapo is esteemed a great delicacy by the natives; but its flesh has a strong, slightly stringent flavour.' These totally herbivorous birds are very fat.

At an unenlightened period when many birds were killed by commercial collectors to be mounted for the museums of the world, as well as for decorative purposes, this species was relentlessly sought as a curiosity. To this day, most major museums throughout the world have numerous specimens. Porter (1934) mentioned that the market was so flooded with skins that they were worth only 7s 6d (37p) each and that, years previously, when Kakapo were plentiful, they were even fed to dogs for meat.

During the first half of this century the decline of the Kakapo or any other species attracted little attention; conservation was not yet fashionable. Then in 1952 the New Zealand Department of Internal Affairs appealed in the journal *Notornis* for assistance in locating Kakapo, the aim being to take steps to conserve it. Between 1958 and the mid-1970s the Wildlife Service made regular expeditions into the Fiordland and north-western Nelson regions in search of the now elusive parrots. Over 60 such expeditions were made to the Milford catchment, where the rugged terrain and high rainfall made field work difficult. Until 1974, when the use of helicopters made extensive searches possible, only eight birds were located and little progress was made in the understanding of the Kakapo's habits. Nevertheless, the earlier expeditions did reveal the rapid retreat of the remnant population between 1960 and 1970.

The highly specialised courtship of the males was studied during the mid-1970s. The first recordings* were made of the booming of the male, which must surely be the strangest sound produced by any parrot. This deep, resonant booming has been described as resembling the noise produced by blowing across the top of a large bottle, also as sounding like distant thunder.

The call was produced in sequences of 20 to 50 booms of approximately half a second duration, repeated at about two-second intervals. Initially, three to five low grunts on a descending scale were given; up to 30 more followed at a slower tempo and increased volume. At the initial stage of booming the thoracic and belly areas are grossly inflated; it is believed that the inflated air sacs enable the bird to produce the resonant bass sound with which he hopes to attract a female. The bird recorded averaged more than 1,000 booms per hour and continued for six to seven successive hours per night. There can be few more extraordinary vocal accomplishments in the entire avian world.

Merton (1975) described the track and bowl system which is part of the male's strategy to attract a mate. Three bowls had been freshly dug or cleaned out and were linked by obvious tracks up to 1 m wide (3 ft) and

20 m (66 ft) or more in length through the scrub and tussock. Bowls are excavated and meticulously maintained by the male. They are often situated against some form of natural reflecting surface which must aid the projection of the low-volume booming call. Although not loud, booming can normally be heard for at least 1 km (0.6 miles) and, under ideal conditions, it has been heard 5 km (3 miles) from the bird.

Booming does not occur every year, but it is invariably produced during the summer months, not having been recorded prior to 26 November or later than the end of March. It is always carried out in or near the bowl. Each bird's bowl system is part of a loose group of such systems on some vantage point in a locality traditionally used as a display ground.

Booming occurs only in years during which Kakapo breed. The erratic booming/breeding cycle is regulated by seasonal and periodic fluctuations in availability and quality of food resources.

Perhaps the first person to record details of the nesting behaviour of the Kakapo over a number of years was Richard Henry, caretaker of Resolution Island. He noted that no male was ever seen near the nest and that the female 'tramps away and carries home food so industriously that she is all draggled and worn' (Henry, 1895). He found several nests, each containing two young. By May the young were balls of fat but the mother was in poor condition. The food supply was by then nearly depleted and Henry thought that many young would die before they learned to forage for themselves.

As the male plays no part in rearing the young, they are left unattended for long periods at night while the female is feeding. After the first few weeks of the approximately ten weeks' nesting period, the female visits the nest only once or twice each night to feed the chicks. Nesting occurs in the late summer and autumn when predatory mammal populations are at a peak; young fledge in May and June (winter) when many carnivores have difficulty in finding food. Young Kakapo stay on the ground, are vocal by day and by night and have a loud call which would certainly attract predators. Taking all these factors into account, plus the fact that the small eggs are easily predated by rats, the wonder is that any young survive to leave the nest.

The adults are also exceptionally vulnerable to predation, because of their unique combination of peculiarities. Their flightlessness renders them almost defenceless and, when confronted by an enemy, they will neither attack nor defend themselves, nor retreat. Their only defence — an inadequate one, despite the cryptic coloration — is to freeze. Their strong scent and tendency to use tracks makes them even easier prey than most flightless birds, as does the lek mating system and unique nesting behaviour.

---

*Kakapo booming is recorded on cassettes VPS429C *Children of Tane* (New Zealand Birds of the Forest) and VPS445C (Birds of New Zealand), and on CD, VPS445CD; available from Viking Sevenseas NZ Ltd, P.O. Box 152, Paraparaumu, New Zealand.

The Kakapo was perfectly adapted for life in pre-historic New Zealand, but its very slow reproductive potential, coupled with the factors already described, do not equip it for survival in the modern world. It is apparently the world's only surviving land bird which is flightless and ground-nesting with altricial young (helpless on hatching). It would almost certainly have been extinct, or effectively extinct (only males surviving) had not a programme of relocation been embarked upon by the New Zealand Department of Conservation (formerly the New Zealand Wildlife Service).

Relocation is a policy with which it has had outstanding success in the conservation of other critically endangered birds. Of 50 transfers to off-shore or outlying islands involving 16 bird species or sub-species, 29 were successful. Of the 15 which failed, at least six did so because too few birds were released and at least four because mammalian carnivores were present or reached the island soon after.

Relocation is not a new idea. During the last years of the nineteenth century, it was practised by Richard Henry, who appears to have fought a lonely battle to conserve the Kakapo long before the word conservation had been coined as a popular term. He trapped between 300 and 400 Kakapo, as well as other flightless birds, with a muzzled dog, and transported them to various islands. Over 700 birds, mainly Kiwi and Kakapo, were relocated on Resolution Island in Dusky Sound. In 1900 his dream of an island sanctuary ended abruptly when a stoat was observed. The Kakapo population declined and transfers ceased.

Henry's attempts did not. In 1904 he captured six birds to send to the bird sanctuary already established on Little Barrier Island. As long ago as 1886 the far-seeing ornithologist Reischek had described Little Barrier as a possible reserve.

Translocation (or marooning, as it is also called) has been tried with various bird species in New Zealand, where there are a few islands in a near pristine state or free from the more efficient introduced diurnal predators. This technique has the advantage that the species remains feral and, after the successful translocation, there are fewer demands on money and manpower than with other methods. There is also the opportunity to establish a population large enough not only to avoid potential genetic and other mishaps, but also to act as a source of birds for other conservation efforts (Williams, 1983).

Merton urged that the Weka and possum eradication programme on another island, Codfish (1480 ha; 3,660 acres), should be greatly intensified in order to prepare it for Kakapo in the shortest possible time. By September 1983 over 3,000 Wekas had been removed and none had been seen for many months. A programme aimed

Track used by Kakapo.

at exterminating the Australian brush-tailed possum (a competitor of the Kakapo for food and roosting sites) was also successful. Thus in late 1987 11 males and five females were transferred to Codfish.

In 1976 three birds, the first of nine, were transferred to Maud Island which was predator-free. In July 1983 three males and two females were still alive but in 1982 a stoat had reached the island. The four survivors, two males and two females, were transferred to Little Barrier Island, New Zealand's largest (3,000-ha; 7,400-acre) predator-free offshore island. Feral cats had been eradicated and the kiore, an introduced rat, was not present.

By the middle of 1985, the Kakapo population was believed to number about 50 birds, 12 of which were females. There were 12 males and nine females on Little Barrier, most of which had been transferred from Stewart Island; on Stewart there were 11 radio-tagged

A Kakapo nest on Stewart Island.

males and three radio-tagged females, plus an additional ten males which had been heard calling; in Fiordland, in the south-west of South Island, one radio-tagged male was known and in the Nelson region, in the north-west of South Island, booming had been heard.

In 1982 two nests (one containing one chick, the other two) were found — the first to be observed and photographed this century. Don Merton and others kept a close watch and were amazed at the energy and total dedication shown by the female. Every night, no matter how wet, cold and windy (and it is often all three on southern Stewart Island in winter), the female sets off on her short legs (the tarsus is only 6 cm [2.4 in] long) and trudges for 1 km (0.6 miles) or more. Up steep hills and through dense scrub, she never deviates until she reaches a rich source of food, such as a patch of berries. When she has eaten as much as she can carry, she turns round and goes straight back, having spent four to six hours feeding. The chicks are then fed by regurgitation. She repeats this twice nightly for at least two and a half months and, in the morning, retires nearby where she can keep an eye on the chicks while resting.

The three young found did not live to leave the nest; one was under two tussocks in semi-open scrub land and the other was under the roots of a small tree in stunted forest.

In his 'Recovery Plan' Merton (1982) described Stewart Island as 'a hazardous refuge for kakapo due to the presence of feral cats'. He stated that although local control of cats in the Kakapo area may be feasible, total eradication is not. In the summer of 1984/85, there were three females on Stewart Island, two of which, Nora and Alice, had hatched chicks in 1981. Nora laid three eggs (measuring about 50 × 38 mm; 2 × 1½ in) which were incubated for about four weeks. She left them once a night for two hours to feed, usually soon after sunset. Only one egg hatched, on February 23; sadly, by March 1 the chick had gone. Alice had laid four eggs by February 17; all were infertile. A video-camera was set up near the entrance to her nest, thus it was a suitable site to which to transfer one of Sue's two fertile eggs. The transfer was not a simple task; it took two hours, aided by a helicopter. Two nights later the chick had hatched; alas, six days later the chick had gone. Sue's remaining egg failed to hatch. However, a young Kakapo was found in June after fledging and near to death from starvation. It was taken into captivity but survived for only a short time.

There is no guarantee that cats can be controlled at a level which is sufficiently low to permit Kakapo to survive, let alone recover, on Stewart Island.

Adult mortality there, due to cat predation, was terrifyingly high: in the order of 50 per cent per annum. Thirty-five cats were trapped in or near the Kakapo area in the 18 months preceding October 1983, and an unknown number were poisoned. Despite these efforts, cat-killed Kakapo were still being found. The rate of predation was dramatically reduced, however, and only two Kakapo were known to have been killed in a year. Of the twenty males and eight females ringed, only about eight males and three females were known to survive in September 1983 (Merton, pers. comm.). Males boomed in the previous summer but neither of the two females fitted with transmitters nested.

Since slaughter by man has ceased, it has been replaced by predation by introduced mammals. By the 1930s man had caused its extinction on North Island, the last acceptable record being from the Huiarau Range in 1927. In addition to direct persecution, dogs, cats, stoats, rats and deer played their part in the decline of this defenceless parrot. Merton (1975) suggests that Polynesian rats (kiore) (*Rattus exulans*),

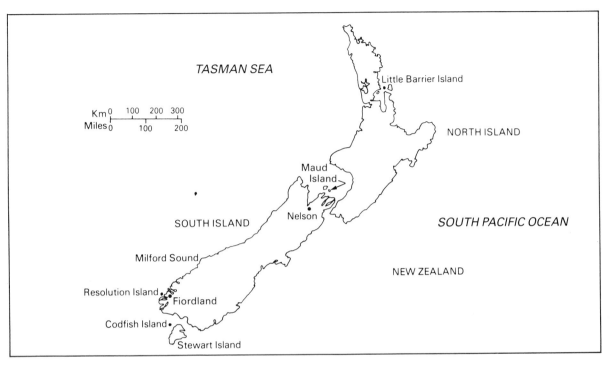

TASMAN SEA

Km
Miles

Little Barrier Island

NORTH ISLAND

Maud
Island

Nelson

SOUTH ISLAND

SOUTH PACIFIC OCEAN

Milford Sound

NEW ZEALAND

Resolution Island
Fiordland

Codfish Island

Stewart Island

introduced by Maoris within the last 1,000 years, may have been a factor in its slow decline from some areas in pre-European times. Others have speculated that by competing with Kakapo for the more succulent food plants, and by eliminating many more palatable species, deer may have caused the final extermination in some areas. There is strong circumstantial evidence to suggest that stoats were the major factor in its rapid decline late in the nineteenth century and during the early part of the twentieth century, according to Merton.

The Milford catchment of Fiordland was the Kakapo's last stronghold in the South Island because deer and chamois have yet to colonise much of the area, thus many vegetation communities survive unmodified. Likewise, brush-tailed possums, introduced from Australia and liberated at Milford early this century have only recently reached the more remote extremities. In New Zealand there are many millions more possums than human beings and they cause incalculable damage by destroying native vegetation. Polynesian rats, not otherwise recorded from the New Zealand mainland for many years, have been trapped in the Milford catchment since 1973.

No Kakapo have been seen outside New Zealand since the early years of the twentieth century. Between 1874 and 1907 London Zoo obtained four, whose average lifespan was 8.2 months. In New Zealand at

Kakapo are now found only on Little Barrier Island, Maud Island and Codfish Island.

that period, these parrots were occasionally kept as pets. Some captured birds were readily tamed (even eating out of the hand on the first day), whereas others apparently remained as fierce as wild cats. Richard Henry recorded that one bird ate little or nothing for the first three days of its captive existence, then consumed two apples and enough green rye grass to feed a goat. Blue peas, oats and gooseberries were other foods taken.

In 1885 it was recorded that one pet Kakapo was fond of the company of the owner's Irish retriever, and was often found asleep in its kennel. It would lie flat on its side with its legs stretched out, and its head under its body or tucked between its legs. A small female was obtained as a mate for the Kakapo and soon became tame; she could be picked up and stroked.

Small pellets of oatmeal were used by a lighthouse keeper named Hansen to rear a week-old Kakapo chick. This bird, with 'lovable characteristics', died at 18 months old. With one notable exception this would seem to represent the maximum survival period in captivity; this must be related to their nutrition, which is lacking in some respect.

Whereas many bird species kept during the early years of the century were short-lived due to inadequate understanding of dietary requirements, more recent attempts to keep Kakapo did not prove successful either. During 1960 to 1967 five were captured in Fiordland. They were kept in large enclosures at Mount Bruce Native Bird Reserve in the Wairarapa district. Each enclosure contained two substantial underground rock caves, 60 × 47 cm (24 × 18 in) to simulate the holes under boulders where Kakapo were thought, at that time, to spend the day under natural conditions. It has since been found that they normally roost above ground under tussock bushes or on low branches with heavy overhead cover. One of these birds died soon after capture, so another was caught. Four of the five, however, died within the first year. The fifth lived for four and a half years. All were males — old birds, and therefore less likely to adapt to captivity than young ones.

Partly because of the sad conclusion of this experiment, for many years the formation of a captive population did not feature in the conservation programme. Don Merton, however, was in favour of this concept. In an interview with Graeme Hyde, in *Australian Aviculture*, he stated (in 1991): 'A recent change of attitude now permits us to intervene in the nesting cycles and to manage the animal in the wild quite intensely. We have also launched into a captive breeding program. This is a major step forward because we wanted to apply aviculture to the kakapo for several years — and finally we've done it. We have had a facility completed recently which cost over $200,000 and we have appointed a most experienced aviculturist on a full-time basis — although at present (March 1991) he has only one bird to look after!

'We have also been working in tandem with the Auckland Zoo and the Avicultural Society of New Zealand developing expertise and techniques for hand-raising the kakapo. We've been working with the kaka and kea to gain experience and to refine our techniques. In the last few weeks we have been able to apply them to the kakapo' (Anon., 1992a).

There is one factor which favours the Kakapo's survival: it is an extremely adaptable bird which can tolerate a wide range of conditions, living in forest, scrub or grassland, from sea-level up to 1,200 m (4,000 ft), in steep or flat country, with high or low rainfall, in subantarctic or subtropical climate. Then there is one factor which weighs heavily against it: it is a K strategist (that is, its level of breeding potential and recruitment is too low to compensate for even a moderate predation rate).

A six-year Kakapo Recovery Programme, costing more than A$2 million, commenced in 1989, as a result of co-operation between the Department of Conserva-tion and the aluminium-maker Comalco. In 1991 600 schools took part in the aluminium recycling 'Canplan' to raise money for this programme. Also in 1989, the importance of supplementary feeding was demonstrated. This means that, instead of breeding every four or five years, Kakapo can be manipulated to breed annually. The 13 males and nine females which had been transferred to Little Barrier Island in 1982 had made no attempt to breed by 1989. Two females attempted to breed in early 1990, a few months after supplementary feeding commenced, but no young survived. In 1991 four females produced eight eggs. Two males were reared — the first young known to survive since 1981.

In 1992 more than 20 track and bowl systems were found on Codfish Island, indicating that most, if not all, of the 20 males released since 1987 had survived. The first sustained booming was heard and at least 11 eggs were laid in four nests. Six chicks hatched — the first to hatch without supplementary feeding since the recovery programme began. However, in March, when the first chicks hatched, Codfish was lashed by gales; the rimu nuts did not ripen. By April, females had to spend more than four hours away from the nest searching for food, and the chicks were starving. Two chicks and two eggs were taken by kiore (Polynesian rats) and, in another nest, one chick was found dead. The other two were in a serious condition, one of them almost on the point of death, after the long struggle to remove them from the almost inaccessible nest. Their mother weighed only 850 g (30 oz) — the lowest weight ever recorded for a female. Supplementary feeding started at once. These two chicks, and later on another, were transferred to Auckland Zoo. All three were desperately needed females. Sadly only one survived. She was called 'Hoki'. At the age of three months, and weighing 1.3 kg (3¾ lb), she was flown to Maud Island. This island will become the centre for captive management.

In September 1993 the known Kakapo population was as follows.

Location	Males	Females
Little Barrier Island	11	6
Codfish Island	c.17	8
Maud Island	3	3
Total	c.31	17

In September 1993 I had the privilege of visiting Maud Island with Don Merton and his wife. It was the highlight of a lifetime's involvement with parrots, for in my wildest dreams I never expected to see a live Kakapo. On two consecutive nights, I visited 'Hoki' in her large enclosure. Inquisitive and playful, she came right up to me and stood on my shoe! The second night was moonlit. I could observe her for an hour, seeing her behave as Kakapo have done for millennia, moving about, often on the run, and feeding on grasses. Hoki is already providing new insights into the behaviour of her species, being the only existing Kakapo which can be readily observed.

A number of extraordinarily dedicated people have devoted years of their lives to working for the Kakapo's survival, yet the disappointments and set-backs have been numerous. For many reasons, but especially the terrain inhabited by this unique parrot, the difficulties have been legion. In 1980 26 female Kakapo were known, only 16 of which are alive today. Since 1981 19 chicks have hatched, only five of which survived to independence. Yet, at last, there is significant progress. The two main populations, on Little Barrier and Codfish, have commenced to breed and, most importantly, can be manipulated to breed annually, instead of perhaps every four or five years. The reasons for lack of nesting success are now well understood and, because the females can be located, the problems can be corrected.

The stage is set for a significant increase in the Kakapo population, which, it is hoped, will signal the start of many productive years for the Kakapo. The name of Hoki, the first captive-reared chick, means 'to return'. Hoki symbolises the hope that this wonderfully endearing species, so unlike any other that ever existed, is indeed returning from the brink of extinction.

17

Parrots of the Pacific Region

The fate of tropical forests will be the major factor that determines the biological wealth of Earth in the future. Those extraordinarily vulnerable ecosystems are the greatest single reservoir of biotic diversification on the planet. A reasonable assumption is that about two-thirds of the species of the tropics occur in the rainforests. If this is correct, then something in the order of two-fifths to one half of all species on Earth occur in the rain-forests, which occupy only 6 per cent of Earth's land surface. These crucial reservoirs remain largely uncatalogued: only about 15 per cent of their species have ever been named, and very little is known about their biology.

PAUL AND ANNE ERHLICH, IN *EXTINCTION* (1982)

A feature of the avifauna of the South Pacific is that on its small islands and island groups occur many species which are endemic to one or a few islands. Because of their restricted distribution in small isolated areas, they are particularly vulnerable to extinction. Indeed, 90 species and sub-species of the South Pacific (excluding Hawaii and the Galapagos Islands) are listed in the ICBP *Red Data Book*; that is, over 20 per cent of all its entries are found on a tiny fraction of the world's landmasses.

It was for this reason that in 1983 the International Council for Bird Preservation selected the region for one of its nine principal conservation themes. An inventory was compiled detailing bird conservation problems on South Pacific Islands in relation to species, habitats and general conservation issues. Such information is essential before embarking on specific field projects.

Three *Cyanoramphus* feature in The *Red Data Book*; of these, only one is accorded specific status. When the data sheet was compiled for the Orange-fronted Parrakeet (*C. malherbi*) in 1977, the entry contained the words: 'This parrakeet has been reported only six times this century, most recently in 1965.' In 1982 a nest was located; the female was captured and her three eggs were taken. All hatched. The young were paired with Yellow-fronted Parrakeets (*C. auriceps*). The resulting progeny plus chromosome analysis suggests that the 'Orange-fronted Parrakeet' from New Zealand was merely a mutation of the Yellow-fronted!

The Yellow-fronted Parrakeet has only two races: the nominate from North and South Islands, the Stewart and Auckland groups and various offshore islands, and *C.a. forbesi*. The range of the latter is minute: 6 ha (15 acres) of forest on Little Mangere Island in the Chatham group, 800 km (500 miles) east of New Zealand. It is a distinctive bird, being larger and brighter than the nominate race; the underparts are a yellower shade of green and the sides of the face a brighter, more emerald, green. The crimson frontal band does not extend as far as the eyes.

This race was formerly found on the larger (112-ha; 275-acre) Mangere Island (now deforested) but was extinct there when a 1937 estimate arrived at the figure

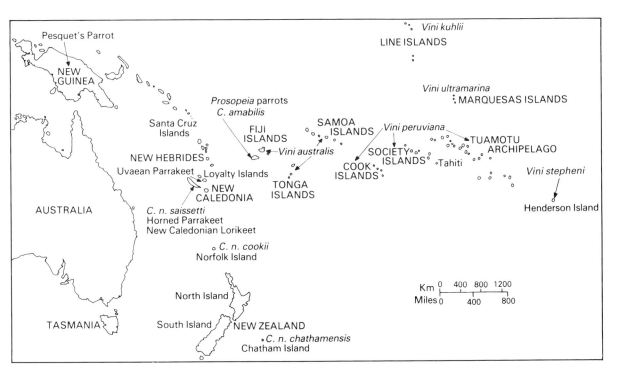

Parrots of the Pacific region.

of over 100 on Little Mangere. Subsequent censuses in 1968 and 1973 suggested that this figure was over-optimistic, since an insidious threat to its existence was discovered. The Chatham Island Red-fronted Parra-keet (*C. novaezelandiae chathamensis*) hybridised with it; then there were reports that a pair of hybrids had displaced a pair of Forbes' Parrakeets. The hybrids were fertile and breeding among themselves. They were therefore eliminated, leaving 16 pure-bred birds. Six of these were taken to the aviaries at Mount Bruce Wildlife Reserve at Masterton, where they have bred (Phipps, 1981).

More recently, a management programme has resulted in a gradual population increase, to an estimated 100 birds. On Pitt and Mangere Islands this parrakeet disappeared as a result of deforestation; it prefers dense unbroken forest or scrub, of which only a 4-ha (10-acre) patch survived at the summit of Little Mangere. This was disturbed by helicopter landings and the parrakeet was on the brink of extinction. Fortunately, wildlife authorities carried out extensive planting on Mangere and there was some natural regeneration of bushland, making it possible for the parrakeet to recolonise the island. It has been suggested that when the numbers of Forbes' Parrakeet increase further, hybridisation will no longer occur. Removal of hybrids and attempts to improve the habitat will continue. The future of this sub-species looks much more optimistic than was the case a decade ago. Once again, intensive management at the twelfth hour averted the extinction of an island race.

It should be pointed out that members of the genus *Cyanoramphus* have a great potential for captive reproduction; the Red-fronted Kakariki, of which the Norfolk Island bird is a sub-species, has proved to be perhaps the most prolific parrot ever kept in captivity, not excluding the Budgerigar. A 1958 census indicated that there were 103 Red-fronted Kakarikis in collec-tions in New Zealand. The numbers were low because a few years previously it had been an offence to keep any native bird in captivity. When its numbers in the wild were known to be declining, permits were issues to allow the keeping of this parrakeet. Six years later there was a staggering captive population of 2,500 Red-frondeds. This species has proved itself supremely suit-able for captive propagation and was soon established in aviaries throughout the world. As an example of its prolificacy, a pair owned by a British breeder known to me hatched and reared 33 young in a period of 12 months. One was killed by the male parent and another in an accident; the rest reached maturity.

Confined to a small island 744 km (460 miles) west of

the northernmost coast of New Zealand, or 1,676 km (1,000 miles) east of Sydney, is another sub-species whose plight is equally desperate. This is the Norfolk Island race (*C.n. cookii*). It differs from the nominate race in its larger size (31 cm [12 in] overall), more robust bill, more extensive crimson on the forehead and crown and darker green coloration. The wonder is that it has survived at all. Its troubles started soon after the island was discovered by Captain Cook in 1774. Settlement commenced in the next decade when a penal station was established but abandoned in 1813. During the period 1825–56 a second penal colony (for the very worst types of offenders) had disastrous consequences for the island fauna. When food supplies failed to materialise, birds were killed for food (Forshaw, 1981). (*See* Plate 21.) They were so common that convicts used sticks to drive them from ripening corn. By 1911 most of the forest had gone. Now the only extensive area of forest is the 465 ha (1,100 acres) in the north, surrounding Mount Pitt. This is about 13 per cent of the island, which extends over 3,500 ha (8,600 acres). In 1981 ICBP proposed that a national park should be created there. This happened in 1986.

The final factor which threatened the existence of this parrakeet was intense cultivation, aided by the rich volcanic soil. Porter recorded of the island: 'It is of comparatively small size, only a few miles in extent, and is now quite thickly populated, there being over a thousand inhabitants. The advent of such a large population has only been during these last few years when, owing to the island being the nearest place to New Zealand where bananas can be grown successfully, there had been a great boom in land prices . . . . Now instead of resembling a typical South Sea Island, it resembles a huge allotment garden where almost every acre is under cultivation. From this it will be seen that there is not much hope for the survival of this interesting Parrakeet.'

At the time of which Porter was writing, the introduction of rats and non-indigenous plants and birds had sounded the death knell for a number of native birds, including a large and fascinating parrot, the Norfolk Island Kaka (*Nestor productus*).

Somehow the parrakeet has survived to this day, mainly in small pockets of native vegetation, although it is known to feed on introduced trees, notably the seeds of the wild olive (*Olea africana*). There now remain two major threats to the existence of the 'Green Parrot', as it is known locally. One of these is the Crimson Rosella (*Platycercus elegans*), or Pennant's Parrakeet, which was introduced from Australia and was established by 1848. It competes with the native parrakeet for food and nesting sites; rosellas are, by nature, aggressive, unlike the more amicable *Cyanoramphus* species. Left to themselves, it would only be a

matter of time before the former ousted the latter. To make matters worse, in 1976 it was discovered that an infectious disease (probably psittacine beak and feather disease, which occurs in a number of Australian parrots in the wild, including the Orange-bellied) rendering permanent damage to the plumage, was rife among the rosella population. In 1977 a Norfolk Island Parrakeet apparently suffering from the same disease was reported (Forshaw, 1981).

'Green Parrots' were said to be still 'reasonably common' in the 1950s. Surveys carried out in 1977/78 and 1981/82 indicated that the population had declined to fewer than 30 birds. It has been suggested that the arrival of the Black Rat (*Rattus rattus*) in the late 1940s, was at least partly responsible for the rapid decline. The parrots had co-existed with the smaller Polynesian Rat (*R. exulans*) for more than 700 years, but the Black Rat spelt danger because it is a more adept tree climber and a more aggressive predator.

A rescue attempt commenced in 1983. The Norfolk Island Government enlisted the help of the Australian National Parks and Wildlife service. The first objective was to set up a captive breeding programme. There was strong community support and the Lion's Club assisted with the construction of an aviary. To date, breeding success has not been great but the captive population now stands at 13. When several chicks are hatched (usually only one or two are reared in the wild), the smaller ones are removed and hand-reared. In one unusual nest where six young hatched, only three survived. Thus the captive population can be increased without expending the wild population.

One pair, which had been caught as adults, did not breed in the aviary. After three years they were released and the female returned to her previous nest site. Over a period of eight months she produced four clutches which resulted in three young fledging. One of the difficulties of aviary breeding was the reluctance of females to accept the offered male, even when this was a wild bird which had courted her through the wire and been trapped in the hope that a successful breeding pair would result.

In December 1988 the estimated minimum wild population was 32 birds (aviary population six). By March 1989 there was a minimum of 28 wild birds and ten in the aviary. Fifteen young fledged from the eight known breeding attempts in 1987/88 and 21 from the 14 attempts monitored in 1988/89 (Hicks and Greenwood, 1989). By 1992 the wild population was believed to number about 40 birds.

Now a new concept is being considered, borrowed from some of New Zealand's conservation success stories. Located 6 km (4 miles) south of Norfolk Island is the small Philip Island, which harbours no predatory rats and cats. Its once lush forests were nearly destroyed by grazing animals and rabbits. The last rabbits were removed in 1988 and the 190-ha (470-acre) island may become a refuge to the Norfolk Island Parrakeet. Then every option will be in play and its future will look immeasurably brighter than it did a decade previously, even though the increase in its numbers has not yet been dramatic.

Fiji, an independent dominion within the British Commonwealth consists of nearly 500 islands. Two of these, Viti Levu (10,386 km^2; 4,010 sq. miles) and Vanua Levu (5,535 km^2; 2,137 sq. miles) together constitute 86 per cent of the land mass. These islands still retain areas of rainforest, deeply dissected by streams, whereas the small islands were denuded many years ago; modification of the natural forest started long before Europeans arrived. In 1983 approximately 8,200 km^2 (3,170 sq. miles) of rainforest survived. About 28 per cent of all forest had been logged out. Since then further deforestation has occurred and there has been extensive planting of pine and other exotic trees. In *Birds of Fiji, Tonga and Samoa*, published in 1982, Dick Watling wrote: '. . . the major threat to the region's avifauna comes from habitat destruction through deforestation. This threat, hitherto unimportant, is now real and pressing, unchecked with regard to the region's wildlife. With only one or two exceptions the endemic land birds of the region are forest species; the majority are totally unable to adapt to open or man-made environments.'

In 1993 I spent three days on Viti Levu, which holds 70 per cent of Fiji's population. I was unprepared for the extent of the deforestation I saw there, apparently with no attempt to regenerate original forest. Vast barren areas could have been replanted. Other areas contained extensive plantations of pine, in which native birds cannot exist. Introduced species of birds, such as Common and Jungle Mynahs (*Acridotheres tristis* and *A. fuscus*) and the tiny Avadavats (*Amandava amandava*) from India were common. Java Sparrows (*Padda oryzivora*) can be seen in rice-growing areas!

Viti Levu measures 146 × 106 km (90 × 66 miles) and, in 1993, had a human population (expanding at the rate of 2 per cent per annum) of more than 0.5 million. It also has one endemic species of parrot — a forest-dweller. This is the Musk Parrot or Yellow-breasted Parrot (*Prosopeia personata*). A strikingly handsome bird, it is mainly green with a black mask and yellow on the underparts. Its total length, including the long, broad tail, is about 47 cm (18 in).

Dick Watling (*in litt.*, 1983) told me that the Musk Parrot was common and in no danger of extinction. But he also stated that it required mature forest for breeding purposes. In *Birds of the Fiji Bush*, published in 1984, Fergus Clunie stated that this parrot is 'common in forest and thick secondary growth'. But a great decline of a forest-dwelling species can occur in a decade when its habitat is ravaged.

I visited the forest reserve in Colo-i-Suva, reputed to be one of the most likely places to see the Musk Parrot. A forest ranger who had worked there for 20 years told me that he regularly saw one or two fly over, rarely up to five or six. They were not common there. I spent two or three hours walking in the forest. There were no large trees! I later discovered that it had been selectively logged in the 1950s and replanted with mahogany. A major problem for the Musk Parrot may now be lack of nesting sites. In *Ecologist* (January/February 1980) it was stated of Fiji: 'Extensive forestry operations are proceeding on the main forested islands and all useful timber with diameter in excess of 33 cm is being extracted.'

My fear for this parrot is that there will be a sudden crash in the population due to lack of recruitment, i.e. death of aged birds which have not bred for years. A study that includes breeding success rate and nest-site availability (not easy to carry out) is surely urgently needed. Unless Viti Levu's forests are preserved and replanted, Fiji will lose one of its most beautiful inhabitants. I did encounter one pair (outside the reserve) — a sighting which will long remain in my memory — the slow, flapping flight, the long-tailed silhouette and the harsh, grating call. An effort must be made to preserve this magnificent bird.

In Chapter 1 of this book the disastrous effects which a logging policy had had on the Thick-billed Parrot were described. In Mexico, the large pines, those whose girth exceeds 40–50 cm (15-20 in), are selectively cut. The resulting loss of nesting sites has been the major factor in the decline of the Thick-bill. A similar situation could arise on Viti Levu.

The Red-breasted Musk Parrot (*P. tabuensis*) is at risk for the same reasons. (*See* Plate 17.) Watling in 1983 reported that 'Kadavu was logged out three to four years ago, yet the parrots are doing well there'. It might be a little early to take a complacent attitude.

This species has a larger range than *P. personata*, and this was extended by human introduction in the eighteenth century. Of the five races, *P.t. splendens* is the most distinctive for it has the head and underparts scarlet; it is found on Kadavu and has been introduced to Viti Levu. The other races, found on Vanua Levu, Taveuni, Qamea, Koro, Gau and in Tonga, have the underparts maroon. Watling (1982) describes it as 'a common and conspicuous species, often aggregating into small noisy parties at favoured feeding sites'.

In years gone by, these birds suffered as a consequence of their beautiful plumage. They were sold to Tongans, or to Samoan residents and traders who plucked their red feathers to decorate mats and to make into leis. The extent of this trade, however, is

On Viti Levu, deforestation threatens the survival of the forest-dwelling Yellow-breasted Musk Parrot.

unlikely to have been great. It was prohibited by the colonial government, as was shooting of all birds, except pigeons during an open season.

Ever extreme rarities in aviculture, the few specimens currently held outside Fiji are not sufficient to establish these birds. There are a few pairs of the Red Shining Parrot but, to my knowledge, only one pair of Masked, which have been together at San Diego Zoo since 1991. The former has been reared occasionally, but not consistently, in at least three collections in the USA. It has not proved easy to breed, merely maintaining its numbers. The same is true of the very few pairs in the UK.

In complete contrast to the large, showy Musk Parrots is the Red-throated Lorikeet (*Charmosyna amabilis*). A tiny, slim, nectar-feeding parrot with a long tail, it is mainly green but for the red cheeks and red throat bordered with yellow. The underside of the tail and the tip is also yellow. This endemic species is found only in mature forest, on Vitu Levu and Taveuni and perhaps also on Ovalau. Wood (Wood and Wetmore, 1926) suggested that it may be extinct there, but a small green bird which inhabits the outer canopy of mountain forest is difficult to locate. For this reason it is impossible to assess its numbers, which have been

tentatively estimated at fewer than 10,000 (ICBP Parrot Action Plan). It seems that it always has been rare; but this species, of all Fiji's parrots, is the most threatened by forest destruction as it alone is confined to mature forest. It is, however, found on Taveuni, where the largest reserve is located; this is the 4,000-ha (9,930-acre) Ravilevu Reserve. In Fiji there are only seven reserves with a total area of only 5,700 ha (14,000 acres). Reserves are difficult to set up because nearly all land is owned by Fijians. Another problem is that conservation or protection forest can be logged at the whim of the Forestry Department (Watling, pers. comm.). On the credit side is the fact that, as yet, there has been no clear felling for government schemes, only for private agriculture.

Much more common and conspicuous is the Blue-crowned Lory, which is also found in Tonga and Samoa. According to Watling (1982), it has ceased to occur on several islands in Tonga and its numbers appear to be decreasing. Nevertheless, it is still common throughout much of its range and, further-more, is found in any habitat where there are flowering trees.

All five species of *Vini* lories are classified as vulnerable or endangered. Two, the Tahiti Blue (*V. peruviana*) and the Ultramarine (*V. ultramarina*) are remarkable for their fascinating behaviour and beauti-ful plumage. The Blue-crowned is bright green, with the cheeks and throat red, also a red and blue patch on the abdomen; the crown is blue, with the unusual shaft-streaked feathers typical of the genus.

According to the Parrot Action Plan: 'The Tahitian Lory has disappeared from most islands within its large range, mainly due to nest predation by Roof Rats . . . . The most promising conservation measure to be taken will be the eradication of these rats from islands in the vicinity of other islands still holding remnant popula-tions of the lory.'

To this end, the Brehm Fund for International Bird Conservation was planning to send two expeditions to the Tuamotu Islands in 1993. They will aim to determine the distribution of the Tahiti Blue Lory and the three species of rats (*Rattus rattus*, *R. norvegicus* and *R. exulans*) and to identify atolls where rat eradication is feasible. If this can be done, lories can be moved to rat-free islands. This Lory is rare; it has been extirpated from most of its former range, including Tahiti and all the larger Society Islands. It was apparently introduced by Polynesians to Aitutaki, Cook Islands, where it is fairly plentiful. The island, however, is only 18 km^2 (7 sq. miles) in extent. In the Society Islands it survives on Scilly and Bellingshausen, on Rangiroa and apparently on other Tuamotu atolls. Population figures given a decade ago by Bruner (1972) were 100 to 200 on Rangiroa which covers 43 km^2 (17 sq. miles) and 350 to 400 pairs on Scilly (350 ha; 860 acres) with possibly a like number on the smaller Bellingshausen which had, then, never been visited by an ornithologist. Its existence there had been con-firmed by the identification of captive birds taken from the island.

According to Dieter Rinke (*in litt.*, 1986) it then occurred on Tikehau, Niau, Ahe and Apataki in the Tuamotus and on the isolated islands of Motu One and Fenua Ura in the Society Islands. Rinke suggested that these islands should be established as reserves. In April 1989 a team of biologists from Wales visited Apataki. They found a 'good population' there, but also evi-dence of a decline.

Its disappearance from Tahiti and Moorea (at the turn of the century) and Bora Bora in the 1920s occurred shortly after the introduction of a harrier (*Circus aeruginosus*) which may have preyed on this lory.

The Ultramarine Lory has one of the most intricate

Immature hand-reared Tahiti Blue Lory.

and beautiful colour schemes of any parrot in existence. Forehead and upper parts are deep sky blue; the crown is mauve, shaft-steaked with pale blue and the lores and part of the cheeks are white. The remainder of the face and upper breast are mauve. Rump and upper tail coverts are bright sky blue and the tail is pale blue tipped with white. The abdomen is mauve and there is a white patch above the thighs. Bill, legs and iris are orange. Length is 18 cm (7 in), slightly larger than the Tahiti Blue Lory.

The Ultramarine is endemic to the Marquesas Islands, north of the Tuamotu and Society groups. There has been a dramatic deterioration in its status, compared with that known when the first edition of this book was published. It then survived on only three islands. On Ua Pou, an island of 104 km^2 (40 sq. miles), it was widely distributed in about a dozen valleys. In 1975, its population there was estimated as 300 ± 50 pairs. On Nuku Hiva, which extends over 337 km^2, the population was said to be about 70 individuals, thinly spread in high valleys and ridges at the north-western end. Ua Huka (78 km^2 or 30 sq. miles) was said to support 225 ± 25 pairs. It is generally found in montane forest at altitudes of 700 to 1,000 m (2,300 to 3,300 ft). Bearing in mind its small size and preferred habitat, it must be difficult to obtain accurate census figures.

However, in November 1991, an expedition spon-sored by the Office of the Environment (FP) and the Zoological Society of San Diego found no Ultramarine Lories on Nuka Hiva or Ua Pou. According to ICBP's Parrot Action Plan, five years after the arrival of rats on Ua Pou the lorikeets had almost disappeared. By the end of the 1980s Roof Rats had been seen on Ua

Huka. The expedition of 1991 found there a population estimated at between 1,000 and 1,500. According to Kuehler and Lieberman (1992): 'Although this population is fiercely protected by the Ua Hukan islanders, its future is of much concern due to the prospect of the construction of a wharf to be built in 1993. Such development will allow the docking of large cargo ships which will lead to the potential invasion of exotic rat species and further anthropogenic activities, i.e. industry, agriculture and urban development. Such factors, in addition to cats, a large goat population, possible presence of avian malaria and the introduction of the common mynah and great horned owl have led to the extinction of the ultramarine lory on all of the other islands.'

Fearing the rapid decline of the only surviving population, the Parrot Action Plan committee made the recommendation to translocate birds to Fatu Hiva. Translocation had been suggested before but Fatu Hiva is the only island with habitat suitable for this species. The uninhabited island of Mohotani would be more suitable in the long term but sheep would have to be removed first, to allow the vegetation to regenerate, and feral cats would have to be eliminated.

In August 1992, personnel from San Diego Zoo and the local Office of the Environment spent ten days mist-netting Ultramarine Lories. Hampered by unseasonal rains caused by Hurricane Omar, it was possible to capture only seven birds. They were kept for six days before being transferred by boat to Fatu Hiva. Local inhabitants saw the birds while still in their holding cages and learned about the translocation programme. The lories were released in a foot-hill valley above Omoa, an area rich in food plants, especially coconut and banana. Released at first light, they began to feed on coconut flowers within minutes. Within an hour, their foraging took them high into the hills.

It is planned that an employee of the Rural Economy Service will make field observations and collect information of sightings by island residents. The translocation will continue on an annual basis in the hope of providing enough founder birds to establish the Ultramarine on Fatu Hiva. In November 1993, seven more were translocated. It was reported that five birds from the first group were seen regularly. On this the most southerly of the Marquesan islands, there are no introduced avian competitors or predators and control of the goat population has allowed it to maintain good primary and secondary forest cover. In addition to banana and coconut palms, there are several species on which this lory is known to feed.

Further steps to conserve this exquisite little bird include a conservation education campaign on Fatu Hiva and the installation of rat-proof nest-boxes on Ua

Tahiti Blue Lories aged eight months.

Huka, to discover whether a population can survive on a rat-infested island. This lory has been protected by law since 1936 and, in French Polynesia, hunting of all birds was prohibited in 1967. Trapping has not been a threat to it, unless there is a local demand. It is unknown in aviculture, except for the few specimens in a collection in the USA and in the Duke of Bedford's collection in the decade from the mid-1930s. John Yealland, curator of the Duke of Bedford's birds, described the Ultramarine as being quite different in temperament from the Tahiti Blue Lory: more arboreal, better tempered, nervous and shy. A single Ultramarine was reared in 1939. This species may not have been kept in captivity outside the Marquesas until the late 1980s, when there was a single bird in France. Should captive breeding be part of the conservation measures taken? In my opinion the answer is that it should, provided that chicks or eggs can be taken with which to found such a population and that there are people experienced in rearing lories to rear the young and to manage the breeding programme. Captive-reared birds are likely to adapt better to captivity than wild-caught adults. However, they would have to be reared with their own species and not permitted to become imprinted on humans. A captive breeding programme in the hands of inexperienced people would be a waste of time, money and precious genetic material; that is my belief. If captive breeding is considered, those responsible should acknowledge that the birds should be placed with specialist breeders of lories.

Ownership of these birds would, of course, remain with the Marquesas Islands, unless captive breeding should prove so successful that the number needed as a captive nucleus was exceeded. I believe this would be unlikely and that this would not be one of the easier lories to rear.

Scarlet below and shades of green above, Kuhl's Lory (*Vini kuhlii*) is a little-known parrot, tiny (19 cm; 7½ in long) and very beautiful. Its natural range was Rimitara, possibly also Tubuai, in the Tubuai or Austral Islands (French Polynesia). It was introduced to Washington (now called Teraina) and Fanning (now Tabueran) Islands in the Line Group, Kiribati. These three islands (Rimitara, Teraina and Tabueran) still maintain small populations — a few hundred birds each. Rats, the bane of the Pacific isles, recently arrived on Rimitara. Unless rapid action is taken, Kuhl's Lory may soon be extinct throughout its original range. The Parrot Action Plan suggests three measures towards its conservation: the erection of rat-proof nest-boxes, to discover if they are acceptable; steps to prevent rats reaching Teraina and Tabueran; and the identification of other rat-proof islands in Micronesia which have small human populations.

Not too different in appearance from Kuhl's Lory, is Stephen's Lory (*Vini stepheni*) from Henderson Island in the Pitcairn Group. It is classified as endangered with a population estimated at between only 500 and 1,000. However, this is another little-known bird — on an island which belongs to Britain! It is also the most easterly island on which a lory occurs.

In this brief review of the *Vini* lories, one fact is very clear. Due to rat predation, their populations are susceptible to declines so rapid that unless their conservation is undertaken *now*, as a matter of extreme urgency, there will be no birds left to conserve — except the more widespread *V. australis* — in perhaps the space of the next decade. That would be a great and irreversible tragedy. In these circumstances, where rats are destroying entire populations in perhaps less than a decade, captive breeding could play an important part. Will the attempt be made? And will it be made in the right way? San Diego Zoo has kept and bred a small number of *V. peruviana* and *V. australis* but the numbers are too small to expect that either species can

be established from these groups. One can envisage the scenario where the numbers of one or more species declines at a terrifying speed to a population of double figures and there is a last-minute scramble to take the few survivors into captivity. I sincerely hope this never happens because by then a captive breeding programme would almost certainly be doomed to failure. Now is the time to plan such a strategy — if it is to be.

In the south-western Pacific, 1,150 km (715 miles) north-east of Sydney, Australia, lie the Loyalty Islands, a dependency of New Caledonia. One of these islands, Ouvea (in fact no more than an islet), has the distinction of being the only home of a parrakeet of special beauty. It and the nominate race found on New Caledonia are the world's only crested parrakeets. Known as the Horned Parrakeet, this species is placed in a genus of its own; however, it is very closely related to *Cyanoramphus* and fertile hybrids between the two genera have been produced.

The Uvaean sub-species has the doubtful distinction of having the smallest range of any parrot living. It is confined to an area of 4 or 5 km (2.5 or 3 miles) on an island only 15 km (9 miles) long (Quinque, 1980). In recent years, the mature, indigenous forest on which this bird relies has been greatly reduced, by felling and by fire. In 1939, when its range included most of Ouvea, its population was estimated at about 1,000 birds. Based on information provided by H. Bregulla, the 1974 estimate given in the *Red Data Book* was 200 at the most. After mentioning this estimate, Quinque (1982) wrote: 'The recent census that I followed with interest revealed that there are, happily, more than 500 pairs. Also, I had the opportunity to see that the nests were recorded and attributed to each family.'

That population estimate seemed very large for such a small area, perhaps indicating that birds displaced by destruction of their habitat were being forced into the isolated forest patches along the coast, thus creating impossible competition for food and nesting sites. However, nothing is known for sure because the delicate political situation on the island makes it impossible for ornithologists to work there. It has been suggested that the population is 'probably below 200'. Although it is legally protected, this counts for nothing if most of its habitat has gone.

Two attempts have been made in the past to establish this parrakeet on the island of Lifou; 100 birds were translocated in 1925 and 14 birds in 1963. The experiment was a total failure because the birds were able to fly the 60 km (37 miles) back to Ouvea!

For this bird, the most practical method of conservation will be captive breeding. As Quinque has pointed out (1982), its habitat will not, for many more years, be able to resist the pressure of human population and the destruction of nature which this entails.

Dr Quinque (1983) made the interesting observation that the Uvaean Parrakeet nests in cavities in coconut palms and that Horned Parrakeets sometimes breed in burrows in the ground.

The nominate form, the Horned Parrakeet (*Eunymphicus cornutus cornutus*) is found on New Caledonia, the largest island (excluding New Guinea) of Melanesia or Polynesia. It extends over 18,700 km^2 (7,200 sq. miles) — an area slightly smaller than Wales. Once found in all forested parts of the island, the parrakeet's habitat, like that of the Uvaean Parrakeet, has been much reduced. Nevertheless, the parrakeet is strictly protected. The people of New Caledonia are apparently sympathetic not only towards conservation of habitat but also towards captive breeding. Dr Quinque writes (1980): '. . . in New Caledonia the government and enlightened bird lovers have created a park at Noumea to save many species, including the Kagu and possibly *Eunymphicus*. These people, in advance of some others, have understood that captivity can contribute to the saving of species in danger. They have come up against fierce defenders of the wild who are opposed to any capturing for captivity. These people certainly had some grounds as long as the environment remained viable for wildlife, but the human population grows more quickly than that of other animals and we must not wait until it is too late to save a species as has so often been the case since the beginning of this century.'

The remarkable breeding successes achieved by Dr Quinque demonstrate quite clearly how successful captive breeding can be as a conservation tool, in the hands of a knowledgeable aviculturist. Due to his efforts, tremendous strides have been made towards establishing endangered birds which are endemic to New Caledonia, especially the unique Cloven-feathered Dove (*Drepanoptila holosericea*) and the Horned Parrakeet. At the time of writing, there were a very small number of Uvaean Parrakeets in Europe. They may be of great importance for the future of this highly endangered sub-species.

Of the 68 bird species found on New Caledonia, 16 are endemic. One of these is the tiny and mysterious lorikeet, the Diademed or New Caledonian Lorikeet (*Charmosyna diadema*). Known to science by only two specimens collected before 1860, one has been lost and the other, the type, is in the Paris Museum of Natural History. Both were females; the male has never been described. There were no reports of its existence since those quoted by Sarasin (1913) in the northern forests. Then Forshaw (1978) gave the exciting news of three unconfirmed sightings reported to Anthony Stokes who visited New Caledonia in December 1976 on behalf of the Australian Museum, Sydney. Forshaw wrote: 'When speaking to Stokes, the observers registered their concern about questionable practices being employed by trappers and collectors coming to New Caledonia in search of this species; apparently local residents are offered financial rewards for obtaining live or dead birds.

'When shown a coloured plate of *Charmosyna diadema*, a resident with an interest in local natural history told Stokes that he had seen one bird in low scrubland near Yaté Lake, in the south of the island, many years ago, maybe in the 1920s. He recalled that the bird was silent during the five minutes it was under observation.

'A senior forestry officer, familiar with local birds, told Stokes that his first record of this species was in 1953 or 1954, on the La Foa to Canala road, when a pair was seen flying from rainforest to open Melaleuca woodland, where they alighted in a low tree. All he could remember about their appearance was that they were predominantly greenish, with some yellow on the abdomen. This observer recorded the species again on 3rd June 1976, to the west of Mt Panie, also in the rainforest-Melaleuca ecotone, when his attention was attracted by a call differing slightly from that of the common Rainbow Lory (*Trichoglossus haematodus*), and on looking up, he saw two small green parrots dart quickly from a tree and fly overhead.'

As has already been mentioned, small forest-dwelling parrots may be overlooked for years. As there is no other parrot on New Caledonia that approached the small size of this lorikeet, it seems that *C. diadema* still survives. What a challenge to an ornithologist possessed of endless perseverence to discover more about the natural history of this enigmatic little bird!

New Caledonia has two other parrot species; neither is endemic. The race of the Green-naped or Rainbow Lorikeet, *Trichoglossus haematodus deplanchii*, is confined to that island and to the Loyalty group. It is nomadic and known to cross the sea between New Caledonia and Lifu and Ouvea in the Loyalty Islands (a distance which takes 15 minutes to fly in a small aircraft). Little is known of its status; possibly it can adapt to altered habitat better than the Horned Parrakeet, which relies on forest.

Finally, there is a sub-species of the Red-fronted Parrakeet or Kakariki, *Cyanoramphus novaezelandiae saissetti*. Within the past two decades there have been conflicting reports concerning its status. Further investigation is needed for this is not a species which is likely to be very tolerant to habitat disturbance.

New Guinea has one of the richest, most varied and fascinating avifaunas in the world. It has over 40 parrot species, being exceeded in this respect only by Australia and Brazil. Numerous as these parrot species are, only two groups, the lories (various species) and cockatoos (two species) are well known in aviculture. Some, such as the Fig Parrots, have been imported only in recent years, since the 1970s, and others such as the Pygmy Parrots (*Micropsitta* species) which also occur in Indonesia, and the *Psittacella* parrots, are totally unknown in aviculture. The Palm Cockatoo (*Probosciger aterrimus*) which is widely distributed in New Guinea and which is also found in northern Australia, is probably the only New Guinea parrot whose numbers have been threatened by trade. The species is now protected however, and its trade prohibited. This did not stop illegal export until Singapore became a signatory to CITES in 1986. Then there was no outlet for the illegally exported birds. At the time, it was a tragedy for the species because hundreds of Palm Cockatoos were held by Singapore bird dealers. Without CITES papers, they could not export them. Either they died or lived a miserable existence as apartment pets.

A New Guinea parrot which is threatened by local trade is the spectacular red and black Pesquet's Parrot (*Psittrichas fulgidus*). The only member of its genus, this huge bird, which has the head partially devoid of feathers, is totally unlike any other parrot. According to Jared Diamond (1972), its red feathers are prized by natives, far more than the plumage of any other bird, including any species of bird of paradise. He wrote: 'Even in a poor area like Karimui, a *Psittrichas* commanded the relatively enormous sum of twenty dollars, equal to the price of a large pig and not much less than the price of a wife. Despite this popularity I saw or heard of only three captive *Psittrichas* in the Karimui area, an indication of its rareness even in areas with sparse human population. This is one of the few montane species whose existence is threatened directly (i.e. as opposed to being threatened indirectly through destruction of habitat) by man.'

As far as it is known (which is saying little, for we know next to nothing about the status of many New Guinea birds), no parrots from Papua New Guinea are endangered. If this is indeed so, the reason is simply that the country has been opened up later than comparable areas. From the point of view of conservation, this is of great advantage because the Territory, by learning from the mistakes made in other parts of the world, can prevent the fatal destruction and pollution of the natural environment from which most highly developed countries already suffer.

To the naturalist, Papua New Guinea is undoubtedly one of the most fascinating places on earth and retains some of the most important wildernesses anywhere in the world. It has a remarkable variety of habitats: tropical rainforest, montane forests, savannah and open grasslands, freshwater marshes, tidal swamps and mangrove formations. Their preservation is of vital

Pesquet's Parrot is hunted by New Guinea natives for its red feathers.

importance. Economic development, especially the mining and timber industries, is expanding at an enormous rate, as is the human population; destruction of habitat and decline of many species is therefore inevitable. Already, forests of montane beech (*Nothofagus* species) and oak have been reduced to an alarming degree. As well as the local need for timber, there is enormous consumption by Japanese companies, and their demand is certain to increase even further.

As we have seen, the Pacific region contains some of the most interesting and unusual of all parrot species, such as the only blue lories, the only crested parrakeets and the spectacular Shining Parrots. All these endemic island forms exist in small numbers which make them vulnerable to dramatic population decreases. Consistent monitoring of the welfare of most species is unlikely, thus the sudden discovery that one or more is in serious jeopardy can be expected within the next few years.

Before it is too late, two steps should be taken which would assist their survival: 1) field work, which up to now has been sparse or non-existent; 2) inauguration of captive breeding programmes in designated collections which have been successful in breeding closely-related species. Experience in rearing other members of the genus in question must surely be very high on the list of priorities when selecting aviculturists or institutions to work with vulnerable and endangered species. A member or members of the same genus as every species mentioned in this chapter is being bred in captivity, therefore the necessary expertise already exists to safeguard the future, albeit in captivity, of the threatened parrots of the Pacific.

18

Indonesia: Too Late to the Rescue?

. . . at present rates, nearly all the lowland forests of the Philippines, peninsular Malaysia, Indonesia, and much of the rest of Southeast Asia will be gone by the turn of the century. This is an area of extraordinary interest to loggers because the dominant trees of the forest, dipterocarps, produce very light, high-quality lumber especially suitable for making veneers and plywood. It is also an area of extraordinarily great biological diversity. The magnitude of the loss of species in Southeast Asia will be far out of proportion to the size of the forest area that disappears.

PAUL AND ANNE ERHLICH, IN *EXTINCTION* (1982)

. . . the country comprises one of the most diverse sectors of the entire rain forest biome — each little island has been able to follow its own evolutionary track in moderate isolation from its neighbours, with the result that certain of the islands feature many endemic species. Hence we can fairly assume that many patches of Indonesian rain forest could well harbour more species than anywhere else on the planet, with the exception of the wettest part of Amazonia.

NORMAN MYERS (1983) OF INDONESIA

Indonesia is a country of astonishing statistics. The nation consists of an archipelago of 17,500 islands, stretching eastward for 5,000 km from Sumatra to Irian Jaya. Nine hundred and ninety of these islands are inhabited by people speaking over 250 languages.

Although occupying only 1.3 per cent of the earth's land surface, 17 per cent of the world's birds (1,532 species) occur in the Republic.

PAUL JEPSON, IN *WORLD BIRDWATCH* (1992)

Indonesia, in south-east Asia, is a 6,400-km (4,000-mile) stretch of islands, reputed to total 13,677, of which 992 are permanently settled (Dalton, 1978). Java is the most densely populated and contains 95 million of Indonesia's 150 million people. The native parrakeet (*Psittacula a. alexandri*) has survived, perhaps because it is able to feed in the paddy fields. Java was originally monsoon forest, dominated by teak and pine.

South-east Asia produces about three-quarters of all tropical hardwoods entering international trade, and Indonesia's output is greater than all other countries of the region combined. One of the most diverse nations of the tropics, two-fifths of Indonesia is still covered with rainforest; about one-fifth has already been destroyed (Myers, 1983). In 1980 it was estimated (*Ecologist*, January/February) that surviving forests did not extend to more than 100 million ha (250 million acres); the official estimate was 120 million ha (300 million acres) — the same figure given in the 1960s, since when large areas had been cleared. Log exports commenced to be significant in 1970 when the volume of 8 million m^3 (280 million cu. ft) was double that of the preceding year. By 1973 the figure was 18.7 million m^3 (660 million cu. ft). Revenue from timber export accounts for about 10 per cent of Indonesia's annual foreign exchange earnings.

In 1980 the rate of exploitation of Indonesian forests was given as 600,000 ha (1.5 million acres) per year in The *Ecologist*, which stated: 'Logging concessions "fill the maps of Sumatra and Kalimantan [the Indonesian part of Borneo] to saturation", concessions have been sold in the Celebes, which is now being logged, and in some outer islands; and West Irian is "in the process of being carved up" . . .'.

What does the future hold for the Indonesian part of New Guinea, West Irian? But for the inaccessibility of large areas, the answer might be: a similar fate to the rainforests of Amazonia. According to Inder (1978), although 75 per cent of the surface of Irian Jaya is covered with forest, only 100,000 ha (250,000 acres) of productive forest were being exploited. Estimates made at that time suggested that there could be a further 650,000 ha (1.6 million acres) of accessible productive forest not yet in use and, in those areas still inaccessible to transport, possibly a further 3.75 million ha (9.3 million acres) of productive forests.

In Papua New Guinea, which is not part of Indonesia but an independent state (a member of the British Commonwealth), it seems that the policy favours large timber companies who can utilise the total produce of forests (timber, wood chips and pulp) and who can create a permanent industry through reafforestation. By 1977, 14,850 ha (36,700 acres) of forest (two-thirds of it pine, which replaced natural pine) had been replanted.

In the first edition of this book I wrote: 'Little or no information is available concerning the status of parrots on most of the Indonesian islands; an important area, rich in parrots, is therefore currently a blank on the map of endangered fauna.'

As in the neotropics, there are two groups which are most vulnerable: the endemics from small islands, and the species, in this case cockatoos, which feature prominently in trade. As with the large macaws, the cockatoos will be unable to tolerate the combined pressures of habitat destruction and trapping for sale on a large scale.

This is especially true of species or distinctive subspecies which have a restricted range, such as the Citron-crested Cockatoo (*Cacatua sulphurea citrino-cristata*) found only on Sumba, an island of 11,180 km^2 (4,300 sq. miles). A survey on Sumba, however, indicated that all parrots occur in reasonably good numbers in selected localities of suitable habitat (Murray Bruce, pers. comm., 1983).

How quickly can a species be almost exterminated by trade! Now, ten years after Bruce's assessment, the Citron-crested Cockatoo is considered to be critically endangered. Its population was believed to have declined by 80 per cent between 1986 and 1989 due to trade and clearance of forest. Less than 16 per cent of the island remains forested. Thousands of these cockatoos were trapped and exported. No one will ever know how many, because the legal quotas were bound to have been exceeded. These quotas declined during the years 1984–86 from 3,000 to 2,000 to only 600.

In 1989 a team of scientists from Manchester Polytechnic in the UK visited Sumba and laid the foundations for a project to be known as the 'Conservation of the Parrots of Sumba'. This expedition provided the first information on the avifauna of Sumba since before Indonesian independence in 1945. Since 1989, field workers have tried to estimate the number of cockatoos which survive there but as yet there is not sufficient information.

Other species of Indonesian parrots, including a number of lories, are exported; but the cockatoos form by far the bulk of the trade, because of the demand, especially from the USA. These birds are found only in Indonesia, New Guinea and Australia, and the latter country prohibits commercial export of all fauna.

Trade in the Indonesian cockatoos has been extensive since the early 1970s and in some, if not most, localities, coincides with the opening up of areas as a result of deforestation or logging activities. Cockatoos would probably not have been exported from some islands had this not occurred.

The natural history of the Eastern Indonesian province of Maluku is one of the most interesting and least known in the world. Formerly known as the Moluccas, the region was originally called the Spice Islands, and the centuries-old trade in spices, notably clove and nutmeg, placed the islands on the map. Spice exports are still sizeable but more important are the exports of timber, marine products and birds, notably cockatoos.

Maluku consists of hundreds of islands, with widely varying geological and climatic conditions. Various combination of physical factors occur on each of the major islands, creating unique habitats that are reflected in the flora and fauna of the forests. Many endemic species have evolved, most of them forest-dwellers; of the 450 bird species, more than a quarter are endemic. Of these endemics, 94 per cent are confined to one island or group of islands. Conservation is therefore of prime importance, in view of the serious environmental threat posed by commercial logging operations. About 90 per cent of all forest in northern and central Maluku is under timber concession, and 17 companies are logging in 22 locations. Moluccan forests attract logging companies because they contain several commercially valuable timber species, distances are short, and large ships can anchor close inshore (Smiet, 1982). There is little government control and companies have free rein, resulting in logging irrespective of steepness, soil fragility or altitude. All this, and the fact that no reafforestation occurs, is in defiance of government regulations. The thin topsoil, heavy rainfall and steep slopes result in severe erosion after the forests have degraded. Smiet states: 'There is no doubt that these fragile ecosystems will be seriously disturbed by this large-scale deforestation.' In these circumstances the creation of reserves will be of vital importance. During a period of 18 months from 1980, Smiet assisted in the selection of 14 conservation areas on all the major islands, totalling 690,000 ha (1.7 million acres). The proposed areas are shown in the table (Smiet, 1982) on this page. By 1992, 10 of the proposed 27 reserves had been gazetted in Malaku, all but one on small off-shore islands.

The creation of these reserves, and many others throughout the world, would be impossible without financial assistance from the Worldwide Fund for Nature (WWF) and the International Union for the Conservation of Nature (IUCN). During the period 1977–81 WWF supported 37 projects in Indonesia (more than in any other country), with a total of more than US$1.5 million. Much of this money was supplied by the Dutch National Appeal of WWF. It was raised through a schoolchildren's campaign which brought in the equivalent of US$10 per head for the Netherlands (Myers, 1983).

The Indonesian government supported WWF and IUCN in their efforts to save its threatened flora and fauna, and committed itself to a conservation campaign that included the setting up of a further 100,000 km^2 (40,000 sq. miles) of tropical forest reserves by 1984. Unfortunately, it has ignored some of these commitments; by 1983 24 km^2 (9 sq. miles) had been felled in an area of central Seram which formed part of a proposed national park — an insignificant area, perhaps, but it demonstrated how easily the principle can be eroded.

In 1983 the nation's network of 96 protected areas covered approximately 4 per cent of national territory. By 1992, 7 per cent of the land area had conservation status. In the Indonesian part of New Guinea, Irian Jaya, an area of 430,000 km^2 (166,000 sq. miles), it is hoped to establish a system of protected areas which will account for 72,800 km^2 (28,000 sq. miles). The Worldwide Fund for Nature assisted in the development of the Manusela National Park as part of its second five-year Indonesian programme. Trade is now under some kind of control, monitored by the PPA (Directorate of Nature Conservation). They stated that, in the four years prior to 1982, 70,000 live birds were exported from Maluku, all species which are not officially protected. Much of the export trade, however, is impossible to register; outside the main towns, law enforcement is difficult and checking the many thousand kilometres of coastline is out of the question.

Proposed Forest Conservation Areas on the Major Islands of Maluku Province

Island	Size km^2	Proposed Reserve size km^2	Altitudinal range m
Morotai	1 800	450	0–1250
Halmahera	18 000	(1) 850	200–1500
		(2) 600	0–1400
		(3) 500	0–1350
Bacan	5700	150	0–2200
Obi	3780	150	500–1750
Sula Islands	6000	150	500–1800
Seram	18 625	(1) 300	50–1100
		(2) 1800	0–3027
		(3) 300	0– 500
Buru	9000	400	0–2800
Wetar	3624	250	0–1500
Tanimbar	5085	200	0– 200
Aru Islands	6325	800	0– 70
		Total: 6900	

According to Smiet: 'In general trade has not yet had a big impact on wild parrot populations. Most parrots, including cockatoos, have a great reproductive capacity, adapt readily to habitat alteration and profit greatly from the widespread introduction of fruit trees throughout Maluku. This, coupled with the fact that large stretches of original habitat still occur on most islands, has helped them to maintain stable populations despite the great hunting pressure, and colourful parrots and white cockatoos are still common in the forests of Seram and Halmahera and occasionally raid crops in nearby villages.'

In the first edition of this book I commented: 'Smiet's assessment might be considered over-optimistic. Personally, I would not consider cockatoos and the other large parrots of Maluku, such as *Eclectus*, to have 'a great reproductive capacity'. In both groups the clutch normally consists of two eggs which are incubated for four weeks; the young fledge after three to four months. If left to rear their own young, cockatoos are normally single-brooded in captivity and the same may apply in the wild. Therefore, the maximum annual production of a pair would be two young. *Eclectus* are continuous breeders in captivity, that is, they ignore the seasons and continue to reproduce all year round. If this also occurs in the wild, a pair could average three young per year. It is true that both groups are potentially long-lived birds; nevertheless, by no stretch of the imagination can this be equated with high reproduction rates when, annually, only a small number of young can be reared. Furthermore, they occur in an area where habitat is diminishing with every year that passes.'

A decade later my fears have proved justified. Two Indonesian cockatoos are considered to be critically endangered (Citron-crested and Red-vented), two are classified as endangered/critical (Goffin's and Moluccan), and the Umbrella or White-crested plus two forms of the Lesser Sulphur-crested (*Cacatua sulphurea sulphurea* and *C.s. parvula*) are endangered. All have suffered catastrophic declines as a result of trade and deforestation; the Moluccan mainly because of trade. The Citron-crested is, of course, a sub-species of the Lesser Sulphur-crested but it is the only truly distinctive sub-species so that aviculturists, at least, tend to think of it as a separate species. It is a bird of great beauty and its extinction in the wild would be a tragedy. Although there are hundreds in captivity, a large number are kept and bred as pets. Males probably outnumber females by at least two to one. Confined to only one island, Sumba, its population suffered a massive decline during the 1980s. By the early 1980s forest covered less than 16 per cent of the island, yet deforestation was still continuing. The most detailed survey, made in 1993, resulted in the population being assessed at between 1,150 and 1,850 individuals. In other words, further study is urgently needed, as is protection of habitat and nest sites. Trade should have been halted in the mid-1980s, as soon as there was some notion of the damage it had done. Enormous fines should have been implemented as a matter of urgency to stop its trapping, which, I fear, will continue as long as there are birds to be trapped. Tardiness in taking action could spell extinction for this wonderful cockatoo. I would implore all breeders of this bird to rear young for breeding — not for pets. Its very survival may one day depend on a few far-sighted aviculturists. (For more information on the Indonesian Cockatoos see Low, 1993.)

The total list of endangered parrots of Indonesia is staggering in its length. Including the above-mentioned, five parrots are judged to be critically endangered (one of these may already be extinct), 32 forms (19 species) are endangered and seven more forms are classified as vulnerable. Thus Indonesia has far more endangered parrots than any other country. It also tops the list for vulnerable bird species in general; of its 1,532 species, 126 are considererd threatened (Jepson, 1992).

With a human population of 180 million and an annual population growth of 2.3 per cent, the future looks grim for Indonesian fauna. It is true that conservation programmes have commenced but, given the increasing human population, it seems unlikely that extinction of some forms can be averted. More and more land will need to be converted for agricultural purposes.

According to Jepson: 'The goverment recognises the importance of Indonesia for conserving global biodiversity, and is working towards integrating environmental conservation with national development.'

PHPA (Directorate General of Forest Protection and Nature Conservation) is to sign an agreement with ICBP for a programme of collaborative work on bird conservation. A programme office has been set up in Bogor. Other government departments will co-operate with ICBP and hope to involve students and local bird clubs in conservation projects. The ICBP programme will aim to promote conservation within endemic areas, promote an awareness of birds and their environment, and provide training to Indonesians with respect to the conservation of birds and their habitats. It will also assess the status and ecology of wild populations of species which are traded to ensure trade is within sustainable limits.

Had these measures been implemented even ten years ago the future for the heavily traded species, especially the cockatoos, would be much brighter today. The harmful effects of trade on the parrots of the Moluccas has been known for some years. During July to September 1985 WWF and IUCN funded an investigation into trade on the island of Bacan in the northern Moluccas and on Warmar in the Aru Islands. The resulting report (Milton and Marhadi, 1987) stated that species of parrots rarely traded were believed to have maintained stable populations. Low abundance was noted in popularly traded parrots, such as the Umbrella Cockatoo and the Chattering Lory; concern was expressed regarding an apparent decline of the Moluccan Cockatoo on Seram. The volume of trade in Moluccan parrots had risen dramatically from approximately 26,000 in 1981 to more than 60,000 in 1984. Almost all of the estimated 180,000–200,000 parrots caught between 1981 and 1984 were of only nine species. Their low abundance suggested that 'temporary severe restrictions or complete bans on their trade be invoked to allow populations to recover. Quotas for the legal harvest of other popularly traded species should be continually evaluated and adjusted to ensure healthy populations are maintained.'

The report was published in February 1987. Clearly, an immediate temporary trade ban should have been enforced. But it was not. Instead, the Moluccan Cockatoo was proposed for Appendix I of CITES. Legislative machinery grinds slowly; it was 1989 by the time that this listing was approved. In the meantime, the trappers on Seram had plenty of time to react. They went into action to clear the forests of every Moluccan Cockatoo they could find. They were so successful, that, shortly before the CITES I listing came into force,

Excessive trade has caused a massive decline in the numbers of Moluccan Cockatoos.

hundreds of Moluccan Cockatoos were shipped from Jakarta to overseas destinations. The last retreat of this species, the Manusela National Park, had been ravaged. As yet, no-one knows how many have survived. Trapping of this species on a large scale commenced in the 1970s. Between 1981 and 1984 over 20,000 were exported legally; subsequently, between 4,000 and 9,000 per annum were believed to have been exported.

The plight of the Moluccan Cockatoo differs from that of most other Indonesian cockatoos in that large areas of its habitat survives. It survives, but it no longer rings with the wonderful quavering call of this magnificent bird. The tragedy of it is that the majority of the Moluccans which were trapped and exported were adult birds. The demand for young birds, whether wild-caught or captive-bred is high, but there is little demand for wild-caught adults. They are extremely easily stressed; few other parrots have such a nervous temperament. There is a limit to the number of people

able to construct the proper accommodation for these large, noisy and destructive birds. Thousands of these adult birds must have been bought as pets and suffered torment from the close confinement of a cage. As has happened with other high-priced parrots, supply exceeded demand because no-one said no. They were imported because they were available and because money was to be made from their trade.

As Roland Wirth (1990) related, in spite of the 'alarming news' of the decline of wild populations, 'the cockatoo trade continued in 1988 and 1989, with the blessing of the Indonesian authorities'.

In some cases, trade was inevitable, as the islands which the cockatoos inhabited had been severely or almost totally deforested. But this was not true of the Moluccan. The plight of this species tears at my heart every time I see a wild-caught adult, so ill at ease in captivity. I wish it was possible to return it to the forests of Seram. But even if the means existed, what point would there be in this action? There is no longer any legal export trade but one can be sure that the illegal trade continues. In 1990 one dealer on Seram took about 1,000 Moluccan Cockatoos to wholesalers on the island of Ambon (Armin Brockner, *in litt.*, 1991). (In Singapore, in March 1993, I saw a consignment of at least 60 recently wild-caught Moluccan Cockatoos.) Even when trade was legal, the illegal trade was substantial. For example, in 1983 and 1984 the numbers of this cockatoo officially exported were 6,415 and 7,655 yet, for the same years, importing countries recorded receiving 9,625 and 9,639.

Illegal trade will continue until it is socially unacceptable to catch and trade parrots. The ICBP programme aims to promote an awareness of birds and their environment. Can it teach the people of Indonesia that their parrots must be cherished and protected? Unless conservation education becomes a successful reality, there can be no future in the wild for most of the parrots of Indonesia.

The unfortunate fate which befell a large group of Goffin's Cockatoos between 1992 and 1993 demonstrates that the desire to protect parrots has yet to be aroused. In 1992 Goffin's Cockatoo (*Cacatua goffini*) was placed on Appendix I of CITES; thus commercial trade was no longer permitted. Unfortunately, no one informed the occupants of the Tanimbar Islands of this fact. Goffin's occurs nowhere else. At the time one dealer possessed 535 Goffin's which were caught in the 'catching season' of January to March when the corn crops ripen. A British TV camera team saw the birds when they numbered only 60 and apparently paid for the birds to be kept where they were rather than being shipped out to a bird market. The World Parrot Trust was asked to help arrange for these cockatoos to be released, then protected in the wild. These birds had originated mainly from the small islands of Seira, Latdalam and Nantabun. Some members of the World Parrot Trust sent donations to ensure these birds were properly cared for until their release.

Unfortunately, some weeks later, the cockatoos were moved to a farm belonging to a Chinese family. Because there were poultry on their premises, thus bringing a risk of introducing disease to the wild population, permission to release these birds was refused, unless they had been properly quarantined, as was permission to export them. The cost of quarantining them was said to be 'tens of thousands of pounds'. How was this figure calculated? When the funds donated by the World Parrot Trust ran out, the cockatoos started to die from neglect. In about March 1993 the survivors, apparently about 200 (and many in poor condition) were released.

Why has no-one considered the fate of captive birds trapped in a sort of 'no man's land' when the species is transferred to Appendix I. They are already in captivity but they cannot legally be sold. Hundreds of Palm Cockatoos died in Singapore when this species was transferred to Appendix I. Those responsible for constructing CITES legislation must address this problem before it claims the lives of hundreds more endangered parrots.

Few Indonesian species have been harder hit by excessive trade than this diminutive cockatoo. It was almost unknown in captivity until mass export commenced in 1971. Trade commenced when the forests were logged. The Tanimbar Islands have a land area of only 5,000 km² (1,900 sq. miles) and the species must have been thriving there. After ten years of trade, in 1983 and 1984, 13,206 and 12,193 Goffin's respectively were imported by various countries around the world during just these two years. The numbers officially exported were just over 9,000 for each year. It was obvious to anyone who ever gave it a thought that such a small area could not sustain trade on this scale for more than a few years without critically endangering the population. Yet trade continued for 20 years until the population was believed to number in the region of 5,000. After a few years demand for it had tailed off and it became the lowest-priced of all cockatoos available. This was yet another case of a species being exported solely because it existed and there were no laws to prevent it. One cannot blame impoverished residents of the Tanimbar Islands, most of whom probably do not even know what an endemic species is. Once again CITES had failed dismally to protect a species from excessive trade.

Little is known about the status of the Blue-eyed Cockatoo (*Cacatua ophthalmica*) from the Bismarck Archipelago of Papua New Guinea. Unlike most other cockatoos, it has not been the subject of commercial

A poster issued in three languages warns against killing, catching or buying the native cockatoo in the Philippines.

trade and is very rare in captivity (Low, 1993). It is found on the islands of New Britain and New Ireland. The size of its population has been suggested as 5,000 (Parrot Action Plan). Mention is made of it here only because it is the least-known of all white cockatoo species.

Another poorly known cockatoo is, alas, now critically endangered. It is the Philippine (Red-vented) Cockatoo (*Cacatua haematuropygia*). In length (30 cm; 12 in), and in shape it is similar to Goffin's but it is most unusually marked for a cockatoo in having red under-tail coverts. It was once widespread throughout the

Philippines, but it was not realised until 1991 how serious was the extent of its decline. In that year it could be found only on the island of Palawan; it was also believed to survive on Dinagat. It was deforestation that led to this species being declared critically endangered by 1992. Never common in captivity, it was almost unknown until logging resulted in new areas being opened up. On Palawan, every known nest has been robbed of its young for years. This means that the surviving population, estimated to number between 1,000 and 4,000 birds, consists solely of aged cockatoos, thus there could be a sudden and dramatic decline in numbers when they cease to breed. When estimated in 1991, it was believed that the population had declined by between 60 and 90 per cent during the previous 10–15 years.

There are different estimates of the severity of deforestation in the Philippines, but all agree that it is very severe indeed. One source indicated that, by the early 1980s, 80 per cent of the forests had been destroyed in the previous 50 years. By now that figure must be much higher.

This species is poorly represented in Europe and the USA, despite the fact that several hundreds were imported during the 1980s. Unlike most cockatoos, mortality among newly imported birds was extremely high, especially among females. It is known that some nest sites in the wild are contaminated with the fungus *Aspergillus*, thus newly captured birds, stressed by their ordeal, succumb to aspergillosis. Psittacine beak and feather disease, which causes feather loss and beak rot, has frequently been encountered in these cockatoos after a few months in captivity.

The captive situation is serious. There are few pairs and few young are being produced, except in the collection of Antonio de Dios in Manila. He has about 20 pairs, some of which are producing young. The first step towards preserving this species in European aviculture was taken in 1993 when an EEP (co-ordinated breeding programme, usually organised by a zoo but also involving private aviculturists) was set up. It was organised by Marc Boussekey of Espace Zoologique, a French zoo. The breeding programme has been linked with a conservation programme for this species in the wild. To this end, an agreement was signed in 1993 by the government of the Philippines and the zoo. The zoo funded and produced a poster in three languages (English and two Philippine languages) for distribution throughout the islands. It emphasises that the cockatoo must be protected. In addition, prints of the poster artwork are sold to help fund the conservation programme. The first priority must be to stop the trapping of this cockatoo. If the species is to survive, young birds must be recruited to the wild population.

Also at risk in the Philippines, for the same reasons,

At least one of the three sub-species of the Red and Blue Lory is already extinct or near to extinction.

is the Blue-naped Parrot (*Tanygnathus lucionensis*). However, it is not an endemic species, being found also on islands of northern Borneo and the Talaud and Maratua Islands of Indonesia. The smallest parrot of the Philippines, the exquisitely coloured Hanging Parrot (*Loriculus philippensis*) has ten sub-species on various islands. One of these, *L.p. chrysonotus* from the island of Cebu, may already be extinct. The other, *L.p. siquijorensis* has a population estimated at fewer than 50 individuals, based on reports by the local people that it still exists. Five other sub-species are threatened. Taxonomic research is urgently required to

In 1992 a dealer in Singapore imported, in one consignment, 60 Red and Blue Lories (probably all *talautensis*).

treated as a sub-species of the Moluccan Hanging Parrot, *L. amabilis*.) Virtually no forest survives on Sangir, the main island of the group. This tiny parrot, just 11 cm (4 in) long, with scarlet rump and forehead, was, reportedly, not plentiful a century ago but it was known to inhabit village gardens as well as forest. On remote islands, seldom or never visited by ornithologists, the passing of a species may go unnoticed or unrecorded. Worse than that, two parrots may have become extinct on this small island. The nominate race of the Red and Blue Lory (*Eos histrio*), from the islands of Sangir and Siao, is also feared extinct. The sub-species *E.h. talautensis* survives, apparently in fair numbers, on the island of Karekelang in the Talaud Islands.

According to Forshaw (1989) two reserves have been proposed to protect 22,000 ha (54,300 acres) in the centre of the island. He believes implementation of this proposal will be critical to the survival of this species. In 1992 its population there was believed to be in the region of 2,000 birds. Nothing is known about the third sub-species, *E.h. challengeri*, which probably survives only on Miangas in the Nenusa Islands — if, indeed, it is still extant.

This species has always been an extreme rarity in captivity, reflecting the fact that little trapping was carried out within its range. However, in about 1990, it attracted the attention of a dealer from Singapore who started to import it, initially in small numbers. When I visited his premises in April 1992 I saw more than 40 crowded into four small cages. Sixty had been imported, all destined to go to one parrot enthusiast in Singapore, who was planning to retain them for breeding. (The same dealer also had a large consignment of Moluccan Cockatoos and greeted with incredulity the idea that they were an endangered species; the trappers had assured him that plenty survived, he said.)

By the late 1980s it was feared that a number of other Indonesian lories were threatened, mainly by loss of habitat. When will it end, the destruction of Asia's rainforests for short-term gain? Will it continue until it is too late — every forest felled and incalculable numbers of birds and other endemic species gone forever? The scale of the problem is immense and shows little sign of abating. In 1980, for example, Japan consumed 35 million m^3 (45 million cu. yd) of tropical hardwoods, three and a half times more than the next nation, the USA. Collar (1986) points out: 'Three quarters of Japan's wood comes from Southeast Asia; in 1981 no less than 74 per cent of Japan's imported Philippines timber had been illegally felled. Caulfield reports that in 1981 a Papua New Guinea company exported 480 million pairs of disposable chopsticks to Japan, some 5 per cent of the latter's annual consump-

investigate the suggestion that some of these may be full species. In addition, research is necessary to formulate management plans, if needed.

The same holds true for the Racket-tailed Parrots (*Prioniturus* species). This is a genus of medium-sized green parrots with softly coloured head markings and ornate racquets on their tails — a feature, in the world of parrots, unique to this genus. Six of the nine species are endemic to the Philippines. A project to study the ecology and conservation needs of these little-known parrots is planned, according to the Parrot Action Plan.

In Indonesia, north-east of Celebes (Sulawesi), are the Sangihe Islands. They have a total area of 777 km^2 (300 sq. miles). The endemic Hanging Parrot (*Loriculus catamene*) is feared to be extinct. (It is sometimes

tion of such items. Suddenly we have the "chopstick connection": ten billion pairs a year, each to last the duration of a single meal. Hamburgers and chopsticks suggest that the ultimate cause of tropical deforestation is nothing more complex than ignorance, indifference, or greed.'

It has already been mentioned that lack of field studies in Indonesia at this date has resulted in an absence of information relating to the status of the parrots which are found there. It should be borne in mind that lack of information does not necessarily mean that a species is rare — it usually indicates that few ornithologists have visited the area in which it is found.

19

The Role of Aviculture in Conservation

. . . captive propagation is the only stock in the conservationist's portfolio that stands between an inexorably increasing number of endangered species and extinction in the face of man's accelerating destruction of habitat.

Endangered bird propagation has been discouraged in the past for fear that it would divert scarce resources from preserving species in nature. Ultimately, however, we must ask ourselves whether having a species in captivity is better than not having it at all; whether preserving even a gradually changing representation of some of the earth's biological diversity is not, of itself, worthwhile?

WILLIAM G. CONWAY, OF THE NEW YORK ZOOLOGICAL
SOCIETY, IN *ENDANGERED BIRDS* (1977)

Parrots have been bred in captivity for more than one century; until the 1960s, however, the larger species were raised only rarely. Sexual determination by laparoscopy (using an instrument developed for human surgery to ascertain whether the bird has testes or ovaries) removed the factor which had previously inhibited breeding successes with many species. It was evolved in the USA during the 1970s and this method reached Europe during the latter part of the decade. It resulted in parrots being raised in aviaries in greatly increased numbers, both as regards individuals and species.

With the primary obstacle removed, captive breeding becomes the only practical method of conservation for most endangered parrots, because protection of natural habitats is fraught with increasing difficulties, or the habitat has been completely destroyed.

Captive breeding has the potential to fulfil three very important roles.

1) The preservation of an endangered species or one which is extinct in the wild. It may or may not be reintroduced to its original habitat, depending upon the circumstances. Alternatively, captive-bred birds can be used to restock wild populations confined to areas too small to sustain genetically viable populations.

2) The development of techniques which can be applied to the breeding and management of endangered birds, both in captivity and in the wild. Captive breeding also increases our knowledge of the breeding biology of endangered birds.

3) Educating the public to the plight of endangered birds, through captive breeding in collections open to the public (zoos, especially, can display informative graphics), and through wider publicity being given to successful breeding programmes.

On the one hand minority groups exist which call for the abolition of all captive collections and studies, whereas on the other there is apathy towards the plight of wild animals resulting from man's destruction of their habitat.

Captive breeding of endangered species remains a contentious and controversial subject. In some instances, 'conservationists' with no knowledge of aviculture refuse even to consider this method as a means of attempting to prevent extinction; apparently they would rather see species lost to us forever than have them survive only in captivity. Some argue, too, that after several generations of captive breeding the birds produced would be unable to survive in the wild because alterations would occur (e.g. tameness) which are deleterious to survival in their natural habitat. Although there may be an element of truth in this, it is invalidated by the fact that the main cause of extinction has been or is likely to be habitat destruction. How can any creature survive in the wild when its habitat no longer exists? Surely it is preferable that it should survive in captivity than that it should disappear from the face of the earth? Scientists may be prepared to go to extreme lengths to preserve genetic material which could, in the future, be used to recreate species which are no longer extant. Is it not more intelligent to use aviculture to preserve birds when their natural habitat no longer exists?

There are signs that some conservationists may slowly be reaching the realisation that this is indeed a more practicable view. In 1981 the International Council for Bird Preservation (ICBP) made certain recommendations to aid the survival of the well-named Imperial Parrot of Dominica. One of these was to initiate a captive breeding programme. I believe that this decision marked a giant step forward in conservation attitudes, even though it was made too late.

Previously, conservationists and aviculturists appeared to be in totally opposing camps on too many occasions. This was in part due to the fact that some conservation organisations confused the role of the field worker with that of the aviculturist when, in fact, one should not be expected to do the work of the other. No aviculturist would suggest that his knowledge of breeding birds qualified him as a field worker, yet field workers in one crucially important project were given the task of captive breeding and rearing chicks of the Puerto Rican Parrot, then the most critically endangered parrot (in populations terms) in the neotropics. The naive manner in which this was carried out horrified the avicultural community. It resulted in an American veterinarian and aviculturist visiting Puerto Rico in 1981 at his own expense and compiling a compendious report on the failings of the operation. An unsuccessful attempt was made to 'lose' the report to prevent its publication. Not long afterwards, practical and political aspects of the breeding programme were completely re-appraised. It had been totally in the hands of the US Fish and Wildlife Service. The government of Puerto Rico insisted in future participation in the programme and a share of the young hatched in captivity. These young were to form the basis of a second captive population (*see* page 89).

Conservationists have failed to realise that the breeding and rearing of endangered parrots is a task which should be entrusted only to the experienced specialist — but aviculturists must not allow this to devalue their opinion of field workers. The latter usually operate under very difficult conditions, especially those obtaining information on parrots; in most types of habitats (except in Australia) these birds are extremely difficult to observe. Long hours in the field, requiring unlimited patience and enduring every kind of inconvenience of the tropics, from mosquitoes and sandflies to torrential rain and searing sun, raging thirst and the dangers of scaling near-vertical mountain sides, are the lot of the field worker.

Organisations such as WWF and ICBP have sponsored some valuable field work which has provided an insight into the dwindling populations of many parrots, especially in the neotropics. This has enabled aviculturists to focus their attention on species whose numbers are dwindling in the wild, when this was not evident as birds were still being exported.

It is to be hoped that before time runs out aviculturists and conservationists will learn to seek the advice of the other and to work together to save endangered birds.

Of course, in a Utopian world it would be preferable to leave these birds to breed in the wild; but we can no longer delude ourselves that this is feasible. Even if the habitat was protected so rigorously that the birds survived unmolested, the political situation in countries where many of these imperilled species occur is unstable. A change of government could result in the sudden reversal of conservation policy. In addition, especially in Latin American countries, the people usually cannot comprehend the purpose of wildlife conservation; indeed, they show little respect for human life.

Captive breeding cannot be considered as a suitable means of conservation for all endangered birds; however, as a group, parrots respond well to confinement. The feasibility of establishing captive breeding groups of endangered species depends on a number of factors, such as the species (some are easier to breed than others) and the number of individual birds available to form the nucleus of a breeding programme. In the hands of experienced, skilled and dedicated aviculturists and zoo personnel, such projects have an excellent chance of success, as is increasingly being proved. If endangered parrots are left to their fate, however, extinction within the next half-century (sooner, in some cases) is inevitable.

Captive breeding programmes must be initiated while the numbers of the more endangered species hover on the three-figure mark: to wait until their numbers are reduced to double figures is to gamble with their extinction. This did happen, and at a cost of millions of dollars, in the case of the Puerto Rican

Parrot (*Amazona vittata*). Had these vast sums been channelled into setting up a centre for breeding all the endangered Caribbean Amazons under the guidance of experienced breeders, the situation would today almost certainly be one of optimism instead of dread at what the future holds for these magnificent birds. Nevertheless, unlike all the other localities in the Caribbean in which parrots are found and which lack the affluence of the USA, Puerto Rico is US territory.

Captive breeding of endangered birds has certain advantages over attempting to protect birds in their natural habitat, as follows.

1) A pair can be managed to produce more young in a given period than would occur in the wild. This is of vital importance in the case of critically endangered species with very small populations. Admittedly, in the case of a single pair there is little genetic diversity among the young, but initially the priority often lies with building up the numbers as quickly as possible. Each individual becomes of the utmost importance and a significant contribution towards the survival of the species.

2) Captive birds have the opportunity of passing on their genes in more combinations than would occur in nature, if correctly managed. They can be mated with different birds (even with more than one in a single season) to increase genetic diversity. (The reverse must be guarded against, i.e. one very successful breeding bird passing its genes on to a large proportion of the captive stock.)

3) Captive birds have a potentially longer life-span when correctly managed because they can be protected from predators (including humans), from food shortages and from adverse climatic conditions. Birds in the wild show extremely high early mortality, probably at least 30 per cent in the first year. (This figure is known for the Puerto Rican Parrot, for example.) In a well-managed captive population of parrots, the mortality (excluding chicks) may not exceed 5 per cent in any year.

4) Captive populations of endangered birds can be located in a country less vulnerable to the natural catastrophes which occur in their natural habitat; for example, the entire populations of the endangered Amazons of St Vincent, St Lucia and Dominica in the Caribbean could be extirpated by a severe hurricane or volcanic eruption, neither of which is uncommon in the region. Captive breeding programmes should be located outside the country of origin as a safeguard. Some of the young produced should be distributed for the same reason.

In the past zoos and aviculturists lost important opportunities to establish breeding programmes; often this was simply due to lack of awareness that a species was declining and lack of foresight that its import would not continue unabated. A new sense of responsibility has been born which should ensure that this will never again be the case.

It is worth noting that private aviculturists, rather than zoological associations, have been responsible for the majority (probably more than 90 per cent) of the parrot species bred in captivity, and of those bred to more than one generation.

Another development is that zoos and private aviculturists are beginning to work together; in the past they usually remained very separate entities. Zoos now, as Robert Wagner (1983) remarked: 'realize the tremendous contributions being made by the private aviculturists and are relying more heavily on the techniques demonstrated in the private sector. On the other hand, the private aviculturist is becoming increasingly aware of the opportunities available in the public exhibition of wild animal species, especially in regard to offering the general public educational information geared towards expressing concern for the growing number of vanishing species and the habitats upon which species depend.'

Commencing in the late 1980s came a new awareness that co-ordinated breeding programmes would be essential for the survival in captivity of certain species. This was partly as a result of growing co-operation between zoos and aviculturists, but also because of information concerning the wild status of a number of species which were well-known in captivity. Moluccan, Citron-crested and Philippine Cockatoos, for example, were added to the growing list of endangered or critically endangered parrot species. It is vital that as many holders as possible of certain species should be able to contact each other through a co-ordinator. The co-ordinator keeps confidential records of birds held by individuals. These are usually published annually, anonymity being maintained where requested. In this way partners can be found for unpaired birds, captive-bred young can be paired with unrelated birds and the co-ordinator can monitor upward or downward trends in captive populations. When these are sufficiently high, it may be deemed no longer necessary to maintain a 'studbook', as it is often called. It is difficult to know how to term these records; the important factor is that they exist and the number of 'studbooks' for species or groups of vulnerable species has shown a spectacular increase for every year of the 1990s so far. Some of these studbooks cover Europe, others a single country such as the UK, and some are maintained mainly for the USA. Appendix 3 lists some of those which exist to date. Many more are certain to be formed.

The participation of private aviculturists shows the increasing concern on their behalf that aviculture will be the means of keeping as many species as possible extant. On the other hand, there are still too many breeders who care nothing about conserving the species which they keep, and whose only motive for keeping them is profit. There are others who do care but fail to register their birds with studbook keepers in case it somehow results in taxation on sales of young birds.

Most of these studbooks are maintained through avicultural societies, especially those catering for certain groups of birds, such as Amazons or lories. In Europe there is another type of breeding programme, known as an EEP. These are mainly for Appendix I species of special value (e.g. Palm Cockatoo, Hyacinthine Macaw) and operate for mammals as well as birds. Administered by zoos, they invite the participation of aviculturists. In most cases, exchanges and transfers occur between zoos without any financial transaction. In the USA studbooks have been established for various animals through the American Association of Zoological Parks and Aquariums (AAZPA). The first formed for a parrot was that for the Golden (Queen of Bavaria's) Conure. Of 67 participants in 1990, 11 were zoos belonging to the AAZPA and 41 were private breeders.

A most important aspect which must not be ignored by private or public breeders of endangered species is genetic management. Ryder (1983) has pointed out: 'While it is true that, to date, genetic research and management have had relatively little impact on propagation programmes for threatened and endangered birds . . . genetic considerations will necessarily play an ever increasing role in captive propagation programmes for endangered birds.'

He emphasises that a proper goal for such a programme 'is to preserve the natural attributes of the species and to minimise changes in its biology because of captive propagation. This goal is tantamount to preserving the gene pool of the species during captive propagation'.

Why is this necessary? Ryder gives three reasons.

1) The captive population must reflect the genetic base of the species as it occurs in nature.
2) It must ensure as far as possible that future changes in the environment can be successfully dealt with. (When deleterious environmental circumstances jeopardise natural populations, such as disease or climatic changes, some individuals may survive because they possess rare forms of a gene [alleles] that increase the likelihood for survival. Therefore, the greater the gene pool, the more likely it is that it contains genes that will enhance survival under adverse conditions.)
3) To enhance the chances for successful reintroduction of captive stock to natural habitat.

Preservation of genetic variation over a period may be an elusive goal, however, as captive breeding inevitably erodes the gene pool. Therefore the tactic becomes one of minimising loss of genetic variability by adapting appropriate breeding strategy.

Ryder suggests that this consists of the following.

1) No hybridising should occur. Even populations classified as different sub-species may be sufficiently distinct genetically that mixing their gene pool would produce individuals different from either pure sub-species.
2) Where possible (seldom where endangered species are concerned), captive breeding programmes should commence with large numbers of birds so that a large proportion of the gene pool is likely to be represented in the founder stock.
3) Inbreeding (the pairing of related birds) should be avoided because of the resulting loss of genetic variability, leading to low fertility, poor hatchability and possibly harmful alterations in the species. As an example, inbreeding of the endangered Hawaiian Goose, also called Néné (*Branta sandvicensis*), led to an alteration in the structure of down in goslings, which rendered them unfit for survival in the wild.
4) The breeder should be aware of the result of genetic drift, i.e. the gene pool of a species will not be constant. Elimination of individuals with unfavourable genetic traits (selection) and mutation will result in changes in genetic variability. Furthermore, not all individuals will leave the same number of offspring and some will leave none. The smaller the size of a population, the greater are the chances that, due to random events, genetic variability will decline. Initially therefore the numbers of a population should be built up as quickly as possible, using double or treble clutching techniques. It may even be advisable, suggests Ryder, to equalise the number of offspring per pair or prevent very successful pairs from 'swamping' the gene pool, so to speak. In practice, however, I doubt that breeders would react sympathetically to the idea; but they should be aware of it.
5) Breeders should beware of selection (purposely preserving variant characteristics) which, again, can reduce genetic variability.

On the other hand, the importance of a large gene pool in the recovery of endangered species may have been over-emphasised. After all, many populations from tiny islands must have originated from a very small number of founders, perhaps only one pair. In the words of Don Merton, New Zealand's 'miracle worker', 'Even when only one viable pair of a species survives, recovery is possible.' He should know. He was instrumental in saving from extinction the Chatham Island Black Robin (*Petroica traversi*). By September 1981 only five birds survived. Two of these were females and only one was fertile. She was nine years old, and most females cease to breed at the age of five or six years. By intensive management of this prolific female and her offspring, the population was increased to 130 birds by February 1991! If ever there was a story to inspire hope, this is it!

This is not a unique instance of the recovery of a species from a single pair. In 1930 only one female Laysan Teal (*Anas platyrhynchos*) survived. Today there are in the region of 400 in the wild and many more in waterfowl collections worldwide.

I hope that the foregoing has shown that genetic considerations are not factors best left to 'the other man'. All breeders of endangered species should be aware that ignoring these aspects can lead to a breeding programme coming to a dead end after a very few generations. If in doubt as to the best way of utilising the birds at their disposal, they should seek advice from a geneticist at a large zoological society or university.

20

A Practical Method of Conservation: Captive Breeding

Endangered species of birds should be regarded as historic monuments left to us by our ancestors; we are their inheritors and keepers. Protection of habitat and maintenance in captivity doubles the chances of survival of species in danger of extinction. Protection of habitat alone, relying on man's goodwill or on repression, is too uncertain and must be supplemented by the safeguard of captive maintenance.

DR H. QUINQUE, IN *AVICULTURAL MAGAZINE* (1982)

Millions of parrots are kept as pets and in aviaries throughout the world. Using the nomenclature of the Parrot Action Plan, with four exceptions* and assuming that the Paradise Parrot and the Glaucous Macaw are extinct, there are 348 species of parrots. Of these, I consider 266 to be known in aviculture in 1993 and 83 species to be unknown. Of the latter there might be a few birds captive in their native country, or even one specimen outside it, but I have judged these species as unknown. They are as follows:

Agapornis swinderniana (Swindern's Lovebird)
Amazona imperialis (Imperial Amazon)
Aratinga brevipes or *A. holochlora brevipes* (Socorro Conure)
Bolbopsittacus lunulatus (Guaiabero)
B. ferrugineifrons
B. orbygnesius

---

*Pionus seniloides is considered a sub-species of *P. tumultuosus*, *Prosopeia splendens* a sub-species of *P. tubuensis*, *Pyrrhura molina* a sub-species of *P. frontalis*, and *Cyanoramphus malherbi* a colour morph of *C. auriceps*.

Charmosyna amabilis (Golden-banded Lorikeet)
C. diadema (New Caledonian Lorikeet)
C. margarethae (Duchess Lorikeet)
C. meeki (Meek's Lorikeet)
C. palmarum (Palm Lorikeet)
C. rubrigularis (Red-throated Lorikeet)
C. toxopei (Blue-fronted Lorikeet)
Eos semilarvata (Blue-eared Lory)
Forpus sclateri (Sclater's Parrotlet)
Geoffroyus species — all
Geopsittacus occidentalis (Night Parrot)
Leptosittaca branickii (Branicki's Conure)
Loriculus aurantiifrons (Ceylon Hanging Parrot)
L. beryllinus, catamene, exilis, flosculus, aurantiifrons tener (Hanging Parrots)
Lorius albidinuchus (White-naped Lory)
L. hypoinochrous (Purple-bellied Lory)
Micropsitta species (Pygmy Parrots) — all
Nannopsittaca species — both
Ognorhynchus icterotis (Yellow-eared Conure)
Pezoporus wallicus (Ground Parrot)
Pionopsitta species — all except *P. pileata*
Poicephalus flavifrons (Niam-Niam Parrot)
Prioniturus species (Racket-tailed Parrots) — except one, or possibly two
Psittacella species — all
Psittacula caniceps (Nicobar Parrakeet)
Pyrrhura albipectus, calliptera, orcesi, viridicata (*Pyrrhura* Conures)
Rhynchopsitta terrisi (Maroon-fronted Parrot)
Tanygnathus gramineus (Rufous-tailed Parrot)
T. heterurus (Black-lored Parrot)
Touit species — all
Trichoglossus rubiginosus (Ponapé Lory)
Vini kuhlii (Kuhl's Lory)
V. stepheni (Stephen's Lory)
V. ultramarina (Ultramarine Lory)

I judged 211 of the 266 species to be established within aviculture, based on the criterion that if not a single bird of the species was ever again taken from the wild into captivity, the species would survive in aviculture.

How can these captive populations benefit the conservation of parrots? There are two ways. Firstly, a captive breeding programme is an integral part of the conservation strategy. In the case of the Puerto Rican Parrot (*Amazona vittata*), young hatched in captivity from wild pairs and from captive pairs were used for release, to augment the wild population and, in some instances, young which would not have survived in the wild were reared in captivity. (The latter is not captive breeding *per se* — but would not have been possible without the existence of the captive breeding programme.) Enough young have been retained to form the basis of a new population in the future, in a different location. Without this breeding programme, the species would probably now be extinct.

Secondly, there is captive breeding within aviculture, rather than a programme aimed at the survival of one particular species. Nearly all captive parrot populations fall in this category. Their existence is some kind of insurance that most species will survive in captivity if they become extinct in the wild. (However, birds from these captive populations would not necessarily be suitable for reintroduction into the wild.) The wild status of many parrots is little known or understood. Unfortunately, it is not impossible that the sudden discovery could be made that a species was near extinction or extinct in its natural habitat; the captive population would ensure that the species was still extant. This seems unlikely, yet it has already happened with a species of dove.

The captive numbers of a few species are already believed to be higher than the wild population. One example is the Hyacinthine Macaw. Unfortunately, the illegal export trade played a major part in its decline. Loss of habitat, shooting and illegal domestic trade could, however, have ultimately taken an equal toll of its numbers in the wild. Captive breeding successes with this macaw have increased so much during the 1980s that it seems unlikely that it will die out in aviculture. While initially the trade in wild-caught birds was enormously damaging to its populations, the long-term effect may be much less so, especially as the point may be reached where the wild population cannot increase beyond a certain point due to lack of suitable habitat. (This has already occurred in other species.)

Since the 1980s private aviculturists have become very efficient at producing, in large numbers, popular species of parrots from many genera, including some endangered species. They have the means and the knowledge to apply this to most species known in aviculture. There are some — but not enough — private aviculturists who can justifiably claim that their form of aviculture is conservation. They specialise in species which are rare in aviculture and which are not popular as pets, with little or no financial gain. Or they have pioneered techniques in breeding certain species.

This work is important because, although parrots are popular zoo exhibits, relatively few parrots are bred in zoos. This is partly because, until recently, many zoos had mixed exhibits of parrot species, in which breeding was unable or unlikely to occur. Another reason is that some zoos make little effort to breed from parrots; in many cases no nest-box is available. This is surprising, because many parrots will breed despite the close proximity of visitors, and their young are a valuable source of revenue or exchange. Susan Clubb (in Beissinger and Snyder, 1992) points out: 'of 85 Neotropical psittacine species reported in ISIS*, only 22 species are represented by 50 or more individual birds (ISIS, 1989). If species survival were to depend on current zoological collections, only a handful of psittacine species would be present in viable numbers . . . . If psittacine species can be adequtely maintained by the private sector, perhaps zoos should encourage such an effort and use their resources to protect species which cannot be maintained privately.'

There are a few species of parrots (such as Swindern's Lovebird) which have been kept on very few occasions for only short periods and have been judged impossible to maintain. However, most of those which are unknown in aviculture are small species and/or canopy dwellers, and are thus not worth the effort of trapping when species for which there is a demand are found in the same locality; alternatively they occur in remote and restricted areas. In the future it is possible that a small number of parrot species will be added to those already known in captivity, as new areas are deforested or become accessible, but most of those currently unknown will forever be so. Some of these are rare (some *Touit* Parrotlets for example) and may become extinct without ever having been in aviculture or the subject of a breeding programme.

Captive breeding is said to benefit conservation because the availability of the resulting young lessens the demand for wild-caught birds. As an aviculturist for several decades, I would like to think that this is true; unfortunately, it applies only up to a point. It certainly does apply to some groups of birds, such as Australian parrakeets, which have been bred in Europe for many generations, following Australia's ban on the export of

---

*International Species Inventory System, in which many zoos worldwide participate.

Blue-throated or Caninde Macaw — an endangered species which aviculturists are breeding.

will certainly apply in countries such as the USA, where there are many commercial breeders who supply the pet trade. In most other countries where parrots are widely bred, the number of species maintained over the long term will probably be higher, provided that there are no licensing or other regulations which make it difficult for breeders to maintain certain species. For example, in the USA, so much long-drawn-out paperwork is involved in the sale of Appendix I species that many breeders avoid them because they are more trouble than they are worth. In Australia, native species cannot be kept in certain states, and the legislation varies from state to state.

A slogan popular with many breeders reads: 'Aviculture *is* conservation'. However, I do not believe this will be true until export ceases of every species which might be threatened by that trade. Many species are now endangered as a result of over-trapping, especially in Indonesia. There are some breeders who claim to be motivated by conservation, yet this is not borne out by their choice of species (which are both high-priced and in high demand) or their total lack of support for conservation projects and lack of interest in joining the World Parrot Trust and other organisations which fund parrot conservation projects.

Inevitably, it is the dedicated specialist who will make the most significant contribution to conservation. A leader in this field is Ramon Noegel, of Seffner, Florida. What he has achieved with the Cuban Amazon and its races is a supreme example of the result of single-mindedness of purpose and an unusual insight into the needs of his parrots (Low, 1979). He was the first to breed in captivity anywhere in the world the endangered Grand Cayman, Cayman Brac and Isle of Pines sub-species (*A.l. caymanensis*, *hesterna* and *palmarum*) of the Cuban Amazon, the Black-billed Amazon (*A. agilis*) from Jamaica, the Tucuman Amazon (*A. tucumana*) from Bolivia and the Yellow-shouldered Amazon (*A. barbadensis*); in addition, after keeping St Vincent Parrots (*A. guildingii*) for only seven months, he reared one youngster and, by 1993, had reared 23.

Growing up in an area of Florida where many Cuban people reside, he noticed over the years that the number of Cuban Amazons kept by expatriates was diminishing. In the 1960s he started to obtain former pets for breeding purposes. Thus he was the forerunner of a crusade — perhaps the first individual to embark upon a private programme of parrot conservation at a time when no-one else could foresee the importance of such work. It was in 1974 that his first success was achieved; three Grand Cayman Amazons were hand-reared from the age of a few days. My own interest in this species derived from seeing those young birds; indeed, Ramon Noegel must have inspired many

fauna in 1959. It does not apply to another commonly bred group, the Lovebirds (*see* pages 91–2). It does apply to the Blue and Yellow Macaw (*Ara ararauna*) because so many are reared annually, but it does not yet apply to the other large macaws. Although many Amazon parrots are reared for sale as pets, the number is still small compared with the totals exported for this purpose. For very many species, the numbers reared in captivity annually fall far short of the numbers currently imported. Inevitably however, when the export of a species ceases, its value rises and a greater effort is made to breed it. Unfortunately, this applies mostly to popular species. If there is no demand, breeders will concentrate on species which they can sell more easily. So, although well over 200 species of parrots could become established in aviculture when all export ceases, what may happen is that many of the less popular species will be virtually lost to aviculture. This

Captive-bred Goffin's Cockatoo (*Cacatua goffini*), aged 26 days. Aviculturists must ensure that sufficient young are retained for breeding purposes.

economic crises, there is no guarantee that such programmes will continue. Also, they may be dependent on the whim of politicians.

It seems unlikely that many more captive breeding projects will be initiated in the country of origin to try to save a single species. But there will always be some aviculturists with a deep interest in conservation (even though these are in the minority) whose priorities lie with breeding multiple generations of one or more endangered parrot species.

There are a number of endangered species which aviculturists are unlikely ever to have an opportunity to work with. Others, however, are available, although some are very highly priced. The following table will guide those with a genuine interest in specialising in one or more endangered species. As knowledge of the wild status of more parrot species becomes available, it will undoubtedly be necessary to add to this list.

Aviculturists should, in the author's opinion, give priority to breeding the species listed below, which are known in aviculture but are either endangered or destined to become so in the wild. The species listed as rare are expensive and not easily obtainable. Those listed as obtainable are readily or fairly readily obtainable. Those listed as intermediate fall between these two categories.

breeders to embark on their own programme of conservation. Thus birds which would have led unproductive lives as pets in the hands of people who did not appreciate their intrinsic value have been able to reproduce their kind.

One of the reasons why private aviculturists have the potential to play an important role in parrot conservation is because their participation costs nothing to the conservation community. All the costs and frustrations and, of course, the joys, are borne by themselves, usually financed by the sale of young or offspring from more common species. Many breeders can afford to keep threatened species only because there is income from more common ones. Captive breeding programmes for single species situated in the country of origin, such as that for the Puerto Rican Amazon and the Echo Parrakeet, involve a number of personnel and are extremely expensive to operate. In times of

Obtainable	Intermediate	Rare
Cockatoos		
Cacatua alba (Umbrella)	*Cacatua haematuropygia* (Red-vented)	
C. goffini (Goffin's)		
C. moluccensis (Moluccan)		
C. s. sulphurea (Lesser Sulphur-crested)		
C. s. citrinocristata (Citron-crested)		
C. s. parvula (Timor Lesser Sulphur-crested)		
	Calyptorhynchus baudinii (White-tailed Black)	

Obtainable	Intermediate	Rare
Lories and Lorikeets		
Eos cyanogenia (Black-winged Lory)		*Eos histrio* (Red and Blue Lory)
E. squamata obiensis (Obi Violet-necked Lory)		
	Lorius domicellus (Purple-capped Lory)	*Lorius lory cyanuchen* (Biak Black-capped Lory)
Trichoglossus haematodus forsteni (Forsten's Lorikeet)		*Trichoglossus haematodus djampeanus*
T. h. mitchelli (Mitchell's Lorikeet)		*T. h. stresemanni*
New Zealand Species		
	Nestor notabilis (Kea)	**Nestor meridionalis* (Kaka)
Other Species		
Agapornis nigrigenis (Black-cheeked Lovebird)		
Amazona autumnalis lilacina (Lilacine Amazon)	*Amazona barbadensis* (Yellow-shouldered Amazon)	*Amazona agilis* (Black-billed Amazon)
A. ochrocephala oratrix (Double-Yellow headed Amazon)	*A. collaria* (Yellow-billed Amazon)	*A. brasiliensis* (Red-tailed Amazon)
A. tucumana (Tucuman Amazon)	*A. ventralis* (Hispaniolan Amazon)	*A. dufresniana* (Blue-cheeked Amazon)
A. viridigenalis (Green-cheeked Amazon)	*A. vinacea* (Vinaceous Amazon)	*A. ochrocephala tresmariae* (Tres Marias Amazon)
		A. pretrei (Pretre's Amazon)

Obtainable	Intermediate	Rare
		A. rhodocorytha (Red-browed Amazon)
Anodorhynchus hyacinthinus (Hyacinthine Macaw)		
A. maracana (Illiger's Macaw)		*Ara ambigua* (Buffon's Macaw)
A. militaris boliviana and *A. m. mexicana* (Military Macaw)		*A. glaucogularis* (Blue-throated Macaw)
	A. rubrogenys (Red-fronted Macaw)	
	Aratinga auricapilla (Golden-capped Conure)	*Aratinga n. nana* (Jamaican Conure)
	A. chloroptera (Hispaniolan Conure)	
	A. euops (Cuban Conure)	
Coracopsis nigra (Lesser Vasa Parrot)		
C. vasa (Greater Vasa Parrot)		
		Cyanoliseus patagonus byroni (Greater Patagonian Conure)
		Eclectus roratus riedeli (Riedel's Eclectus)
	Eunymphicus cornutus cornutus (Horned Parrakeet)	*Eunymphicus cornutus uvaeensis* (Uvean Parrakeet)
Guaruba guarouba (Golden (Queen of Bavaria's) Conure)		
Lathamus discolor (Swift Parrakeet)		

* Available only to zoos in New Zealand

Obtainable	Intermediate	Rare
Loriculus philippensis (Philippine Hanging Parrot)		
		Pionus menstruus reichenowi (Reichenow's Blue-headed Pionus)
		Poicephalus robustus robustus (Cape Parrot)
	Psephotus c. chrysopterygius (Golden-shouldered Parrakeet)	
	Pyrrhura cruentata (Blue-throated Conure)	
	P. leucotis (White-eared Conure — all Brazilian sub-species)	
	Rhynchopsitta pachyrhyncha (Thick-billed Parrot)	
	Tanygnathus lucionensis (Blue-naped Parrot)	
		Triclaria malachitacea (Purple-bellied Parrot)

The inclusion of certain species, such as the Hyacinthine Macaw and the Moluccan Cockatoo, might be questioned by some. They are bred in substantial numbers in the USA and in increasing numbers in some other countries. The problem is that the majority are hand-reared for pets. While some of these may eventually end up with breeders, they will not necessarily be suitable for breeding. Some parrots that are hand-reared and then isolated from other parrots from a very early age never learn the normal behaviour which allows them to socialise with their own species. They become totally imprinted on humans. This is especially true of the Moluccan Cockatoo. It is not hand-rearing, *per se*, which causes the problem; hand-reared parrots which are kept with their own species from the age of a few weeks are just as suitable for breeding purposes as parent-reared young. There is a danger that insufficient young of certain species which are popular as pets will be retained for breeding purposes. Responsible aviculturists who care about the future in aviculture of the above-listed species will not only breed them but also adopt the following practices.

1) Maintenance of at least two unrelated pairs of the species in question so that all or some of the offspring (depending on the species) can be sold to other breeders in the form of unrelated pairs. The service of chromosome sexing available in the USA (and surely destined to be available in many other countries eventually) enables breeders to have young sexed while they are still in the nest.

2) Keeping back sufficient young birds to ensure that their own breeding programme continues for an indefinite number of generations.

3) Refraining from hybridising.

4) Ringing or micro-chipping their young and keeping records which allow them to trace the parentage of every bird reared.

5) Putting the welfare of the individual bird above financial gain; in other words, not selling their birds to people obviously unsuitable to care for them properly.

Their collections, although not open to the public, are usually accessible to those with like interests. Data obtained, concerning breeding behaviour and other details which would be difficult or impossible to compile without keeping birds in captivity, are published in avicultural journals throughout the world.

In many cases such information would be of great value to anyone studying the species, or other members of the genus, in the wild. Worldwide, there are countless aviculturists who have made a significant contribution to the pool of knowledge of avian breeding behaviour.

21

Is Reintroduction Feasible?

Most reintroduction programs take years of sustained effort to build up a population to the point where it is self-sustaining and can continue to grow without recurring additions of captive-bred individuals. The well-known Peregrine Falcon program in the eastern United States has tried to come to grips with this by using computer-generated population models to predict how long it will take to achieve the program's goal of a self-sustaining wild population. The estimates are that it will take decades of releasing birds. Sustaining public and institutional support of a program over such a time period, which is not atypical of what would be required for other species, is a major challenge.

STANLEY A. TEMPLE, IN *JEAN DELACOUR/ IFCB SYMPOSIUM* (1983)

Some people assume that the principal purpose of the captive breeding of endangered birds is to release the young produced into the species' natural environment. With very rare exceptions, notably the famous Peregrine Falcon programme, this is not so. The very factors which have led to the endangerment of a parrot, or any animal, tell against the release of captive-bred individuals. The rare exceptions are principally birds of prey endangered by toxic chemicals, resulting in thin-shelled eggs and low hatchability. Once this factor was corrected, the habitat was repopulated with captive-bred birds. Alas, in other cases it is not so simple. A multitude of factors make releases of captive-bred birds totally impracticable.

In most cases the birds themselves are not suitable subjects for release. Close association with humans has caused them to lose their fear of people. This is, perhaps, not insurmountable. Peregrine Falcons received negative conditioning to human presence prior to release (Temple, 1983): they were repeatedly frightened by the use of noisemakers and became wary of human approach. Would this work with parrots reared in captivity? I doubt it. They would eventually realise that no harm resulted from the noise; a parrot's curiosity often overcomes its fear.

This is not to say, however, that all captive-bred parrots would be useless for release. In favourable conditions, preferably in an area of low human population density, the chances are that a fair number would revert to the wild with total success. In any case, with today's sophisticated telemetry devices, released birds can be monitored and those which prove incapable of adequately fending for themselves can be recaptured. This, however, assumes the necessary funding for these devices, and the money may not be available. With endangered birds, though, it might be argued that releases should not be made unless telemetry was used.

In 1982, in the Dominican Republic, what I can only describe as a cruel and unnecessary experiment was carried out — unnecessary because the outcome was totally predictable to anyone with a modicum of knowledge of parrot behaviour.

Thirty-six Hispaniolan Amazon Parrots (*Amazona ventralis*) were used, 23 raised in the Puerto Rican Field Station (used in connection with the *A. vittata* captive breeding programme) and 13 donated by the Parque Zoologico Naciónal in Santo Domingo. Most of the birds were at least partially hand-raised; they varied in age from three months to five years. They were divided into two groups of 18 birds. One group was force-released together away from the area in which they had been held; they were not familar with the natural foods of the area. Members of the other group were held in a field aviary in full view of the eventual release area. Their usual diet was supplemented with fruits and seeds which occurred naturally there. After 9–12 days of 'conditioning' the birds were allowed to leave the field aviary at will. They were allowed to return to it for shelter, food and water.

All birds wore plastic wing tags which were individually coded and nine birds in each group were fitted with radio-transmitter collars. Their activities were monitored from three towers in emergent trees on hillsides overlooking the release valleys as well as from several ground stations. Wiley (1983) recorded: 'The non-conditioned parrots dispersed immediately from the release site, displayed little flock cohesion, and demonstrated aberrant foraging behaviour.' By day 7 six birds had lost an average of 17.9 per cent of pre-release body weight.

He noted: 'In contrast, the pre-conditioned birds displayed good flock cohesion, normal feeding behaviour, and no immediate dispersal. The group members had a high survival rate and eventually integrated into wild parrot populations. As in the non-conditioned group, there was no difference in survival among age classes . . . .'

No mention was made of how many birds were known to survive, nor of the fact that some of them were killed and eaten by Haitian farmers (Temple, 1983).

Obviously, prior to releasing any captive-bred parrots it is advisable to familiarise them with the native foods they will be most likely to encounter and select. In my view, however, it is unlikely that a parrot would starve in the midst of plenty. I once watched a tame, hand-reared escaped Golden (Queen of Bavaria's) Conure, which had been at liberty for 24 hours in mid-winter, gorge itself on the small fruits of a tree which it could never have encountered previously, while its owner stood below. After about 20 minutes, when it had finished feeding, it climbed down the tree and flew to its owner! I do not believe that any parrot released in an area where only unfamiliar food is available would fail to find it.

Also, there is no reason to believe that released captive-bred birds would not breed as successfully as those reared in the wild. Aviculturists know that most parrots imprinted (fixated) on humans can eventually be used successfully for breeding. There are stubborn

exceptions — generally long-term cage pets who are greatly attached to one person — but the release of such birds should not be considered. As formerly imprinted birds will breed under the artificial conditions imposed by captivity, there is little doubt that unimprinted captive-bred parrots would breed in their natural habitat, where they are free to select their own mates and nesting sites.

Major considerations in the release of any parrots would be that they were full-winged, healthy and carrying no excess weight. For preference young birds would be released as they are more adaptable to a new environment than are adult birds.

In my view, however, it is unlikely that many aviary-bred parrots will ever be released to the wild for the simple reason that suitable habitat is not available. Unless intensively managed (as is the Puerto Rican Parrot), released birds would be equally as vulnerable as their wild counterparts to the factors which caused the decline in the first place. Also, wastage would be very high. It is known that only a third of Puerto Rican Parrots (whether parent-hatched or aviary-hatched then fostered into wild nests) survive their first year. Large numbers of captive-bred young would therefore have to be produced for reintroduced birds to make any significant impact on the wild population. Most of those birds would be better employed in building up the numbers of captive birds. Only when the captive population was comparatively large could releasing significant numbers be justified. Also, the larger the scale of such an experiment, the greater the likelihood of success.

There is another reason why releasing small numbers would not be realistic in an attempt to repopulate an area rather than augment an existing population. It concerns genetics and the importance of maintaining genetic variability (*see* pages 152–3 for a discussion of this aspect).

If a situation arose where it seemed that captive-bred birds could be used to augment a declining wild population, the first step would be to carry out intensive field studies. It would be essential to assess the impact that captive-reared released birds would have on the wild population and to ensure that the released birds could be absorbed and would not be displaced due to scarcity of food or nesting sites or other factors. Suppose for example (and this is a fantastic hypothesis) that a captive population of Echo Parrakeets was suddenly discovered and it was decided to release 50 into the wild to bolster the near-extinct population on Mauritius. From recent continuous studies we know that it would not be possible for that number to survive because there is insufficient native food (on which Echo Parrakeets feed exclusively) available. Without such studies, reintroduction might be carried out when it was not in the best interests of the species concerned.

In 1986 occurred the first reintroduction of a parrot to a part of its range where it had long been extinct. The Thick-billed Parrot (*see* pages 14–15) was then found only in Mexico. Formerly, it occurred in the pine forests of Arizona and New Mexico, USA. It was one of two species of parrots found there, the other being the Carolina Parrakeet. Both species are said to have been seen for the last time in the USA during the 1930s, the Carolina in the cypress swamps along the Santee river of South Carolina and the Thick-billed in the Chiricahua mountains of south-eastern Arizona in 1938 (Snyder, Snyder and Johnson, 1989). Both species were shot out of existence, the Thick-billed (like the Passenger Pigeon), for food. Fortunately, it survived in Mexico.

It was never popular as a cage bird or as an avicultural subject but, in 1985 and 1986, quite large numbers were smuggled from Mexico into the USA. All those located were confiscated; nearly all were adults. A proposal was made to use them to try to re-establish the Thick-billed Parrot in Arizona. The location chosen was the Chiricahua mountains. Most of the early records came from this area which is now managed for recreation, wildlife and watershed values. The diversity of food trees, more than a dozen species each of conifers and oaks, compares well with the Thick-billed's habitat in Mexico. This species is dependent on temperate coniferous and mixed deciduous–coniferous woodlands.

Most of the birds available for release could not fly. Some had permanent damage to the feather follicles of the wings; these were suitable only for captive breeding programmes. Others had had their flight feathers cut, rendering them temporarily unable to fly. Parrots do not moult all their flight feathers simultaneously; thus it could be two years before the cut feathers were replaced. It was decided to use a process called 'imping' — splicing and gluing in replacement feathers, a practice which is sometimes used by falconers on birds of prey. However, their lives do not depend on the ability to fly strongly; that of the released Thick-billeds did. Some of the released birds had six or more feathers on each wing imped, although it was known that they would not be as strong as normal feathers. Prior to release they were held in a 2.5-m^3 (8-cu. ft structure) — not adequate to provide wing exercise for any parrot of this size.

The first releases occurred in the early autumn of 1986 — 29 birds, some of which were wearing radio-collars. Seven birds were quickly lost, apparently to hawk predation. (Their release coincided with migratory birds of prey passing through the area.) Eight were observed heading south towards the Mexican border

and 14 remained in Arizona. In the spring of 1987 a few more were released, which, by June, had increased the flock size to 17 birds. They spent the summer along the Mogollon Rim of central Arizona. In September, one year after release, nine returned to the release area in the Chiricahuas. Birds of this species move long distances in search of food. In the autumn of 1988 the flock included two easily distinguished light-billed immatures. The first breeding success had occurred! However, the hope of a sedentary population quickly becoming established in the Chiricahuas was not fulfilled. Such a population was hoped for because, in other areas, people would not be familiar with the re-establishment project and might molest the Thick-billeds.

The supply of confiscated birds soon ceased. Captive-bred birds were essential to maintain the release programme. The problem was that they were nearly all hand-reared birds. A group which was conditioned for six months prior to release included only one parent-reared Thick-billed. During the conditioning period, all learned to feed on pine cones. On release, the hand-reared birds showed no tendency to flock and dispersed in all directions. They appeared not to recognise pine cones as food, even when perched next to them. By late afteroon of the following day it seemed unlikely that they could survive; therefore they were recaptured. The parent-reared bird joined the wild flock on the first day. Unfortunately, it was taken by a raptor on the following day.

Will this species ever become established in Arizona? According to Snyder, Snyder and Johnson: 'Thick-billed Parrots appear to be highly dependent on flocking for protection from raptors, and in the long run they may not be able to sustain themselves in groups smaller than a certain size. Thus, a full test of the possibility of re-establishing the species in the USA depends on releasing many more birds than the numbers presently flying the skies of Arizona.'

This experiment demonstrates two factors which, I believe, could easily have been predicted: a) parrots hand-reared in the normal manner (i.e. with constant contact with humans) are useless for release; and b) it is pointless releasing small numbers because heavy losses will occur.

In this instance, one has also to question the wisdom of releasing imped birds. Surely, only normally full-winged parrots should be used for release purposes. Birds held or hatched in captivity will encounter enough hazards; to release birds which are disadvantaged in any physical aspect is not only foolish but cruel.

Later releases were carried out in a more sensible manner. In 1990 the Avicultural Breeding and Research Centre (ABRC) in Loxahatchee, Florida, USA, embarked on a programme to breed Thick-billed

Parrots for release, after making an agreement with the Arizona Game and Fish Department and the US Fish and Wildlife Service. A one year 'amnesty' had been negotiated whereby Thick-billeds kept by people in the USA could be donated to this breeding programme without being charged with unlawful possession or transport. Illegal importation or sale across state lines without a permit is a felony under the Endangered Species Act and the Lacey Act, as the Thick-billed is treated as a native species. The penalty could be up to five years' imprisonment or a fine of up to $250,000. The birds at ABRC, whether bred or donated, are donated to the state of Arizona. They may be held in Florida for breeding purposes or released in Arizona. At ABRC a very large aviary has been built to allow the birds destined for release to learn flocking and feeding behaviour. It contains a simulated cliff face where they learn how to find water. The aviary measures 47×7.7 m (150×25 ft) and 5.2 m (17 ft) high. The Thick-billeds are provided with pine cones as feeding on cones is apparently learned behaviour, not instinctive. In short, these birds are prepared in every possible manner for life in the wild (Clubb, 1991). (Further information on this release project can be obtained from ABRC, 1471 Folsom Road, Loxahatchee, Florida 33470 or Thick-billed Parrot Program, Arizona Game and Fish Department, 222 West Greenway Road, Phoenix, AZ 85023–4399).

ABRC has also provided birds of another species, the Military Macaw, for release in western Guatemala. The demise of this macaw was the region's first documented vertebrate extinction in historical times. In 1989 and 1990 the Fundación Interamericana de Investigación Tropical (FITT) pioneered the breeding and release of local and US-bred Spectacled Owls and Bat Falcons. In 1990 they contacted ABRC concerning the possibility of releasing captive-bred Military Macaws. Beforehand, they had inventoried and studied the flora and fauna of the Santa Maria region for two years, in conjunction with the University of Texas. ABRC was keen to participate and offered captive-bred macaws, aged between one and two years, from eight different blood lines.

The release site is the south-western slope of Santa Maria volcano in the department of Quezaltenango. Pristine climax forests along intermediate elevations of the volcano contain Resplendent Quetzals, Ornate Hawk Eagles and many other spectacular birds (Clubb, 1991). In November 1991 the first Military Macaws, four males and a female, were released. Two males immediately set off for the mountains and were seen as high as 1,300 m (4,265 ft) at 8 km (5 miles) away from the release point. The other three stayed in the vicinity. All had been held at the release site for several months; their mates were still caged. On the first night three roosted near the cage area; the other two returned on the following day. They were not fitted with radio collars as originally planned (presumably for practical reasons — perhaps the macaws would not tolerate them) but all were implanted with micro-chips so that they could be identified. It was planned slowly to reduce the food offered at the feeding station. To protect the birds, the release site was manned by armed guards (Anon., 1992b). The release of more birds was planned, the outcome of which will be followed with great interest by many.

It has already been noted that as habitat loss or degradation is the major factor in the endangerment of parrot species it is unlikely that many reintroductions to former habitat will occur. Could captive-bred birds, however, be introduced to new areas, outside the species' natural or present range, where conditions were more favourable? Temple (1983) believed that: '. . . possibilities for interisland transfer of endangered birds probably exist with groups like the *Amazona* parrots of the Caribbean region.'

There is only one species which might be reintroduced to islands where it occurred formerly: the Bahaman race of the Cuban Amazon. Some of the smaller Bahaman islands have low human population densities and probably contain suitable habitat. Also, strict legislation protects most Bahaman birds — although, as elsewhere, it is not always enforceable. I suspect that new populations of parrots on other islands in the Caribbean region would be wiped out by hunters, whatever the law stated.

However, in March 1993 I received a letter from Ramon Noegel following his visit to the islands of Grenada and Martinique in the south-eastern West Indies. Grenada, which covers 310 km^2 (120 sq. miles) still has 'vast rainforest preserves and undeveloped areas — forests too thick to penetrate'. He commented: 'What a perfect place to establish an island Amazon!' Martinique, an overseas department of France since 1946, has even greater possibilities within its 1,090 km^2 420 sq. miles). Rainforest covers six large mountains. The island is prosperous and conservation is taken seriously. Considering that conservation measures on St Lucia have resulted in an increased population of the St Lucia Parrot which, like the St Vincent Parrot, may already have reached the maximum capacity for the amount of surviving rainforest, why should a second population not be established on another island? There are no native parrots on these two islands. What is there to lose? Provided that enough birds were transferred and an intensive education programme was mounted, the chance of success would surely be quite high. First, however, a study of the vegetation would be necessary to ascertain adequate food sources. These are unlikely to be lacking.

It seems appropriate here to point out the difference between reintroduction and re-stocking. These terms are defined by IUCN (Anon., 1987) as follows: 'Reintroduction is the release of a species of animal or plant into an area in which it was indigenous before extermination by human activities or by natural catastrophe . . . . Restocking is the release of a plant or animal species into an area in which it is already present.'

Re-stocking might be used when a population is dangerously depleted, as in the case of Spix's Macaw, for example. Superficially, it might seem an easy solution to bolster small, declining populations, especially if the species breeds readily in captivity. Restocking was carried out some years ago in New Zealand with the Red-fronted Kakariki or Parrakeet (*Cyanoramphus novaezelandiae*). Hundreds were released because it is such a free-breeding aviary bird. But they did nothing to bolster the wild population. These days no releases would occur without investigation into the cause of the decline. We now know that hundreds of thousands of Kakarikis could have been released without making any impact on the long-term population level. The birds could not survive in large numbers due to the presence of introduced mammals which were predators and/or food competitors. There was possibly another factor involved, however.

The largest member of the genus *Cyanoramphus* is the Antipodes Green Parrakeet (*C. unicolor*) found on islands with a total area of about 21 km^2 (8 sq. miles). The treeless Penguin-inhabited Antipodes Isles must be one of the strangest habitats of any parrot. Despite this there is a large population of about 3,000 birds which is believed to be stable. Some years ago it was decided to establish a captive population as an insurance against the wild population being overcome by some disaster. The 12 captured in 1967 increased only slowly at first, to 30 by 1979. Twenty were maintained at a bird reserve in Wairarapa and ten were transferred to other aviaries in New Zealand. In 1980 a female died from psittacine erythroblastosis, which had not previously been identified in *Cyanoramphus* species. Over the next four years, 30 of the 37 Antipodes Parrakeets held at this reserve and in three other aviaries died. The disease apparently has an incubation period of between three and four months.

At these four locations Yellow-fronted Kakarikis (*C. auriceps*) and Red-fronted Kakarikis were kept and sometimes used as foster parents for the larger Antipodes Parrakeets. A similar disease, causing anaemia and sporadic deaths, was found in both the smaller species. Young affected birds lacked tail feathers. This feather abnormality has been observed in Yellow-fronted Kakarikis in the wild, but not in the parrakeets from the Antipodes. It might even be one of the factors involved in the decline of this species.

Imagine the disastrous impact on the wild population if captive-bred Antipodes Parrakeets had been used to 're-stock' their native islands! This story perfectly illustrates a serious threat inherent in any re-stocking attempt — the introduction of disease to the wild population. The growing number of serious diseases now found within captive populations of parrots will surely be destined to limit the usefulness of captive breeding for reintroduction and re-stocking purposes. Disease is a threat which cannot be ignored.

However, birds used for re-introduction purposes do not have to come from avicultural sources. In Costa Rica, for example, there are several sites where Scarlet Macaws once abounded but were extirpated during the 1970s and 1980s. Vaughan, McCoy and Liske (1991) suggest that surplus birds could be harvested from the Carara Biological Reserve and reintroduced to areas which apparently offer adequate food, roosting and nesting requirements and, above all, protection. A possible site is the Curu National Wildlife Refuge and Hacienda, an 800 ha (2,000 acres) forested zone only 10 km (6 miles) from the Carara Reserve, across the Gulf of Nicoya. The Scarlet Macaw was last seen there in 1950.

This idea could be applied to other species and makes much better economic sense than captive breeding for release. More importantly, however, birds with a knowledge of living in the wild are infinitely superior for release purposes.

In Chapter 15 mention is made of the release of captive-bred (parent-reared) Orange-bellied Parrakeets This occurred on Tasmania, where the species breeds. However, it migrates to Australia for the winter. Two captive-bred birds were identified by their rings in Victoria in May 1993. Later that year, they migrated back to Tasmania, thus demonstrating the success with which even a migratory parrot species can be used to restock its natural habitat.

22

CITES

Trade in endangered species is closely monitored by all countries which are signatories to the treaty known as CITES (Convention on International Trade in Endangered Species of Wild Fauna and Flora) or the Washington Convention. It came into effect in 1975 and establishes rules for commercial and non-commercial trade. To date, over 100 countries have ratified the CITES agreement.

The species covered are listed in three appendices. Appendix I contains the names of species or sub-species which are endangered and for which trade is authorised only in exceptional circumstances. Appendix II lists species which are not presently threatened but which could become so unless trade was subject to strict regulation; commercial trade is permitted for these species. Appendix III contains species identified by a party country as being subject to conservation regulations within its jurisdiction and requiring the co-operation of other parties to make such regulations effective.

At a meeting held in 1982 an unprecedented step was taken: all parrots not on Appendix I were placed on Appendix II, with the exception of the Budgerigar, Ringneck Parrakeet and Cockatiel.

This move was strongly opposed by two party countries: the USA and Switzerland. The Berne criteria of 1976 established procedures for determining which species should be listed and specifically required that certain biological and trade data be produced before listing a species on Appendix II. The data should indicate that the species in question is subject to

a decreasing or very limited population size or geographic range and that there should be evidence of actual or expected trade in such a volume as to constitute a potential threat to survival of the species.

The USA maintained that to place all parrot species not already on Appendix I on Appendix II affects the credibility and integrity of CITES because it is obvious that not all parrot species are threatened and, further-more, the wholesale listing of an entire order distorts the purpose and meaning of the Treaty and of the Berne criteria.

Trade in Appendix II and III species is permitted only with an export permit issued by the scientific or management authority in the country of origin. Where specimens are re-exported through a third country, a certificate of re-export is issued by that country's management authority, and the original export permit need not accompany the shipment, In the USA under the Lacey Act, the original export permit must be presented to customs upon entry into the country. In Britain, the Department of the Environment normally but not always issues a licence to import Appendix II species on request.

Trade in Appendix I species is much more difficult; commercial trade is not normally allowed. It is necessary to obtain an export permit from the country of origin and an import permit from the country of destination. In theory, permits are issued only after a separate authority determines that trade or shipment of the species will not be detrimental to its survival. It can take several months to obtain the necessary permits.

The Vinaceous Amazon (*Amazona vinacea*) is one of the species included in Appendix I of CITES.

At the time of going to press, the following parrot species were listed on Appendix I of CITES.

Amazona arausiaca (Red-necked Amazon)
A. barbadensis (Yellow-shouldered Amazon)
A. brasiliensis (Red-tailed Amazon)
A. guildingii (St Vincent Parrot)
A. imperialis (Imperial Parrot)
A. leucocephala (Cuban Amazon)
A. pretrei (Pretre's [Red Spectacled] Amazon)
A. rhodocorytha (Red-crowned Amazon)
A. tucumana (Tucuman Amazon)
A. versicolor (St Lucia Parrot)
A. vinacea (Vinaceous Amazon)
A. vittata (Puerto Rican Parrot)
Anodorhynchus glaucus (Glaucous Macaw)
A. hyacinthinus (Hyacinthine Macaw)
A. leari (Lear's Macaw)
Ara ambigua (Buffon's Macaw)
A. glaucogularis (Blue-throated Macaw)
A. maracana (Illiger's Macaw)
A. militaris (Military Macaw)
A. rubrogenys (Red-fronted Macaw)
Cacatua goffini (Goffin's Cockatoo)
C. haematuropygia (Red-vented Cockatoo)

C. moluccensis (Moluccan Cockatoo)
Cyanopsitta spixii (Spix's Macaw)
Cyanoramphus auriceps forbesi (Forbe's Parrakeet)
C. novaezelandiae (Red-fronted Kakariki [Parrakeet])
Cyclopsitta (= Opopsitta) diophthalma coxeni (Coxen's Double-eyed Fig Parrot)
Geopsittacus occidentalis (Night Parrot)
Neophema chrysogaster (Orange-bellied Parrot [Parrakeet])
Ognorhynchus icterotis (Yellow-eared Conure)
Pionopsitta pileata (Red-capped Parrot)
Probosciger aterrimus (Palm Cockatoo)
Psephotus chrysopterygius (Golden-shouldered Parrot [Parrakeet])
P. pulcherrimus (Paradise Parrot [Parrakeet])
Psittacula eques (echo) (Mauritius [Echo] Parrakeet)
Psittacus erithacus princeps (Príncipe Grey Parrot)
Pyrrhura cruentata (Blue-throated Conure)
Rhynchopsitta pachyrhyncha (Thick-billed Parrot)
R. terrisi (Maroon-fronted Parrot)
Strigops habroptilus (Kakapo)

Unfortunately, some countries which are signatories to CITES are finding it impossible to enforce the terms of the treaty. One such is Indonesia, which became a member in 1978. In a report made to IUCN (International Union for the Conservation of Nature) in November 1982, it was stated that implementation of the provisions, particularly in terms of monitoring quotas and controlling the export of endangered species, had been far from effective. Much of the problem lay in the administration of so many islands and the sheer numbers of birds involved (over 389,000 in 1978). In addition to the difficulties with regulating legal trading, illegal export is substantial and well organised.

The report stated: 'The current permit system has many loop-holes which may be easily abused by unscrupulous dealers. Birds may be transported under false names, large shipments may have incorrect numbers entered up, some individuals were disguised by being painted with water-colours, and the permits themselves used several times over. Quotas are not set for captures, and export quotas are not based on biological criteria: many quotas are too high, and no account is taken of mortality between capture and final shipment.'

Anomalies in CITES arise through illogical classification, especially the failure to take into account the fact that several species which are rare in the wild are extremely common in captivity. Because sub-species of *Cyanoramphus novaezelandiae*, the Red-fronted Kakariki (New Zealand Parrakeet), are endangered, the species is placed on Appendix I. A common bird in captivity, it is so prolific (exceeding even the Budgerigar in this respect) that in the Netherlands this species was being offered at £3 each in 1982. Bird-garden owner in Kent, Peter Taboney, decided to import a couple of pairs. On arrival at Heathrow Airport they were confiscated because he did not have the necessary DoE licence for this 'endangered' species.

Formerly on Appendix I, the Splendid (Scarlet-chested) Grass Parrakeet (*Neophema splendida*) is a rare and local species in the interior of Australia. In fanciers' aviaries throughout the world, however, it is common, and bred in thousands annually. As it occurs only in Australia and that country does not permit the export of its native fauna, wild-caught Splendid Grass Parrakeets are never traded and there would be no point in smuggling out such an inexpensive species. The fact that it was ever placed on Appendix I indicates how important it is for aviculturists as well as ornithologists to be consulted regarding the Appendix on which species are listed.

In the future an increasing number of parrots are likely to have captive populations which far exceed those in their natural habitat. Because of the difficulties in obtaining a licence for species on Appendix I, aviculturists will be penalised if species are incorrectly placed on this Appendix. They should note, however, that under Article VII, paragraph 4, of CITES, it is stated that: 'Specimens of an animal species included in Appendix I bred in captivity for commercial purposes, or of a plant species included in Appendix I artificially propagated for commercial purposes, shall be deemed to be specimens of species included in Appendix II.'

It also states (paragraph 5) that: 'Where a Management Authority of the State of export is satisfied that any specimen of an animal species was bred in captivity or any specimen of a plant species was artificially propagated, or is a part of such an animal or plant or was derived therefrom, a certificate by that Management Authority to that effect shall be accepted in lieu of any of the permits or certificates required under the provisions of Articles III, IV or V.'

23

Turning the Tide of Destruction

The environmental problem . . . is frequently invisible to the eye; it works slowly, silently and undramatically; when diagnosed it often requires actions that are in conflict with deeply rooted social and religious values, life styles, and economic systems. In other words, the crisis is potentially lethal because it can only be met through levels of international cooperation unknown to world history.

ROBERT DISCH, IN *THE ECOLOGICAL CONSCIENCE* (1970)

The parrots of the eastern Caribbean are unique symbols of nationhood. Despite being protected for nearly a century, most species are under threat of extinction from hunting, hurricanes, the pet trade, and habitat destruction. A decade ago there was little hope for their survival, but now they have a chance as the result of innovative conservation education programs taking place in Saint Lucia, Saint Vincent and the Grenadines, and Dominica. Through songs, dance, theater, and the mass media, forestry departments of these islands are using pride to promote species preservation. Local attitudes are changing and parrot populations are on the increase.

PAUL BUTLER, IN *PARROTS, PRESSURES, PEOPLE, AND PRIDE*, IN NEW WORLD PARROTS IN CRISIS (IN BEISSINGER AND SNYDER, 1992. SEE REFERENCES CITED)

What can be done to reverse the tide of destruction to habitats and fauna? How can that which survives be protected? There is no simple solution; for the problem is a complex one, all too often involving politics or personal gain. It is proving impossible to prevent the destruction of forests throughout the tropics, thus it is vitally important to protect the fauna that remains in the surviving forests and other habitats. As yet, no wholly effective way has been found to do this. Conservation laws (where they exist) are impossible to enforce. Even if the habitats were of a type which could be controlled by wardens, most of the countries and islands of the tropics are not affluent enough to do this; their priorities lie with such basic problems as feeding and housing their people. The majority of these are poor; many are short of food — and parrots are traditional items of food or trade, whatever the law may state to the contrary.

Nevertheless, there are a number of ways in which this hitherto tide of destruction can be turned into a tide of conservation. Effective conservation measures are already being practised on a small scale. In the more enlightened future all will, hopefully, come to be regarded as standard practices. They can be divided into two categories: a) general practices; b) measures which conserve rainforest.

In the first category are the following.

1) Education and promotion.
2) Large fines for breaking conservation laws.
3) Banning firearms.
4) Establishing more national parks and reserves.
5) Preserving potential nest sites.

6) Captive breeding.

7) Reduction in trade of wild-caught fauna.

8) Specific projects funded by international conservation organisations such as the Worldwide Fund for Nature, the World Parrot Trust and Birdlife International (formerly called the International Council for Bird Preservation).

In the second category the following must be considered.

1) Less wasteful forestry practices.

2) Replanting.

3) Improving yields of existing cultivated areas.

4) Survey of surviving rainforest to assist in future land use.

GENERAL PRACTICES

Education and promotion   Peoples in the tropics must be taught the importance of their own fauna. How can this be done? Perhaps only by promoting the concept of wildlife as a national asset. Where the standard of living is low, however, this is extremely difficult to achieve. One of the few countries where such promotion is beginning to take effect is St Lucia, in the Caribbean. Within two months of a new government being elected in September 1979, the St Lucia Parrot (*Amazona versicolor*) had been declared the national bird. A hazard to its small population, then numbering between 100 and 150, was shooting. To celebrate the parrot's new status, a week of activities included radio and television programmes about it, also a newspaper supplement, and a children's essay competition (in conjunction with which 300 youngsters were taken on a walk through the rainforest). Since then the St Lucia Parrot has featured prominently on posters and T-shirts, and information packs referring to it have reached 20,000 children in biology, English and geography classes.

In Dominica, the Forestry Division visited over 50 schools in 1980, with financial support from WWF. Its purpose was to educate children in the importance of wildlife, especially the two parrot species. The undesirability of hunting was highlighted in a weekly radio programme entitled 'Parrot Poachers'. The newly formed Environmental Education Unit revived the conservation education newspaper *VWA Diablotin* which had ceased publication due to lack of resources. It appears as a supplement to a national newspaper. In January 1989 Paul Butler of the RARE Center for Tropical Bird Conservation started an eight-month programme to heighten public awareness of the plight of Dominica's two parrots. He distributed posters and a questionnaire to ascertain current awareness, and

visited all the schools. The most novel aspect of his campaign was the staging of a musical featuring the parrots (Evans, 1991).

The infectious enthusiasm for conservation possessed by Paul Butler is a great asset in an education programme. Two others who share this gift are Carl Jones, who leads the Mauritius conservation effort, and Don Merton of the New Zealand Department of Conservation. They all possess the charisma which makes compelling television viewing. Programmes featuring these conservation biologists have captured the imagination of millions of viewers worldwide.

There are a few dedicated private individuals who are trying to instill into the people of tropical countries an awareness of the dangers which local parrot populations face. One of these is Dr J.P. Ehrenberg in Yucatán, Mexico. In Mérida he will open, probably in 1996, a centre for the conservation and rehabilitation of Mexican parrots. There he plans to educate the public on all aspects of their conservation, using birds exhibited in aviaries, slide shows, films, a library and every other means at his disposal. At the time of writing, he was organising a concert by popular Mexican singers, all the proceeds of which were to be donated to Amerycop (Asociación Mexicana para la Rehabilitación y Conservación de los Psitácidos).

Conservation workers involved with specific projects can do much to heighten local awareness of a species' plight with promotional material. For example, those working with Lear's Macaw gave T-shirts featuring it to a few important local people (the shirts soon became collectors' items); woven patches illustrating the macaw were given to those who helped with the census, and bumper stickers were given to everyone.

The World Parrot Trust and RARE initiated and sponsored a highly popular method of promoting conservation awareness. The idea is simple but its execution is expensive. It is a mobile centre; in other words, a conservation bus. The first one, the 'Jacquot Express', took off on St Lucia in 1991. A renovated vehicle was painted with forest motifs and fitted with various displays, slide projector, video-cassette-recorder and television. Open mouths and looks of disbelief, followed by radiant smiles, greeted the bus wherever it went. In February 1992, the *Sisserou Express* arrived on Dominica. This was also decorated with a forest motif, dominated by an Imperial Parrot. In 1993 the *Vincie Express* arrived on St Vincent. Each bus cost about £25,000 and has demonstrated that joint projects between specialised charities can be remarkably successful.

When Third World countries take practical steps to educate their young in environmental matters the future becomes tinged with hope. This has happened in Indonesia. The appointment in 1982 of a Minister for

Environment and Development Supervision hopefully heralds a dawning of awareness of the environment in that country. The Minister mobilised the education system to stimulate 'environmental awareness' among the citizens and called upon 28 state universities to establish environmental study centres.

Large fines The penalty for those who break conservation laws must be high, or the law is no deterrent. In St Lucia, since 1980, fines of the equivalent of £1,000 can be imposed on anyone attempting to smuggle birds off the island, and any yacht or aeroplane used in the attempt can be impounded. Realistic fines have also been introduced in Dominica (*see* page 73), and other countries must follow.

Banning firearms Ironically, it seems that laws which directly protect wildlife are less effective than those banning the possession of guns, for reasons unconnected with conservation. On Jamaica prohibiting firearms has had a markedly beneficial effect on the fauna. A gun law which came into operation in 1974 to repress criminals resulted in all rifles being collected by the constabulary. Within a few years most of the land

The *Jacquot Express* tours St Lucia, educating its people on the importance of conserving the forest and its parrots.

birds had become more numerous, particularly doves and parrots, both of which are considered good eating. Contravening the anti-gun and anti-hunting law resulted in a mandatory prison term, with or without fines that ranged from Eastern Caribbean $50 to $1,000.

Laws which discriminate between bird species, protecting, for example, parrots but not pigeons, may be ineffective. Blanket protection is therefore desirable because one of the principal enemies of parrots is the pigeon-shooter. Pigeons and certain parrots are not dissimilar in size, shape and style of flight and there may be either genuine misidentification or the excuse that parrots were shot in mistake for pigeons.

National parks and reserves More countries in the tropics are realising the importance of establishing and maintaining national parks and reserves — not only for intrinsic reasons but for the wider ecological benefits. Brazil is an excellent example.

After the devastation of natural habitats which occurred on an enormous scale, Brazil produced the Plano Naciónal de Parques. It includes proposals for 1,560,000 km² (600,000 sq. miles) of well-sited parks and reserves. This is equal to 18 per cent of the entire territory.

Paul and Anne Ehrlich (1982) consider Brazil's 'official policy turnaround on Amazonia, from uncontrolled exploitation to a mix of conservation and ecologically sound development, is the single most encouraging event on the extinction front in our memory'.

Will this ambitious plan, however, be overtaken by the continuing destruction of forests? By 1992 8.5 million acres of Brazilian rainforest were being destroyed annually. Unless the reserves are rapidly implemented on the ground, they may never exist. Prior to 1979 the only national park existing within the forested region of Amazonia was the 1,258,000-ha (3.1-million-acre) Amazonia National Park, located mainly to the west of the Rio Tapajós, but including a 10-km (6-mile) wide buffer zone on its eastern side. During 1979 and 1980 four more national parks and three biological reserves were decreed in Brazilian Amazonia. These include two very large national parks: the 2,200,000-ha (5.4 million-acre) Pico da Neblina (continuous with the 1,360,000-ha [3.4 million-acre] Serrania da Neblina National Park in Venezuela) and the 2,272,000-ha (5.6 million-acre) Jaú National Park (Rylands and Mittermeier, 1982).

As yet not a great deal has been accomplished; but at least the Amazonian countries are becoming increasingly aware of the need for established and effective conservation policies, as well as of the necessity of preserving large tracts of forest and the varied Amazonian ecosystems. In 1975 Brazil, Venezuela, Ecuador, Bolivia, Peru and Colombia formed an Intergovernmental Technical Committee for the Protection and Management of Amazonian Flora and Fauna (CIT) to co-operate on the standardisation of conservation policies and legislation, and on the formation of parks and reserves. In general priority is given to the conservation of ecosystems; little emphasis is placed on fauna.

In Peru, CEDIA (Center for the Development of the Amazon Indian) is well advanced in its work to protect 28,000 m² (11,000 sq. miles) of rainforest — one of the last very large undisturbed areas of rainforest on earth. Funds are raised through Friends of the Peruvian rainforest (see Appendix 3). Over 24,000 ha (9,400 sq. miles) of this rainforest surround the 18,200-km² (7,000-sq. mile) Manu Biosphere Reserve, where eight species of macaw are being studied.

Preserving potential nest sites Large live trees of low commercial value or standing dead trees with suitable cavities should be left by foresters for nesting sites (*see* pages 14–15), where appropriate.

Provision of nest-boxes Lack of nest sites has been mentioned throughout these pages as one reason for low reproduction rates in some parrot species. How successful are the results of providing artificial nest sites? This probably depends on how carefully the habits of the birds involved have been studied and on the type of nest provided. It appears that the nearer they are in appearance to natural sites, the more acceptable they are.

Some interesting experiments have been carried out. One factor limiting breeding success of the Norfolk Island Parrakeet (*see* page 132) was lack of nest sites. Between 1984 and 1987 53 boxes of varying shapes and sizes were hung in the national park where these birds occur. They were a great success with the introduced Starlings (*Sturnus vulgaris*) who occupied 44 of them! The introduced Crimson Rosellas nested in three boxes, rats occupied four, and four were occupied by bees. None were used by the parrakeets. In a similar experiment on New Zealand for the nominate subspecies, the Red-fronted Parrakeet (*Cyanoramphus novaezelandiae novaezelandiae*), more than 500 boxes were erected, but only one was used by the birds for which they were intended (Hicks and Greenwood, 1989). In Mauritius, nest-boxes were erected for Echo Parrakeets. Over several seasons, counting each box once per season, 22 of the 40 boxes were occupied by alien animals (Jones and Duffy, 1992).

An interesting and successful experiment was carried out with the Green-rumped Parrotlet (*Forpus passerinus*) in Venezuela. These little parrots, only 12 cm (5 in) long, normally nest in holes in trees, termitaria or even in clothesline supports. One study found that hollowed fenceposts were often used. One hundred artificial nest-boxes were designed, using the same dimensions of fencepost cavities. The study area that contained 100 nest-boxes in 1989 contained ten known semi-natural nest sites in fenceposts from 1985 to 1987. Assuming that not all the nests were found, and that twice as many existed, the area would have contained only a quarter of the number of nests which were occupied. In 1988 there were 58 nesting attempts in 40 boxes; in 1989, when 100 boxes were erected, there were 119 nesting attempts in these boxes. In 1988, 39 of the 40 were visited at least once and, in 1989, 96 of the 100 boxes were visited. In this case, the provision of boxes resulted in a three- to four-fold increase in nesting birds (Beissinger and Bucher, in Beissinger and Snyder, 1992). My own opinion is that such a high success rate with species other than parrotlets or

Lovebirds would be most unlikely. Because of their small size, they do not have to repel any large avian species, and because they are aggressive they are well able to fend off any small avian nest competitors — if such exist. Although the provision of nest sites may have limited application, it can clearly be very effective in some cases.

Munn *et al.* (1991) described early experiments in providing nest sites for large macaws at the Tambopata Research Center in Peru. In October and November 1990 23 heavy palm-trunk nests and three large wood-lined plastic barrels were mounted in the canopy of emergent trees. With hindsight it was felt that these were erected too late in the season. However, that season, 23 of these nests were visited and many of them had been excavated inside. One nest was successful in fledging a young Scarlet Macaw in March 1991. In the previous season Blue and Yellow Macaws used and fledged young from three out of ten smaller, less well-constructed nest-boxes. In the case of large parrots, where nest sites are at a premium, it seems likely that providing artificial nests could be a very successful method of increasing reproduction rates. This is an area which needs to be investigated with many other parrot species.

Captive breeding   The importance of captive breeding as a means of conservation is discussed in Chapters 19 and 20.

Reduction in trade of wild-caught fauna   The volume of worldwide trade in wild-caught parrots is, at the time of writing (1993), excessively high. Banning trade in the most vulnerable species has led to other formerly common species being threatened. For example, the Yellow-fronted Amazon (*Amazona ochrocephala ochrocephala*), formerly widespread and common in Venezuela, may soon reach threatened status there due to the huge numbers captured for the national and international trade. Quotas (limiting the numbers captured per species per year) *must* be established for all species — and adhered to.

Specific projects funded by international conservation organisations   The founding, in 1961, of the World Wildlife Fund, which later changed its name to the Worldwide Fund for Nature, marked the start of a new era for conservation. Previously there had been no truly co-ordinated or worldwide conservation projects, only local ones. WWF took off in a way which few could have predicted, pinpointing the great need which had existed for such an organisation. Initially, it was the more spectacular creatures, such as the tiger, which were the subject of international campaigns, with a strong element of emergency action. As funds and

The Yellow-winged sub-species (*Amazona aestiva xanthopteryx*) of the Blue-fronted Amazon is endangered in Argentina by nest robbing and destruction of nest sites to reach the young.

knowledge increased, programmes to save entire habitats became more common. Then in the late 1970s WWF gave support and financial assistance to World Conservation Strategy, a statement of global conservation priorities, and plans for achieving them.

In the 1970s at least two parrot studies were undertaken as a result of WWF funding. The very first project of the Australian division of WWF was a study of the Orange-bellied Parrakeet, for which A\$45,000 were allocated. This commenced in 1979 (*see* Chapter 15).

The organisation known as TRAFFIC (Trade Records Analysis of Flora and Fauna in Commerce) produced a report on macaws which was funded by WWF. Published in 1980, under the title of 'Macaws: traded to extinction', it provided data and recommendations concerning the huge numbers of macaws in trade.

There was no extensive involvement in parrot conservation by the major conservation societies until the late 1980s. By then, ICBP, which had already helped to fund several parrot projects, was involved with many more. One of the most ambitious was the long-term management plan for a tropical forest, the location being Dominica. The study is to be conducted jointly with the Forestry Division, placing particular emphasis on determining the minimum size and structure of forest areas necessary for maintaining species diversity and stability, identifying key links in the structure of co-evolved food webs, and facilitating the co-existence of forestry and agriculture.

Compared with the number of endangered parrots, lamentably few conservation projects to assist these species had been launched by the 1980s. There was a clear and urgent need for an organisation devoted solely to parrot conservation. It was Michael Reynolds, director of Paradise Park (which concentrates on breeding and showing to the public endangered birds) in Cornwall, UK, who had the foresight and the dedication to do something about it. In 1989 he launched the World Parrot Trust. It aimed to educate the public about the threats to parrot survival, to seek their interest, concern and support, and to promote a high standard in the keeping of parrots. In the four and a half years (at the time of writing) of its existence, it has achieved remarkable success in funding and sponsoring conservation projects for the Hyacinthine Macaw, Lear's Macaw, various Amazon species in the Caribbean and Brazil, Echo Parrakeet, Red-tailed Black Cockatoo and many others. It publishes a quarterly magazine, *PsittaScene*, which is unlike any other publication devoted to parrots, in that it focuses on parrot conservation projects and news of endangered species, as well as containing items of interest to the aviculturist, book reviews, fund-raising appeals, etc. Considering its significant success in a short period, WPT is destined to play in the future a leading role in conserving parrots (see Appendix 3).

Special fund-raising projects Dedication and enthusiasm alone are not sufficient to make fund-raising successful. In my experience, the printed word is not very effective because few respond to this type of appeal. One has to try to take advantage of gatherings such as symposia or other places where visitors are likely to be interested in conservation, such as zoos and wildlife parks. For example, at the First International Parrot Convention at Loro Parque, Tenerife, in 1986, I organised an appeal on behalf of the endangered parrots of Dominica. From 500 people at the gala dinner, more than $20,000 was raised. I also encouraged zoos in the UK to instal collecting boxes. This sparked off the idea for the National Federation of

Zoos 1988 'Parrots in Peril' appeal which raised £12,000. Another zoo which I contacted came up with a very simple and effective idea. In one of their exhibits was a pond in which people often threw coins. The erection of a notice concerning the Dominican Parrot Appeal increased the flow of coins which were then channelled to this cause, and quickly mounted up to hundreds of pounds. Generally speaking, collecting *boxes* do not achieve such good results. A more novel idea is needed, such as a specially adapted and decorated parking meter in an American zoo.

MEASURES WHICH CONSERVE RAINFOREST

Less wasteful forestry practices A major area of waste is that which relates to current logging procedures. The potential for improvement is enormous. The crown of a giant forest tree may measure as much as 0.4 ha (1 acre); when it falls it injures neighbouring trees, both directly and because the crown is usually linked to that of other crowns by lianas and vines. It would be a simple matter, states Norman Myers (1983) to sever the linking plants before the chainsaw is applied. This would add in the region of US$5 to the US$200 it costs per cubic metre of timber exported from Indonesia.

Damage to residual forest could be further reduced if logs were extracted by helicopters. Although timber corporations claim this is too expensive, they practise this form of extraction in hilly terrain without losing their competitive edge in the market.

Thirdly, greater care could be taken with directional felling, ensuring that a tree being felled falls away from its principal neighbours. Myers estimated that were this simple practice to be implemented in Indonesia, the logger's damage (which now leaves between a third and two-thirds of residual forest injured beyond recovery) could be reduced by a least 50 per cent.

Timber-exporting countries could earn more from hardwood exports if all logs were processed into plywood or veneers before export. In this way the income would be as great but the number of trees cut would be considerably reduced.

According to Secrett (1986), in Malaya, 55 per cent of the forest is destroyed to harvest only 10 per cent of the trees. And in soil compacted by heavy machinery and vulnerable to erosion, regrowth is virtually impossible. For every 1 m^3 (1.3 cu. yd) of wood sold, at least 1.25 m^3 (1.6 cu. yd) is lost in the processing. Also, secondary disturbed forests could provide many of the main timber products. Plantations are being established at only a tenth of the felling rates.

Replanting Indonesia has adopted an excellent scheme which should be noted elsewhere in the tropics.

Please Help Save
The Imperial Parrot

$40,000 is needed to save it from extinction.

Only 50 of these magnicent parrots survive on the island of Dominica in Caribbean. Your donation will help fund a three year study and to build an education centre to help Dominica's people to protect their parrots.

Thank you for your donation.

Dominican Parrot Project
International Council For Bird Preservation
219c Huntingdon road,
Cambridge CB3 ODL

Collecting boxes in zoos and bird parks help to raise much-needed funds for conservation projects. This one, for the Imperial Parrot, was installed by the author at Loro Parque, Tenerife.

Timber corporations have to post a performance bond of $4 per cubic metre of exportable hardwood against an undertaking to plant trees as replacements for those cut down. If they fail to do so, no refund is given on the bond.

Plantations of pines or other exotic trees in the tropics can generate ten times as much usable timber per acre as can natural forest. In Indonesia it is planned to establish such plantations quickly, in order to relieve some of the exploitation on such patches of virgin forest as may still have a chance of surviving the century.

Ruined croplands and degraded savannahs can be used for planting forests of pine and eucalypts; although these will not provide habitat for displaced animals or result in the former ecolocial diversity, they prevent further needless destruction of rainforest.

There are, however, practical measures that can prevent further deforestation. Yields can be improved in areas already under cultivation, in preference to clearing virgin forest.

Damage to the ecosystem is reversible where small areas are concerned in tropical rainforests: they will undergo successional changes and automatically revert to a climax state if further disturbance does not occur. Unfortunately, this is not true of large areas in which the soil deteriorates and other changes occur, to the degree where it is impossible to re-establish the forest.

Tariffs on 'rainforest' beef Importing countries should ensure that beef produced at the expense of rainforest is discouraged through tariffs and quotas, suggests Secrett (1986). Since 1950, almost two-thirds of Central America's lowland rainforests have been cleared or seriously degraded to produce cheap beef. Of this, 90 per cent is exported to the West.

Ecotourism   Not until the late 1980s came the realisation that macaw populations in accessible areas were worth conserving as tourist attractions. For instance, in Costa Rica, only a two-hour drive on a paved highway from the major tourist area, the most accessible population of Scarlet Macaws in Central America is located. Visiting these macaws has become a major day trip and tourist attraction. Tourists bring dollars and jobs to the area, the Carara Biological Reserve. However, there is a problem. The local people do not benefit. Most of the tourist dollars are spent in the Central Valley but leave the country through foreign investment in hotels, airlines and tour agencies. Unless there is direct economic benefit to the several hundred people living in the area of the reserve, they have no reason to be interested in conserving the macaw population. Vaughan, McCoy and Liske (1991) suggest that incentives to the local people could include additional ranger positions in the reserve, stimulation of local souvenir sales and a tourist tax for local community development.

In Brazil and Peru, rainforest tourism is growing at an extraordinary rate and is destined to expand much further. In some areas tour lodges are the fastest-growing and most lucrative businesses. One Peruvian company expanded its revenue from US$7,000 in 1985 to US$240,000 in 1989 (Munn, in Beissinger and Snyder, 1992). In the Pantanal region of Brazil, Hyacinthine Macaws are generating substantial income through ecotourism (*see* page 42) and the potential to increase this income is enormous.

Surveying the surviving forest   One of the most important steps taken in Brazil in recent years, which gives some cause for optimism, is Project Radar Amazon. The combination of airborne radar remote sensing systems and ground surveys are being used to analyse the Amazon basin. Maps are being produced for the first time that show the characteristics of the soil, the basic geology and forest types, and the agricultural potential of Amazonia. This will assist in future use of the land which, it is to be hoped, will not involve the scandalous waste which occurred during the 1970s.

* * *

On Caribbean islands, areas of rainforest in which parrots survive are small; although they can be considered quite large in terms of providing wardens to protect them and their fauna, and to enforce the law. In South and Central America, areas of rainforest are vast in comparison — so vast that wardening is impractical and law enforcement almost impossible.

What, then, can be done to protect the parrots which inhabit these areas? Although prohibiting the export trade does have a beneficial effect, its impact is reduced by the fact that parrots which formerly were caught by natives to be sold alive are now shot for food. In addition, several parrots would be eaten to replace the amount of food which could be bought with the proceeds of the sale of one live parrot. I am not condoning the trade in live parrots, which has reached unacceptable proportions since 1960, merely pointing out that laws which protect parrots from trade can also work against their survival.

The only effective method of conserving most parrots, without taking them into captivity, lies in prohibiting any further reduction of their habitat. Alas, the most extreme optimist knows that this is a wildly Utopian idea. Some countries have had the foresight to protect small areas which are designated as national parks or reserves but these are all too often ineffective, as explained in Chapter 1.

Protective legislation and the formation of reserves are major steps forward; but laws may be broken and reserves desecrated. What is needed is a change of attitude not only by those who shoot or poach or trap, or by politicians and leaders, but also by men and women who will never see a tropical forest. In other words, what is vital to the continuing existence not only of the forests and of their fauna, but to our very selves, is the worldwide development of an ecological conscience.

In the book of that name, *The Ecological Conscience* (1970), Robert Disch reaches straight to the heart of the matter: 'The conscience of ecology must teach man that there is no natural right to exterminate a form of life; that one is not entitled to desecrate earth, air, or space merely because he happens to own, control, or occupy some portion of it; and that the fact of "legality" in a human court cannot remove ecological crimes from having planetary implications for all mankind.

'The development of our ecological conscience will require an unflinching reassessment of past traditions and present practices, both of which are tainted by a blinding western egocentricity, a mental state that confuses the destruction of the conditions necessary for life with the assertion that man has somehow "conquered nature".

'. . . Expert in the moral dilemmas and concerns of humanity, the humanism of the West never brought the wisdom of ecology into the mainstream of its tradition.'

Are we so bound by tradition that it is not possible to change our ways? Or, at this crucial stage in man's history, can we make amends before it is too late? As Barry Commoner wrote with so much foresight: 'A new conservation movement is needed to preserve life itself.'

Those who ask why it is important to preserve any

form of life must be made to realise that in ensuring the future of other forms of life, from the lowliest amoeba, we are safeguarding our own future, for all species are interdependent. There is, perhaps, an analogy in the old adage 'Look after the pennies and the pounds will look after themselves.' No creature should be deemed insignificant or unworthy of attention. Ecologically, the smallest insect is as important as the most beautiful parrot. Many people can relate to birds, and especially parrots, which by tradition are much-loved pets, whereas few would show concern about less known, less conspicuous or less endearing creatures. The knowledge that a parrot species is endangered evokes more reaction than the loss of a species of snail, for example. Much as the public might support or applaud the principles of conservation, however, without the necessary habitat to carry out conservation all will be lost.

Aldo Leopold (1970) said: 'A rare bird or flower need remain no rarer than the people willing to venture their skill in building it a habitat.' He also pointed out that: '. . . a sufficiently enlightened society, by changing its wants and tolerances, can change the economic factors bearing on land.'

This is true. Only one force can halt the destruction of forest and the abuse of the environment: public concern, and the knowledge that if this concern is expressed loudly enough politicians are forced to heed it. In the USA in 1969 the National Wildlife Federation commissioned two poll organisations to investigate American attitudes on the environment. They resulted in the conclusion that most people are very concerned about environmental problems and would have prefer-

red that a greater proportion of their taxes were devoted to the cost of solving them. Over 50 per cent of those interviewed felt that the government was devoting insufficient attention to environmental problems; over 80 per cent felt a personal concern about the environment and most of these registered 'deep concern'. If these polls reflect the true attitudes of those interviewed, it is clear that it is not apathy that results in so little being done but, as Frank M. Potter (1970) suggests, because 'we are too easily convinced of our own political impotence'. He also points out that '. . . when they are really aroused, people can take and have taken effective action'.

Nevertheless there is hope. The younger generation seem to be more aware of the dangers of pollution and other abuses of the environment than their elders. Can they begin to correct the mistakes of the technological age in which we live, mistakes which will be irreversible unless some action is taken within the next few years? To do so, fundamental moral changes are required, changes in human habits.

These young people, and others who are acutely aware of what is happening to our environment, are making their voices heard, they are beginning to turn the tide. If they can make headway in one of the less affluent nation states, the Dominican Republic, there is hope. In 1982 reafforestation was being carried out in many places there, people were being educated against the tradition of cutting and burning and advised on how to limit the size of their families.

We can only hope that through the wider awareness of the vital necessity to conserve natural resources the tide of destruction will be turned just in time . . . .

Epilogue

New Zealand songwriter Syd Melbourne penned the following words, ascribing them to a highly endangered bird of the forest, the Kokako. Yet could anything more appropriate have been written on behalf of the parrots of the world?:

Many birds suffered for the use of mankind. Your survival once depended on us. Now our survival depends on you. What are you going to do about it? That is the challenge.

Appendix 1: Parrot Extinctions

Species	Endemic Area	Last Known	Reason for Extinction
Lophopsittacus mauritianus (Broad-billed Parrot)	Mauritius, Indian Ocean	Early 17th century	Hunting?
Necropsittacus rodericanus (Rodrigues Parrot)	Rodrigues I., Indian Ocean	18th century	Hunting?
Cyanoramphus ulietanus (Society Parrakeet)	Raiatea (Ulieta), Society Is., Pacific Ocean	1777	Rats?
C. zealandicus (Black-fronted Parrakeet)	Tahiti, Society Is., Pacific Ocean	1844	Rats?
Mascarinus (=Coracopsis) mascarinus (Mascarene Parrot)	Réunion I., Indian Ocean Mauritius?, Indian Ocean	After 1834?	Hunting?
Nestor productus (Norfolk Island Kaka)	Norfolk I. and Phillip I., Pacific Ocean Australia	1850s	Hunting
Ara tricolor (Cuban Macaw)	Cuba	1864	Hunting
Psittacula exsul (Newton's Parrakeet)	Rodrigues I., Indian Ocean	1875	Hunting?
Cyanoramphus novaezealandiae subflavescens (Lord Howe Island Parrakeet)	Lord Howe I., Pacific Ocean	c. 1890	Hunting? Rats?
C. n. erythrotis (Macquarie Island Parrakeet)	Macquarie I., Pacific Ocean	1870–90	Shooting (crop pest)
Psittacula wardi (Seychelles Parrakeet)	Mahé I., Silhouette I., Indian Ocean	Before 1906	Shooting (crop pest)
Conuropsis (=Aratinga) carolinensis (Carolina Conure)	South-eastern USA	1926	Shooting
Anodorhynchus glaucus (Glaucous Macaw)	Argentina Uruguay Brazil	Unknown	Loss of habitat
Psephotus pulcherrimus (Paradise Parrakeet)	Australia	Unknown – 1960s?	Habitat degradation?

Appendix 2: 'Studbooks' and EEPs for Endangered and Threatened Species

International

Guaruba guarouba (Golden [Queen of Bavaria's] Conure): Alan Lieberman, San Diego Zoo, PO Box 551, Ca. 92112–0551, USA.

Europe (EEP = European Breeding Programme)

Amazona tucumana (Tucuman Amazon): Matthias Reinschmidt, Schwanenstrasse 13, 7580, Buhl, Germany.

Anodorhynchus hyacinthinus (Hyacinthine Macaw): Dr H. Lücker, Zoo Dresden, Tiergartenstrasse 1, D01219, Dresden, Germany.

Cacatua haematuropygia (Red-vented Cockatoo): Marc Boussekey, Espace Zoologique, St Martin-la-Plaine, 42800 Rive-de-Gier, France.

Guaruba guarouba (Golden [Queen of Bavaria's] Conure: Bengt Holst, Copenhagen Zoo, Sdr Fasanvej 79, Frederiksberg, DK2000, Denmark.

Probosciger aterrimus (Palm Cockatoo): Dr Roger Wilkinson, Chester Zoo, Caughall Road, Upton-by-Chester, CH2 1LH, UK.

UK

Amazona autumnalis lilacina (Lilacine Amazon) and *A. viridigenalis* (Green-cheeked Amazon): Mark Pilgrim, Chester Zoo, Caughall Road, Upton-by-Chester, CH2 1LH.

Anodorhynchus hyacinthinus (Hyacinthine Macaw): Colin Bath, Paignton Zoo, Totnes Road, Paignton, Devon.

Ara ambigua (Buffon's Macaw), *A. macao* (Scarlet Macaw) and *A. rubrogenys* (Red-fronted Macaw): David Woolcock, Paradise Park, Hayle, Cornwall TR27 4HY.

Cacatua goffini (Goffin's Cockatoo): David Woolcock, Paradise Park, Hayle, Cornwall TR27 4HY.

C. haematuropygia (Red-vented Cockatoo): c/o The Parrot Society, 108b Fenlake Road, Bedford, MK42 0EU.

C. moluccensis (Moluccan Cockatoo): Rob Colley, Penscynor Wildlife Park, Cilfrew, Neath, Glamorgan, South Wales.

C. ophthalmica (Blue-eyed Cockatoo): Dr Roger Wilkinson, Chester Zoo, Caughall Road, Upton-by-Chester, CH2 1LH.

Eos reticulata (Blue-streaked Lory): c/o The Parrot Society, 108b Fenlake Road, Bedford MK42 0EU

Guaruba guarouba (Golden [Queen of Bavaria's] Conure): c/o The Parrot Society, 108b Fenlake Road, Bedford, MK42 0EU.

Rhynchopsitta pachyrhyncha (Thick-billed Parrot): David Jeggo, Jersey Wildlife Preservation Trust, Les Augres Manor, Trinity, Jersey, Channel Islands.

USA

Coracopsis species (Vasa Parrots): Dave Blynn 6727 Windfaire Drive, Norcross, GA 30093.

Probosciger aterrimus (Palm Cockatoo): Mike Taylor, White Oaks Plantation, 726 Owens Road, Yulee, FLA 32097.

International Loriinae Society, c/o J. van Oosten, 8023 17th NE Seattle, WA 98115.

Appendix 3: Organisations which Aid the Conservation of Parrots

Amerycop (Asociación Mexicana para la Rehabilitación y Conservación de los Psitácidos, Apdo Postal 4–174 Izimna, Mérida, Yucatán, Mexico.

Friends of the Abaco Parrot (*Amazona leucocephala bahamensis*), donations to Barclay's Bank, (a/c no 1074526), Marsh Harbour, Abaco, Bahamas.

Friends of the Peruvian Rainforest, 668 Public Ledger Building, Philadelphia, PA 19106, USA.

Birdlife International (formerly International Council for Bird Conservation), Wellbrook Court, Girton Road, Cambridge CB3 0NA, UK.

World Parrot Trust, Glanmor House, Hayle, Cornwall TR27 4HY, UK.

Zoologische Gesellschaft für Arten- und Populationsschutz, Franz-Senn Str.14, 81377 München, Germany.

References

Anon, 1926, 'Avicultural Notes', *Avicultural Magazine:* 158.

1974, *Madagascar: The Malagasy Republic,* Sterling Publishing, New York.

1982, *Study of Impact of Logging on the Dominica Parrot,* Caribbean Consultants for Caribbean Conservation.

1986, 'No chance for Spix's Macaw?', *World Birdwatch,* 8 (3): 5.

1987, *Translocation of Living Organisms, IUCN Position Statement,* Gland, Switzerland, 20pp.

1991, 'A discussion with Don Merton of New Zealand', *Australian Aviculture,* 46 (5): 109–12.

1992, 'Military Macaws released into wild', *The Majestic Macaws,* 3 (1): 8.

Albornoz, M., Rojas Suárez, F. and Sanz, V., 1992, 'Conservación y Manejo de la Cotorra (*Amazona barbadensis*) en la Isla de Margarita', *1° Simposio sobre la Biologiá y Conservación de los Psitácidos Venezolanos.*

Anderson, Charles, Dedman, Valda and Doughty, Chris, 1980, 'The Orange-Bellied Parrot: species endangered by improperly assessed development', *Victorian Naturalist,* 97: 235–47.

Andrle, Robert F. and Patricia R., 1975, 'Report on the status and conservation of the Whistling Warbler on St Vincent, West Indies, with additional observations on the St Vincent Parrot', *Bull. Internat. Council Bird Preserv.,* xii: 245–51.

Arman, Mr and Mrs J., 1983, 'Breeding the Jamaican Yellow-billed Amazon Parrot', *Avicultural Magazine:* 89(1):21–6.

Arndt, T., 1989, 'Zum Status der Gelbschulteramazone', *Papageien,* 2: 57–60.

Atkinson, I.A.W., 1985, 'The spread of commensal species of *Rattus* to oceanic islands and their effects on island avifaunas', in *Conservation of Island Birds,* ed. P.J. Moors, Cambridge, ICBP Technical Publication No. 3: 35–49.

Azara, F. de, 1805, *Apuntamientos para la Historia Natural de los Pajaros de Paraguay y Rio de la Plata,* Vol. 3, Madrid.

Barbour, Thomas, 1943, *Cuban Ornithology,* Cambridge, Massachusetts.

Beissinger, R. and Snyder, N. eds, 1992, *New World Parrots in Crisis,* Smithsonian Institution Press, Washington.

Benson, C.W., 1960, 'The birds of the Comoro Islands: results of the British Ornithologists' Union Centenary Expedition 1958', *Ibis,* 103B: 5–106.

Bertagnolio, Paolo, 1981, 'The Red-tailed Amazon and other uncommon South American parrots', *Avicultural Magazine,* 87: 6–18.

Blackwell, Chris, 1982, 'Consistent success with an endangered conure', *Cage and Aviary Birds,* November 6: 1, 5.

Bond, J., 1929, 'On the birds of Dominica, St Lucia, St Vincent and Barbados, British West Indies', *Proc. Acad. Nat. Sci. Philad.* 80: 523–45.

Boshoff, A., 1991, 'What is happening to the parrots of southern Africa?', *Quagga,* No. 27: 7–10.

Boussekey, M., Saint-Pie, J. and Morvan, O., 1991, 'Observations on a population of Red-fronted Macaws *Ara rubrogenys* in the Río Caine valley, central Bolivia', *Bird Conservation International,* 1 (4): 335–50.

Bowden, John, 1983, Editorial 'Concoms Ban', *Queensland Aviculture,* August: 6–7.

Bradley, P.E., 1986, *A Report of a Census of Amazona leucocephala caymanensis, Grand Cayman and Amazona leucocephala hesterna, Cayman Brac,* George Town, Grand Cayman: Cayman Islands Government Technical Publication, No. 1.

Britt, Kent, 1981, 'Costa Rica steers the middle course', *National Geographic Magazine,* July: 32–57.

Brown, P., 1991, 'The Orange-bellied Parrot recovery effort', *PsittaScene,* 3 (2): 5–8.

Brown, P.B. and Wilson, R.I., 1980, *A Survey of the Orange-bellied Parrot* (Neophema chrysogaster) *in Tasmania, Victoria and South Australia,* National Parks and Wildlife Service, Tasmania, 65 pp.

1981, *A survey of the Orange-bellied Parrot,* Neophema chrysogaster, *in Tasmania, Victoria and South Australia,* National Parks and Wildlife Service, Tasmania, 57pp.

1982, 'The Orange-bellied Parrot' in *Species at Risk: Research in Australia,* eds R.H. Groves and W.D.L. Ride, Australian Academy of Science, Canberra.

Bruner, P.L. 1972, *The Birds of French Polynesia,* B.P. Bishop Museum, Honolulu.

Bucher, E.H., *et al.,* 1992, 'Status and management of the Blue-fronted Amazon Parrot in Argentina', *PsittaScene,* 4 (2): 3–6.

Butler, P., 1990, 'The conservation of Lesser Antillean Amazons', *Proceedings, Second International Parrot Convention* Loro Parque, Tenerife.

Cade, Tom J., 1977, 'Manipulating the nesting biology of nesting birds', in *Endangered Birds,* ed. Stanley A. Temple, University of Wisconsin Press, Wisconsin: 167–70.

Chapman, P., 1990, 'Realising a life-long ambition', *Birds International,* 2 (1): 23–33.

Chisholm, Anne, 1972, *Philosophers of the Earth*, Sidgwick and Jackson, London.

Clubb, K.J., 1991, 'The reintroduction of Military Macaws in Guatemala', *PsittaScene*, 3 (2): 2–3.

Clubb, S.L., 1991, 'Thick-billed Parrots; homecoming for native US parrot, *PsittaScene* 3 (4): 7–9.

Collar, N.J., 1986, 'Tropical forest birds: another hostage crisis', *World Birdwatch* 8 (1): 6–7.

Conway, W.G., 1977, 'Breeding endangered birds in captivity: the last resort', in *Endangered Birds*, ed. Stanley A. Temple, University of Wisconsin Press, Wisconsin: 225–30.

1983, 'The summing up', *Proceedings: Jean Delacour/IFCB Symposium on Breeding Birds in Captivity*.

Cruz, Alexander, and Fairbairn, Patrick, 1980, *Conservation of Natural Resources in the Caribbean: The Avifauna of Jamaica*, paper presented at N. American Wildlife and Natural Resources Conference, Miami.

Cuddy, J., 1993, 'The St Vincent's Amazon – conservation success or potential dilemma?', *Magazine of the Parrot Society*, XXVII (5): 157–9.

Dalton, Bill, 1978, *Indonesian Handbook*, Moon Publications.

Davis, Shelton M., 1977, *Victims of the Miracle*, Cambridge University Press.

DeLoach, Juanita, 1982, 'The breeding of the Red-fronted Macaw', *Avicultural Bulletin*, July: 18–20.

Desenne, P. and Strahl, S.D. 1991, 'Trade and the conservation status of family Psittacidae in Venezuela', *Bird Conservation International*, 1 (2): 153–69.

Diamond, A.W. and Lovejoy, T.E. eds, 1985, *Conservation of Tropical Forest Birds*, ICBP Technical Publication No.4, Cambridge.

Diamond, Jared M., 1972, 'Avifauna of the eastern Highlands of New Guinea', *Pubs of Nuttall Orn. Club* No. 12, Cambridge, Mass.

Disch, Robert, ed., 1970, *The Ecological Conscience*, Prentice-Hall Inc., New Jersey.

Dutton, Hon. and Rev. F.G.., 1898, 'Parrot notes', *Avicultural Magazine*, II: 173.

Erhlich, Paul and Anne, 1982, *Extinction: The Causes and Consequences of the Disappearance of Species*, Victor Gollancz, London.

Evans, P.G.H., 1979, 'Status and conservation of the Seychelles Black Parrot', *Biological Conservation*, 16: 233–40.

1991, 'Status and conservation of Imperial and Red-necked Parrots *Amazona imperialis* and *A. arausiaca* on Dominica', *Bird Conservation International*, 1(1): 11–32, ed.

1993, Dominica Multiple Landuse Project: 1992 Report.

Fairbairn, Patrick, 1981, 'Parrot conservation in Jamaica', *Conservation of New World Parrots*, Proceedings of the ICBP Parrot Working Group Meeting, ed. R.F. Pasquier, Smithsonian Institution Press, Washington, 95–101.

FAO, 1988, *An Interim Report on the State of Forest Resources in the Developing Countries*. Forest Resources Division, Forest Dept FO: MISC/88/7. FAO. Rome.

Forshaw, Joseph M., 1973, *Parrots of the World*, Lansdowne Editions, Melbourne.

1978, ibid. (2nd revised edition).

1981, *Australian Parrots* (2nd revised edition), Lansdowne Editions, Melbourne.

1989, *Parrots of the World* (3rd revised edition), Lansdowne Editions, Melbourne.

Gale, Nathan, B., 1983, 'Avifauna and aviculture of Panama', *Proceedings: Jean Delacour/IFCB Symposium on Breeding Birds in Captivity*, 1–4.

1987, 'Conservation in Panama: update', *Proceedings: Jean Delacour/IFCB Symposium on Breeding Birds in Captivity*: 451–8.

Goriup, P.D. and Collar, N.J., eds, 1983, ICBP/University of East Anglia, 'Report on an expedition to survey the status of the St Vincent Parrot, *Amazona guildingii*', ICBP, Cambridge, 64pp.

Gould, John, 1848, *The Birds of Australia*, Vol. 5, London.

Greenway, James C., Jnr., 1967, *Extinct and Vanishing Birds of the World*, Dover Publications, New York.

Gregoire, Felix, 1981, 'The Dilemma of the *Amazona imperialis* and *Amazona arausiaca* parrots in Dominica following Hurricane David in 1979', in *Conservation of New World Parrots*, Proceedings of the ICBP Parrot Working Group Meeting, ed. R.F. Pasquier, Smithsonian Institution Press, Washington.

Groen, H.D., 1962, *Australian Parrakeets*, published by the author, Haren, Holland.

Guerin, R., 1940, *Faune Ornithologique Ancienne et Actuelle des Iles Mascareignes, Seychelles, Comores et des Îles Avoisinantes*, published by the author, Port Louis, Mauritius.

Hanbury-Tenison, 1980, *Mulu — The Rain Forest*, Weidenfeld and Nicolson, London.

Hayward, Jim, 1980, 'Breeding a rare and queenly Conure', *Cage and Aviary Birds*, January 5: 5.

Henry, Richard, 1895, 'On Dusky Sound', *TNZI*, 28: 50–51, Board of Governors of the Institute, Wellington.

Hicks, J. and Greenwood, D. 1989, 'Rescuing Norfolk Island's Parrot', *Birds International*: 1 (4): 35–47.

Hill, W.C. Osman, 1939, 'Breeding of the Queen of Bavaria's Conure (*Eupsittula guarouba* [Gmelin]), in Captivity', *Avicultural Magazine: 338–9*.

Hoy, G., 1969, 'Addendas a la avifauna saltena', *Hornero*, 11: 53–6.

Hutton, F.W. and Drummond, James, 1905, *The*

Animals of New Zealand: An Account of the Colony's Air-breathing Vertebrates, Whitcomb and Tombs, Christchurch: 136–40.

Imboden, C., 1992, 'The wild bird trade', *World Birdwatch*, 14 (1): 6–7.

Inder, Stuart, ed., 1978, *Pacific Islands Year Book*, Pacific Publications, Sydney.

Ingels, Johan, Parkes, Kenneth C. and Farrand, John, Jr., 1981, 'The status of the macaw generally but incorrectly called *Ara caninde* (Wagler)', *Le Gerfaut*, 71: 283–94.

Jeggo, D.F., 1982, 'Captive breeding programme for the St Lucia Parrot *Amazona versicolor*, at Jersey Wildlife Preservation Trust', *Dodo*, 19: 69–77.

Jeggo, D.F., Taynton, K.M., and Bobb, M., 1982, 'A survey of the St Lucia Parrot', *Dodo*, 19: 33–7.

Jepson, P., 1992, 'Indonesia — ICBP conservation priority', *World Birdwatch* 14 (2): 10–11.

Jones, C.G., 1980, 'Parrot on the way to extinction', *Oryx*, 15: 350–54.

1987, 'The Larger Land-birds of Mauritius', in *Studies of Mascarene Island Birds*, ed. A.W. Diamond, Cambridge University Press, Cambridge: 208–300.

Jones, C.G. and Duffy, K. 1991, 'Field work on the Echo Parrakeet (*Psittacula eques*)', *PsittaScene* 3 (4): 6–7.

1992, 'The conservation of the Echo Parrakeet', *PsittaScene* 4 (4): 7–10.

Juniper, T., 1990, 'Last of a kind', *Birds International*, 3 (1): 10–17.

King, Warren B., 1977, ed., 'Endangered birds of the world and current efforts towards managing them', in *Endangered Birds*, University of Wisconsin Press.

1979, *Red Data Book*, Vol. II, Part 2, IUCN, Morges, Switzerland.

1981, *Endangered Birds of the World*, ICBP Bird Red Data Book, Smithsonian Institution Press, Washington DC.

Kuehler, C. and Lieberman, A. 1992, 'French Polynesia', *PsittaScene*, 4 (4): 11–12.

Lambert, F., Wirth, R. *et al.*, 1992, *Parrots, An Action Plan for their Conservation 1993–1998*, ICBP, Cambridge. Draft report.

Lanning, Dirk V., 1982, 'Survey of the Red-fronted Macaw (*Ara rubrogenys*) and Caninde Macaw (*Ara caninde*) in Bolivia, December 1981–March 1982', unpublished report made to ICBP and New York Zoological Society.

Lanning, Dirk V. and Shiflett, James T., 1981, 'Status and nesting ecology of the Thick-billed Parrot (*Rhynchopsitta pachyrhyncha*)', in *Conservation of New World Parrots*, ed. R. F. Pasquier, Proceedings of the ICBP Parrot Working Group Meeting, Smithsonian Institution Press, Washington: 393–401.

1983, 'Nesting ecology of the Thick-billed Parrot', *Condor*: 66–73.

Lawson, Peter W. and Lanning, Dirk V., 1981, 'Nesting and status of the Maroon-fronted Parrot (*Rhynchopsitta terrisi*)', in *Conservation of New World Parrots*, ed. R.F. Pasquier, Proceedings of the ICBP Parrot Working Group Meeting, Smithsonian Institution Press, Washington: 385–92.

Legrand, H., 1964, 'Le Perroquet Noir de l'Isle de Praslin (Archipel de Seychelles)', *Oiseaux Revue Fr. Orn.*, 34: 154–8.

Lehmann, F.C., 1957, 'Contribuciones al estudio de la fauna de Colombia', *Noved Columb*. XII, 3: 101–56.

Leopold, Aldo, 1970, in *The Ecological Conscience*, ed. Robert Disch, Prentice-Hall Inc., New Jersey.

Low, Rosemary, 1972, *The Parrots of South America*, John Gifford, London.

1976, 'Birds seen during a short stay on Grand Cayman Island', *Avicultural Magazine*, 82: 90–93.

1979, 'New Age for Amazon breeding', *Cage and Aviary Birds*, October 20: 1, 4.

1980a, *Parrots, their Care and Breeding*, Blandford Press, Poole.

1980b, 'Citron-crested Cockatoo', *Cage and Aviary Birds*, March 15: 3, 5.

1980c, 'Goffin's Cockatoo provides an important opportunity for aviculturists', *Cage and Aviary Birds*, October 4: 3.

1980d, 'Imperial Parrot — the king from Dominica', *Cage and Aviary Birds*, August 30: 4, 6.

1981a, 'Need to breed the Double Yellow-head,' *Cage and Aviary Birds*, November 14: 5.

1981b, 'The Yellow-shouldered Amazon (*Amazona barbadensis*)', in *Conservation of New World Parrots*, Proceedings of the ICBP Parrot Working Group Meeting ed. R.F. Pasquier, Smithsonian Institution Press, Washington: 209–14.

1982a, 'The Black Parrots of Praslin', *Cage and Aviary Birds*, May 22: 5, 9.

1982b, 'Breeding the Cape Parrot', *Avicultural Magazine*, 88: 1–11.

1982c, 'Replies to "A dissenting view of aviculture"', *Avicultural Magazine*, 88: 117–19.

1983a, 'The Yellow-shouldered Amazon', *Amazona barbadensis*, *Avicultural Magazine*, 89: 9–20.

1983b, 'Contrasting methods of leading parrot breeders', *Cage and Aviary Birds*, August 27: 5, 6.

1987, 'Status of the Lilacine Amazon Parrot', *Avicultural Magazine* 93 (4): 223–5.

1990, *Macaws: A Complete Guide*, Merehurst, London.

1992a, *Parrots, Their Care and Breeding*, (3rd revised edition) Blandford Press, London.

1992b, 'Improved outlook for the Bahamas Parrot on Abaco', *PsittaScene*, 4 (1): 5–6.

1993, *Cockatoos in Aviculture*, Blandford Press, London.

Mann, Mr and Mrs R., 1982, 'Breeding the Red-topped Amazon Parrot, *Amazona dufresnia* [sic] *rhodocorytha*', *Avicultural Magazine*, 88: 12–14.

Mayr, E., 1965, 'Avifauna: Turnover on islands', *Science*, 150: 1587–8.

Merton, D.V., 1975, 'Kakapo', in *Wildlife* — a review. New Zealand Wildlife Service, Wellington, New Zealand, Dept. Internal Affairs, 6: 39–51.

1982, 'The Kakapo: A Recovery Plan', report to New Zealand Wildlife Service.

Merton, D.V., Morris R., and Atkinson, I.A.E., 1984, 'Lek behaviour in a parrot: the Kakapo *Strigops habroptilus* of New Zealand', *Ibis*, Vol. 12: 1–7.

Milton, R.R. and Marhadi, A. 1987, *An Investigation of Parrots and their Trade on Pulau Bacan (North Moluccas) and Pulau Warmar, Aru Islands*, WWF/IUCN.

Mittermeier, Russell A., *et al*, 1982, 'Conservation of primates in the Atlantic forest region of eastern Brazil', *International Zoo Year Book*, Zoological Society of London, 22: 2–17.

Moors, P.J., Atkinson, I.A.E. and Sherley, G.H. 1992, 'Reducing the rat threat to island birds', *Bird Conservation International*, (2): 93–114.

Myers, Norman, 1983, 'Indonesia: signs of a new day dawning? *Zoonooz*, vol. LVI, no. 8: 4–9.

Newton, A. and Newton, E., 1876, 'On the Psittaci of the Mascarene Islands', *Ibis*, 3rd ser., 23: 281–9.

Nichols, H.A.J., 1976, 'Parrot watching in the Caribbean', *SAFE Newsletter*, 6: 1–8.

Niles, Joseph J., 1981, 'The Status of psittacine birds in Guyana', in *Conservation of New World Parrots*, Proceedings of the ICBP Parrot Working Group Meeting, ed. R.F. Pasquier, Smithsonian Institution Press, Washington: 431–8.

Nisbet, Ian C.T., 1977, Concluding remarks, *Symposium on Management Techniques for Preserving Endangered Birds*.

Noegel, Ramon, 1981, '*Amazona leucocephala*: status in the wild and potential for captive breeding', in *Conservation of New World Parrots*, Proceedings of the ICBP Parrot Working Group Meeting, ed. R.F. Pasquier, Smithsonian Institution Press, Washington, 73–9.

1982, 'We are hand rearing a St Vincent chick', *Magazine of the Parrot Society*, September: 272.

1983, 'Caribbean Island Amazons, captive breeding for conservation', *Proceedings, Jean Delacour/IFCB Symposium on Breeding Birds in Captivity*: 187–92.

Noegel, R. and Moss, G. 1993, The St Vincent Parrot, A Long Range Captive Breeding Program Based on DNA Fingerprinting. In press.

Noegel, R., Wissman, M. and Moss, G., 1990, 'Captive breeding the St Vincent Parrot, *Amazona guildingii*', *PsittaScene* 2 (3): 1–4.

Nores, M. and Yzurieta D., 1983, 'Distribución y situación actual de grandes psitacides en Sudamerica Central', *Second Iberian–American Meeting of Ornithology, Xalapá, Mexico*.

Oren, David C. and Willis, Edwin O., 1981, 'New Brazilian records for the Golden Parrakeet (*Aratinga guarouba*)', *Auk*, 98: 394–6.

Orfila, R.N., 1936, 'Los Psittaciformes Argentinos', *Hornero*, 6: 197–225.

Ottenwalder, José, A., 1978, 'Las cotorras del Caribe, Rev. Parque Zool. Nac.', *Zoodom* 3 (1): 19–28.

Pasquier, Roger F., ed., 1981, *Conservation of New World Parrots*, Proceedings of the ICBP Parrot Working Group Meeting, Smithsonian Institution Press, Washington.

Patrick, A., 1991–92, 'Mystery bird makes a reappearance, but for how long?' *Australian Birdkeeper* 4 (12): 584–6.

Pavord, A., 1989, 'The land of few bananas', *BBC Wildlife* July: 452–6.

Penny, Malcolm, 1965, 'Bristol University Seychelles Expedition. Part 3: The Black Parrots of Praslin', *Animals* 7 (7): 184–7.

Phipps, Graeme, 1981, 'The Kakarikis', *Australian Aviculture*, June: 126–39.

1983a, 'The Kakarikis', *AFA Watchbird*, February/March: 4-11.

1983b, 'What the Australian experience means to world aviculture', *Proceedings, Jean Delacour/IFCB Symposium on Breeding Birds in Captivity*: 307–16.

Pinto, Oliverio, M. de O., 1978, *Novo Catalogo das Aves do Brazil*, la., São Paulo.

Pittman, T., 1992, 'The Glaucous Macaw – Does it still exist?' *Magazine of the Parrot Society*, XXVI (II): 366–71.

Porter, S., 1929, 'In search of the Imperial Parrot', *Avicultural Magazine*, Ser. 4, Vol. VII, 240–46, 267–75.

1934, 'Notes on New Zealand Birds: The Kakapo or Owl Parrot (*Strigops habroptilus*)', *Avicultural Magazine*: 205–8.

1939, 'The Norfolk Island Parrakeet', *Avicultural Magazine*: 408.

Potter, Frank M., 1970, in *The Ecological Conscience*, ed. Robert Disch, Prentice-Hall Inc., New Jersey.

Poulton, Sarah, 1982, *Kakapo — A Bibliography*, New Zealand Wildife Service, Dept of Internal Affairs, Wellington.

Pugh, P.B. 1978, 'Puerto Rican Parrot fights against extinction', *Cage and Aviary Birds*, October 19: 3, 4.

Quinque, Henri, 1980, 'Breeding the Horned Parrot', *Avicultural Magazine*: 187–94.

1982, 'Reply to "A dissenting view of aviculture"', ibid.: 179–83.

1983, 'Breeding the Cloven-feathered Dove, *Drepa-*

noptila holosericea, and three other rare species from New Caledonia', *Proceedings of Jean Delacour/IFCB Symposium on Breeding Birds in Captivity*: 267–73.

Ridgely, R.S., 1976, *A Guide to the Birds of Panama*, Princeton Univ. Press, Princeton, New Jersey.

1977, Report to WWF-US on the status of Middle American Parrots.

1981, 'The current distribution and status of mainland neotropical parrots', in *Conservation of New World Parrots*, Proceedings of the ICBP Parrot Working Group Meeting, ed. R.F. Pasquier, Smithsonian Institution Press, Washington: 233–384.

1989, 'Hyacinth Macaws in the wild', *Birds International*, 1 (1): 9–17.

Rodriguez-Vidal, J.A., 1959, *Puerto Rican Parrot (Amazona vittata vittata) Study*, Puerto Rican Dept. Agric. and Commerce Monogr, 1: 1–15.

Rudran, R. and Eisenberg, J.F., 1982, 'Conservation and status of wild primates in Venezuela', in *International Zoo Year Book*, ed. P.J. Olney, Zoological Society of London, 22: 52–9.

Ruschi, A., 1979, *Aves do Brasil*, Editoria Rios Ltda., São Paulo.

Ryder, Oliver, A., 1983, 'Genetic considerations in breeding threatened and endangered birds', *Proceedings, Jean Delacour/IFCB Symposium on Breeding Birds in Captivity*: 551–65.

Rylands, Anthony B. and Mittermeier, Russell A., 1982, 'Conservation of primates in Brazilian Amazonia', in *International Zoo Year Book*, ed. P.J. Olney, Zoological Society of London, 22: 17–37.

Sarasin, F., 1913, 'Die Vogel Neu-Caledoniens und der Loyalty-Inseln', in G.F. Sarasin and J. Roux, *Nova Caledonia*, Vol. 1, Wiesbaden, C.W. Kreidels Verlag.

Secrett, C., 1986, 'And now some answers', *World Birdwatch*, 8 (1): 11.

Sempe, E., 1992, 'Research on the Ground Parrot in Barren Grounds Nature Reserve (NSW–Australia)', *PsittaScene* 4 (3): 3.

Serventy, D.L. and Whittell, H.M., 1976, *Birds of Western Australia*, 5th ed., Perth, Univ, W. Aust. Press.

Short, L.L., 1975, 'A zoogeographic analysis of the South American Chaco avifauna', *Bull. Amer. Mus. Nat. Hist.*, 154: 163–352.

da Silva, C.P., Munn, C.A. Cintra, R., Renton K., Valqui, M. and Yamashita, C., 1991, 'Breeding ecology of Hyacinth Macaws', *PsittaScene*, 3 (3): 1–3.

Smiet, Fred, 1982, 'Threats to the Spice Islands', *Oryx*, 16 (4): 323–8.

Snyder, N.F.R., 1977, 'Puerto Rican parrots and nest site scarcity', in *Endangered Birds*, ed. S.A. Temple, University of Wisconsin Press, Madison: 47–53.

Snyder, N.F.R and Taapken, J.D., 1977, 'Puerto Rican parrots and nest predation by Pearly-eyed Thrashers',

in *Endangered Birds*, ed. S.A. Temple, University of Wisconsin Press, Madison: 113–20.

Snyder, N., Snyder, H.A. and Johnson, T.B. 1989, 'Gunned down north of the border', *Birds International*, 1 (2): 44–5.

1989, 'Parrots return to the Arizona skies': 41–3, 46–50, 52.

Stevens, J., Herremans, M. and Louette, M. 1992, 'Conserving the endemic birds on the Comoro Islands, II: population fluctuations on Ngazidja', *Bird Conservation International*, 2 (1): 81–91.

Stonehouse, Bernard, 1981, *Saving the Animals*, Weidenfeld & Nicolson, London.

Suárez, F. Rojas, 1992a, Biologia reproductiva de la Cotorra: *Amazona barbadensis* (Aves: Psittaciformes) en la Peninsula de Macanao', *1° Simposio sobre la Biología y Conservación de los Psitácidos Venezolano*.

1992b, 'Situación actual y aspectos de la biología de Ñangaro (*Aratinga acuticaudata neoxena*) en la isla de Margarita', *1° Simposio sobre la Biología y Conservación de los Psitácidos Venezolano*.

Tavistock, the Marquess of, 1928, 'The Queen of Bavaria's Conure', *Avicultural Magazine*: 255–6.

1929, 'Queen of Bavaria's Conures', ibid.: 229–30.

Temple, Stanley, A., 1976, 'Conservation of endemic birds and other wildlife on Mauritius, Progress Report and proposal for future activities, unpublished report to ICBP, Washington DC.

1977, *Endangered Birds*, ed., University of Wisconsin Press, Madison.

1978, 'The life histories and ecology of the indigenous landbirds of Mauritius (non passerines)', unpublished manuscript, 116pp.

1983, 'Is reintroduction a realistic goal?', *Proceedings, Jean Delacour/IFCB Symposium on Breeding Birds in Captivity*: 597–605.

Temple, S.A., Staub, J.J.F., and Antoine, R., 1974, 'Some background information and recommendations on the preservation of the native flora and fauna of Mauritius', unpublished manuscript summarised in J. Procter, 1975, *Conservation in Mauritius 1974*, IUCN, Morges, Switzerland.

Varty, N., 1990, 'Hurricane Gilbert — Jamaica counts the cost', *World Birdwatch*, 12 (1–2): 6–7.

Vaughan, C., McCoy, M. and Liske, J. 1991, 'Scarlet Macaw (*Ara macao*): ecology and management perspectives', *Proceedings of the First Mesoamerican Workshop on the Conservation and Management of Macaws*, Center for the Study of Tropical Birds.

Vickers, M.C., 'Psittacine erythroblastosis — a new disease of Antipode Island and New Zealand Parrakeets (*Cyanoramphus* spp.)', unpublished report.

Villiard, M., 1978, in *F.A.O.* (1980).

Wagner, Robert O., 1983, 'The private and the public aviculturist', *Proceedings, Jean Delacour/IFCB Sympo-*

sium on Breeding Birds in Captivity: 11–15.

Watling, Dick, 1982, *Birds of Fiji, Tonga and Samoa*, Millwood Press, Wellington.

Wells, Don, 1981, 'Red-fronted Macaws', *Avicultural Bulletin*, July: 3–7.

Wells, D.R., 1971, 'Survival of the Malaysian bird fauna', *Malay Nat, J.,* 24: 248–56.

Wiley, James, 1981, 'The Puerto Rican Amazon (*Amazona vittata*): its decline and the program for its conservation', in *Conservation of New World Parrots*, ed. R.F. Pasquier, Proceedings of the ICBP Parrot Working Group, Smithsonian Institution, Washington: 133–59.

    1983, 'The role of captive propagation in the conservation of the Puerto Rican Parrot', *Proceedings, Jean Delacour/IFCB Symposium on Breeding Birds in Captivity*: 441–35.

Wiley, J.W., 1991, 'Status and conservation of parrots and parakeets in the Greater Antilles, Bahama Islands, and Cayman Islands', *Bird Conservation International*, 1 (3): 187–214.

Williams, G.R., 1983, 'Aviculture and the birds of the *Red Data Book of New Zealand*', *Proceedings, Jean Delacour/IFCB Symposium on Breeding Birds in Captivity*: 17–32.

Wirth, R., 1990, 'Moluccan Cockatoos and other Indonesian parrots', *Proceedings, Second International Parrot Convention*, Loro Parque, Tenerife.

Wood, C.A. and Wetmore, A., 1926, 'A collection of birds from the Fiji Islands', Part III, Field Observations, *Ibis*, 12th ser., 2: 91–136.

Woods, C., 1987, 'The threatened and endangered birds of Haiti: lost horizons and new hopes', *Proceedings: Jean Delacour/IFCB Symposium on Breeding Birds in Captivity*, 385–430.

Woolcock, D., 1990, 'Spix's Macaw — the dilemma of the world's rarest bird', *PsittaScene* 2 (4): 9–10.

Wright, Carol, 1974, *Mauritius*, David and Charles, Newton Abbot.

Index of Scientific Names

General Index